ORIGEN OF ALEXANDRIA

His World and His Legacy

Christianity and Judaism in Antiquity

CHARLES KANNENGIESSER, SERIES EDITOR

Volume 1

ORIGEN OF ALEXANDRIA

His World and His Legacy

Edited by Charles Kannengiesser
and
William L. Petersen

University of Notre Dame Press

Library of Congress Cataloging-in-Publication Data

Origen of Alexandria: his world and his legacy / edited by Charles
Kannengiesser and William L. Petersen.
    p. cm. – (Christianity and Judaism in antiquity; 1)
Papers from the Origen Colloquy held at the University of Notre
Dame, Apr. 11-13, 1986.
    ISBN 0-268-01501-5
    1. Origen – congresses. I. Kannengiesser, Charles. II. Petersen,
William Lawrence, 1950-. III. Origen Colloquy (1986: University
of Notre Dame) IV. Series.
BR1720.07075 1988
270.1'092'4–dc19   88-40319

Manufactured in the United States of America

CONTENTS

Preface   vii

I. The World of Sacred Scripture   1

Origen's Old Testament Text: The Transmission History
of the Septuagint to the Third Century, C.E.
Eugene Ulrich   3

The Text of the Gospels in Origen's Commentaries on
John and Matthew
William L. Petersen   34

Origen in the Scholar's Den: A Rationale for the
Hexapla
John Wright   48

Straw Dogs and Scholarly Ecumenism: The Appropriate
Jewish Background for the Study of Origen
Roger Brooks   63

Origen, the Rabbis, and the Bible: Toward a Picture of
Judaism and Christianity in Third-Century
Caesarea
Paul M. Blowers   96

Origen and the *Sensus Literalis*
Charles J. Scalise   117

Allegory and Spiritual Observance in Origen's
Discussions of the Sabbath
Daniel J. Nodes   130

Divine Deception and the Truthfulness of Scripture
Joseph W. Trigg   147

Poetic Words, Abysmal Words: Reflections on Origen's
Hermeneutics
Patricia Cox Miller   165

II. Spirituality--Philosophy--Theology   179

Origenian Understanding of Martyrdom and Its Biblical
      Framework
      Pamela Bright   180

The Role of Prayer in Origen's Homilies
      Daniel Sheerin   200

Looking on the Light: Some Remarks on the Imagery of
      Light in the First Chapter of the *Peri Archon*
      John Dillon   215

Divine Trinity and the Structure of *Peri Archon*
      Charles Kannengiesser   231

Sacrifice in Origen in the Light of Philonic Models
      Jean Laporte   250

Origen's Ecclesiology and the Biblical Metaphor of the
      Church As the Body of Christ
      Verlyn D. Verbrugge   277

The Place of Saints and Sinners After Death
      Lawrence R. Hennessey   295

Moses and Jesus in *Contra Celsum* 7. 1-25: Ethics,
      History and Jewish-Christian Eirenics in
      Origen's Theology
      Peter J. Gorday   313

Origen and Early Christian Pluralism: The Context of
      His Eschatology
      Jon F. Dechow   337

Elements of Fourth Century Origenism: The
      Anthropology of Evagrius Ponticus and Its
      Sources
      Michael O'Laughlin   357

PREFACE

This collection of papers results from the Origen Colloquy held at the University of Notre Dame, Indiana on April 11-13, 1986.

Owing to the large variety of topics presented, we could not include all the papers delivered at the Colloquy within the limits imposed by the present volume. The key-note address by Henri Crouzel, S.J. has appeared in the Fall, 1988 issue of *Theological Studies*.

The Colloquy, *Origen of Alexandria: His World and His Legacy*, was conceived as a properly American celebration of the eighteenth centennial of Origen's birth. It was sponsored by the Department of Theology at the University of Notre Dame.

A special word of thanks for the preparation of this volume is due to Colleen McEvoy-Smith, Paul Blowers, and Jon Bailey.

Charles Kannengiesser

William L. Petersen

LIST OF ABBREVIATIONS

BIOSCS	Bulletin of the International Organization for Septuagint and Cognate Studies
BLE	Bulletin de littérature ecclésiastique
CCSL	Corpus christianorum, series latina
CPG	Clavis patrum graecorum
GCS*	Die griechischen christlichen Schriftsteller der ersten drei Jahrhunderte
HTR	Harvard Theological Review
JQR	Jewish Quarterly Review
JTS	Journal of Theological Studies
LThK	Lexikon für Theologie und Kirche
NovT	Novum Testamentum
NTS	New Testament Studies
PG	Patrologia graeca
PL	Patrologia latina
PO	Patrologia orientalis
RB	Revue Biblique
RSPhTh	Revue des sciences philosophiques et théologiques
SC	Sources chrétiennes
StPatr	Studia patristica
SVF	Stoicorum veterum fragmenta
TU	Texte und Untersuchungen
VC	Vigiliae christianae
ZKG	Zeitschrift für Kirchengeschichte
ZNW	Zeitschrift für die neutestamentliche Wissenschaft

*   Volume numbers from the writings of Origen cited in the critical editions of the GCS are those of Origenes Werke and not the general series.

I. The World of Sacred Scripture

ORIGEN'S OLD TESTAMENT TEXT: THE TRANSMISSION HISTORY OF THE SEPTUAGINT TO THE THIRD CENTURY, C.E.

Eugene Ulrich
University of Notre Dame

Origen is still commemorated 1800 years after his birth, and one of the many reasons is the Hexapla which he composed—his monumental work striving toward exactness in the text of the Old Testament scriptures.[1] As Bigg has noted, Origen was perhaps "the first who distinctly saw that for the

---

[1]That is, the Jewish translation of their scriptures into Greek, the Septuagint, which the early Christian church accepted. "Old Testament" is used predominantly in this article insofar as it reflects Origen's position and denotes the wider canon of scripture. For the most recent comprehensive study of the Septuagint, see Sidney Jellicoe, *The Septuagint and Modern Study* (Oxford: Clarendon, 1968); this supplements, rather than replaces, the still valuable 1902 work by H. B. Swete, *An Introduction to the Old Testament in Greek* rev. by R. R. Ottley (New York: Ktav, 1968). For a highly useful study concerning the relationship of the Septuagint to the Hebrew Bible and the use of it in OT textual criticism, see Emanuel Tov, *The Text-Critical Use of the Septuagint in Biblical Research,* Jerusalem Biblical Studies 3 (Jerusalem: Simor, 1981). For bibliography on the Septuagint, see Sebastian P. Brock, C. T. Fritsch, and S. Jellicoe, eds., *A Classified Bibliography of the Septuagint,* Arbeiten zur Literatur und Geschichte des hellenistischen Judentums 6 (Leiden: Brill, 1973); for subsequent bibliography, see the "Record of Work" in the annual *Bulletin of the International Organization for Septuagint and Cognate Studies.*

theologian, whatever may be [the] immediate object, controversy, edification, or doctrine, the prime necessity is a sound text."[2] Though Origen may have been the first Christian, he was not, as Bigg suggested, "the first" to see this, for he clearly followed and built on the work of a long line of Jewish textual scholars.[3] Bigg's statement, however, does point in the right direction: in order to understand Origen correctly, just as it is necessary to know his historical context, his educational and philosophical context, and his religious and theological context, so too is it necessary—since Origen and his works were so thoroughly rooted in the Bible—to know the character, the evolving character, of the biblical text which he used.

The purpose of this article is to provide a focus on the nature of the Old Testament text used by Origen. What would "the OT text," the Septuagint, have looked like in Origen's day? What was the character of the text that Origen would have picked up and begun to use when he started reading, praying over, preaching from, and writing commentaries on "the OT text"?

That question necessarily requires a diachronic perspective, for the biblical text which Origen used was the product of a historical process. But this is a complex undertaking, if for no other reason, because Origen himself significantly changed the shape of that text. Origen primarily used "the Septuagint," and what later theologians, such as Eusebius, Jerome, or

---

[2]Cited by Jellicoe (*Septuagint*, 101) from *The Origins of Christianity*, ed. T. B. Strong (Oxford, 1909) 423.

[3]Not only did Origen fill his hexaplaric columns with the content of the recensions of Aquila and Theodotion, but his methods were similar to theirs; see D. Barthélemy, *Les devanciers d'Aquila*, Supplements to Vetus Testamentum 10 (Leiden: Brill, 1963); and K. G. O'Connell, "Greek Versions (Minor)," *The Interpreter's Dictionary of the Bible*, supplementary volume (Nashville: Abingdon, 1976) 377-381.

Pamphilus would think of as "the Septuagint text" looked noticeably different from "the Septuagint text" which Origen first took in hand. We should presume, for example, that "the Septuagint text" of Jeremiah, or Psalms, or Daniel cited by Origen early in his career would read differently from "the Septuagint text" cited by Origen late in his career, because he devoted a substantial amount of time to re-editing that "Septuagint text."

Thus, understanding the character of "Origen's Old Testament text" means understanding the origins and developments that formed it. Indeed, there are several more complicating factors, each of which needs its trajectory carefully charted. The first concerns the transmission of the text during the century or two after Origen. The oldest extensive MSS of the Septuagint which are extant are dated in the fourth century, at least a century after Origen, so that we cannot always be certain that our "Septuagint text" corresponds to that of his day (either in its pre-Origenic or post-Origenic form).

The second complicating factor concerns the transmission of the text during the centuries before Origen. Numerous changes and numerous types of change, both intentional and unintentional, buffeted the Septuagint on its journey from Jewish Alexandria in the third and second centuries B.C.E., to Christian circles in Egypt and Palestine in the third century of the common Jewish and Christian era.

A third complicating factor, only rarely suspected[4] prior to the
discovery of the Qumran scrolls, is the shape of the Hebrew text of which the
Septuagint was a translation. For a number of books the variation in the
Hebrew text[5] was as significant as that in the Greek text between the second
century B.C.E. and the late first century C.E.

Thus, my goal is to study some aspects of the text of the Greek Old
Testament and of Origen's use of it. But since that text is an evolving text,
we must first consider its origins and character, secondly its early

---

[4]Lagarde (*Anmerkungen zur griechischen Übersetzung der
Proverbien* [Leipzig: 1863] 3) had already formed and elaborated the principle,
summarized by Jellicoe (*Septuagint*, 6): "In a choice between alternative
readings preference is to be given...to one which represents a Hebrew original
other than MT." It is regrettable that many modern scholars, in religious
loyalty to the MT, have failed to pay sufficient attention to this empirical
principle, especially since it has been amply confirmed by the Qumran
textual evidence.

[5]Cf., e.g., S. R. Driver, *Notes on the Hebrew Text and the
Topography of the Books of Samuel*, 2d ed. (Oxford: Clarendon, 1913); F.
M. Cross, "The Evolution of a Theory of Local Texts," *1972 Proceedings:
IOSCS and Pseudepigrapha*, ed. R. A. Kraft (Missoula: Scholars, 1972) 108-
126; D. Barthélemy, *Les devanciers* [n.3 above], and "Origène et le texte de
l'Ancien Testament," *Epektasis, Mélanges patristiques offerts au Cardinal
Jean Daniélou* (Paris: Beauchesne, 1972) 247-261, esp. p. 252; repr. in D.
Barthélemy, *Études d'histoire du texte de l'Ancien Testament*, Orbis biblicus
et orientalis 21 (Fribourg, Suisse: Éditions Universitaires, 1978) 203-217;
S. Talmon, "The Textual Study of the Bible—A New Outlook," *Qumran and
the History of the Biblical Text*, ed. F. M. Cross and S. Talmon
(Cambridge, MA: Harvard University, 1975) 321-400; E. Tov, "The Literary
History of the Book of Jeremiah in the Light of Its Textual History,"
Empirical Models for Biblical Criticism, ed. J. Tigay (Philadelphia:
University of Pennsylvania, 1985) 211-237; J. Trebolle, "Redaction,
Recension, and Midrash in the Books of Kings," *BIOSCS* 15 (1984) 12-35;
E. Ulrich, *The Qumran Text of Samuel and Josephus*, Harvard Semitic
Monographs 19 (Missoula: Scholars, 1978), and "Characteristics and
Limitations of the Old Latin Translation of the Septuagint," *La Septuaginta
en la investigación contemporánea (V Congreso de la IOSCS)*, (Textos y
Estudios «Cardenal Cisneros» 34, ed. N. Fernández Marcos (Madrid: Instituto
«Arias Montano» C.S.I.C., 1985) 67-80.

transmission history, and then thirdly some aspects of Origen, his Hexapla, and his use of the "Septuagint" text.

I. The Origins and Character of the Old Greek Text

DEFINITIONS

At the outset it is important to sort out the various entities for which we use the term "Septuagint" and to clarify our terms for them. There is no fully acceptable definition or consistent usage for the term "Septuagint."[6] The term originally designated the pristine translation of the Torah (only the first five books of the Hebrew Bible) by the seventy (*septuaginta*) or seventy-two elders commissioned to go from Jerusalem to Alexandria for that purpose—but all this *as narrated* in the *Letter of Aristeas*. But the *Letter of Aristeas* is legendary in content and, though epistolary in form, is really "a propaganda work."[7] Thus, historically, we cannot document any "72 elders" who were the original translators of the Torah nor, *a fortiori*, of the entire Hebrew Bible. But the term "Septuagint" in its strictest usage refers only to the Pentateuch and only to the original Greek translation of it.

By extension, however, it legitimately[8] designates the original

---

[6]Swete, *Introduction*, 9-10; Kraft in E. Tov and R. A. Kraft, "Septuagint," *The Interpreter's Dictionary of the Bible*, supplementary volume (Nashville: Abingdon, 1976) 807-815, esp. 811.

[7]Jellicoe, *Septuagint*, 30; cf. P. Kahle, *The Cairo Geniza*, 2d ed., (Oxford: Blackwell, 1959) 211; and J. Wm Wevers, "An Apologia for Septuagint Studies," *BIOSCS* 18 (1985) 16-38, esp. 16-19.

[8]Justin is probably the first Christian to use the term (*Dialogue with Trypho* lxviii.7) in extant material, and his context shows that the term is already being used in a way that includes Isaiah and extends to the whole OT; see Jellicoe, *Septuagint*, 41-42; cf. Swete, *Introduction*, p.9, n.1.

Greek translation of the entire Old Testament, including both the books later accepted as the Hebrew Bible and the Apocryphal or Deutero-Canonical books. But it is excessive elasticity when the term is stretched further to mean "the Greek Old Testament," i.e., any Greek form of the OT without regard to specific Greek textual tradition.

More accurate terms would be:

(1) *the Old Greek* for the original, single, or singly-influential, translation of each different book (many writers now use "the Old Greek" as a term preferable to "Septuagint," since "the OG" is not necessarily confined to the Pentateuch, and since it clearly distinguishes from later forms of the Greek text);[9]

(2) *the early Greek text(s)* for the gradually-evolving forms which developed from that original translation;

(3) *the early recensions* of Proto-Theodotion (and perhaps Theodotion), Aquila, Symmachus, and possibly of others ("Quinta," etc.);[10]

(4) *the Hexaplaric recension* for the text which Origen produced in his fifth column, "o´" (= "LXX"="70"); and

(5) *the Lucianic recension* for the fourth-century Antiochene recension of certain books .[11]

The ideal object of the quest for many Septuagintalists is "the text as it left the hand of the [original] translator," or even the Hebrew text behind

---

[9]See E. Tov and R. A. Kraft, "Septuagint" [n. 6 above].

[10]See Barthélemy, *Les devanciers* [n.3 above]; O'Connell, "Greek Versions (Minor)" [n.3]; and section II below.

[11]See n. 31 below. The "Proto-Lucianic" text tradition may belong to the second or third category above.

the LXX.[12] But the practical object of the quest, that sought by the Göttingen critical editions, is the oldest recoverable text of each book, and this would be called "the Old Greek."[13]

This leads us to the final, and for the study of Origen and other ancient writers a very important, distinction: the distinction between the text of the Old Greek as the original Jewish translation of the Hebrew Scriptures, and the text of the Greek Old Testament as the living Bible of the on-going church during the early Christian centuries. The former signals the translation's importance as a witness, in fact one of the most important witnesses, to the early Hebrew text. The latter signals the text's importance as the living scriptures of the developing church. These are two different focuses, the Greek OT at two different points in its history, serving two different historical-theological purposes.

The two focuses can be clearly exemplified by the works of Emanuel Tov and Marguerite Harl. Tov's book is entitled *The Text-Critical Use of the Septuagint in Biblical Research*,[14] and his aim is to understand the LXX and to use a retroversion of it, wherever and insofar as this be possible, as a witness to a form of the Hebrew text—a witness which predates extensive Hebrew MS documentation of the OT. Thus, he studies the LXX to see how it can help us get further and more reliably back to earlier or superior forms of the Hebrew Bible. Harl's project of a French translation of the LXX focuses on the use of scripture in the early church and envisions that:

---

[12]See Jellicoe's first and last pages (*Septuagint*, 1, 359).

[13]See Kraft, "Septuagint" [n. 6 above] 811.

[14]See n.1 above.

la Septante sera prise pour elle-même, non pas comme une traduction mais comme *un texte* au sens plein du terme: le texte de la Bible du Judaïsme hellénistique et de l'Eglise ancienne, le texte tel qu'il fut lu par des lecteurs qui n'avaient aucunement recours à l'original hébreu pour tenter de le comprendre, un texte qui s'explique à l'intérieur du système linguistique grec de son époque.[15]

From the perspective of Origen, both focuses are necessary, for one of his goals was to restore "the translation of the Seventy," and another was to explain and expound the scriptural text of his church. Therefore, we must look at the original Septuagint, and the developed text which Origen used, and thus the intervening evolutionary process which produced the text he used.

SEPTUAGINT ORIGINS: THE DATA FROM EARLY MANUSCRIPTS AND QUOTATIONS

Rather than beginning with the *Letter of Aristeas*, which is legendary material, I think that it is preferable to begin with Septuagintal MS evidence and with quotations of the Septuagint by ancient authors. The evidence usually cited is the following:[16]

---

[15]M. Harl *BIOSCS* 13 (1980) 7. Professor Harl is aware of the difficulties: "Un premier travail est d'établir le catalogue de ces difficultés, de les étudier, de proposer des solutions. Il faudra notamment décider quelle tradition textuelle de la Septante on choisira de traduire, faute de pouvoir rendre compte de la pluralité des états textuels" (p. 8).

[16]See, e.g., Swete, *Introduction*, 369-380, and Jellicoe, *Septuagint*, 237-239. With all the advances in LXX research over the past decades, however, this evidence should be closely restudied; see, e.g., the following note.

•Demetrius the Hellenist quotes the Greek Genesis in the late third century B.C.E.

•Eupolemos, a Hellenistic Jewish historian of the mid-second century B.C.E., bases a part of his narrative on the Greek Chronicles.[17]

•The Prologue of Ben Sira, written shortly after 132 B.C.E., refers to "the law . . ., the prophecies, and the rest of the books" which had been translated.

•The John Rylands Library of Manchester has small papyrus scraps of the Greek Deuteronomy, dated (by C. H. Roberts) to the second century B.C.E.

•Papyrus Fouad 266, also containing small portions of Deuteronomy, comes from the late second or early first century B.C.E.

•Qumran has yielded five early Greek MSS of Genesis-Deuteronomy: 4QLXXLev[a] (late second century B.C.E.), 7QLXXExod (ca. 100 B.C.E.), 4QLXXLev[b] and 4QLXXNum (probably first century B.C.E. or the opening years of the first C.E.), and 4QLXXDeut,[18] in addition to the Greek Minor Prophets scroll and a fragment of the Letter of Jeremiah.

---

[17]See the caution already expressed by Montgomery (*A Critical and Exegetical Commentary on the Book of Daniel* , ICC [Edinburgh: T. & T. Clark, 1927] 38): "On rather scanty evidence, that the Jewish historian Eupolemus, *c.* 150 B.C. (text given by Swete, *Int.*, 370 = Eus., *Praep.*, ix, 31) knew **G** of 2 Ch. 12^{12}ff., Torrey holds, p. 82, that the OGr. tr. of Ch.-Ezr.-Neh. (containing 2 Esd.) existed by the middle of the 2d cent."

[18]See C. H. Roberts, quoted in P. Kahle, *The Cairo Geniza*, 223; and E. Ulrich, "The Greek Manuscripts of the Pentateuch from Qumrân, Including Newly-Identified Fragments of Deuteronomy (4QLXXDeut)," *De Septuaginta: Studies in Honour of John William Wevers on his Sixty-Fifth Birthday*, ed. A. Pietersma and C. Cox (Mississauga, Ont.: Benben, 1984) 71-82. The derivative date in Jellicoe, *Septuagint*, 276, should read: ". . . assigned to the late second [not "the late first"] or the first century B.C. or the early first A.D." I should stress that the palaeographically assigned dates quoted above for the Greek MSS at Qumran are rough and preliminary and need more thorough analysis.

•Papyrus 967 is an early third century C.E. MS containing portions of Ezekiel, Daniel, and Esther.[19] For Daniel, this MS displays a "pre-hexaplaric" text, i.e., a text which is a developed form of the OG, such as Origen would have used as a basis for the "o´" column, but which shows no admixture of elements from the Hexapla. In this case, 967 is for the most part very close to what Origen listed as the "o´" text of Daniel (and clearly at variance with the Theodotionic text which became universally used and displaced the older "o´" text); but it does not yet have the demonstrably Origenian hexaplaric changes and additions taken from the Theodotionic text which are now found in the single extant Greek witness to Origen's revised "o´" text, MS 88.

The conclusions indicated by the evidence from manuscripts and citations are that the Torah was translated by the late third century B.C.E. and probably by ca. 250, that the Former Prophets were translated before the middle of the second century B.C.E. and probably by ca. 200 because they would have been translated prior to Chronicles which was circulating by the mid-second century B.C.E. The Latter Prophets would very likely have been translated at the same time as the Former Prophets, and of the Writings many books would very likely have been translated about the same time as Chronicles.

---

[19]For bibliographic information on the several volumes, see S. Pace, "The Stratigraphy of the Text of Daniel and the Question of Theological *Tendenz* in the Old Greek," *BIOSCS* 17 (1984) 15-35, esp. pp. 18-19 and n. 9; see also now S. Pace Jeansonne, *The Old Greek Translation of Daniel 7-12*, Catholic Biblical Quarterly Monograph Series 19 (Washington: Catholic Biblical Association, 1988) 11.

SEPTUAGINT ORIGINS: HYPOTHESES

The *Letter of Aristeas* purports to be a letter written in the mid-third century B.C.E., sent by Aristeas to his brother Philocrates, describing the events surrounding the original translation of the Hebrew Torah into Greek for the Ptolemaic king's library. It was taken at face value as historical as early as Philo, and continued to be taken as such by Josephus, early church writers such as Jerome, and others all through the centuries until 1705. The question of LXX origins was considered answered, indeed narrated in detail, by the *Letter of Aristeas.* Jellicoe traces the transmission history[20] of the *Letter*, including the steady embellishment as it went from hand to hand, all connected with the inspired and authoritative character of the LXX as the Greek form of God's word to Israel.

But in 1705 Hody studied the letter and declared it legendary. John Wm. Wevers has recently presented a current view concerning it, again emphasizing that it is legendary in character, and that "it would be methodologically sound not to accept anything stated in the *Letter* that cannot be substantiated elsewhere."[21]

Since late in the 19th century, Lagarde's theory of LXX origins has held sway, except for a brief period when the influential figure of Paul Kahle propounded a diametrically opposed theory. Lagarde thought that the widespread variation in our extant MSS led us back to three major recensions of the Greek text, differentiated geographically; and behind those three recensions one could arrive at a single translation of the Hebrew Bible into Greek.

---

[20]Jellicoe, *Septuagint*, 38-47.

[21]"An Apologia for Septuagint Studies," *BIOSCS* 18 (1985) 16-38, esp. 17.

Kahle, in contrast, thought that the Septuagint arose as did the targumim--from a plethora of individually produced partial translations, which after a period of multiplication, were supplanted by a single translation now endorsed by rabbinic decision as being authoritative. In 1915 he claimed that the letter, though fictionally set in the third century B.C.E., was actually written as propaganda to assure the outcome for one side of a conflict over the authority of competing Greek texts in the late second century B.C.E.[22]

Thus, Lagarde saw an original single translation gradually branching out both chronologically and geographically, whereas Kahle saw many targumim being displaced by a single standard translation. Lagarde's view, however, appears confirmed by nearly a century of multifaceted research by a wide spectrum of Septuagintal specialists and by the data available from the Qumran and other very early MSS, whereas Kahle's view finds no support in detailed research by Septuagintalists.[23]

There remain two schools of thought on the degree of intentional fidelity in the OG translations: one, that the translators generally intended and attempted to render in the Greek language what they perceived to be said in the Hebrew original; the other, that the translators viewed themselves as in a certain measure free to adapt the original meaning to conform with contemporary historical knowledge or theological *Tendenz*. Though the case differs from book to book, I think that in general the former describes the situation more accurately.[24]

---

[22]P. Kahle, "Untersuchungen zur Geschichte des Pentateuchtextes," *Theologische Studien und Kritiken* 88 (Gotha, 1915) 399-439, esp. 410-26; and *The Cairo Geniza*, 212.

[23]Cf. Jellicoe, *Septuagint*, 61-63.

[24]Contrast, e.g., the articles of Trebolle and van der Kooij in *BIOSCS* 15 (1982)12-35, 36-50. For an example of disproof of the *Tendenz* hypothesis, see S. Pace, *BIOSCS* 17 (1984)15-35. It should be noted that

SUMMARY

The OG of the Pentateuch was translated starting near the mid-third century B.C.E., the last of the books (e.g., Daniel) being translated probably by the late second or early first century B.C.E. Thus the OG of the Pentateuch antedated Origen by about 450-500 years and the latest of the books by about 300 years.

The earliest nearly-complete codices of the Greek Bible date from the fourth (Vaticanus) and fifth (Alexandrinus and Sinaiticus) centuries C.E., a century or two after Origen. But fragmentary MSS are preserved as far back as the second century B.C.E., and quotations by Hellenistic Jewish authors apparently document the Greek Genesis as far back as the late third century B.C.E.

Lagarde's view that the present variation in LXX MSS is traceable back through three ancient recensions to a single original translation receives confirmation by nearly a century of extensive research by a wide spectrum of Septuagintal specialists and by the data available from the Qumran and other very early MSS.

For each biblical book there seems to be an original translation from the Hebrew into Greek. The translations, however, display differing translation techniques, and thus each book's translation should be presumed to derive from a different translator.

---

the issue is not whether the translation is "literal" or "free"; we find both literal and free styles of translation in both "faithful" and "interpretative" translations. The question is: do the translators attempt to reproduce in Greek the meaning they find already in the text, or do they feel free to change the original meaning in light of new or current ideas, whether literary, historical, cultural, or theological, or whether private or communal?

Though it is often not done, one must carefully consider the relationship of the Old Greek translation to its Hebrew *Vorlage*. Not infrequently, differences from the MT either in individual words or phrases or even in the form of the larger book (e.g., Jeremiah[25]) are due not to theological *Tendenz* but to faithful translation from a different Hebrew parent text.

Thus, as far as we can tell, originally the OG would have been a collection of papyrus or leather scrolls, each normally containing one biblical book, each apparently translated by a different translator, and all (or many) attempting to reproduce in Greek the intended meaning of the Hebrew text (Masoretic, Qumran, or other) from which it had been translated.

II. The Transmission of the Early Greek Text up to the Hexapla

The collection of scrolls produced from the mid-third to the early first centuries B.C.E., containing the original Greek translations from varying Hebrew texts of the scriptures, traversed a somewhat complex history of transmission, knowledge of which is essential for understanding the work of Origen—a history partially chartable, mostly lost in the darkness of the past.

We do not, and Origen did not, have extant for any book what anyone would consider the original form of that translation. All manuscripts display a considerable amount of textual development—certainly unintentional changes, such as the well-known panoply of errors, but also intentional changes, such as clarifications, revisions, doublets, and harmonizations.

---

[25]See E. Tov, "The Literary History," [n. 5 above].

Moreover, for some books, we no longer have even the changed, corrupted, and developed copies of the OG. In these cases all our extant MS evidence is traceable only to a later recension which either by chance or by conscious decision supplanted the original Greek. The Book of Daniel furnishes an example in which this loss and supplantation was complete, except for one manuscript, MS 88, the single extant Greek witness to Origen's "o´" text.[26]

With regard to the Hebrew *Vorlage* or parent text, the transmission history becomes simplified: the evidence suggests that there were no variant Hebrew MSS generating further Greek variants due specifically to correction toward Hebrew readings at variance with the MT after approximately the beginning of the second century C.E. The Hebrew scrolls found at Murabba^cat, dated prior to 135 C.E., conform very closely to the MT and indicate that the rabbinic bible was already standardized both in general contents and in consonantal text by the Second Jewish Revolt.

A number of additional sources help illuminate parts of the transmission history of the early Greek text. Study of sources such as the Vetus Latina,[27] quotations of the Hebrew Bible or the LXX in the NT and in Jewish and Christian authors in antiquity, and ancient biblical manuscripts provides us with windows on the past, enabling us to glimpse what the early Greek text looked like in certain places and specific points in time.

---

[26]See the description of Papyrus 967 in section I, above.

[27]See E. Ulrich, "The Old Latin Translation of the LXX and the Hebrew Scrolls from Qumran," *1980 Proceedings IOSCS—Vienna: The Hebrew and Greek Texts of Samuel*, ed. E. Tov (Jerusalem: Academon, 1980) 121-165; and J. Trebolle, "From the 'Old Latin' through the 'Old Greek' to the 'Old Hebrew' (2 Kings 10:23-25)," *Textus* 11 (1984) 17-36.

Regarding the *devanciers d'Aquila*, as Barthélemy terms them, the predecessors of Aquila, we should not take the hexaplaric order as a chronological indicator.   The text which circulated under the label "Theodotion" can more accurately be labelled "Proto-Theodotion"; i.e., the main systematic revision which characterizes that text was done around the turn of the era, early enough to influence possibly Philo, the NT, and Justin.[28]

For Proto-Theodotion, Aquila, and Symmachus, it is important to stress that these were not new translations from the Hebrew but recensions, i.e., systematic revisions, of earlier Greek texts. For Proto-Theodotion, the OG (but already in developed form) was used as the basic text, and it was revised according to definite principles. The principles operative in the Proto-Theodotionic recension involve bringing the early Greek text into much closer conformity with the Rabbinic Hebrew Text (the consonantal text which would later become the vocalized "Masoretic" Text). This conformity embraced both quantitative and qualitative aspects. Quantitatively, material in the Greek not found in the rabbinic bible was excised, and material in the Hebrew not matched by the Greek was filled in. Qualitatively, there was insistence on much greater, much more literal, fidelity to the details of the Hebrew text: lexically, Greek roots were matched much more consistently and mechanically with Hebrew roots, even if some violence was done to meaning; and the syntax of the Greek, already awash with semiticisms, was forced into even greater conformity to the syntax of the Hebrew, even if some syntactic violence occurred.

_____

[28]See P. Katz, *Philo's Bible* (Cambridge, 1950) 12, 102-103, 114-121; Jellicoe, *Septuagint*, 83-94; and P. Katz, "Justin's Old Testament quotations and the Greek Dodekapropheten Scroll," *Studia Patristica* 1/1 (Berlin, 1957) 343-353.

Aquila's recension was based on Proto-Theodotion but carried the systematic revision of Proto-Theodotion to even further levels of mechanical conformity toward the rabbinic text of the second century C.E. Aquila's recension is so systematic that Joseph Reider and Nigel Turner were able to compile *An Index to Aquila*,[29] which gives the Greek equivalents used by Aquila for the Hebrew roots in the biblical text.

Symmachus, about whom little is known,[30] produced a recension also based on Proto-Theodotion but aimed at good Greek style. Variants in which "the Three" (a' σ' θ') agree against the OG usually signal words revised in the Proto-Theodotionic recension and adopted but not further revised by Aquila and Symmachus.

Thus, the task of tracing the transmission of the Greek OT during the early rabbinic and early church period is a multifaceted task, for that text differed for each century and for each geographical region.[31] Book by book,

---

[29]*VTSup* 12; Leiden: Brill, 1966. Since 1968 a series of dissertations [see n. 32 below] have also been produced, exploring and charting the recensional developments of the Proto-Theodotion, or *Kaige*, recension.

[30]See Jellicoe, *Septuagint*, 94-99.

[31]Cf. H. Dörrie, "Zur Geschichte der Septuaginta im Jahrhundert Konstantins," *ZNW* 39 (1940) 57-110. P. A. de Lagarde (ed., *Librorum Veteris Testamenti Canonicorum Pars Prior Graece* [Göttingen, 1883]) attempted but failed to determine the Lucianic text of fourth-century Antioch. N. Fernández Marcos has recently contributed to this endeavor through *Theodoreti Cyrensis Quaestiones in Octateuchum: editio critica*, Textos y Estudios «Cardenal Cisneros» 17, ed. N. Fernández Marcos y A. Sáenz-Badillos (Madrid: Instituto «Arias Montano» C.S.I.C., 1979); and *Theodoreti Cyrensis Quaestiones in Reges et Paralipomena: editio critica*, Textos y Estudios «Cardenal Cisneros» 32, ed. N. Fernández Marcos y J. R. Busto Saiz (Madrid: Instituto «Arias Montano» C.S.I.C., 1984). The same chronological and geographical diversity obtains for the Old Latin; cf. Ulrich, "Characteristics" [n. 5 above] 68-70, 80.

we are learning the detailed characteristics of the Old Greek, the developments within the early Greek texts, and the characteristics of the subsequent recensions.[32]

Finally, to envision the "Septuagint" text which would have been available to Origen in the early third century one can study Codex Vaticanus or Papyrus 967. Both are codices containing all or many of the biblical books, inscribed in uncial script, with a text that is pre-hexaplaric. Both have numerous errors, and both display expansions clearly attributable to the vulnerabilities inherent in the process of transmission history. The "Septuagint" text, in varying forms, was the text used in the churches; the texts of Aquila, Symmachus, Theodotion, and others (such as "Quinta" and "Sexta"), mostly known to be Jewish and more closely based on the Hebrew, would also by now have been available.

III. Some Aspects of Origen and his Hexapla

So Origen began with the ordinary, somewhat corrupted, somewhat developed, koine Greek text of his day (called "the Translation of the Seventy" or simply "Septuaginta"), and he produced a text which was neither the original Old Greek translation nor the purified, inspired "Translation of the Seventy."

In this third section I would like to bring a Septuagintalist's eye to focus on three aspects of Origen and his work: (1) whether Origen knew

---

[32]In addition to the Göttingen LXX editions by R. Hanhart, J. Wm. Wevers, and J. Ziegler, for recent monographs dealing with Exodus (O'Connell, Sanderson), Joshua (Greenspoon), Judges (Bodine), Samuel (Ulrich), Kings (Shenkel, Trebolle), Isaiah (van der Kooij), Jeremiah (Tov), and Daniel (Schmitt, Pace Jeansonne), see the annual bibliographic "Record of Work" in *BIOSCS*.

Hebrew; (2) whether the Hexapla contained a column with Hebrew characters; and (3) an evaluation of Origen's hexaplaric labors as a contribution to the history of the Greek Bible.

(1) First, Origen's alleged knowledge or use of Hebrew centers on three areas: (a) his Hebrew tutor(s); (b) references to "the Hebrew" in his writings; and (c) the first column of the Hexapla. Let me begin by stating what would be a minimalist position on these three points:

(a´) Perhaps Origen knew no Hebrew or very little Hebrew, so little that it was virtually non-functioning. (b´) When Origen speaks of "the Hebrew," the basis of his knowledge is the Greek versions of Aquila, Symmachus, and Theodotion, i.e., the Hebrew indirectly, as witnessed by literal Greek renditions, not the Hebrew text itself in Hebrew script.[33] (c´) The extant Hexaplaric MS fragments contain no Hebrew column, perhaps because there never was a "first" column which contained the Hebrew characters.[34] One is hardpressed to move beyond this minimalist position, but let us see what can be established or plausibly conjectured.

(a´´) Eusebius says that Origen took great pains to learn Hebrew and had copies of the Jewish scriptures in the Hebrew script.[35] Jerome makes a similar assertion.[36] Now this may be attributed to the panegyric style of Eusebius and Jerome; but just because they are waxing eloquent about their hero, that does not mean that what they say is false, it simply means that we

---

[33]Barthélemy, "Origène" [n. 5 above], 254;   Pierre Nautin, *Origène: Sa vie et son œuvre* (Christianisme Antique 1; Paris: Beauchesne, 1977) 337.

[34]Nautin, *Origène*, 303, 312, 337, and *passim*.

[35]*Hist. Eccl.* vi.16; see also Swete, *Introduction*, 59.

[36]*De Viris Ill.*, 54; see also Swete, *Introduction*, 59.

cannot *ipso dicto* consider the statements accurate without further verification. On the one hand, it is quite possible that Origen learned some Hebrew both from "his second teacher in Scripture..., the unnamed 'Hebrew,' son of a rabbi, earlier converted to Christianity in Palestine,"[37] and later from learned Jews through direct conversation or debate. On the other hand, that remains nebulous, and it is only possible to determine whether he knew Hebrew and how much he knew through his actual uses of it in specific writings.

(b´´) To what specifically is Origen referring in his commentaries, homilies, etc. when he speaks of "the Hebrew"? when he relates the Christian "OT" to "the Hebrew"? I have not found any loci where Origen uses Hebrew[38] in such a way that he is free of possible dependence on a Greek intermediary, such as Aquila or the Greek transcription of the Hebrew,[39] or possible dependence on well-known early Christian tradition, such as the discussion of Isa 7:14 by Justin, Irenaeus, Tertullian, and others.[40]

On the contrary, Origen can be seen referring to the Hebrew at least once[41] where his argument founders because the Hebrew of the Masoretic *textus receptus* is other than he says; and it seems unlikely that we may appeal to a Hebrew different from the Masoretic, because the context demands

---

[37]Kannengiesser, unpublished CJA seminar notes, p.2. See Nautin, *Origène*, p. 347 and 417, where he refers implicitly to Origen's autobiographical note in the *Letter to Africanus* 11.

[38]Also Barthélemy ("Origène," 254) says that Origen "se comporte toujours comme s'il ignorait l'hébreu."

[39]Cf. Nautin, *Origène*, 337.

[40]Cf. Barthélemy, "Origène," 250.

[41]*Cont. Cels.*, I.34. I am grateful to Jeffrey Oschwald for pointing out this example to me.

precisely the word found in the MT.[42] The passage under discussion is Isaiah 7:14, and the Hebrew quoted is "Aalma" [=עלמה] which, of course, does occur in Isaiah 7:14. Origen argues that the word "Aalma" here means "virgin" and not simply "young woman." For support, he appeals to Deut 22:23-26, a legal text in which the point centers specifically on a virgin. Origen says that "the word Aalma, which the Septuagint translated by 'parthenos' (virgin) and others [i.e., Aquila and Theodotion] by 'neanis' (young woman), also occurs, so they say, in Deuteronomy applied to a virgin,"[43] and he proceeds to quote the full text of Deuteronomy. Immediately, one suspects that Origen's qualifier "so they say" indicates that he is getting his argument second-hand. And yet, one would think that such an indefatigable scholar as Origen on such a much-argued point as the virgin-mother of Christ would certainly have checked the passage in Hebrew if he could have. Had he done so, he would have seen that "Aalma" does not occur in that passage, but rather $na^cr[ah]$ (youth) and the required betûlah (virgin). But it is the presupposition here, not specifically Origen's knowledge of Hebrew, which emerges as problematic: Origen was not sufficiently "indefatigable"—at least not at this point. For even if Origen knew no Hebrew, had he, as presupposed, made the effort to consult even the Greek transliteration, he would have found that his argument from Deuteronomy was baseless. Thus, even this argument where he errs with regard to the

---

[42] A quick check of the unpublished scrolls from Qumran Cave 4 finds that, as for the published MSS from the other caves, Deut 22:23-26 is not preserved. But even if it were, one would not expect that it would display עלמה as a variant, since בתולה is necessary for the legal point made therein.

[43] Cont. Cels., I.34.

Hebrew does not prove that he did not know Hebrew, but rather that he simply did not check his sources, in Hebrew or in Greek transliteration.

In sum, one could conjecture from the evidence and the lack of it that Origen may possibly have learned some Hebrew at some time, but that his lack of display of that knowledge quite probably points to at most a modicum of acquired Hebrew, and that his Hebrew was virtually non-functioning.

(c´´) If Origen's knowledge of the Hebrew language is in serious doubt, that would seem to lend support to Nautin and cast serious doubt as well on whether his Hexapla contained a "first" column in the Hebrew script, and to this we now turn.

(2) Secondly, then, was there in the Hexapla a column written in the Hebrew script? It is with regard to the Hebrew column of the Hexapla that the minimalist position stated above, echoing Nautin,[44] seems too minimal to me. The Mercati fragments of the "Hexapla," the Ambrosian palimpsest O 39 sup.,[45] contain no Hebrew column, nor do the other Hexaplaric remains.[46] Does this prove, however, that there never was a

---

[44]Nautin, *Origène*, 303, 312, 337, and *passim*.

[45]Giovanni Mercati, ed., *Psalterii Hexapli Reliquiae...*, Pars Prima: *Codex Rescriptus Bybliothecae Ambrosianae O 39 sup. phototypice expressus et transcriptus* (Vatican City, 1958). See also B. M. Metzger, *Manuscripts of the Greek Bible: An Introduction to Greek Palaeography* (New York: Oxford University, 1981) pl. 30 and pp. 108-109; and E. Würthwein, *The Text of the Old Testament*, tr. E. R. Rhodes (Grand Rapids, MI: Eerdmans, 1979) pl. 34 and pp. 188-189. For fuller discussion see Jellicoe, *Septuagint*, 130-133.

[46]See Nautin, *Origène*, 303-309. F. Field (ed., *Origenis Hexaplorum quae supersunt sive veterum interpretum Graecum in totum Vetus Testamentum fragmenta*, 2 vols. [Oxford, 1875] 1. XIV-XV) lists some examples which contain a Hebrew column, but he does not give the source, and thus it is difficult to ascertain whether there are in fact remains of the Hexapla which preserve the Hebrew column.

"first" column which contained the Hebrew characters? Barthélemy, having published his article prior to Nautin's book, assumes with the majority of scholars that there was a Hebrew column.[47] My colleague John Wright[48] is convinced by Nautin, but I am not.

Beginning with the data, we note that the ninth- or tenth-century Mercati MS has as its initial column the transliteration of the Hebrew in Greek characters, followed by Aquila, Symmachus, the "o´," and a fifth column, customarily labelled "Theodotion" but in Psalms probably Quinta. The side margins are preserved, and it appears certain that there was no column with Hebrew characters prior to the transliteration column in this manuscript. Similarly, the other three synoptic fragments with excerpts of the Hexapla (the marginal notes in Ambrosian codex B 106, the Cambridge fragment from the Cairo Geniza, and the Vatican codex Barberinus 549)[49] contain no column in the Hebrew script.

Starting from a different angle, it appears that the Greek transliteration column was clearly an element of the original Hexapla. It, with or without the Hebrew first column, is the key to the vertical format of the Hexapla. It is implausible that the Greek transliteration would have been added later by Origen or added to Origen's work between the third and eighth centuries had it not been there from the start. The question is whether Origen also had a column with the Hebrew text in Hebrew characters which preceded the transliteration.

---

[47] Barthélemy, "Origène," 255.

[48] See J. W. Wright's paper in this volume.

[49] See Nautin, *Origène*, 303-309.

Nautin bases his assertion that there was no column in the Hebrew script on the format of the four preserved Hexaplaric fragments and a critique of Eusebius' description.[50] But, turning first to Eusebius, Nautin's critique does not disprove Eusebius. Nautin admits that Eusebius had seen the Hexapla,[51] and quotes Eusebius' statement that Origen had learned the Hebrew language and had acquired personal copies of the Jewish scriptures in Hebrew characters.[52]   The statement that Origen had learned the Hebrew language may well be eulogizing praise, founded or unfounded; but the statement about copies of the Hebrew scriptures sounds more like a statement of fact, a description of something Eusebius had seen in the libary at Caesarea.

Nautin says that Eusebius "manifestly wants to give a complete description but makes no mention of a column containing Hebrew characters" (314); thus, he concludes, there existed no such column.

Now Nautin is correct that in this passage Eusebius does not explicitly state that there was a column with Hebrew characters as the first

---

[50]Ibid., 303-309 (Hexaplaric fragments) and 311-316 (Eusebius). Nautin begins his chapter on the Hexapla (303) with a description which omits this column. He prepares his reader: "On observera qu'il n'existe pas de colonne contenant l'hébreu en caractères hébraïques, ce qui concorde tout à fait, nous le verrons, avec le témoignage d'Eusèbe" (305). And after his discussion of Eusebius (311-316) he discounts Epiphanius' testimony: "Mais il est contredit par celui d'Eusèbe . . ., qui mentionne une seule colonne d'hébreu, celle de la translittération" (320).

[51]"Eusèbe a regardé les synopses qu'il trouvait dans la bibliothèque de Césarée" (ibid., 312), and "Eusèbe avait une connaissance directe de la synopse" (320).

[52]"...qu'il acquit personnellement les Écritures prototypes conservées chez les Juifs et écrites avec les charactères hébreux eux-mêmes..." (Ibid., 312; πρωτοτύπους αὐτοῖς Ἑβραῖων στοιχείοις γραφάς Hist. Eccl. vi.16).

column of the Hexapla. He is also probably correct that τῆς Ἑβραίων σημειώσεως means the Greek transliteration. But though he makes the curious remark (causing one to wonder what presupposition lies behind) that the LXX comes only in the third rank among the four Greek versions (305), he does not bring to our attention that Eusebius does not describe the columns in order but is content to mention the LXX in one phrase, but the versions of Aquila, Symmachus, and Theodotion together in a separate phrase. Nor does he bring to our attention that Eusebius mentions τῆς Ἑβραίων σημειώσεως after, not before, the other Greek versions.

In my view, just as Eusebius spoke of the LXX and "the Three" in one natural way of speaking, but not in a precise description order, so he began this passage by speaking of Origen's Hebrew bible "in Hebrew characters" and immediately continued describing—without having precisely stated that the Hebrew was inscribed in the first column—the other elements of the Hexapla. Eusebius is patently not giving the type of precise description required to support the weight of Nautin's conclusion. Put another way: why is it possible to conclude that, since Eusebius makes no explicit mention of a column containing Hebrew characters, therefore there existed no such column, if one is not prepared to say that, since Eusebius explicitly mentions the LXX in one phrase but the versions of Aquila, Symmachus, and Theodotion together in a separate phrase, therefore the columns of the Hexapla were precisely in the order he described?

Nautin's well-intentioned cross-examination appears more rigorous than Eusebius' words were meant to bear. At the level of concepts, Nautin has elaborated one provocative, perhaps possible reconstruction of the Hexapla. But at the level of judgment, he has not at all proved that the traditional (ancient and modern) reconstruction is incorrect, nor has he proven that his is correct; each of his conclusions still needs to be tested.

Turning now to Nautin's assessment of the Mercati MS, before considering his judgment it is important to state explicitly, as Nautin does not in his opening treatment of the MS, that the Mercati MS is not *the* Hexapla but a *ninth- or tenth-century copy* of excerpts from the Hexapla. In fact, our earliest fragments of the Hexapla date only from the eighth century, 500 years after Origen. We should expect there to be very few Christians after Origen and before the date of the four surviving fragments of the Hexapla who could transcribe the Hebrew column,[53] and it would be extremely unlikely that for each instance of copying during those 500 years there was someone who both knew Hebrew and saw a need to preserve the Hebrew column.

Furthermore, I am not at all sure that all four fragments support Nautin's conclusion. The 12th century (or later) marginal notes in the Ambrosian codex B 106 list 5 columns (the Greek transliteration, then presumably Aquila, Symmacus, the Septuagint, and Theodotion or Quinta); but prior to the Greek transliteration column there are four points arranged, according to Nautin, in a diamond shape. Mercati wondered whether these points would not have been put in place of the Hebrew letters; but Nautin says that "This supposition has no foundation since Eusebius himself did not find the column in Hebrew characters . . . and furthermore [the Mercati fragment] does not have it. These four points can have no other function than to mark the beginning of the citation or to signal the use of Hebrew words."[54]

---

[53] Jerome was one of the few Christian authors after Origen and before the 12th century who studied Hebrew.

[54] Nautin, *Origène*, 306-307, n.5.

However, Nautin's argument does not hold up. Against the three parts of his statement: first, I have argued above that Nautin has not proved that Eusebius did not see a Hebrew column in the Hexapla; secondly, the absence of the Hebrew column in the ninth- or tenth-century Mercati copy does not prove that the third-century Hexapla did not have a Hebrew column; and thirdly, the scribe's four points do, I would agree, signal the use of Hebrew words; but I would assume that these signalled Hebrew words were in the Hebrew script from the first column, where in fact the points are properly placed. In contrast, Nautin, if his argument is to be consistent, apparently assumes that these "Hebrew words" are the Greek transliteration in what is traditionally considered the "second" column. This point, however, must remain unresolved until it can be determined, from other usage in the MS or elsewhere, whether the four points substitute for words in the Hebrew script, seen, not copied, but their presence marked, or whether they simply indicate that the following words which were copied are foreign words, though written in Greek script.

Thus, for Nautin's denial of the Hebrew column on the basis the MS evidence, (a) I question his data on one of the four MSS, and (b) I think that the 500-year hiatus between Origen and the preserved fragments neutralizes his evidence, for one would not expect Christians either to have been able, or to have always wanted, to copy the column with the Hebrew script. Nautin has argued the case for one possible reconstruction of the Hexapla, but in my view he has not proved that the traditional reconstruction is wrong, and I still find myself holding the traditional understanding.

I would also point out that it may well be that none of the four fragments are really copies of "the Hexapla" but simply excerpts, or copies of excerpts, from the Hexapla. Three of the four are from the Psalms, and the citation in Vatican codex Barberinus 549 is a citation of one verse excerpted from the Hexapla (Ἐκ τῶν ἑξάπλων)—only a citation from Hosea 11:1, in connection, as it itself says, with Matthew's quotation of it in his Infancy Narrative. The Hosea usage is clearly Christian, and the Psalms usage may very well have been. Thus, a minimalist interpretation here would be that the Greek columns of the Hexapla of Psalms were copied and used, and excerpts were occasionally made from a copy of the Hexapla for Christian exegetical purposes.

Be that as it may, from a larger perspective the point of the Hebrew column may be of little consequence, if Origen did not know or use the Hebrew. I think that, whether Origen's Hexapla contained a Hebrew column or not, the transliteration column arose earlier as a column in parallel with a column containing the Hebrew characters. Origen borrowed and placed in his Hexapla either the Hebrew text and the transcription (the traditional view) or simply the transcription (Nautin's view). It is quite conceivable that Origen borrowed a Jewish source which already had in parallel columns the Hebrew, a Greek transliteration, and Aquila's exactly corresponding version—and possibly even Symmachus' version as well for intelligibility or elegant style.

The picture which emerges is that Origen was confronted with MSS of the Greek Bible used by the church which disagreed with each other, and that he was confronted by argumentation (live or literary) with Jews whose Bible differed significantly from that of the church, and he had enough balance to understand that the Hebrew had a certain priority. So he took "the Hebrew" (probably in Hebrew script and also in Greek transliteration, possibly only the latter), Aquila, Symmachus, Theodotion, and whatever other ἐκδόσεις were available plus the "Septuagint" in forms then current in Alexandria or Palestine, and had his copyists and calligraphers (probably including Hebrew) compile a work which he in his extant writings does not, but which Eusebius does, call "the Hexapla." In its fifth column he produced "the Hexaplaric recension" a revised edition of the "Septuagint," with the quantitative changes marked by the Aristarchian symbols, with the qualitative changes including transposed word order not marked, and ineluctably with some copyists' errors.

(3) Thirdly and finally, what evaluation do we render concerning Origen's Hexapla in relation to the transmission history of the Greek Bible? From Driver[55] to Barthélemy, the judgment has been negative. Barthélemy even uses the word "catastrophique," and notes that for us to arrive at the original OG, "il nous faut commencer par purifier le texte de la Septante de toute contamination hexaplaire...."[56]

The key to the problem engendered by the Hexapla is that by Origen's time the rabbinic Hebrew Bible had been standardized and there was a general assumption that it was the "Hebraica Veritas." Origen assumed that the single Hebrew text-type used by his contemporaries was identical to that from which "the LXX" had been translated. Deviations of the Greek from the Hebrew were considered problems or infidelities in the Greek. It is precisely in Origen's carrying out of his objective that he obscured and lost most: it is in his changing the Greek "back" toward agreement with the rabbinic text that he lost, sometimes forever, many superior readings and many attestations to variant traditions.

Nautin and Trigg[57] think that Origen should not be blamed. They rather blame his followers who did not maintain his critical standards. But here again, I must disagree. Origen deserves high marks for industry, good

---

[55]S. R. Driver, "Notes" [n. 5 above] xliii.

[56]Barthélemy, "Origène," 247.

[57]Nautin, *Origène*, 359-361;   J. W. Trigg, *Origen: The Bible and Philosophy in the Third-century Church* (Atlanta: John Knox, 1983) 85.

intentions, and perhaps the highest standards conceivable and achievable in his era. But he did not achieve the "incorrupta et inmaculata septuaginta interpretum translatio" as claimed by Jerome.[58] Neither did he achieve the original Old Greek translation, in the sense of the goal of the modern text critic; on the contrary, he moved further away. Nor did he produce a text which would long stand as a purified text for the Eastern churches (in his sense of conforming to the Hebrew). Nor did he even have the luck to bequeath a very useful tool for the modern scholar—in that it is scarcely preserved, and what is preserved is confusedly preserved.

What is the difference between the Hexaplaric Septuagint and the Septuagint which we use today? The Göttingen critical editions, and even Rahlfs' hand edition, have attempted to purify the text of any hexaplaric influence, and the Cambridge Septuagint chooses Vaticanus as its diplomatic text precisely because it is largely pre-hexaplaric. Is this "purification" good and desirable? The textual critic, attempting to drive further back toward earlier and "superior" forms of the Hebrew biblical text, would assent. One seeking the bible of the early church may perhaps start by dissenting, but would soon have to agree that Origen moved the bible away from the form that the church had previously known and produced yet another form of the varying LXX manuscript tradition—a form which, soon afterwards at the hand of Lucian, spawned future diffusion in the transmission history.

On the positive side, Origen was the pioneer of biblical textual criticism for the Christian tradition. He also pioneered the path of integration of critical scholarship with theology and spirituality. He did achieve the removal of a number of mistakes from the text, and he brought the Christian

---

[58]*Epistula* CVI, 2.2, *Sancti Eusebii Hieronymi Epistulae* II, *CSEL* 55, ed. I. Hilberg (Vienna, 1912) 248-249.

text into greater conformity with the rabbinic Hebrew Text of the third century, so that dialogue continued to be possible. A principal achievement was that he bolstered Christian confidence in the soundness of the Greek Old Testament they used, and this should be reckoned a significant milestone in the Christianization of the Hebrew Bible.[59]

---

[59]This final idea and a significant amount of clarification throughout this paper I owe to Jeffrey Oschwald's insightful discussion.

THE TEXT OF THE GOSPELS IN ORIGEN'S COMMENTARIES ON JOHN AND MATTHEW

William L. Petersen
University of Notre Dame

Writing in 1928, Kirsopp Lake, Robert Blake and Silva New observed that "perhaps the most important piece of work which remains is the double task of collecting and studying the quotations from the other Gospels in Origen and Eusebius."[1] This is because the evidence of Patristic writers "is always the guiding star of the textual critic in his effort to localise and date a text."[2]

Since the time of Griesbach, classification of the gospel text used by Origen has been attempted.[3] Origen is a particularly attractive subject for

---

[1]K. Lake, R. Blake and S. New, "The Caesarean Text of the Gospel of Mark," *HTR* 21 (1928), 277.

[2]Ibid., 258.

[3]See the survey of researches in Kwang-Wan Kim, *The Matthean Text of Origen in His Commentary on Matthew*, unpublished Ph.D. dissertation, Univ. of Chicago (1946), 135-41. In addition to the other studies cited in this article, reference should be made to P. Koetschau, "Beiträge zur Textkritik von Origenes' Johanneskommentar," TU 28,2 (1905) and E. Klostermann and E. Benz, "Zur Überlieferung der Matthäuserklärung des Origenes," TU 47, 2 (1932).

investigation for three reasons. First, he is an early father, whose literary output coincides with the beginning of the third century. Second, he is regarded as the first Christian text critic, whose interest in the text is evidenced by his *Hexapla*, commentaries and literary/textual observations.[4] Third, the two cities in which Origen lived and wrote, Alexandria (from his birth until 231-2 C.E.) and Caesarea (c. 232-253/4 C.E.), are, coincidentally, the presumed homes of two of the major text types of the New Testament: the Alexandrian, and the Caesarean.

Erwin Preuschen, in the introduction to his 1903 GCS edition of Origen's *Commentary on John*, investigated Origen's text type. His findings dismayed him:

> Es war wohl die schlechteste Auskunft, auf die man überhaupt verfallen konnte, wenn man annahm, dass Origenes sich bei seinen Citaten an keine Textform gebunden habe, sondern wahllos bald der und bald der Autorität gefolgt sei.[5]

Further work on Origen's text was done by B.H. Streeter, in his 1924 study which brought the Caesarean text to light: *The Four Gospels*.[6] Relying on the variants noted by Preuschen, Streeter found, from the field of

---

[4] B.M. Metzger, "Explicit References in the Works of Origen to Variant Readings in New Testament Manuscripts" in *Biblical and Patristic Studies in Memory of Robert Pierce Casey*, J. Neville Birdsall and R.W. Thomson, edd. (Freiburg, 1963), 78-95.

[5] E. Preuschen, *Origenes Werke IV, Der Johanneskommentar* GCS 10 (Leipzig, 1903), p. xci.

[6] B.H. Streeter, *The Four Gospels, A Study of Origins* (London, 1924).

24 variants identified by Preuschen, what he thought were significant agreements with his Caesarean text.[7] This position was refined by Kirsopp Lake, Robert Blake and Silva New, in their exposition of "The Caesarean Text of the Gospel of Mark," published in the *Harvard Theological Review* of 1928.[8] Noting that only the first *five* (not twelve) books of the *Commentary* had been authored in Alexandria,[9] they examined the citations more closely, and came to the conclusion that after chapter twelve in Mark (which was, coincidentally, about Bk. XII in the *Commentary*), Origen's text of Mark became predominately Caesarean.

Their conclusion is accurately reflected in Sir Frederick Kenyon's *The Text of the Greek Bible*:

Origen may have used the Caesarean text before he left Alexandria; . . . he certainly used the Alexandrian text on his first arrival at Caesarea; and . . . for the rest of his life at Caesarea he certainly used the Caesarean text.[10]

This statement "certainly" reminds one of the worried Roman of antiquity who, not knowing which religion was "true," joined them all. Kenyon's statement, which reflects the position of Lake, Blake and New,

---

[7]Ibid., 96-102.

[8]*HTR* 21 (1928), 207-404.

[9]Origen, *Comm. Io.*, VI.2.8; see the comments and analysis of Lake, Blake and New, 259-261.

[10]F.G. Kenyon, *The Text of the Greek Bible*, rev. and aug. A.W. Adams (London, 1975[3]), 191.

leaves virtually every possibility open, in essence saying nothing, while appearing to say something.

The publication of Klostermann's edition of Origen's *Commentary on Matthew* in 1935 permitted the first comparative studies of Origen's text in the two cities. R.V.G. Tasker published two studies, including collations, one on Bks. I and II of the Alexandrian-authored *Comm. Io.* (logging 13 variants), and one on Klostermann's edition of the Caesarean-authored *Comm. Mt.* (logging 73 variants).[11] The "irresistible" conclusion was that in Bks. I and II of the *Comm. Io.*, Origen was "using a predominantly Neutral (= Alexandrian) text."[12] In Caesarea, Tasker's findings on the *Comm. Mt.* supported the conclusions of Lake, Blake and New's investigation into Origen's text of Mark: it was Caesarean.

After the Second World War, Kwang-Wan Kim wrote a dissertation on the Matthean text in the *Comm. Mt.*,[13] and published the results in two articles.[14] While limited to the Caesarean-authored *Comm. Mt.*, Kim's work is significant, for it noted one of the obstacles in categorizing Origen's text type, and, under the supervision of E.C. Colwell, used the "Method of Multiple Attestation" (a predecessor of the Claremont Profile Method) to resolve the issue. The problem is best seen in an example. In his *Comm.*

---

[11]R.V.G. Tasker, "The Text of the Fourth Gospel Used by Origen in his Commentary on John," *JTS* 37 (1936), 146-55; idem, "The Text of St. Matthew Used by Origen in his Commentary on St. Matthew," *JTS* 38 (1937), 60-64.

[12]Ibid., "Fourth Gospel," 149.

[13]Kim, *The Matthean Text of Origen* .

[14]K. W. Kim, "The Matthean Text of Origen in his Commentary on Matthew," *JBL* 68 (1949), 125-39; idem, "Codices 1582, 1739, and Origen," *JBL* 69 (1950), 167-175.

Io. II.224, Origen interpolates *ἀκούειν* before *ἀκουέτω* in Mt. 11.15. This agrees with א C L Z in the Alexandrian text; Θ *f*¹ *f*¹³ in the Caesarean text; syr^c lat in the Western text; and W syr^{p.h} M(ehrheitstext) in the Koine (Byzantine) text.[15] But it is *omitted* (that is, against Origen's reading) in: B in the Alexandrian; 700 in the Caesarean; and D *k* syr^s in the Western text. How does one decide from which family Origen took the reading? Major witnesses in each of the families support the reading; major witnesses in three of the families also dissent from the reading.

Kim resolved this problem by logging the variants, their support, and only then seeing with which Origen agreed. If they were dominantly Western, for example, then Origen's reading was Western. Kim found that MSS 1 and 1582 were closest to the 120 variants he noted in Origen's text of Matthew in the Caesarean-authored *Comm. Mt*. Since Origen did not follow Θ, the premier "Caesarean" witness, Kim was loath to call Origen's text Caesarean, even though many text critics would lump these two MSS in with the Caesarean witnesses.

The next enquirer into Origen's text type was Gordon D. Fee. His first study was limited to the fourth chapter of John, and he conluded that "Origen's text of John 4 is a 'primary' Neutral."[16] A second study of the text of Luke in Origen's treatise *On Prayer* and the *Comm. Io*. indicated that Origen's text was "very close to p^75 B in the gospels."[17]

---

[15]Family membership was determined on the basis of B. Metzger's classification, *The Text of the New Testament* (Oxford, 1968²), 212-219.

[16]G.D. Fee, "The Text of John in Origen and Cyril of Alexandria," *Biblica* 52 (1971), 370. Fee's "primary" Neutral group consists of p^66 p^75 B C.

[17]Idem, "Origen's Text of the New Testament and the Text of Egypt," *NTS* 28 (1982), 358; by "gospels," Fee must mean Luke, for that is the scope of this study. See also Fee's "p^75, p^66 and Origen: The Myth of

The most recent work has been indirect, in that it focused on the text of Serapion of Thmuis. Following Fee's lead, and against the findings of earlier researchers, Alexander Globe concluded that Serapion's text was similar to Origen's, which he called "Neutral" (= p^{66} p^{75} ℵ B).[18]

The study in hand is intended to clarify these issues, or, failing that, to present more data for analysis. One of the failings of the work of earlier researchers is the small number of passages collated. Preuschen noted 24 variants; Tasker logged 86; Kim, 120. Our study involved complete collations of large portions of two commentaries, which logged 379 variants. Further, given the movement of Origen from Alexandria to Caesarea, a collation of works from both cities should make possible a comparison of the text type Origen used in these two cities. Any shift in Origen's text type should become immediately apparent. Heretofore, only Tasker has made such a comparison.

From Origen's Alexandrian period, the first five books of his *Commentary on John* were selected.[19] Origen himself states that these were written in Alexandria (*Comm. Io.* VI.8); they are dated between 226 and 229 C.E. From Origen's Caesarean period, books X and XI of his *Commentary on Matthew* were selected.[20] This work dates from circa 244 C.E. These

---

Early Textual Recension in Alexandria," in *New Dimensions in New Testament Study*, ed. R.N. Longenecker and M.C. Tenney (Grand Rapids, MI, 1974), 19-45; idem, "Codex Sinaiticus in the Gospel of John: A Contribution to Methodology in Establishing Textual Relationships," *NTS* 15 (1968-9), 23-44.

[18]"Serapion of Thmuis as Witness to the Gospel Text Used by Origen in Caesarea," *NovT* 26 (1984), 97-127.

[19]*Origène, Commentaire sur S. Jean, I*, ed. C. Blanc, SC 120 (Paris, 1966).

[20]*Origène, Commentaire sur l'Evangile selon Matthieu, I*, ed. R. Girod, SC 162 (Paris, 1970).

commentaries were selected because they afford several advantages. First, they are available in the original Greek, not a Latin translation. Second, the manuscript tradition is identical: the most ancient copy of both is the same MS, Monacensis graecus 191. The MS dates from the twelfth or thirteenth century; other MSS are descendants of this archetype. Finally, excellent new editions of both works are available in the series Sources Chrétiennes.[21]

While limitations of space prevent presentation of the actual collations here, examples will be given to illustrate the type of variants found, along with examples which point out some of the pitfalls one encounters in attempting to conclude which text family Origen favored (or used) at any given location or date.

A few words must be said about method, for in patristic works it is difficult to define what constitutes a gospel quotation (as opposed to an allusion or echo) or where the quotation begins and ends. To circumvent these problems, only obvious quotations were collated. Where Origen appeared to have deliberately reordered the text, or altered it (deleting a proper name, for example, because the name was already in the sentence which introduces the quotation), the passage was ignored.[22] Further, short two or

---

[21]On the dating of Monacensis: E. Preuschen, *Origenes Werke IV*, GCS 10, p. ix; that Monacensis is the archetype for the other MSS in *Comm. Io.*, p. xl. E. Klostermann, *Origenes Werke X, Origenes Matthäuserklärung I*, GCS 40 (Leipzig, 1935) calls it "unabhängig" from the next oldest MS of the *Comm. Mt.*, 14th-century Cantabrigiensis Coll. S. Trinit. 194 (p. viif.).

[22]An example can best illustrate the problem: at *Comm. Io.* X.21, the text in the gospel runs, "Jesus said, 'Destroy this temple . . . ' " (Jn. 2.19). Origen omits the "Jesus said" introduction. For a fuller treatment of the problems involved, and methods for solution, see, W. L. Petersen, *The Diatessaron and Ephrem Syrus as Sources of Romanos the Melodist* (Louvain, 1985), pp. 55-59.

three word quotations were excluded, for, especially in such brief snippets of text, it is hard to tell if one has a real quotation or only an echo. Finally, variants unattested in the apparatus of our collation base (the 26th edition of Nestle-Aland's *Novum Testamentum Graece*) and H.F. von Soden's *Die Schriften des Neuen Testaments* have been excluded, for they cannot help locate Origen's text type.

Although Kim's study, using the "Method of Multiple Attestation," attempted to resolve the problems of simple collation as a mode of fixing Origen's association with a particular textual family, his method is still not totally reliable. Observing *agreements* with a particular text family can be misleading, for Origen may also be going against major representatives of that same text family (e.g., Kim's finding of agreement with 1 and 1582, but against Θ). Therefore, it is necessary to record both agreements and *disagreements* with a text family.

In our study, therefore, three sets of figures are presented for each collation: agreements, disagreements, and singular agreements--that is, agreements which are unique in that they are between Origen and the representatives of a *single* text family.

For the *Commentary on John*, penned in Alexandria, 148 quotations were isolated. From them, 34 attested variants were found. The table below sets out the raw number of agreements (N=), disagreements and singular agreements, as well as percentages (%=) for each.

	ALEX.	CAESAR.	WESTERN	KOINE
Agreements:				
N=	21	20	23	18
%=	.61	.59	.68	.53
Disagreements:				
N=	24	22	18	21
%=	.70	.65	.53	.62
Singular agreements:				
N=	3	2	4	2
%=	.27	.18	.36	.18

(there were 11 singular agreements, leading to a different divisor)

In raw numbers, agreements between Origen and the first three text families are virtually identical. In a sample of this size, the difference is not significant. The Koine is clearly not a major influence. Regarding the disagreements, Origen's reading is contradicted equally as often by the Alexandrian, as by the Caesarean and Koine texts. It is interesting, however, to note that the *fewest* number of contradictions comes from the Western text. When we turn to the "singular agreements," that is agreements unique to a single textual family,[23] there are more with the Western text than with any other family, although the sample size is too small to speak of statistically significant differences. Be that as it may, it is nevertheless a confirmation of the Western text's fewer number of disagreements.

Turning to the Caesarean-authored *Commentary on Matthew*, 231 quotations were isolated; 62 were paralleled in the apparatuses. The data is as follows:

---

[23]It must be pointed out that our basis for determining such "singular agreements" (as well as "agreements" and "disagreements") is, of course, proscribed by the range of witnesses listed in the critical apparatuses. Hence, it is acknowledged as incomplete and inaccurate, even though it uses the most complete and best data available today.

	ALEX.	CAESAR.	WESTERN	KOINE
Agreements:				
N=	31	47	31	34
%=	.50	.75	.50	.54
Disagreements:				
N=	39	28	38	36
%=	.63	.45	.61	.58
Singular agreements:					
N=	2	8	5	1
%=	.13	.50	.31	.06

(there were 16 singular agreements, leading to a different divisor)

In this case, Origen's agreements with the Alexandrian, Western and Koine texts are statistically undifferentiated. The agreements with the Caesarean text are, however, significantly higher. A similar pattern is to be found in the disagreements: there are fewer between Origen and the Caesarean text. Finally, in singular agreements, the Caesarean is again obviously more significant.

In reflecting upon these findings, several observations can be made. First, the higher agreements with the Caesarean text in the Caesarean-authored *Comm. Mt.* is rather to be expected. But it is interesting to note that in the Alexandrian-authored *Comm. Io.*, the major families (excluding the Koine, which is of little import) are virtually equal. Indeed, if, based on our collations, one were to give preference to any of the families in this Alexandrian-authored work, it would be difficult not to point to the Western text: it has the most agreements, fewest disagreements, and most singular agreements.[24]

---

[24]These singular agreements with the Western text are not superficial, either:

  1. *Comm. Io.* II.74: ἔιτη] βλασφημήσῃ with syr[s.c] at Mt. 12.32

  2. *Comm. Io.* I.50: omit ἐν ἡμῖν ὡς ἐλάλει ἡμῖν with syr[s.c] *c e* at Lk. 24.32.

In both works, the type of variants is often trivial. While there are significant variants,[25] more often than not the variant is one of style or word order. These bespeak arbitrary stylistic improvements, and usually are of minor import for locating a text type. Some examples are:

At *Comm. Io.* I.19 (apud Mt. 23.8): κληθῆτε] καλέσητε

At *Comm. Io.* I.68 (apud Mt. 26.13): ἄν] ἐάν

At *Comm. Io.* II.116 (apud Mk. 12.26): τοῦ] τῆς

At *Comm. Io.* II.215 (apud Jn. 1.27): ἐγὼ ἄξιος] ἄξιος ἐγώ

At *Comm. Mt.* X.1 (apud Mt. 13.36): + αὐτοῦ post οἰκίαν

At *Comm. Mt.* X.14 (apud Mt. 13.52: ἐκβάλλει] προφέρει

At *Comm. Mt.* X.21 (apud Mt. 14.4): ὁ Ἰωάννης αὐτῷ] αὐτῷ ὁ Ἰωάννης

At *Comm. Mt.* XI.16 (apud Mt. 15.22/harmonization Mk. 8.6): κακῶς] δεινῶς

There is one rather minor variant which, however, when taken in the context of Origen's accompanying commentary, raises grave questions about the integrity of the text transmitted. When quoting Mt. 14.13, Origen twice omits the difficult reading ἐν πλοίῳ, having Jesus ἀνεχώρησεν εἰς ἔρημον τόπον, rather than ἀνεχώρησεν ἐκεῖθεν ἐν πλοίῳ εἰς ἔρημον τόπον. It is omitted at *Comm. Mt.* X.23 and XI.5. What is striking is that Origen specifically speaks of the boat, and allegorizes it later in X.23: διὸ λέλεκται ἐν πλοίῳ, τουτέστι τῷ σώματι.[26] Now, it must be

---

[25]See, for example, those listed in the preceding note.

[26]In R. Girod's edition (supra, n. 12), the omissions are located at p. 252, lined 1-3 (X.23) and p. 288, line 20 (XI.5). The full reading (with ἐν πλοίῳ) is given at p. 252, lines 9-10 (X.23).

granted that when quoting the passage a third time (also in X.23[27]) Origen *does* give the full reading. One is puzzled, however, by the deliberate allegorization of the "boat," which Origen omits two of three times. Why allegorize a difficult reading which is not present in one's text?

The only solution which suggests itself is that the citations in Origen's works may have been "Vulgatized" by later scribes,[28] that is, brought into conformity with a later "standard" text. This would explain the absence in two lemmata of the very *lectio difficilior* which Origen is attempting to allegorize away. The later scribes substituted their "standard text," in two places, thus removing the reading Origen knew, but did not revise the commentary itself, or, inexplicably, the third lemma.

If this suggestion is correct, then it raises questions about the reliability of our twelfth or thirteenth century MS of the commentaries and, consequently, the validity of conclusions based on collations of their Biblical texts. Rufinus' preface to *Peri archon*, in which he admits rewriting Origen at points, is a clear precedent for revisions and "corrections" of Origen's works.

The results of our investigation confirm the findings of Preuschen in some respects.[29] While in Alexandria, there is no discernible tendency to favour one text type over another. Perhaps the most striking feature is the

---

[27]Ibid., p. 256, lines 38-9.

[28]On "Vulgatization," see Petersen, *The Diatessaron*, 26, 29f, 34, 41; also Tasker, "St. Matthew": "There was a tendency to correct the text of the Fathers in order to bring their biblical quotations into line with the standardized Byzantine text" (64).

[29]Our findings parallel a brief remark found in an anonymous notice (probably by D. Leon Sanders) of Preuschen's edition in the "Bulletin" section of *RB*, n.s. 1 (1904), 298.

slight prominence of the Western text, but this must be mitigated by remembering that:

> its date of origin must have been extremely early, perhaps before the middle of the second century. Marcion, Tatian, Justin, Irenaeus, Hippolytus, Tertullian, and Cyprian all make use to a greater or less extent of a Western form of the text.[30]

It may well be that this most ancient text form, the Western text, was a (the?) major manifestation of the gospel text in Alexandria at the time Origen wrote there, and that what scholars now call the "Alexandrian" text is indeed what Peter Corsson, professor at Berlin, called it in 1892:

> Der distillierte Text den die Modernen aus einigen griechischen Uncialen gewonnen haben,...ist nur ein Spiegelbild einer willkürlich fixierten Recension des vierten Jahrhunderts.[31]

Once in Caesarea, more readings from the Caesarean text appear in Origen's writings. Even then, however, the Caesarean text does not displace the other textual families in Origen's writings. Rather, it becomes first among what, in Alexandria, at least, had been equals. This serves to remind the present-day scholar of the evolving nature of the Biblical text, and the dangers of

---

[30]Metzger, *Text*, 132.

[31]Quoted by J. Rendel Harris, *Four Lectures On the Western Text of the New Testament* (London, 1894), p. vii. One should not ignore the opinion of C.R. Gregory that ℵ and B "would suit very well as a pair of the fifty manuscripts written at Caesarea for Constantine the Great" (p. 345, *The Canon and Text of the New Testament* (New York, 1907). This is based on Eusebius, *Vit. Constant.*, IV.36. See also Metzger, *Text*, 7.

imposing the arbitrary boundaries of modern text types on the subtle eclecticism of the gospel text used by second and third century writers.

ORIGEN IN THE SCHOLAR'S DEN:
A RATIONALE FOR THE HEXAPLA

John Wright
University of Notre Dame

From all indications Origen's Hexapla was one of the most massive textual projects in the history of the text of the Hebrew Bible.[1] Yet for all of its magnitude, it remains shrouded in mystery. It seems to have suffered destruction with the library in Caesarea in the Islamic conquest of the region without ever being copied in full. The work itself, while referred to by Origen in his extant writings, is never given a name by him, nor described by him in a thorough and consistent manner as we might desire.[2] The matter is further complicated by inconsistencies between the descriptions of the work

---

A version of this paper was given in the CJA Seminar on January 15, 1986. I benefited greatly from the discussion and suggestions by the faculty and students and have incorporated many of them into the paper.

[1]Henry Swete estimated its size as 6500 pages, based upon the size of Codex Vaticanus. Even this approximation, however, seems to underestimate the bulk of the Hexapla, as will be argued below. See H. Swete, *An Introduction to the Old Testament in Greek* (Cambridge: Cambridge University, 1900), 74.

[2]I will discuss these passages in further detail below.

and the few remains that we actually possess.[3] In short, there is little concerning the Hexapla that is straightforward and unproblematic. We are therefore forced to deal in the realm of probability and reasoned speculation in undertaking a historical reconstruction of this massive work.

In light of these uncertainties, it is not surprising to discover a wide range of answers to the question of why Origen wrote the Hexapla in the first place. The extreme magnitude of the work, which seems to have taken fifteen years to complete, raises this question with some urgency. What rationale possessed Origen to devote the energy and effort to compose such a work? Various scholars have arrived at diverse answers to this question, ranging from a Hebrew primer[4] to the restoration of *the* text of the LXX, meaning a "purified" LXX, revised to the MT tradition.[5] I will argue in this paper that the rationale for the project was to form a compilation of texts that might be easily compared for a variety of detailed exegetical work, foremost

---

[3]This is most obvious in the lack of asterisks and obeli in the Mercati fragments.

[4]See H. Orlinsky, "The Columnar Order of the Hexapla," *JQR* (n.s.) 27 (1936-37): 137-149.

[5]The most recent presentation of this position is P. Nautin in his *Origène: Sa vie et son oeuvre* (Paris: Beauchesne, 1977): 303-361, especially 344-353. Other scholars who have held this view include H. Swete, *The Old Testament in Greek* and S. Jellicoe, *The Septuagint and Modern Study* (Oxford: Oxford University, 1968), 74-146. Other current positions on the issue are S. P. Brock, "Origen's Aims as a Text Critic of the Old Testament," *Studia Patristica* 10 (1970): 215-218 and D. Barthélemy, "Origen et le texte de l'Ancien Testament," *Études d'histoire du texte de l'Ancien Testament* (203-213). Brock argues that Origen composed the Hexapla for apologetic reasons to protect the Church against polemics by the Jews. Barthélemy argues that Origen compiled the Hexapla as "an ample collection of data" (p. 203). As will become immediately apparent, although differing in many details with Barthélemy's argument, my ultimate sympathies are with his position.

of which was the possibility of establishing a corrected text of the Old Testament. To support this position, I will examine three facets of the evidence for the Hexapla: (1) the structure and form of the work; (2) Origen's own statements concerning the work; and (3) the base text used by Origen in his *Homilies on Jeremiah* and his evaluation of textual variants within these homilies.

The Structure and Form of the Hexapla

Two works, a recent study by P. Nautin[6] and an older study by I. Soisalon-Soininen,[7] contribute greatly to our understanding of the structure and form of the Hexapla--Nautin in regards to the work's basic structure and Soisalon-Soininen on the mechanics that produced the LXX column of the Hexapla. These works will form the basis for the following discussion.

P. Nautin devotes nearly a seventh of his work on Origen to the Hexapla. Through a critical examination of the data, he convincingly dispels the tradition of a column of Hebrew characters and establishes the seven column format of the Hexapla as follows (in order): a Greek transcription of the MT, Aquila, Symmachus, the LXX text (with asterisks and obeli), Theodotian, followed by the fifth and sixth versions that were recovered by Origen.[8]

---

[6]Nautin, *Origène*, especially pp. 303-333.

[7]Ilmari Soisalon-Soininen, *Der Charakter der Asterisierten Zusätze in der Septuagint* (Helsinki, 1959). Soisalon-Soininen summarizes his conclusions on pp. 193-196.

[8]Nautin, *Origène*, p. 321.

How were these columns constructed? According to Eusebius and confirmed by the Mercati fragments, Origen arranged the columns in "cola"--"small units of meaning of which each, corresponding to a Hebrew word, occupies a line in a manner that the reader, in surveying a line in the different columns, sees how the same word was rendered in the different translations."[9] Such an arrangement was ideal for a comparison of all the versions and the construction of the column that has received the most attention--the critically markedly LXX column.

There is a danger of narrowing the question of the rationale of the Hexapla to the rationale of the LXX alone.[10] While the Hexapla contained six more columns that we may not disregard in examing Origen's rationale for the Hexapla, we cannot dispute the centrality of the LXX column for the Hexapla.

As is well known, in this column Origen marked the MT additions to the LXX with asterisks and LXX segments not in the MT, with obeli. He borrowed these critical markings from the ancient Alexandrian grammarians. The asterisks marked additions that merited close attention, while the obeli denigrated the worth of a reading.[11] Soisalon-Soininen has studied Origen's

---

[9]Ibid., p. 314.

[10]This narrowing pervades the secondary literature. This is largely due to Origen's own statements that refer to this column, the significance of this column for the transmission of the text of the LXX, and the late 19th century critical reconstruction of this column by F. Field.

[11]See Swete, *The Old Testament in Greek*, pp. 70-71. Barthélemy disagrees with this, but in the *Comm. in Matt.*, Origen states that he uses obelis because he does not "dare to remove" the longer LXX passages entirely (*Comm. in Matt.* XV, 14). This implies that Origen saw the obeli as lessening the worth of a passage as in the Alexandrian grammarians.

utilization of these signs with interesting and relevant results for this paper.[12]

Soisalon-Soininen discovers that Field's critically reconstructed LXX column of the Hexapla employs asterisks and obeli in an extremely mechanical fashion. The critical markings are characterized by a technical-translational nature, with great concern to arrive at a word-for-word correspondence between the MT and LXX in regards to length. Such a detailed comparison "extends often into the smallest grammatical features."[13] In the asterisked sections, Origen does not translate directly from any Hebrew text, but employs the other versions, with Theodotian (the column that followed the LXX column) the most prominent.[14] This minute attention to an exact word-for-word correspondence, however, results in a linguistically coarse translation, often even to the point that an incongruence is found between the old text and the additions.[15]

Yet despite this careful attention and comparison to the texts, Origen largely disregards variants. He does not alter the LXX text, except where he saw freely translated sections as possible additions or omissions. We may see this purely mechanical process that produced the LXX column as a direct

---

[12]Soisalon-Soininen works with Field's critical edition of the septuagintal column, and may assume greater stability in the accuracy of the current placement of the critical signs than is possible. The main lines of his findings, though, are established with sufficient strength to make this inconsequential for the purposes of this paper.

[13]Soisalon-Soininen, *Der Charakter der Asterisierten*, p. 105.

[14]Ibid., p. 107.

[15]Ibid., pp. 193-194. Such an approach also brought extreme havoc upon the history of the LXX text.

result of the cola-format that facilitated comparison and as a key to the rationale for the entire work.

What are the implications of this structure and form of the Hexapla for Origen's rationale? First, the cola structure would seem to demand a codex, rather than a scroll, and imply that Swete's estimate of 6500 pages may have significantly underestimated the size of the project.[16] The Hexapla would not have been a readily portable work, with easy reference to a passage in a public debate[17] or for liturgical use. Origen's private scholar's den, where he prepared his homilies and commentaries, or might want to check a passage for a treatise or a dispute, seems a much more likely setting.

The structure and form of the Hexapla also reveal that the rationale was not to restore the LXX-column to the pristine purity of the MT. First, Origen could have accomplished this task without the bother of writing out the other versions, thus shortening his task immensely. Second, the fifth and sixth versions (if not also Symmachus and Theodotion) would become entirely superfluous for this purpose. Yet the fact of the matter is that Origen included all available versions in a format whereby he might achieve a comparative analysis of the versions at a glance. Third, Origen, through his uses of the Alexandrian signs, did move towards forcing the LXX into the MT's mold; but he stopped short of dropping or adding sections without

---

[16]The cola-form would take more space than continuous writing because of the gaps to set the columns apart. See Mercati fragments for the extent of the space such a format would demand.

[17]This would seem to discredit Brock's view that the Hexapla was written for public disputes with the Jews. The Hexapla could be used to prepare for debates in checking various passages, but the awkwardness of its bulk would seem to prohibit its employment within a live debate. In addition to this, such a rationale would not demand that Origen compile the complete Hebrew Bible; controverted passages, especially those that carried special import for Christians, would have sufficed.

notice. Most importantly, though, he did not change the wording of the LXX where it varied from the MT. A rationale to "restore" the LXX to the "true" text--the MT of the Jews--would demand the harmonization of variants between the two versions.[18] The structure and form of the Hexapla made such a harmonization possible, but it left the decisions open for the scholar to evaluate as he had occasion. The format of the work would greatly facilitate this process.

The structure and form of the Hexapla suggest that the rationale for the project was to form a compilation of texts that might be compared easily in detail. From its location in a "study" or a library,[19] Origen had an invaluable resource for homilies, scholarly works, or even for preparation for public disputes. His exegetical options were opened to the maximum degree through the structure and form of the Hexapla.

Origen's Statements on the Rationale for the Hexapla

Origen's statements in *Ad Africanum* and his *Commentary on Matthew* usually form the point of entry into the discussion of the rationale for the Hexapla. From this perspective, the scholar then progresses to the structure and form of the Hexapla, usually concentrating on the LXX column. By reversing this method, it becomes possible to accomplish two matters: (1) Our preunderstanding of the statements are broadened by the structure of

---

[18]Swete asserted that Origen "tacitly corrected" the LXX as a key point in his argument for his "restoration" view of the rationale for the Hexapla. Soisalon-Soininen, of course, had not conducted his study at the time of Swete's work. See Swete, *The Old Testament in Greek*, p. 68.

[19]The Hexapla seems to have made its way eventually to the library at Caesarea where Eusebius examined it later and copied the LXX column.

the Hexapla itself; and (2) We may read the texts more critically and account for the diversity in Origen's two statements.

His *Commentary on Matthew* contains the locus for the restoration-of-the-LXX view for the purpose of the Hexapla. Again, Origen openly states that he has, "with God's help, devised to heal the divergence in the texts of the Old Testament, using the remaining versions as a criterion [κριτήριῳ]" (*Comm. in Matt* 15, 14). In contrast to *Ad Africanum*, the asterisks and obeli now contain editorial significance, with the Hebrew text granted more authority than the LXX. He utilizes the obeli because he does not "dare" to drop those passages, even though they do not correspond to the Hebrew text.

The Hexapla could serve this function well for Origen. Yet, as I have argued, there were easier methods available to him and such a rationale does not explain several aspects of the structure and form of the Hexapla. Thus, these statements are suspect as a rationale for the whole work.

We may discover the function of these statements in the context of the *Comm. in Matt*. The description of the Hexapla functions to aid Origen in explaining the divergences between the Gospels in the story of the "Rich Young Man/Ruler" (Matt 19:16-22; Mark 10:17-22; and Luke 18:18-23).[20] This, then, functions to support a textual emendation that Origen makes in his exegesis on Matthew. This use of the reference to the Hexapla therefore functions to support a particular interpretation of Matthew. We may not generalize it to *the* rationale for the Hexapla.

---

[20]The divergence that draws Origen's attention is that Matthew has Jesus respond to the young man as "If you wish to be perfect," while Mark and Luke read differently.

Ad Africanum provides the locus for the apologetic-against-the-Jews view for the purpose of the Hexapla.[21] Indeed, Origen emphasizes an apologetic rationale for the work, and the Jews figure prominently in his polemic. But the apologetic extends further than the Jews and includes "those who seek a starting point, who wish to slander the average [believer] by appearing to denounce it [the LXX] among the common people." Origen's concern here (as throughout *Ad Africanum*) is to defend the LXX against claims by others, of whom the Jews are the major adversaries. Origen did not write this section as a rationale for the Hexapla; the Hexapla, however, with its use as a tool for apologetics, expecially for comparative purposes, ideally fit the momentary need of Origen to defend the LXX against its critics.

This interpretation is strengthened by Origen's mention of the obeli and asterisks. Rather than weighing the worth of the readings of the LXX (with the LXX being weighed less) as in *Comm. in Matt.*, here they were said to have been employed only "for the sake of distinction" (*Ad. Afr.* IV). He thus protects the LXX from any criticism that might be inherent in the Hexapla itself. It is thus important not to transfer the apologetic use described in *Ad Africanum* to the rationale for the Hexapla itself. While the work could easily facilitate this apologetic work of Origen, its rationale encompassed a broader aim.

These "classical" references to Origen's own statements on the Hexapla, therefore, are of limited value in discovering the rationale for the entire work. Yet in *Ad Africanum*, immediately preceding the mentioning of the polemical use of the Hexapla, he describes a more general purpose to his textual endeavors:

---

[21]See Brock, "Origen's Aims as a Text Critic."

And I do not say these things with hesitation to search also the Jewish Scriptures, and to compare them to all of ours, and to observe the differences in them. Because, if it is not burdensome to say, we have worked much on this to the extent of our strength, seeking their sense in all the versions and their differences. We have sought the interpretation of the LXX much more ... (*Ad. Afr.* IX).

The description given here accords exactly with the implications of the structure and form of the Hexapla discussed above. Origen describes his endeavors as a comparison in order to discover the differences between the texts. This process is for general exegetical purposes: to understand the meaning of the versions, with special emphasis on the LXX. The data discovered could then be used in a variety of ways, including apologetical; nonetheless, the basic purpose of the Hexapla was the general understanding of all available versions of the Old Testament. It remains to be seen if this is consistent with Origen's actual practice in the *Homilies on Jeremiah*.

Origen's Evaluation of Textual Variants in the *Homilies on Jeremiah*

Origen's utilization of the text of Jeremiah in his *Homilies on Jeremiah* provides indirect insight into the rationale for the Hexapla. These homilies, still surviving in Greek,[22] would provide ample opportunity for Origen to use his Hexapla, due to the vast difference between the LXX and

---

[22]Origéne, *Homélies sur Jérémie*, 2 Vols. Traduction par Pierre Husson et Pierre Nautin. Edition, Introduction, et Notes par Pierre Nautin (Paris: Les Éditions du Cerf, 1983).

MT texts.[23] I will examine first the base text of the homilies and then review the evaluation of the variants by Origen.

Pierre Nautin appeals to the base text of the *Homilies on Jeremiah* as support for his restoration view of the purpose of the Hexapla. On the basis of the text of Jer 20:2-6 in *Hom* XIX, Nautin argues that Origen's Bible was not the LXX, but "the text revised after the other versions that he had established in constructing the Hexapla."[24] This holds true for Jer 20:2-6. Nautin errs, however, in ascribing normative status to the exception. A revised LXX text does not even remain consistent throughout all of Hom XIX, as in vv. 7-11 the text largely follows the LXX version[25] against the MT. As evidence for this, I will present the three variants found in v. 7:

Origen:	ἐκράτησας καὶ ἠδυνάσθης
LXX:	ἐκράτησας καὶ ἠδυνάσθης
MT:	חזקתני ותוכל

---

[23]The LXX text of Jeremiah is 1/7th shorter than the MT, with a transposition of a major section. A comparison of the LXX with 4QJer has indicated that the LXX most likely represents a shorter Hebrew *Vorlage* of the book. For detailed discussions of the text of Jeremiah, see J. G. Janzen, *Studies in the Text of Jeremiah* (Cambridge, Mass.: Harvard University, 1973) and E. Tov, *The Septuagint Translation of Jeremiah and Baruch* (Missoula: Scholars Press, 1976). Tov has summarized an evaluation of the Qumran, LXX, and MT texts in his "Some Aspects of the Textual and Literary History of the Book of Jeremiah," in *Le Livre de Jérémie*, pp. 145-167 (Leuven: University Press, 1981).

[24]Nautin, *Origène*, p. 345. This view is also given by Nautin in his "Introduction" in *Homélies sur Jérémie*, p. 116.

[25]By the Septuagintal text of Jeremiah, I mean the critically reconstructed text of the Göttingen edition, edited by Joseph Ziegler, *Ieremias* (Göttingen: Vandenhoeck and Ruprecht, 1957).

Origen:	πᾶσαν τὴν ἡμέρην
LXX:	πᾶσαν ἡμέρην
MT:	כל־היום
Origen:	διετέλεσα μυκτηριζόμενος
LXX:	διετέλεσα μυκτηριζόμενος
MT:	כלה לעג לי

In these three instances, the two more significant readings follow Origen = LXX ≠ MT, while the mere addition of an article shows Origen = MT ≠ LXX. This "mixed text" continues throughout the remaining three verses of the passage for the homily. We may find this non-revisional nature of Origen's base text the remaining verses of this homily, or for that matter, in any homily; it is dramatically apparent, however, in *Hom* IX where he follows the shorter LXX text in omitting the expansion of vv. 7-8. Thus, the whole text for this homily has not been consistently revised towards the MT via the versions, but witnesses to the mixed nature of the Septuagintal text that Origen had at his disposal in Caesarea.

Rather than Origen's text of Jer 20:2-6, Nautin should have chosen a more representative portion of the text that Origen used. His text of Jer 3:6-10, the textual basis for *Hom* IV, provides such a passage. We may characterize the text as basically following the LXX while displaying indications of an assimilation towards the MT, but also containing isolated idiosyncrasies. I would like to give v. 8 as an example of this text:

Origen:	διότι περὶ πάντων ὧν κατελείφθη ἐν οἷς ἐμοιχᾶτο
LXX:	διότι περὶ πάντων ὧν κατελήμφθη [ἐν οἷς ἐμοιχᾶτο]
MT:	כי על־כל־אדות אשר נאפה

Origen: ἡ κατοικία τοῦ Ἰσραήλ   ἐξαπέστειλα αὐτὴν

LXX: ἡ κατοικία τοῦ Ἰσραήλ καὶ ἐξαπέστειλα αὐτὴν

MT: משבה ישראל שלחתיה

Origen: καὶ ἔδωκα αὐτῇ βιβλίον ἀποστασίου εἰς τὰς
χεῖρας αὐτῆς

LXX: καὶ ἔδωδκα αὐτῇ βιβλίον ἀποστασίου

MT: ואתן את ספר כריתתיה אליה

Origen: καὶ οὐκ ἐφοβήθη ἡ ἀσύνθετος Ἰούδα

LXX: καὶ οὐκ ἐφοβήθη ἡ ἀσύνθετος Ἰούδα

MT: ולא יראה בגדה יהודה אחותה

While this verse contains more unique Origenic readings than usual, it clearly shows that the text used by Origen has not been revised towards the MT.[26] Thus, while the text he used does witness the gradual process of assimilation of the LXX towards the MT in isolated instances, it is not sufficient to hypothesize a revision of the text by Origen. Rather, we may explain the data best by concluding that Origen used as a base text in his *Homilies on Jeremiah* a Septuagintal text that was circulating within the church in Caesarea, a text that was typical of Septuagintal texts of that time in a modest degree of assimilation towards the MT.[27]

---

[26]This is not to say that Origen's text never follows the MT against the LXX. One of the many examples may be found in Hom VII on the text of Jer 5:19:

Origen: ἀνθ' ὧν ἐγκατελίπετέ με καὶ ἐδουλεύσατε θεοῖς ἐτέροις

LXX: ἀνθ' ὧν ἐδουλεύσατε θεοῖς ἀλλοτρίοις

MT: כאשר עזבתם אותי ותעבדו אלהי נכר

[27]See Eugene Ulrich, "Origen's Old Testament Text," in this volume.

Origen, in adopting this text, is conscious of the differences between the LXX and the MT. In seven, possibly eight instances, he discusses variants between the LXX and the "remaining versions."[28] He treats the variants in two different manners. On the one hand, Origen evaluates the variants to establish the superior reading, either due to an error in transmission (e.g., XV 5, 16-17) or to the homiletical value of the variant (XVI 5, 17-25). On the other hand, he at times embraces both readings, providing exegetical comments on each (e.g., XIV 3, 6-8). His comparison of the versions, obviously facilitated by the Hexapla, leaves his options open and he takes advantage of this wide gamut.

The implications of the data provided by the *Homilies on Jeremiah* are entirely consistent with our findings above. Origen does not emerge as a thorough "purifier" of the LXX text. The Hexapla provides the opportunity for such a move, and he does opt for it on occasion. But more fundamentally, he operates with the LXX version of his church and uses the comparative Hexaplaric data for a wide range of exegetical resources. The biblical text is a mine for divine treasures for the skilled miner, and the Hexapla increased the availability of golden divine nuggets.

Conclusion

I have argued that Origen's rationale for the Hexapla was to obtain a compilation of biblical texts for comparative analysis that would increase his understanding of the various versions and would provide an exegetical

---

[28]The clear references to variants are found in VIII 1, 17-21; XIV 3, 1-8; XV 6, 13-18; XVI 5, 17ff; XVI 10, 1-5, XVIII 6, 74-85; and XX 5, 16-24. In *Hom.* XIX 12, 10-12 Origen refers to a phrase found in the MT, but not in the LXX. It is not clear, however, whether Origen merely mentions the phrase itself of refers to the fact that it is added in the MT.

resource for a wide range of applications. Such an interpretation accounts for the total structure and form of the Hexapla and the diverse rationales given by Origen himself. It is further confirmed by his use of the biblical text and his evaluation of textual variants in the *Homilies on Jeremiah.*

This rationale reveals Origen as a transitional figure in the history of the biblical text. St. Jerome may provide a foil to him at this point. It is anachronistic to read into Origen Jerome's complete concern for the *hebraitas veritas.* On the one hand, Origen stands with the ancient scribal practice of adding doublets into the sacred text in order to preserve the most complete version of the text[29] and the Qumran community's practice of maintaining different versions of the same book in their library. Such a practice does not demand, or even desire, the strictly controlled standardization that Jerome did. On the other hand, Origen represents a significant step towards the complete standardization of the sacred text through his employment of the critical signs with their evaluative connotations and his usage of the versions to establish superior readings. Here he is a precursor to Jerome, and prepared the way for Jerome's translation project of the Old Testament from Hebrew into Latin.

In its own way, therefore, the Hexapla represents the capstone of the scribal practices of the Ancient Near East and the beginning of the process of standardization resulting in the Göttingen edition of the Septuagint. It stands as a monument to the utter seriousness and thoroughness with which Origen approached his exegetical task and the impact that he has made, even 1800 years after his birth.

---

[29] See S. Talmon, "Double Readings in the Massoretic Text," *Textus* 1 (1960): 144-184.

STRAW DOGS AND SCHOLARLY ECUMENISM: THE APPROPRIATE JEWISH BACKGROUND FOR THE STUDY OF ORIGEN

Roger Brooks
University of Notre Dame

> Heaven and Earth are not humane
>
> They regard all things as straw dogs;
>
> The sage is not humane
>
> He regards all people as straw dogs.

> *-The Way of Lao Tzu,* 5

The world of third-century Caesarea, in which Origen lived and wrote, we may imagine as a series of concentric (or at least overlapping) circles of culture. In this picture, Origen himself stands at the center of the

---

This paper took shape as a presentation to the Christianity and Judaism in Antiquity Seminar at the University of Notre Dame. My thanks go to the seminar's coordinator for 1985-1986, Professor Charles Kannengiesser, who encouraged me along the way, and to each of the other participants who kindly added their criticisms and suggestions. I also gratefully acknowledge the help I receive from my teacher, Professor Jacob Neusner, whose advice continues to guide my studies.

circles. Ringing around him would be the early Christian world, with its institutions and social networks.[1] A still larger circle of culture might take into account the Greco-Roman setting in which Origen thrived.[2] Finally, cutting across these various concentric circles is the band of Jewish culture so prominent and available to Origen, both in Alexandria, and to a greater extent in Caesarea.[3] To use the words of Nicholas de Lange:

---

[1] See, for example, Wayne Meeks, *First Urban Christians: Social World of the Apostle Paul* (New Haven: Yale University Press, 1983), pp. 51-139.

[2] The Greco-Roman setting of Caesarea is described fully in Lee Levine, *Caesarea Under Roman Rule* (Leiden: E.J. Brill, 1975). See also Martin Goodman, *State and Society in Roman Galilee. A.D. 132-212* (Totawa, N.J.: Rowman and Allanheld, 1983).

[3] On Jewish life in Alexandria, see Victor Tcherikover, *Hellenistic Civilization and the Jews* (Philadelphia: Jewish Publication Society, 1961), pp. 272-285; on Judaism in Caesarea, see Levine, *Caesarea*, and Mary Smallwood, *The Jews Under Roman Rule* (Leiden: E.J. Brill, 1981), pp. 516-579.

Origen stands, historically, in the transition period, when the Christian symbolism had already become highly developed, but before the triumph of Christianity had brought about the final break between the Christian and Jewish traditions.[4]

Origen and the Jews in Modern Scholarship

Some recent studies have focused their attention neither on Origen's role of leadership within the Christian community, both as writer and presbyter, nor on Origen as member of the educated elite in these provincial centers.[5] Instead, they have aimed at the intersecting cultural context, namely, Judaism in the late-second and early-third centuries.   These investigations proceed from two types of motivations. The first is factual: Origen's *Contra Celsum* contains references to Jews and Judaic practice, and Christianity, of course evidences a historical affinity with, and similarity to, Judaism. Thus in these works we read suggestions that the Iuollos to whom Origen referred probably was Hillel, the second son of the Patriarch Gamaliel;

---

[4]Nicholas R. de Lange, *Origen and the Jews: Studies in Jewish-Christian Relations in Third-Century Palestine* (Cambridge: Cambridge University Press, 1976), p. 116. Further discussion of the emerging split between Jewish and Christian communities may be found in Robert Wilken, *John Chrysostom and the Jews* (Berkeley: University of California Press, 1983), pp. 29-33, 68-79. Wilken sees the split as occupying several hundred years and continuing well into the fourth century.

[5]See, e.g., de Lange, *Origen*, and Bietenhard, *Caesarea, Origenes und die Juden* (Berlin: W. Kohlhammer, 1974). On Origen's biography, see Jean Daniélou, *Origène* (Paris: La Table Ronde, 1948), pp. 19-64; Pierre Nautin, *Origène: sa vie et son oeuvre* (Paris: Beauchesne, 1977); René Cadiou, *La jeunesse D'Origène: histoire de l'école d'Alexandrie au debut du III° siècle* (Paris: Beauchesne, 1935).

or that some of Origen's discussions of Jews must be understood to refer to Rabbi Hoshaya, an important Talmudic sage reported to have lived in Caesarea around 230; or again, we may have the admission that while such identifications *in particular* present us with extreme difficulty, still they remain *generally* suggestive.[6]

The second influence stems from the recent movement toward improved Jewish and Christian relations. Once again, I cite Nicholas de Lange, now from the closing paragraph of his book:

> At a time when the Church and Synagogue find themselves drawing closer together once more in the face of a new paganism, it is edifying and instructive to contemplate an era when, despite powerful antagonisms, Jews and Christians could live in close harmony and derive mutual benefit from their intercourse.[7]

This scholarly ecumenism, as I have termed it, has led academics to many interesting avenues of study--not just of Origen, but also with regard to the study of the other Church Fathers, of Christianity and Judaism in antiquity, and of Pauline Christianity. Consider, for example, Wayne Meeks' instructive but short chapter on Urban Judaism, or Robert Wilken's study of Jewish and Christian interaction in Antioch.[8] Each of these studies takes

---

[6]These particular examples come from de Lange, *Origen*, pp. 89-102.

[7]De Lange, *Origen*, p. 135.

[8]Meeks, *First Urban Christians*, pp. 32-39; Wilken, *John Chrysostom*.

seriously the diversity of Judaism in shaping the early Christian world.

Yet in the recent studies of Origen and the Jews, a relatively simple-minded theory of cultural diffusion seems to underlie the fascination with Jewish practice in Caesarea. Whether Judaism and Christianity represented competing schools of thought in Caesarea, or the enemies of a common foe--namely, the pagans--these two groups, it is claimed, shared many aspects of life. The one scholarly given is that there existed a large area of common ground between Jews and Christians, "especially when the two groups were faced with similar attacks by pagans."[9]

This type of study proceeds from an intimate knowledge of Origen's own works, and isolates themes and issues to investigate in Judaism. The scholar searches Rabbinic literature for corroboration of Origen's depiction of Jewish institutions and ideas, and, I hasten to add, such confirmation is readily found.[10] For example, de Lange claims that inquiry into Rabbinic interpretation of the Hebrew Bible provides a central and profitable way of understanding Origen's use of Scripture. One should also look for Jewish views on topics like Law, Election, and Messiah.[11] Furthermore, the scholar must compare Origen's statements on institutions like the

---

[9]De Lange, *Origen*, p. 11.

[10]While other types of Jewish literature from the first several centuries often are invoked in these discussions, attempts to confirm Origen's depiction of Jewish institutions in Caesarea in the mid-third century turn almost exclusively to contemporaneous Rabbinic literature, in particular, the Talmud of the Land of Israel (under formation perhaps as early as 275 C.E., redacted probably between 350 and 400; see Louis I. Rabinowitz, "Talmud, Jerusalem," in *Encyclopaedia Judaica* (Jerusalem: Keter, 1973), Vol. 15, pp. 772-779).

[11]See de Lange, *Origen*, pp. 78-102.

Patriarchate and Jewish sects with the depiction of those same institutions in Rabbinic sources.

Such study produces useful results. De Lange's book (which he himself terms preliminary) teems with information necessary to a full understanding of Origen's writings and interests. Yet we must also see the problem posed by this simple method. For in such work, one side of the dialogue sets the entire scholarly agenda. Origen discussed only some of the issues of interest to Jews during his era. It is misleading to look at only those issues in the Jewish world of the late-second and early-third centuries. To state the same thing from the other side: Jewish literature from the early- and mid-third century contains essay-length discussions on many topics never even mentioned by Origen.[12] If we ignore this data, we overlook important evidence regarding the Jewish sphere of life in which Origen lived. We glimpse only bits and pieces of Judaism, taken from here and there, which add up to a distorted view of this important context.

What might serve as a remedy to this one-sided vision? Our goal should be to ask what Judaism looked like, in the period at hand, *without* the framework supplied by Origen. Here, however, we encounter a vexing problem: whence shall we derive information regarding the Jews and Jewish practices in the Land of Israel during the third-century? Jewish writings of the late second and early third centuries, as I indicated, constitute one common source of data. Early Rabbinic literature--in particular the Talmud

---

[12]For example, the Mishnah and the Tosefta focus in a detailed way upon the manner in which liquids can cause food to become subject to ritual uncleanness (see Lev. 11:34, 37-38; Tractate Makhshirin); as I show below, however, Origen's *Homilies to Leviticus* never mention such rules. If our interest remains only in Origen and topics he mentions, we miss a crucial feature of Rabbinic literature.

of the Land of Israel--is taken to represent a movement of Jews emerging, in the third century, into the forefront of Jewish life.[13] Yet nascent Rabbinism did not immediately supplant all other forms of Jewish life. In third-century Caesarea, we surely would find groups of Jews for whom apocalyptic hopes still burned; or for whom Philo's synthesis of Judaism and Greco-Roman philosophy still proved thoroughly convincing.[14] On the other side, we must not assume that whatever may be found in the Talmud of the Land of Israel, compiled between 350 and 400, indicates accurately the Rabbinic synthesis 100 or more years earlier, as it existed in Origen's own day and age.[15] These concerns point out the need for historical review: we must see the Land of Israel in a context larger than just the second and third centuries in order to understand the Judaism(s) of that time.

---

[13] Such a view is problematic, for it ignores several fine details: even if the Rabbinic movement produced its first documents no earlier than 200 C.E., still, we know of Rabbinic figures who flourished at least 150 years earlier (compare Gamaliel, mentioned in Acts 5:35 and the Pharisees of the Synoptic Gospels). So this movement must be studied with an eye toward a much longer span of time than the 35 years since the appearance of the Mishnah.

[14] See Levine, *Caesarea*, for information on Caesarea as a cosmopolitan center with various, competing forms of Judaism; see also Wilken, *John Chrysostom*, pp. 55-65.

[15] One possible touchstone for such comparisons might be found in the so-called "Caesarean Tractates" of the Talmud of the Land of Israel (the three parts of Tractate Nezikin: Baba Qamma, Baba Mesia, and Baba Batra). See Saul Lieberman, *Talmudah shel Kisrin*, Supplement to *Tarbiz* 2:4 (1931), pp. 9-20, for the claim that these three parts of the Talmud derive from Caesarea itself and were probably composed between 275 and 300 C.E. On the dating of other parts of Rabbinic literature, see Moshe D. Herr, "Midreshei Halakhah," in *Encyclopaedia Judaica*, Vol. II, pp. 1521-1523; Idem, "Tosefta," Vol. XV, pp. 1283-1285; see also Ephraim Urbach, "Mishnah," Vol. XII, pp. 93-109, and Louis I. Rabinowitz, "Talmud, Jerusalem," Vol XV, pp. 772-779.

The Land of Israel under Roman Rule

In painting Jewish history leading up to the third century, let me first sketch a gradual loss of Jewish sovereignty over two centuries.[16] In 64 B.C.E., Rome instituted provincial rule over Syria-Palestina, and then (upon Jewish request) formally annexed the Land of Israel one year later; we also have the fall of Jerusalem in 37 B.C.E., and the corresponding decimation of the judiciary (forty five judges are reported by Josephus to have been executed) under the authority of the provincial governor, Herod;[17] in 70 C.E., Rome put down an attempted grasp at self-rule, in the process destroying the Temple in Jerusalem and forever changing the face of Jewish life. Similarly, in 135 C.E., the Romans defeated another rebellion, now under the leadership of the Messiah, Simeon Bar Kokhba. And during this same period of time, the Romans appointed a Patriarch, their local representative, who, despite the fact that he wielded some independent power, nonetheless was a sign of continuing Roman dominance over the Jews.

In addition to these political and military events, we might also point to heavy increases in Roman taxation and confiscation of land, especially after the imposition of direct Roman rule of the province of Judea in 6 C.E.,[18] and then again after the persecutions and rebellions in

---

[16]See Sean Freyne, *Galilee from Alexander the Great to Hadrian* (Notre Dame: University of Notre Dame Press, 1980), pp. 57ff.

[17]For the date of Jerusalem's fall, see Smallwood, *Jews Under Roman Rule*, pp. 565-567; see Idem, pp. 63-64, for the persecution of the judiciary.

[18]See Ibid., pp. 119, 150-151.

Alexandria in 115-117 C.E. and in Palestine in 135 C.E.[19]

By rehearsing these events I hope to point out the long process of Roman domination, which in some respects reached a head near the middle or end of the second century. Yet these events are not the only features for us to keep in mind when asking about Judaism at the beginning of the third century. For we must also take account of the recent flurry of messianic movements in Judaism, between 150 B.C.E. and 150 C.E. We may look at the Samaritans, with their annointed High Priest offering sacrifices at Mount Gerizim and their eschatological prophet, the *taheb*;[20] the Essenes at Qumran with their proto-messianic figure, the Teacher of Righteousness;[21] Christian Judaism, with its proclaimed annointed Son of God;[22] or the messianic

---

[19]See Goodman, *Roman Galilee*, pp. 146ff.

[20]See James Purvis, *The Samaritan Pentateuch and the Origins of the Samaritan Sect* (Cambridge: Harvard University Press, 1968), p. 89, and Richard J. Coggins, *Samaritans and Jews: The Origins of Samaritanism Reconsidered* (Atlanta: John Knox Press, 1975), on the Samaritans and their high priest.

[21]See Geza Vermes, *Qumran in Perspective* (Philadelphia: Fortress Press, 1981), pp. 185-186, on the Teacher of Righteousness as a messianic figure.

[22]As a sidelight, I note that for Origen and other Palestinian Christians like him, we must recognize the different nature of their Messianic movement from the earlier Jewish messianism. The rapid influx of gentile converts had two profound effects: first, it seems to have kept Christianity alive in era of declining Jewish Messianism, and second, it served to separate Christianity from Judaism. Of course, we must be careful not to see too sharp a break between these two communities. Outsiders saw Jews and Christians as similar or the same larger people. In the same way, we have evidence of social interchanges between the two groups well into the fifth century. Origen himself "was conscious of addressing on Sunday some who had been to synagogue the previous day" (de Lange, *Origen*, p. 36; cf. p. 93).

general, Bar Kokhba, proclaimed by Rabbi Aqiba.[23] By 150 C.E., the result in each case was the same. None of these movements had produced any real consensus in the Jewish world. None of these messianic figures had succeeded in bringing about meaningful changes in the social situation or political structure in which the people of Israel found itself.

Origen's birth in 185 C.E, and his move to Caesarea around 230 C.E., placed him wholly within this historical and cultural context. Jew and Christian alike lived in the aftermath of the political struggles between Rome and the Judean province.[24] When we ask what type of Judaism Origen knew, we point first to a country and populus governed by foreigners, though perhaps at a time of toleration conditioned by utter victory.

A Rabbinic Response: The Mishnah

To return to our main inquiry, we ask: how did the Jewish world react and respond to these two and one-half centuries of ever-increasing control by Rome? The major cultural creation of this era must be seen as the

---

[23]See Peter Schäfer, Der Bar-Kokhba-Aufstand: Studien zum zweiten jüdischen Krieg gegen Rom (Tübingen: J.C.B. Mohr, 1981), pp. 55-72; Yigal Yadin, Bar Kokhba: The Rediscovery of the Legendary Hero of the Second Jewish Revolt against Rome (New York: Random House, 1971), pp. 172-183; and Emil Schürer, A History of the Jewish People in the Age of Jesus Christ (175 B.C. - A.D. 135), Revised and Edited by Geza Vermes, Fergus Millar, and Matthew Black, (Edinburgh: T&T Clark, 1973), Vol. I, pp. 534-557, for more on Bar Kokhba's messianic claims.

[24]See Goodman, Roman Galilee, pp. 135-174; Stuart Miller, Studies in the History and Traditions of Sepphoris (Leiden: E.J. Brill, 1984); Daniel Sperber, Roman Palestine: 200-400. I. Money and Prices (Ramat Gan: Bar Ilan University Press, 1974); II. The Land (Ramat Gan: Bar Ilan University Press, 1978).

Mishnah. This law code (together with its supplement, the Tosefta) is the only surviving literary evidence of any type of Judaism that was produced during Origen's lifetime. So if we wish to know about Jewish reaction to these events, we must turn our attention, first, to this earliest document of the Rabbinic movement.[25] What does the Mishnah, redacted at the end of the second century, tell us about the setting of Judaism in the late-second and early-third centuries?

In terms of its content, the Mishnah is conditioned by two main issues. First, the Mishnah presents a view of the world far removed from the Jewish messianic movements that had preceded it.[26] The Mishnah contains

---

[25]Two other bits of Jewish literature are sometimes held to stem from this era. The first, *Liber Antiquitatum Biblicarum* indeed was translated into Latin in the third century, but was composed perhaps one-hundred years earlier; second, we have mystical texts, such as the Heikhalot literature or the book *Shi^cur Qomah*. In both cases, recent scholarship asserts these books to have been redacted and edited only centuries later; see Peter Shäfer, *Synopse zur Heikhalot Literatur* (Tübingen: J.C.B. Mohr, 1981) and Martin Cohen, *Shi^cur Qomah: Liturgy and Theurgy in Pre-Kabbalistic Jewish Mysticism* (Washington, D.C.: University Press of America, 1983), pp. 66-67). This being the case, we must point to the Mishnah as an attempt by some Jews to summarize, in a new and fresh book, their reactions to their recent history. But the paucity of other types of literature need not blind us of two facts: (1) other Judaisms are likely to have remained on the scene during this part of the third century, if not expressing themselves anew in literature; (2) yet other forms of Judaism, it is likely, might perfectly well reflect the situation in Palestine during the era in question, even if they produce tangible literary remains only quite a bit later. While I find necessary further study of these other possible Jewish contexts for the study of Origen, still, I believe we are warranted in placing a good deal of emphasis on the one group of Jews from the early third century who *did* produce a new book, namely the Rabbis who stood behind the Mishnah.

[26]For this characterization of the Mishnah as essentially non-Messianic, see Jacob Neusner, *Messiah in Context: Teleology in Formative Judaism*, Foundations of Formative Judaism, Vol. I (Philadelphia: Fortress Press, 1984), pp. 17-53.

only two explicit references to the Messiah in its entire 64 tractates (some 1200 pp. in the new English translation). Furthermore, those two references to the Messiah occur merely as parts of lists of ordinary matters. M. Sotah 9:9-15 mentions the "footsteps of the Messiah" in a list of tragic events that led to the moral decline of the Israelites. The other reference, M. Berakhot 1:5, is to the messianic age; again, this mention appears routinely in a short explanation of why Jews include a paragraph regarding the exodus from Egypt in their daily liturgy. In and of themselves, "the days of the Messiah" hardly figure as crucial events in the holy life of Israel, as *explicitly* depicted in the Mishnah.

For the most part, however, the Mishnah's message must be seen as a reaction to Rome's takeover of God's Holy Land, the Land of Israel. Throughout the various tractates, one uncovers the assertion that although seemingly defiled, the Land of Israel remains holy; although seemingly possessed by Rome, the Land of Israel remains the exclusive property of God; although seemingly governed and ruled by Rome, the people of Israel remains eternally subject to God's sovereignty. Within the Mishnah, these various points are made by invoking the Priestly Code of Leviticus, with its emphasis on order, holiness, regularity, and proper attention to those natural categories established by God at Creation.[27]

So the Mishnah formed a two pronged polemic, one side negative, one side positive. Its framers ignored the messianic and apocalyptic styles that had characterized centuries of Jewish writings. At the same time, the

---

[27]Examples may be found throughout the six major Divisions of the Mishnah. For a specific instance of this sustained polemic, see Roger Brooks, *Support for the Poor in the Mishnaic Law of Agriculture: Tractate Peah*, Brown Judaic Studies 43 (Chico: Scholars Press, 1983), pp. 1-12.

Mishnah's authors looked back to a different age of Jewish history, one in which everything seemed in place. They skipped back over 700 years to the regulations found in Leviticus, and took as their base the principles underlying that priestly work of law. In the Mishnah, the earliest Rabbinic authors emphasized order, not chaos; holiness, not defilement; and the Israelites' power, not helplessness.[28]

This review of Jewish history and this brief look at the Mishnah should help us grasp the Rabbinic world at the beginning of the third century. But another, larger problem remains before our pursuit of the Jewish background appropriate to the study of Origen. How may we avoid the use of categories to look at Judaism that are not intrinsic to Judaism? How do we isolate those categories that truly represent Rabbinic thought?

The problem is acute. Onward from George Foot Moore, the great systematician of Jewish thought, many prominent scholars of Judaism have argued that one cannot extract theology from Judaism. Rabbinic literature, it has been claimed, simply does not allow that type of analysis. In Moore's own words:

> Judaism, in the centuries with which we are concerned, had no body of articulated and systematized doctrine such as we understand by the name theology.[29]

---

[28] For this reconstruction, see Jacob Neusner, *Judaism: The Evidence of the Mishnah* (Chicago: University of Chicago Press, 1981), pp. 217-229.

[29] George Foot Moore, *Judaism in the Age of the Tannaim* (Cambridge: Harvard University Press, 1927), Vol. I, p. 357.

This seemingly strange notion, that Judaism has no theology, emerges from a particular theory of the formation of Rabbinic literature. The Mishnah, it has been argued, contains the record of many centuries of *ad hoc* judgments handed down to satisfy particular juridical situations as they arose.[30] Since these laws are occasional and *ad hominem,* they cannot add up to a cohesive theology at all, let alone on topics that are essentially Christian. In other words, since the Mishnah reports legal rulings as they happened, we should not expect the text to provide us with sustained essays, but rather with a mere legal record.

The work of Jacob Neusner, in *Judaism: the Evidence of the Mishnah,* may give us reason for hope. Neusner adopts a quite different interpretive scheme. He sees the Mishnah not as a mere record of hundreds and thousands of decisions; rather, Neusner employs Hegel's tripartite historical framework to understand the creation of the Mishnah: Rabbinism emerged from a long period of Messianic hope (Thesis: the several messianic movements I alluded to above, but especially the Bar Kokhba Revolt); this then followed by failure and disappointment (Antithesis: the two wars with Rome, finally ending in the defeat of the Messiah's army), all culminating in the redaction of the Mishnah (Synthesis: a holy book, meant to reflect upon-- and move beyond--Israel's current situation).[31] For Neusner, the Mishnah contains a set of extended essays, combining various topics with particular formulary patterns, meant to argue in behalf of crucial points of the Rabbinic

---

[30]This theory of the formation of the Mishnah pervades almost all scholarship prior to the 1970's. See Jacob Neusner, Ed., *The Modern Study of the Mishnah* (Leiden: E.J. Brill, 1973).

[31]See Jacob Neusner, *Judaism in Society: The Evidence of the Yerushalmi* (Chicago: University of Chicago Press, 1983), pp. 19-25.

world view.[32]   As Neusner lays things out, then, the Mishnah constitutes
the Rabbis' reaction to their history.

Rabbinic Systematic Theology: The Legacy of the Mishnah

The Mishnah had a profound effect upon Judaism in the third and
later centuries. First, seeing the Mishnah as an independent set of essays
making the Rabbis' own points necessarily raised several questions: Who is
telling me this? Why? On whose authority?[33]   In context, the next
Rabbinic documents all took up this problem.   Sifra, Sifre, and Leviticus
Rabbah, three works of Scriptural exegesis from the third through fifth
centuries,[34] each aimed at grounding the Mishnah's rules in Scripture. Far
from mere exercises in prooftexting, these books tried to establish the
absolute Scriptural authority of the Mishnah.[35]   Then in the fourth century,
the Talmud of the Land of Israel took as one of its starting points the

---

[32]See Jacob Neusner, *A History of the Mishnaic Law of Purities*
(Leiden: E.J. Brill, 1977), Vols. XXI and XXII.

[33]We should recall that the Rabbinic movement made its first real
pitch for authority at this point in time, not earlier. Thus the opening lines
of Tractate Abot, "Moses received *torah* at Sinai, and passed it on to Joshua,
...who passed it on to Hillel and Shammai," ought to be seen as an attempt
to justify the authoritative stance of the Mishnah. See Jacob Neusner, *A
History of the Mishnaic Law of Damages* (Leiden: E.J. Brill, 1975), Vol. IV.

[34]For these dates, see Hermann L. Strack, *Einleitung in Talmud und
Midrasch,* Revised and Edited by Günter Stemberger, (Munich: C.H. Beck,
1982).

[35]See, for example, Neusner, *Mishnaic Law of Purities*, Vol. VII,
which discusses in detail the relationship between the Mishnah and Sifra.

problem of relating the Mishnah to Scripture.[36]

In similar fashion these documents also attempted to deal with the Mishnah's non-messianic attitude. One major problem left open for these successive generations was how to integrate the Mishnah's strong teleology of holiness with an appropriate amount of messianism. This interplay between Sanctification and Salvation served as one of the primary foci of the Talmud of the Land of Israel and of the Talmud of Babylonia.[37]

But the legacy of the Mishnah extended further than to these problems taken up by the immediately succeeding generations. For the Judaism produced in this era, according to such scholars as George Foot Moore, Gershom Scholem, and Ephraim Urbach, was somehow normative for 1600 years.[38] These thinkers see this long period in one way or another as a unity, showing only small amounts of cultural and intellectual change. Rabbinic thought, from its inception to the advent of modernity, formed a single, larger conceptual whole.

What could these scholars possibly have meant by their insistence that Rabbinic culture continued uninterrupted from 200 C.E. to 1800? Clearly, their view is *culturally* inaccurate: we easily may document a wide

---

[36]So Neusner, in *Judaism in Society*, pp. 78-79, and in *The Talmud of the Land of Israel: A Preliminary Translation, Vol. 35: Introduction: Taxonomy* (Chicago: University of Chicago Press, 1983), pp. 52-56.

[37]See Neusner, *Messiah in Context*, pp. 79-130, 167-231.

[38]Neusner's work has shown without doubt that we cannot speak of the Mishnah's Judaism as "normative," as Moore or Urbach wish. Nonetheless, as Neusner himself points out, "Rabbinic Judaism," as it emerged from the Mishnah and on through the Talmuds, became the state constitution of the Jewish people. See Jacob Neusner, *The Way of Torah*, Third Edition (Belmont, CA: Wadsworth, 1979), pp. 12-16.

variety of cultures in the period at hand. Synchronically, consider the vast differences, in the second and third centuries, between Jews in Palestine and those in Babylonia. Or, diachronically, consider the variety of cultures before and after the Arab conquest around 640. The assertion of an uninterrupted Jewish culture is also *intellectually* problematic. The claim that such movements as Jewish Philosophy and Jewish Mysticism worked themselves out principally within the confines of the Rabbinic system is true, but beside the point. For we must just as soon point out that these two systems shared scarcely a single aspect of their world views.

In what way can we speak of the legacy of the Mishnah as a single, unified whole?

This document represents the best efforts of the Rabbis to compose essays (or at least connected discourses) on a variety of topics, topics chosen not to represent everything in Scripture,[39] but to divide life into its component parts as the Rabbis themselves saw things. The Mishnah therefore comprised the first document of Rabbinic Systematic Theology. Certainly the Mishnah and early Rabbinism knew of no such categories as Providence, Miracles, Election, Messiah, Prayer, Worship, Free Will, Sin, Repentance, Evil, Immortality, or Angelology. On these categories of *Christian* systematics, Rabbinic literature has nothing but episodic and scattered comments.[40] But if by systematic theology we mean sustained,

---

[39]See Neusner, *Judaism: Mishnah*, pp. 167-172, 217-229.

[40]These comments may be gathered together and arranged into chapters, as Moore and Urbach have done. But we must realize that such categories are totally foreign to the Rabbinic system these authors attempt to describe. For a full critique of this methodology, see Neusner, *Judaism: Mishnah*, pp. 5-14.

rational discourse on God, his relationship to humans, and his communications to them, then the Mishnah certainly constitutes *Judaism's* first systematics.[41] And if we turn to the categories utilized by the Rabbis who composed the Mishnah, we will find their theology.

The Mishnah's Systematic Categories

Without reference to all of the sub-categories and individual tractates of the Mishnah, let us look at the six major divisions of the Mishnaic law, and lay out the basic questions posed by the Mishnah.

I. *ZERAᶜIM:* THE DIVISION OF AGRICULTURE:

How does God's ownership of the Land of Israel affect Israelites' use of that Land and its produce? [A sample sub-division: *Demai*, dealing with buying and selling produce in a doubtfully tithed status.]

II. *MOᶜED*: THE DIVISION OF APPOINTED TIMES:

How does God's interaction with Israel in history serve to orient the calendar, marking out special times requiring special actions by Israelites? [Sample sub-division: *Shabbat*, spelling out various aspects of Sabbath law and observance.]

III. *NASHIM*: THE DIVISION OF WOMEN:

How does the special sanctity demanded of Israelites by God affect their relationships with that "most dangerous of creatures," woman?

---

[41]For this definition, see Louis Jacobs, "Theology," in *Encyclopaedia Judaica*, Vol. 15, pp. 1103-1110.

[Sample sub-division: *Ketubot*, specifying rules for transfer of woman from father to husband.]

IV. *NEZIQIN*: THE DIVISION OF DAMAGES:

How does the unity and equality of God's holy people Israel demand special action in business, government, and day-to-day dealings? [Sample sub-divisions: *Baba Qamma*, on torts; *Baba Mesia*, on civil law; *Baba Batra*, on property law.]

V. *QODASHIM*: THE DIVISION OF HOLY THINGS:

How does the worship of God demand special action in the Temple, God's holy locus? [Sample sub-division: *Zebahim*, concerning the various procedures for animal sacrifice.]

VI. *TOHOROT*: THE DIVISION OF PURITIES:

How does extending the holiness required in God's Temple to everyday life demand special attention to all aspects of life *vis-à-vis* cultic purity? [Sample sub-divisions: *Tohorot*, on sources of uncleanness, and *Miqva^{c}ot*, on modes of purification.]

This Rabbinic effort to select which topics to talk about--a task undertaken during the entire period from before 70 until about 185--succeeded beyond the mere details of the Mishnah's rules. For the categories set up in the Mishnah became the categories for all later Rabbinics. Early Rabbinic documents such as the Tosefta (ca. 300), the Talmud of the Land of Israel (ca. 350-400), and the Talmud of Babylonia (ca. 450-600) each organized their quite independent discussions around the topics dealt with in the Mishnah. This is true to such an extent that these documents, despite their diverse interests and intents, all are commonly described as "commentaries" to the Mishnah. Similarly, the great Rabbinic law codes of Medieval times--that of

Rabbi Isaac Al-Fasi and, to a degree, those of Maimonides and Joseph Caro[42]--each systematically take up a variety of topics and sub-topics first dealt with in the Mishnah.

In order to show this continuity and development in action, let me discuss two separate examples, one an entire Division of the Mishnah (*Mo*^{c}*ed*, Appointed Times), and the other a single tractate (Tractate Peah, Poor-Relief).

Within the Mishnah, as I have indicated, the Division of Appointed Times claims that the home and village, on holidays, attain a measure of holiness, just as the Temple would have on those same days. Now the Mishnah's authors knew that the home was not the same as the Temple; hence home and village were deemed to be not an exact parallel to the Temple, but rather its mirror image.[43] On the festivals, Israelites at home and in the village were governed by rules precisely opposite of those that had ruled the cult that the Israelites no longer possessed. Within this larger scheme, therefore, the Division presents two types of essays, (1) those dealing with the maintenance of holiness during the festival Temple service, and (2) those dealing with attaining a measure of holiness in the home during these special times. Individual tractates go over the ground of many of the festivals found in the Hebrew Bible--Passover (*Pesahim*), Tabernacles (*Sukkot*), the New Year (*Rosh Hashanah*), and the Day of Atonement

---

[42]I note, of course, that such later law codes contained other influences and interests. So, for example, while Maimonides formally objects to the categorical scheme of the Mishnah, he replaces it with a conceptual-topical scheme quite akin to that of the Rabbis' first document. See Isador Twersky, *Introduction to the Code of Maimonides: Mishneh Torah* (New Haven: Yale University Press, 1980), pp. 238-310.

[43]On this point, see Neusner, *Judaism: Mishnah*, pp. 182-188.

(*Yoma*)--and also discuss the functioning of the cult throughout the year (*Ta^{c}anit, Hagigah*, and *Sheqalim*). Finally, several tractates deal with the home and village during these same festivals (*Shabbat, Erubin, Besah*, and *Mo^{c}ed Qatan*).

How did this Mishnaic exposition of festival law set the agenda for later Rabbinic work? To begin with, the second generation of Rabbinic documents--the Tosefta and the Talmuds--all used precisely these categories and carried forward the overall point that the home must provide the mirror image of the now lost Temple. Similarly, the later law codes took their cues from the Mishnaic law, adding their own developments here and there. Thus, for example, Maimonides called Book III of his *Mishneh Torah "Zemanim"* -- Times--and covered within it each of the topics found in the Division of Appointed Times, in the order presented first in the Mishnah. At the broadest levels, then, the Mishnah's Divisions determined the shape of Rabbinic thinking.

Let us now turn to a second example, an individual tractate, Tractate Peah--Support for the Poor. The Mishnah,[44] in a break with the scattered and episodic approach found in Scripture, introduced the subject of poor-relief as a category appropriate for separate and full exposition. In the later documents, thinkers continued to define, refine, and develop the laws, rights, and obligations incumbant upon wealthy farmers. And these later thinkers added to this topic when they felt it necessary. For instance, charity did not form part of the Mishnaic system of poor-support, which was conceived only as a part of the system of tithes. Since charitable gifts could not be seen as

---

[44]For the Mishnaic and Toseftan texts here described, see Brooks, *Support for the Poor*, pp. 150-156.

agricultural dues, the Mishnah's authors excluded them from discussion in the setting of Tractate Peah. Yet within a few generations, some attention was paid to this topic *as part of the discussion of poor-support.* In the Tosefta (about 300 C.E.) and in the Talmud of the Land of Israel (350-400), charity formed a minor, but nonetheless essential part of the discussion of poor-relief. And by the thirteenth century, in Maimonides' code of Jewish Law, charity occupied several chapters of this discussion.[45] Even on a tractate-by-tractate basis, therefore, I think it fair to say that the Mishnah's legacy--Rabbinic Systematic Theology--is long-lived indeed.

So to review, in the second through fourth centuries the Rabbis attended to recent history by systematizing and organizing Jewish thought. I have already explained how three centuries of Roman domination over the Land of Israel helped to form the content and message of the Mishnah, with its assertion that God alone ruled sovereign over the Land; and later Rabbinic literature--the early Midrash compilations and the Talmuds--endorsed this statement, to the extent that such books took the Mishnah as the constitution of the Jewish nation (however removed from power it might have been). The Jews' stuation as a defeated people forced them to retreat into a systematic never-never land, in which Rome played little or no part whatsoever.   But their circumstance also led them to create real and lasting social structures, within which they could live under Rome, yet apart from the Empire. Rabbis emerged as leaders, if not quite political figures; through their books, the Rabbis purported to guide the daily routine of the Jews in all its aspects

---

[45]Despite Maimonides' stated rejection of the categorical scheme presented in the Mishnah, note that one of his broad "concept-topics", namely, poor-relief, clearly reflects Tractate Peah in both the Mishnah and the Talmud of the Land of Israel. See Twersky, *Introduction to Mishneh Torah*, pp. 265-266, 274.

(hence their focus both on "secular" and "religious" topics). By the beginning of the third century, these same Rabbis had established institutions of learning, the Rabbinic academies. Set throughout lower Galilee, these schools are represented as having strongly defined networks of authority, teachers and students sitting in assigned seats that indicated their merits within the emerging Rabbinate, studying a common curriculum, working out an ordered, ordained livelihood.[46]

Judaism under Roman domination and taxation faced no crisis; it did not die away. On the contrary, under the tutalege of the Rabbis, the Jews of the second, third, and fourth centuries prospered and produced literary monuments that remain formative for Jews into our own day--the Mishnah and the Talmud. These Jews created the social institutions--the Rabbinate and the academy--that sustained their nation then and now. In place of the Temple as the locus of worldly power and authority, they created a religion of the mind, in which the paramount virtue was found in study of the Mishnah's various rules regarding the Temple cult and proper maintenance of its purity-- in short, through study of Torah they reconstructed the world taken away from them. Jews faced the encounter with Roman subjugation and won their battle.

Origen and Rabbinism

We now must inquire about the appropriate Jewish background for understanding Origen. To pose a direct question: how much did Origen really know about the emerging Rabbinic synthesis and system *in its own right?*

---

[46]See Goodman, *Roman Galilee*, pp. 32-33, 75-81.

We must immediately move beyond the few details of exegesis and lore known to Origen (found mostly in the *Contra Celsum*), which have been so ably catalogued by several writers. My interest lies not so much in Origen's depiction of the abstract religion, piety, and ethics of Judaism. That information hardly is definitive of the only Judaism about which we have firm evidence stemming from Origen's day. Rather, to use the words of Frank Porter (imported from another context),

> We should look for more [information] about the Mishnah itself, about its systematic arrangement of the laws, its methods of argument and of bringing custom and tradition into connection with the written law, and more of its actual contents and the total character of those actual rules of life, that "uniformity of observance" which constituted the distinction of the Judaism of the Rabbis.[47]

Origen's *Peri Archon* represents one logical starting point for this investigation. For just as the Mishnah's categories were taken by later Rabbinic Jews as a basis for their own Judaic thought, so too *Peri Archon,* in retrospect, may be seen as "the first Christian system of theology and the first manual of dogma."[48] As one of the first systematicians of Christian doctrine, Origen set out the broad categories that formed the starting point for

---

[47]Frank C. Porter, "Review of G.F. Moore, *Judaism*," in *Journal of Religion* 8 (January 1928), p. 42.

[48]Johannes Quasten, *Patrology*, 3 Vols. (Utrecht-Antwerp: Spectrum, 1966), Vol. II, p. 57.

much of later Christian thought. I find this formal parallel suggestive: in this period of time, both Christianity and Judaism produced the systems that would later become normative and definitive of the movements, and these systems were composed by officials who led schools of disciples in the proper interpretation and understanding of the Hebrew Bible.

In other words, the formation and establishment of the Christian and Judaic movements in the second through fourth centuries took place under common historical circumstances, within the same backyard. Alexandria and Caesarea during the third century were vibrant and cosmopolitan centers of Greco-Roman culture and influence. One can scarcely imagine life within those cities without the constant, dull throbbing of Roman domination over both peoples with a claim to Israelite heritage, the Rabbis and the Christians. Is it any wonder, then, that these two groups built similar edifices within which to protect and nurture their fledgling movements? The academy and school, acting along parallel lines, each provided refuge in the Hebrew Bible, the common Scripture of Jews and Christians; and each emerging group had taken up the challenge of the day by claiming that their traditions included not just the ancient texts, but also new and innovative interpretations, explanations, and expansions. Whether the move was to the documents of the New Testament and the early Church Fathers, on the one side, or to the Mishnah, Midrash compilations, and Talmuds, on the other, these two communities confronted their concrete historical situation and, with an eye toward tradition, forged a new reality. So we ought to look toward *Peri Archon*, the system created by Origen at the beginning of the third century. Here we hope to find substantive indications of Origen's understanding for the Judaic system constructed at precisely the same time.

But even a quick glance shows that *Peri Archon*, in its structure and contents, bears no resemblance to, or knowledge of, formative Rabbinism.

Consider the major sections of Origen's document:[49]

FIRST EXPOSITION (Parts 1:1 - 2:3):

    - On the Nature of God, Christ, and Holy Spirit

    - On Rational Natures

    - The World and Its Creatures

SECOND EXPOSITION (Parts 2:4 - 4:3):

    - One God of Creation, Law, and Apostles

    - Christ Jesus begotten, incarnate

    - Holy Spirit

    - Souls: their substance, merits, punishments and rewards

    - Free Will and Choice

    - Origins of Sin and Souls

    - Angelic Nature and the Origin of the competing powers

    - World: Beginning and End

    - Scriptures: Obvious and Hidden Meanings

RECAPITULATION (Part 4:4):

    - Trinity exceeds all comprehension

    - Mystery of the Trinity in Creation

    - Rational Creatures must participate in the Trinity

    - nature of Father, Son, Holy Spirit eternal

    - Father, with Son and Holy Spirit, stands alone in his knowledge

---

[49]For this outline of *Peri Archon*, I rely upon Charles Kannengiesser, "Divine Trinity and the Structure of *Peri Archon*," delivered at the Origen Colloquium, University of Notre Dame, April 12, 1986, and published in this volume.

The entirely different character of this work from the Mishnah implies a *prima facie* claim that the two share nothing but their systematic natures! And that is certainly understandable. For the overall purpose of *Peri Archon*--namely, exposition of God's relationship with the world, in particular the mystery of the Trinity that pervades all creation and revelation-- is as different from the aim of the Mishnaic system as we might imagine.

Similarly, the content of *Peri Archon* is far removed from that of the Mishnah. For the Rabbis, the Temple and its proper service within the cult remained a crucial issue long after the Temple had been destroyed. Thus the greatest part of the Mishnah and other early Rabbinic literature dealt directly with the maintenance of the cult (the Divisions of Holy Things and Purities), its agricultural dues (the Division of Agriculture), and the impact of its required holiness upon the Israelite home and village (the Divisions of Appointed Times, Women, and Damages). In answer to Roman domination, the Temple--symbol of God's ownership and sovereignty over the Land (although no longer standing)--was to be the focus of every aspect of daily life. For Origen, by contrast, the problems that followed upon the destruction of the Temple were not clearly in sight (as they had been for some earlier Christians, like the author of the Epistle to the Hebrews). Instead, Origen's interest lay in setting forth the allegorical and spiritual dimensions of Scripture; he urged an understanding of the Biblical tradition not as law, but as spirit; all was packaged as an allegory, far from a legal understanding.

For Origen, this spiritual understanding of Scripture stood in sharp contrast to the "literal" or "historical" interpretation that characterized "Jewish" reading of the Bible. But did Origen specifically intend to exclude the type of discussion one would find in the Mishnah, in which the reality of the law found in the Hebrew Bible remained an absolute fact?

The answer to this question leads us away from *Peri Archon* to a preliminary examination of Origen's own discussions of Scripture. In particular, I turn to his *Homilies on Leviticus.*[50] As I explained above, this book, with its priestly concerns for order and sanctification, provided the vision for much of the Mishnaic law. Did Origen's discussions of Leviticus--either in their depiction of Jewish exegesis or in their own spiritual interpretations--show any familiarity on Origen's part with the substance of nascent Rabbinism?

To begin, I note that Origen's homilies addressed only five passages within all of Leviticus that have any relevant material within the Mishnah:

LEVITICUS	HOMILIES	MISHNAH	TOPIC
4:2-26	2:1	Horayot 1:3-5	Sin Offerings
5:2-3	3:2-6	Shebu^cot 2:5, 3:5	Corpse Uncleanness
12:1-7	8:2-4	Keritot 6:9	Childbirth Purification
13:2	8:5	Nega^cim 6:8, 9:2	Leprosy
25:29-31	15:1-3	Arakhin 9:5-7	Property Redemption

Furthermore, in only one of these cases, that concerning corpse uncleanness, did Origen explicitly mention the interpretation of the Jews. Thus in his discussion of Lev. 5:1-16, Origen said:

> Among the Jews, observance of this law [regarding corpse uncleanness] is quite unbecoming and useless. Why should someone who had touched a dead animal or a human corpse, for

---

[50]See Marcel Borret, *Origène: Homélies sur le Lévitique*, Vols. I-II, in SC, Nos. 286-287 (Paris: Les Éditions du Cerf: 1981).

example, be regarded as impure? What if it were the body of a prophet? What if it were the body of a patriarch or even that of Abraham himself? Furthermore, what if one touched bones: will he be impure? What if he touches the bones of Elisha, which resuscitate the dead? Will whoever touches them be impure? And do the prophet's own bones render impure even that person whom they resuscitate from the dead? You see how incoherent this Jewish interpretation is![51]

Note that Origen shows no knowledge of the Rabbinic system of corpse uncleanness, found in the Division of Purities. Missing, for example, is any reference to the spread of uncleanness, as in Mishnah Tractate Ohalot: we find no discussion of the "tent of uncleanness" that surrounds a dead person; no portrayal of the uncleanness itself filling the entire room like some sort of thick gas. Neither does Origen mention the various types and severities of uncleanness, fully spelled out in Tractate Kelim: in the Rabbinic system, human bone carries a lower level of uncleanness than a corpse itself, and animal bone is not deemed unclean at all!

In providing the "Jewish understanding" of corpse uncleanness and in pointing out the inconsistencies in Jewish practice, Origen showed himself

---

[51]Ibid., Vol. I, p. 128; Homily III, 3:

Haec quidem apud Iudaeos indecenter satis et inutiliter observantur. Ut quid enim immundus habeatur, qui contigerit, verbi causa, animal mortuum aut corpus hominis defuncti? Quid si prophetae corpus sit? Quid si patriarchae vel etiam ipsius Abrahae corpus? Quid si et ossa contigerit, immundus erit? Quid si Helisaei ossa contingat, quae mortuum suscitant? Immundus erit ille, qui contingit, et immundum faciunt ossa prophetae etiam illum ipsum, quem a mortius suscitant? Vide quam inconveniens sit iudaica intelligentia.

rather ignorant of the Rabbinic system, both in its details and as a whole. Instead, Origen imputed to the Jews merely a straightforward reading of Scripture. In his view, Judaic practice was simply "Old Testament" law, acted out directly and without change. This of course ignores all those places where Rabbinic interpretation of the laws of uncleanness innovated and added to the Biblical law, as well as those places where the Rabbis simply ignored Biblical law. The Jews were Origen's "straw dogs"--he had no attachment to them, and sacrificed them as a set up for his own allegorical understanding of Scripture.

So much for Origen's discussion of "Jewish interpretation." In two other of the passages I listed, regarding property redemption rights and childbirth purification, Origen referred to the "literal" or "historical" sense of the Scriptural verses. In both of these cases, however, Origen's "literal interpretation" bore no resemblance to Rabbinic interpretation as reflected in the Rabbinic legal system of the Mishnah.

To make this point, let me discuss one of these cases by comparing the Mishnah's and Origen's treatment of Lev. 25:29-31, which discusses the rights a person has to redeem a house he has sold. Within the Mishnah, the passage is seen as providing property rights for individuals: for one full year after selling real estate, according to the Mishnah's reading of Leviticus, the seller has the right to recant and repurchase his property. This overall point stands within the Mishnah's concern for maintaining the *status quo* in property transfers--since God alone owns the Land of Israel and divided it evenly among the Israelite tribes, Jews must take pains to allow anyone to regain control of property he sold to raise cash. This assures, for the most part, that no Israelite will be unfairly deprived of his portion of the Land and its product.

Origen begins his treatment of these verses by providing an

explanation of their meaning "according to history;" but in this literal interpretation, he simply repeats and paraphrases the various laws.[52] No attempt was made to understand these laws in the setting of Jewish practice or understanding. In his own spiritual exegesis, however, Origen imputes a far different meaning to these verses. For him, the discussion of "houses" is something of a "highly mystical" nature, not referring to real estate at all. Instead, "house" here refers to the credit one builds up in Heaven for good works and a pure heart. Since, through one's sins, one might have to "sell" this house--that is, sin might cause a person to lose some of the heavenly credit he has built up--the divine legislator has provided a means through which each person may "repurchase" his divine house--that is, through repentance and good works one may again acquire merit.

Perusal of the remaining passages of Leviticus that both Origen and the Rabbis dealt with leads to similar conclusions: in these cases Origen rarely even referred to the literal, historical, or Jewish understanding of the law at hand. And when, as in the cases I have discussed, Origen *did* use a discussion of the literal sense of a passage to set up his allegorical understanding, he did so without any reference to prevailing Rabbinic understanding of his day. In no case within Leviticus do we find Origen commenting upon verses that underlay portions of the Mishnah and at the same time reflecting anything akin to the Rabbinic understanding of those verses.

Further evidence emerges when we consider the information missing in Origen's writings. Many, many parts of Leviticus are treated in Mishnah, but then lead nowhere in Origen. A simple-minded example makes the point:

---

[52]Ibid., Vol. II, pp. 251-257; Homily XV, 1-2.

the Mishnah and the Tosefta, in Tractate Makhshirin, focus in a detailed way upon the manner in which liquids can cause food to become subject to ritual uncleanness (see Lev. 11:34, 37-38); but Origen's homilies do not even touch upon this passage, which provides the basis for a whole tractate of Mishnaic law and for an interesting essay on the effects of human intention.

The result of a straightforward reading of Origen's *Homilies on Leviticus* is striking: Origen's school and the Rabbinic academies may have prospered in the same city; students in each may have discussed portions of the Bible together; Origen himself may even have studied some Hebrew with a Rabbi; Origen and the Rabbis may have produced parallel systems to regulate life under the Roman Empire. Nevertheless, a warning bell ought to sound. The Jewish background and culture available to Origen throughout his life seems to have been remarkably superficial. Certainly Origen had some familiarity with a few scraps of Jewish exegesis--he knew some fine details of Rabbinic Sabbath law, for example.[53] Yet, on the whole Origen simply had no understanding of the Rabbinic movement gaining prominence around him.

Why then do we find in recent literature such an emphasis on Origen's knowledge of and intercourse with Jews? I think this to be a misguided application of scholarly ecumenism. Writing about Christian thought and hermeneutics in the post-Holocaust era, Glenn Earley has stated that the fresh look at Judaism and Christianity in their formative ages has been spurred on by

. . . (1) the ever-increasing knowledge of the *Sitz-im-Leben* of the

---

[53]See de Lange, *Origen*, pp. 39-40.

earliest communities of Jesus-followers and the nature of the change of these communities from Jewish sect to Gentile Church, and (2) the urgent need to work out the relation of the Church to the Jewish People after the Holocaust. In fact, it is the latter--the similarity of the concerns in the church's present horizon to the concerns of . . . [the early Christian world]--which has enabled . . . [the scholar] to cut through the sedimental layers of reinterpretation to find the answer to *our* problem in the very terms in which, [for example], Paul worked out the answer to *his* problem.[54]

In an attempt to lay the foundations for modern rapprochement between Jews and Christians, scholars have rendered far too positive an evaluation of Origen's relationship to, and reliance upon, Rabbinism. Let me recall once again the words that close Nicholas de Lange's study: ". . . *it is instructive to contemplate an era when, despite powerful antagonisms, Jews and Christians could live in close harmony and derive mutual benefit from their intercourse.*"

This image of harmonious interchange and shared knowledge masks the raw, sometimes bitter polemics that characterized Origen's relations with the Jews. Such a view sits atop our studies of Origen like the Emperor's new clothes; but we need only take another look to realize the naked truth: Origen probably knew a few Jews; he probably studied a bit of Jewish law and lore here and there; but he knew little of the Rabbinic system of thought within which those few details resided.

---

[54]See Glenn David Earley, "The Radical Hermeneutical Shift in Post-Holocaust Christian Thought," in *Journal of Ecumenical Studies*, Vol. 18, No. 1, Winter 1981, pp. 16-32.

ORIGEN, THE RABBIS, AND THE BIBLE:
TOWARD A PICTURE OF JUDAISM AND
CHRISTIANITY IN THIRD-CENTURY CAESAREA

Paul M. Blowers
University of Notre Dame

A series of excellent recent monographs have helped to illuminate Origen's relation to the Judaism of his time. In the most exhaustive study to date, Nicholas de Lange has exposed abundant, if sometimes episodic, evidence of Origen's contacts with Jewish institutions and traditions.[1] Other studies have enhanced our knowledge of the social and religious history of third-century Palestine, the period of Origen's tenure in Caesarea.[2] I wish in this brief paper to stand back for a moment and observe the broader historical

---

[1]Cf. N. R. M. de Lange, *Origen and the Jews: Studies in Jewish-Christian Relations in Third-Century Palestine,* Cambridge Oriental Publications 25 (Cambridge, 1976); also H. Bietenhard, *Caesarea, Origenes und die Juden* (Stuttgart, 1974); G. Sgherri, *Chiesa e Sinagoga nelle opere di Origene,* Studia patristica mediolanensia 13 (Milan, 1982).

[2]Cf. L. Levine, *Caesarea under Roman Rule,* Studies in Judaism in Late Antiquity 7 (Leiden, 1975), especially chaps. 4-7; R. Kimelman, *Rabbi Yohanan of Tiberias: Aspects of the Social and Religious History of Third-Century Palestine* (diss., Yale University, 1977); M. Goodman, *State and Society in Roman Galilee, A. D. 132-212* (Totowa, N. J., 1983).

spectrum of Origen's connection with Judaism. How "typical" is his confrontation with the Jews of the patterns of Jewish-Christian relations we see emerging in the second, third, and fourth centuries? Conversely, how can these larger patterns help to fill in our picture of the encounter between Origen and the Jews in Caesarea?

Research on Origen's contacts with Judaism has proceeded in the shadow of a larger debate on the actual extent of Judaism's impact on the emerging Church in late antiquity. Numerous scholars have followed Marcel Simon's basic position that Judaism continued to be a vital force, rivaling the Church in Palestine and the cities of the Diaspora well beyond the disastrous Bar Kochba Revolt of 132-135 C. E.[3] Only recently, however, David Rokeah has revived Adolf Harnack's original thesis that Jewish proselytism disappeared altogether after Bar Kochba. The Jews accordingly became passive "middlemen" in the prevailing conflict between Christianity and paganism,[4] and Christian polemic *adversus Judaeos* degenerated merely into edifying propaganda for the Church.[5] Rokeah cites Origen's *Contra Celsum*, with its theoretical defense of Judaism, and reticence to censure the

---

[3]Cf. M. Simon, *Verus Israel: Étude sur les relations entre chrétiens et juifs dans l'empire romain (135-425)*, 2nd. ed. (Paris, 1964); more recently, *int. al.* R. L. Wilken, *John Chrysostom and the Jews: Rhetoric and Reality in the Late Fourth Century*, The Transformation of the Classical Heritage 4 (Berkeley, 1983); H. Drijvers, "Jews and Christians at Edessa," *Journal of Jewish Studies* 36 (1985): 88-102. See also Y. Baer, "Israel, the Christian Church, and the Roman Empire from the Time of Septimius Severus to the Edict of Toleration of A. D. 313," *Scripta hierosolymitana* 7 (1961): 79-149.

[4]Cf. D. Rokeah, *Jews, Pagans and Christians in Conflict*, Studia Post-Biblica 33 (Jerusalem and Leiden, 1982), pp. 47ff, 78.

[5]Ibid., pp. 47, 65-76.

Jews, as evidence that the Synagogue no longer hindered the Church's designs on the pagan world.[6]

Were the Jews in fact only harmless bystanders lurking in the background of Origen's ministry in Caesarea? Scattered evidence from his Caesarean writings, including the *Contra Celsum,* point to a more dynamic pattern of Christian-Jewish relations in third-century Palestine. Common interests and frontiers engendered a tacit competition which occasionally gave way to open strife. I will examine here three interrelated fronts of this contention: (1) Origen's personal contacts with the rabbis; (2) the wider missionary conflict between Church and Synagogue in Palestine; and (3) Origen's exegetical-homiletic disputations with the rabbis.

I.

Origen's allusions to his private *magister hebraeus,* and to other Jewish Christians and Jews who assisted him in his biblical scholarship, are, along with his testimony to various contemporary Jewish traditions and institutions, well-documented elsewhere and need not be covered here.[7] The turning-point in Origen's relation with Judaism was his relocation in Caesarea around 233, at a time when Caesarean and Galilean rabbinism was just beginning to reach the zenith of its power. He founded his school within only a few years of the academy of R. Hoshaya in Caesarea, which helped to train some of the greatest halakhists in third-century Palestine: R.

---

[6]Ibid., pp. 69-71.

[7]Cf. G. Bardy, "Les traditions juives dans l'œuvre d'Origène," *RB* 34 (1925): 221-223; de Lange, *Origen and the Jews,* pp. 15-37. See also S. Krauss, "The Jews in the Works of the Church Fathers," *JQR* 5 (1983): 139ff (on Origen).

Yohanan of Tiberias, R. Eliezar b. Pedat, and Resh Laqish.[8] Origen may have come across one or more of this elite group in his discussions with "men whom the Jews allege to be sages" (οἱ λεγόμενοι παρὰ 'Ιουδαίοις σόφοι).[9]

Rabbinic sources confirm that Tannaitic and early Amoraic rabbis in Palestine bore certain traits of late antique popular philosophers, a fact which Morton Smith has noted of first-century Pharisees.[10] Origen himself used Josephus' description of the Pharisees as philosophers to characterize the rabbis of his own time: they are "the pre-eminent rank (τάξις) and school (αἵρεσις) in Judaism, professing a well-balanced lifestyle and precision in interpreting the law and prophets"; though "brash and ostentatious", they "separate themselves from the entire Jewish nation, as surpassing in their wisdom (φρόνησις) and way of life (βίος). . ."[11] Origen had heard of certain esoteric practices within rabbinic academies.[12] He had probably

---

[8]Cf. Levine, *Caesarea*, p. 88.

[9]*C. Cels.* 1.45, GCS 1.95.3f; ibid. 1.55, GCS 1.106.3f; ibid. 1.56, GCS 1.107.27f; ibid. 2.31, GCS 1.159.1f. (GCS references include volume number in the Origenes Werke, page, and where appropriate, lines. Translations of primary texts are my own unless otherwise noted).

[10]Cf. M. Smith, "Palestinian Judaism in the First Century," repr. in *Essays in Graeco-Roman and Related Talmudic Literature* (New York, 1977), pp. 195-196.

[11]*Comm. in Joann.*, frag. 34, GCS 4.510.2-8. Cf. Josephus, *Bell.* 2.162-166; *Ant.* 18.11-17.

[12]Cf. *Comm. in Cant.* Prol., GCS 8.62.22-30, where Origen specifically mentions how certain texts of scripture, the so-called δευτερώσεις, were withheld from immature students, who were to be initiated in these writings only by the sages.

observed first-hand the school of R. Hoshaya in Caesarea, which was more than a sedentary institution, having distinct ascetic features.[13]

The rabbis are known in some cases to have exploited this philosophical repute. Not only did Greek ethical and philosophical idioms influence moral discourse within certain Tannaitic circles,[14] but some rabbis actively sought a larger hearing for their teachings. Writes Martin Goodman, "As Greek philosophers were expected to teach practical ethics as physicians of souls rather than impractical theorisers, so the rabbis meted out moral advice in the midrash they delivered to the wider public on Sabbaths."[15] They also engaged pagans and Christians in public debates.

The rabbinic literature unfortunately never affords details of the rabbis' encounters with various *minim* (heretics), but it does report certain instances where the rabbis confuted Christian "philosophs" (philosophers) and other *epiqursim* ("Epicureans") who distorted scripture or questioned Israel's election. These derisive labels, far from suggesting an anti-philosophical attitude on the part of the rabbis, were aimed at branding the opponents petty sophists in comparison with the erudite sages.[16] R. Gamaliel II (early second century) reportedly confronted a "philosopher",

---

[13]Indeed, its precursors included the "open-air" academies in Palestine, teaching groups meeting in everything from marketplaces to vineyards, "touring" academies like that of R. Gamaliel (Tosefta *Pesahim* 2.16), and the like. See the discussion of M. Goodman, *State and Society*, pp. 76ff; also the study of S. Krauss, "Outdoor Teaching in Talmudic Times," *Journal of Jewish Studies* 1 (1948-49): 82-84.

[14]Cf. J. Goldin, "A Philosophical Session in a Tannaite Academy," *Traditio* 21 (1965): 1-21.

[15]*State and Society*, p. 74.

[16]Cf. Goldin, "A Philosophical Session," p. 20-21.

probably a gentile Christian, perhaps a trained orator,[17] who cited Yahweh's "withdrawal" in Hosea 5:6 in order to dispute Israel's election.[18] R. Yohanan, Origen's contemporary from Tiberias, warned against gentile as well as Jewish "Epicureans" who wreaked havoc on the Torah.[19] Another celebrated pericope[20] records how R. Hoshaya, Origen's major Jewish counterpart in Caesarea, answered a "philosopher's" query about circumcision. If circumcision was so precious, why did God create Adam uncircumcised? R. Hoshaya responded that all of God's hexaemeral creations needed perfecting, and circumcision was conducive to man's perfection. Wilhelm Bacher, the great rabbinics scholar, surmised a century ago that this philosopher was Origen himself contending with R. Hoshaya.[21] Yet this particular derogation of circumcision is found earlier in Justin,[22] and was probably a stock argument in Christian polemic against Jewish observances.

It is little surprise, then, that Origen too should boast to Celsus of his victories in debate with the sages, often pitting his knowledge of their teachings against Celsus' Jewish persona.[23] Some of his confrontations

---

[17]This is T. Herford's view in *Christianity in Talmud and Midrash* (London, 1903; repr. ed., New York, 1975), p. 148.

[18]*Midrash Ps.* 10.8; cf. B. Yebamot 102b. See also *Genesis Rabbah* 1.9; B. *Shabbat* 116a. References to the Babylonian Talmud are cited under "B" and specific tractate; those to the Talmud of the Land of Israel under "J" and specific tractate).

[19]B. *Sanhedrin* 38b.

[20]Genesis Rabbah 11.6.

[21]W. Bacher, "The Church Father, Origen, and Rabbi Hoshaya," *JQR* 3 (1891): 357-360.

[22]Cf. *Dial. c. Trypho* 19, PG 6.516C.

[23]Cf. *int. al. C. Cels.* 2.31, GCS 1.159.1-5.

with the rabbis were probably informal discussions in private,[24] but others were public debates or symposia before an audience, focusing on interpretations of scripture, the miracles of Jesus and Moses, and the like.[25] Lee Levine notes that Caesarea, like other Graeco-Roman cities, had a meeting-place for religious controversies where the Bible, New Testament, and other Jewish and Christian texts were deposited for easy reference.[26] Such debates no doubt played an important role in securing the popular appeal and intellectual integrity of Judaism and Christianity in late antiquity.

Origen respected the skills of his rabbinic opponents enough to be concerned that Christians might shame themselves in these public disputes.[27] Perhaps he composed the Hexapla in part for the purpose of controverting the sages on the text of scripture.[28] At any rate, he leaves little doubt that the Jewish scholars were a force to be reckoned with if Christianity was successfully to appropriate the Hebrew Bible. We may reasonably assume that Origen himself was no weakling in debate. His inquiries into the Hebrew language may well have scandalized the rabbis in view of the Caesarean Jewish laity's ostensible ignorance of Hebrew;[29]

---

[24]Cf. *Ep. ad Afr.* 6, PG 11.61B.

[25]Notably, *C. Cels.* 1.45, GCS 1.95.3-5.

[26]*Caesarea*, pp. 82-83.

[27]*Ep. ad Afr.* 5, PG 11.60B-61A.

[28]So argues S. P. Brock, "Origen's Aims as a Textual Critic of the Old Testament," *StPatr* 10 (TU 107; Berlin, 1970), pp. 215-218.

[29]The Shema was recited in Greek in at least one of Caesarea's synagogues because the congregants did not read Hebrew (cf. J. *Sota* 1.21b). On the extensive use of Greek among Jews in hellenized towns like Caesarea, see S. Lieberman, *Greek in Jewish Palestine*, 2nd. ed. (New York, 1965), pp. 37-59. Notably, Lieberman suggests (pp. 2, 39) that the rabbis in towns like

moreover, his ability to cite biblical texts at will, and his knowledge of certain Jewish haggadic traditions, would very well have impressed Jewish and non-Jewish audiences alike. Perhaps Origen, among others, inspired R. Yohanan's poignant remark that "a gentile who studies the Torah deserves capital punishment."[30]

II.

Religious debates over shared scriptures were only the outward sign of an implicit competition, and broader coincidence of interests, between the Church and the Synagogue in the second and third centuries. Marcel Simon argues that if Judaism had not been proselytizing in this period, this conflict would have been merely "un lutte toute théorique, livresque et stérile controverse autour des textes sacrés"; if proselytizing, Judaism would constitute "un rival véritable et dangereux" to Christianity.[31] Simon has of course vigorously argued for the latter, insisting that early Hadrianic bans on circumcising gentiles never extinguished the Jewish mission. He contends that rabbinic dicta favorable to proselytism presume its reality, and that epigraphical allusions, patristic references, and Constantinian counter-measures adequately attest its persistence well into the fourth century.[32]

Caesarea preached in Aramaic but illustrated passages in Greek for the sake of the townspeople. Yet Levine (*Caesarea,* p. 198, n. 124) rightly argues that Aramaic preaching would be hard to imagine in Caesarea, where, not only was the Shema recited in Greek, but the speaker frequently addressed gentiles as well as Jews.

[30]B. *Sanhedrin* 58b.

[31]*Verus Israel,* p. 315.

[32]Ibid., pp. 323-351.

David Rokeah denies Simon's conclusions, and cites, among other things, select negative comments of the rabbis about proselytizing.[33] In reality, the rabbis' statements vary greatly in this period, indicating a constant alternation between the desire for expansion and disillusionment with unfaithful converts.[34]

For our purposes, it is especially significant that in third-century Galilee, R. Yohanan and other leading sages sought stricter regulation of ritual entry requirements (i.e., circumcision and baptism),[35] but still encouraged Jewish missionary activities.[36] Origen himself complained of Judaizing Christians being lured to the synagogue by Jewish missionaries,[37] and portrayed the success of Christian proselytism precisely in terms of the spiritual Israel usurping the carnal.[38] Caesarean Jews were probably incited

---

[33]*Jews, Christians and Pagans in Conflict*, pp. 42-43.

[34]See the relevant texts gathered by B. Bamberger, *Proselytism in the Talmudic Period*, rev. ed. (New York, 1968), pp. 149-173.

[35]B. *Yebamot* 46a.

[36]Cf. *int. al.* R. Yohanan in B. *Nedarim* 32a. See also M. Avi-Yonah, *The Jews under Roman and Byzantine Rule* (New York, 1976), p. 82, who observes that all of R. Yohanan's outstanding pupils endorsed proselytism. Independent testimony of Jewish proselytism specifically in Caesarea is offered in a funerary inscription mentioning a particular convert to Judaism: Μεμοριον της προσσυλητου [προσηλυτου] Αστη και Παρηγοριου Ευχαριστουσα, as recorded by B. Lifshitz in his "Inscriptions greques de Césarée en Palestine (Caesarea Palaestinae)," *RB* 68 (1961): 115-116 (no. 2).

[37]*Hom. in Matt.* 16, GCS 11.29-31.

[38]Cf. *Hom. in Luc.* 5, GCS 9.87.24-88.3: *Nunc autem populi credentium accedunt ad finem Jesu, et angeli, quibus creditae fuerant ecclesiae, roborati praesentia Salvatoris multos adducunt proselytos, ut congregentur in omni orbe conventicula christianorum. Quapropter consurgentes laudemus Dominum et fiamus pro carnali Israhel spiritualis Israhel.*

by competition with Christian missionaries for the same pool of potential converts.[39]

The competition for proselytes gave rise to an ideological exchange as well. Classic arguments *adversus Judaeos* were probably leveled in just this context, the destruction of the Temple and dispersion of the Jews being seen as divine punishment for the execution of Jesus.[40] Origen mentioned a Jewish response to such allegations from a debate with the sages over the Servant Songs in Isaiah: Israel's chastisement and subsequent diaspora were a providential means for her to make proselytes of the nations.[41] This very rationale was espoused by R. Eliezar b. Pedat, a Galilean contemporary of Origen, and seconded by R. Yohanan.[42] The rabbis took the offense too at times. R. Yohanan was probably reacting to Christian notions of original sin when he insisted that the gentiles ("idolaters") were contaminated only by not having participated in the lawgiving at Sinai,[43] for which he apparently prescribed proselytism as the solution.[44] Confronted by Christian attempts to spiritualize the Law, the rabbis asserted the eternal and universally binding

---

[39]On this mass of potential proselytes, cf. *Hom. in Jesu Nave* 9.9, GCS 7.354-355.

[40]Cf. int. al. *C. Cels.* 2.8, GCS 1.134-135; ibid. 4.22, GCS 1.291-292. See also Sgherri, *Chiesa e Sinagoga,* pp. 78-132; Kimelman, *Rabbi Yohanan,* pp. 266-271.

[41]*C. Cels.* 1.55, GCS 1.106.5-8.

[42]B. *Pesahim* 87b.

[43]B. *Shabbat* 145b-146a; =B. *Yebamot* 103b. See also the discussion of this passage in Kimelman, *Rabbi Yohanan,* pp. 255-256.

[44]See above, note 34.

validity of the *mitzvot*.[45] A missionary universalism thrived on both sides: if Christianity was a moral leaven and "army of piety" quietly undergirding the imperial order,[46] Judaism was a stabilizing "hedge to the world".[47]

The actual missionary success of the Church and the Synagogue of course depended on various factors. Judaism enjoyed the greater antiquity and an ancient moral code that accorded well with the pagan κοιναὶ ἔννοιαι. Certain of its customs were venerable and inspiring, and Origen knew this when he complained of Judaizing Christians who persisted in hand-washing before meals,[48] attending synagogue,[49] and observing Passover.[50] Yet Origen was also well aware that these rituals could be a stumbling block to pagans.[51] Christianity could in turn appeal to the simplicity of faith in Jesus and the universal need for moral regeneration.[52] Origen maintained in his *Commentary on Romans* that Israel believed only after observing Yahweh's miracles, but Abraham (the prototype of believers) had the truly

---

[45]Cf. J. *Aboda Zara* 2.1.40c, cited by Levine, *Caesarea,* p. 84 and 209, n. 251.

[46]Cf. *C. Cels.* 8.73-74, GCS 2.290-291; also ibid. 3.50-61 *passim.*

[47]R. Yohanan in *Exodus Rabbah* 2.5.

[48]*Comm. in Matt.* 11.8, GCS 10.47.5-15.

[49]*Hom. in Lev.* 5.8, GCS 6.349.4; *Sel. in Exod.* 12.46, PG 12.285; *Hom. in Jer.* 12.13, GCS 6.100.

[50]*Hom. in Jer.* 12.13, GCS 6.99-100. On the appeal of Jewish traditions and customs to Judaizing Christians in an analogous context in fourth-century Antioch, see Wilken, *John Chrysostom and the Jews,* pp. 66-94.

[51]Cf. *Comm. in Rom.* 2.11, PG 14.897A: *Ridicula etiam ipsis gentibus fiunt.*

[52]*C. Cels.* 1.9-11, GCS 1.61-64.

virtuous faith which demanded no such wonders.[53] Yet Resh Laqish similarly lauded gentile proselytes to Judaism as dearer to God than Israel at Sinai, because they had not witnessed the miraculous signs on the mountain, but were converted through spontaneous piety.[54]

Perhaps, however, the singularly most important instrument in luring proselytes both to Judaism and to Christianity continued to be their shared treasure: scripture, the Hebrew Bible in Greek recensions.[55] A number of second-century rabbinic allusions suggest that gentiles contemplating conversion to Judaism busied themselves with reading scripture, and expressed their reservations to Jewish friends whose answers were often determinative.[56] *Sifre Deuteronomy* tells of a "philosopher" who was martyred for protesting the burning of the Torah scroll (presumably during the Bar Kochba war).[57] Though sophisticated pagans sometimes derided scripture as crude or distasteful,[58] Origen still recorded in the third

---

[53]*Comm. in Rom.*, frag. 6.1 (ed. J. Scherer, Cairo, 1957), pp. 182, 184.

[54]*Tanhuma B. and N. Lek Leka* 6, selected and quoted by Bamberger, *Proselytism,* p. 155.

[55]On the use of Greek recensions for Jewish proselytism, see Simon, *Verus Israel,* pp. 348-351. On the importance of scripture in general in the early Christian mission, see W. H. C. Frend, "The Missions of the Early Church 180-700 A. D., " in *Miscellanea Historiae Ecclesiasticae* 3 (Louvain, 1970), pp. 4-5.

[56]See the relevant evidence adduced and assessed by I. Heinemann, "The Attitude of the Ancient World toward Judaism," *Review of Religion* 4 (1940): 387-388.

[57]*Sifre Deut.* 307.4.

[58]Cf. e. g. Arnobius, *Adv. gentes* 1.58, CSEL 4.39.8ff; and Celsus in *C. Cels.* 6.49-65 (against the Mosaic cosmogony); ibid. 7.1-26 (against the OT prophecies).

century that the Church converted souls principally "through readings of the Bible and explanation of the readings" (δι᾽ ἀναγνωσμάτων καὶ διὰ τῶν εἰς τὰ ἀναγνώσματα διηγήσεως).[59] Isaak Heinemann has reasonably concluded that converts both to Judaism and to Christianity "were won less through dogmas and rites than through Scripture, to which other religions in antiquity, both official and mystery, had nothing comparable to oppose."[60]

Jews and Christians, nevertheless, were not the only ones using scripture for proselytism. Gnostic and Marcionite sects in Palestine also sought adherents, and exploited the popularity and availability of the Bible. Already in the second century, the so-called "two powers" heretics had begun to show their heads in Palestine, raising exegetical questions about the unity of the Godhead, theodicy, and the like. Caesarean and Galilean rabbis championed the cause of biblical orthodoxy, propounding rules of monotheistic exegesis for sensitive passages like Genesis 1:26-27.[61] Marcionism was a common enemy of Christianity and Judaism, attacked by Origen in his homilies,[62] by R. Yohanan,[63] and later in the third century by R. Abbahu of Caesarea.[64] Alan Segal's observation about the rabbis'

---

[59]C. Cels. 3.50, GCS 1.246.17-19.

[60]"The Attitude of the Ancient World," p. 388.

[61]Cf. R. Yohanan in B. Sanhedrin 38b.

[62]Cf. int al. Hom. in Luc. 16, GCS 9.108; Hom. in Num. 7.1, GCS 7.38. On one occasion, Origen actually borrowed from a Jewish midrash to refute an exegesis of Apelles concerning the dimensions of Noah's ark (Hom. in Gen. 2.2, GCS 6.28f).

[63]Cf. Exodus Rabbah 13.3; and Kimelman, Rabbi Yohanan, pp. 179-182.

[64]See S. Lachs, "Rabbi Abbahu and the Minim," JQR 60 (1969): 209ff.

dilemma with these sects could also apply to Origen's: "Although the answers to the heretics were worked out by the academies, the questions must have been raised in relation to Bible-reading and by groups who were interested in hearing the Jewish Bible expounded."[65]

III.

This wider missionary struggle between the Church and the Synagogue in Palestine, in which scripture doubtless played a crucial role, intensified their rival claims to the Bible and its legitimate interpretation.[66] Christian-Jewish confrontations in this period were therefore more than trivial or bookish disputes over the scriptures; they were genuine struggles for credibility. Newly ordained and burdened in Caesarea with the responsibilities of a preacher, Origen took Jewish exegesis to task in his commentaries and homilies. Despite his deeper appreciation for the rabbinic hermeneutics, he perpetuated the "myth of Jewish literalism",[67] as de Lange has called it, because it continued to be an effective rhetorical *reductio ad absurdum* with which to oppose Judaism.

---

[65]*Two Powers in Heaven: Early Rabbinic Reports about Christianity and Gnosticism*, Studies in Judaism in Late Antiquity 25 (Leiden, 1977), p. 154.

[66]On the centrality of biblical intepretation in Christian-Jewish exchanges throughout late antiquity, see the recent studies of M. Simon, "Le Bible dans les premières controverses entre juifs et chrétiens," in *Le monde grec ancien et la Bible,* ed. Claude Mondésert, Bible de tout les temps 1 (Paris, 1984), pp. 107-125; also J. Maier, *Jüdische Auseindersetzung mit dem Christentum in der Antike,* Erträge der Forschung 177 (Darmstadt, 1982).

[67]Cf. *De princ.* 4.3.2, GCS 5.326; *C. Cels.* 2.4-6, GCS 1.130-132; and de Lange, *Origen and the Jews,* pp. 82-83.

Origen persistently refused, for example, to admit any rationale at all for the literal interpretation of the ceremonial laws. He was aware of current Jewish *halakhah* which sought to revise Sabbath regulations so as to make them more practicable in extenuating circumstances. He refuted such qualifications as endlessly bothersome: the wearing of one kind of sandal a burden, another not, *ad infinitem*.[68] With similar bluntness he argued that the impossibility of Jews making their paschal offerings in the Temple (Deuteronomy 16:6f) after its destruction was adequate grounds for discontinuing all such rituals.[69] Though many Jews admirably studied the Torah from infancy to old age,[70] their literalist teachings were nothing but "myths and rubbish" (μύθοι καὶ λῆροι)[71] without the higher (Christian) interpretation of the Law.

Origen likewise warned against the Jews' literalism in interpreting the prophets: "The prophets also do not limit the meaning of their sayings to the obvious history and to the text and letter of the law."[72] Yet in one of his debates with the rabbis, the sages themselves interpreted Isaiah's Servant

---

[68]*De princ.* 4.3.2, GCS 5.326.

[69]*Comm. in Rom.* 2.13, PG 14.906ff. For a fuller discussion of such arguments, see de Lange, *Origen and the Jews*, pp. 89-102; Bietenhard, *Caesarea, Origenes und die Juden*, pp. 48-52.

[70]*Comm. in Rom.* 2.14, PG 14.915C: *Videmus plurimos Judaeorum ab infantia usque ad senectutem semper discentes.*

[71]*C. Cels.* 2.5, GCS 1.132.12. On Jewish "fables" (μύθοι), see also *Hom. in Gen.* 6.3, GCS 6.69ff; *Hom. in Exod.* 5.1, GCS 6.184; *Hom. in Lev.* 3.3, GCS 6.306.

[72]*C. Cels.* 2.6, GCS 1.132.25-27. The translation here is H. Chadwick's from his magisterial *Origen: Contra Celsum* (Cambridge, 1953; rev. ed., 1965), p. 71.

Songs allegorically, rendering the Servant as the whole people of Israel.[73] Origen's response was predictable: their allegory simply did not fit. Rather than confuting an allegorical interpretation as such, he resorted merely to an *ad hominem* argument: "Why is this man said to have been led to death because of the iniquities of the people of God, if he is not different from the people of God?"[74] Rhetorically speaking, the rabbis failed to take the prophecy "literally" enough. The rabbis could, of course, respond in kind. Origen mentioned a Jewish response to another prophecy used by Christians as a pivotal Christological *testimonium*: Zechariah 9:9-10. Granted Jesus' entry into Jerusalem "on an ass", when did he ever "cut off" the "chariot from Ephraim", the "war horse from Jerusalem", or the "battle bow"? Why indeed did he have to ride into Jerusalem at all, when the journey was so short?[75]

One other aspect of these ongoing exegetical disputations in third-century Palestine has only recently been examined closely: Origen's exchanges with rabbis over the Song of Songs. The Song had been elevated by the sages to a kind of "nationalist ode on the chosenness of Israel",[76] and its interpretation had become a veritable battleground for Jewish and Christian claims to divine election. Here there was an initial consensus on the *peshat* (plain sense) of the text: for the rabbis, the allegorical interpretation of the Song was the only possible *peshat*,[77] a love song

---

[73]Ibid. 1.55, GCS 1.106.

[74]Ibid. GCS 1.106.23-24, trans. Chadwick, p. 51.

[75]*Comm. in Joann.* 10.27, GCS 4.199ff, cited by de Lange, *Origen and the Jews*, p. 100.

[76]S. Baron, *A Social and Political History of the Jews,* vol. 2, 2nd ed. (New York, 1952), p. 145.

[77]Y. Muffs, "Joy and Love as Metaphorical Expressions of Willingness and Spontaneity in Cuneiform, Ancient Hebrew, and Related

between God and Israel; for Origen it was an allegory of Christ's marriage to his Church.

Building on Ephraim Urbach's earlier work, Reuven Kimelman has demonstrated a thoroughgoing cross-fertilization in Origen's exegetical disputations with R. Yohanan.[78] In Song 1:2, for example, R. Yohanan found that the mystical "kiss" of God was destined for Israel at Sinai,[79] and to obviate the potential anthropomorphism, he introduced into his exegesis an angelic mediator who kissed the Holy One.[80] Origen countered by claiming that the "kiss" was Christ's and intended for the Church; he downplayed the meditorial role of an angel, asserting that angels merely brought down the Law to the Church (cf. Galatians 3:19).[81] Origen's equations of Bridegroom=Christ and Bride=Church, which denigrated the idea of the kiss being a mediation of the Torah, in turn triggered R. Yohanan's attempt to show that God gave the commandments directly at Sinai,[82] with

---

Literatures," in *Christianity, Judaism and Other Graeco-Roman Cults* 3, Studies in Judaism in Late Antiquity 11 (Leiden, 1975), p. 21; cited by R. Kimelman, *Rabbi Yohanan,* p. 239, n. 1. Origen himself, of course, was aware of the esoteric esteem in which the rabbis held the Song as a sourcebook for allegorical and mystical speculation (cf. *Comm. in Cant.* Prol., GCS 8.62.22-30).

[78]Cf. E. E. Urbach, "The Homiletical Interpretations of the Sages and the Expositions of Origen on Canticles, and the Jewish-Christian Disputation," Scripta hierosolymitana 22 (1971): 247-275; R. Kimelman, "Rabbi Yohanan and Origen on the Song of Songs: A Third-Century Jewish-Christian Disputation," *HTR* 73 (1980): 567-595 (=ch. 6 of Kimelman's dissertation, *Rabbi Yohanan,* cited above, note 2 and *passim*).

[79]Cf. Urbach, "The Homiletical Interpretations," p. 254.

[80]*Song of Songs Rabbah* 1.2.2.

[81]*Comm. in Cant.* 1, GCS 8.90.

[82]*Pesikta Rabbati* 21.5, quoted by Kimelman, "Rabbi Yohanan and Origen," pp. 575-576.

Moses playing the role of an arranger of the rendezvous between Yahweh and Israel.[83]   Other examples notwithstanding,[84] this exchange will suffice to show that in the debate over the Song, Origen refuted the rabbis precisely by attempting to best their allegories.   He in no way underestimated the profundity or the appeal of the rabbis' homilies.   In fact, in his sermons on Ezekiel, as David Halperin has discovered, Origen actually exploited the colorful Sinai and ascension imagery of Galilean rabbis' Pentecost homilies in order to embellish his own preaching.[85]

The dispute over the Song of Songs clearly shows that Origen was capable of entering into extensive and sophisticated exegetical controversies with the rabbis.   The upshot was nonetheless the same.   His aim was not to attack any certain mode of Jewish exegesis, but to undermine the entire Jewish claim to the authoritative interpretation of the Bible.   In his disputes with the rabbis, there was no shared, highly articulated language about the method of rendering texts.   Such debates thrived on rhetorical strategies and *ad hoc* arguments.   For the same reasons, therefore, that he dismissed the literal interpretation of Jewish laws, Origen rejected the rabbis' allegorical exegeses or tried to outstrip them.   In so doing, he testified to the skill of the

---

[83]*Song of Songs Rabbah* 1.2.3.

[84]Kimelman ("Rabbi Yohanan and Origen," pp. 574-595) finds no less than five "topics" of this ongoing disputation on Song 1:1-6:   a covenant mediated by Moses vs. one negotiated by him; the NT vs. the Oral Torah as "superseding" scripture; Christ vs. Abraham; the heavenly vs. the earthly Jerusalem; and Israel being repudiated vs. Israel being disciplined.

[85]See David Halperin, "Origen, Ezekiel's Merkabah, and the Ascension of Moses," *Church History* 50 (1981):   261-275.

rabbinic preachers who, like himself, addressed the concrete needs of a religious community.[86]

IV.

Because Origen's allusions to his contacts with rabbinic Judaism are fairly scattered and episodic, we are hard-pressed to fill in the gaps in his picture of the Christian-Jewish encounter in third-century Caesarea. The rabbis he debated publicly and in his preaching--not to mention those Jews who assisted him privately[87]--are elusive figures never clearly identified by Origen. By comparing Origen's evidence with parallel rabbinic traditions, and with analogous developments in Christian-Jewish relations throughout this period, his confrontation with Judaism begins to take shape. We see Judaism not only as a resource in Origen's scholarly background, but as a vibrant rival community in the foreground of his commentaires and homilies composed in Caesarea.

Indeed, the Jews in Origen's purview did not stand idly by in Christianity's ongoing engagement with the pagan world. Inspired by a strong rabbinate of scholars and preachers with their own missionary vision, the Jews of Caesarea, as in the Diaspora cities, were very much in the thick of current religious controversies. As Han Drijvers emphasizes in a recent study of their relations in Edessa, Jews, Christians, and pagans did not live in some idyllic isolation in the setting of an ancient town, where most of life was lived in public and privacy was almost unheard of. Their mutual

---

[86]As Levine notes (*Caesarea*, p. 102), the Caesarean rabbis in particular were distinguished by their heavy involvement in preaching and the practical affairs of synagogue life.

[87]See above, note 7.

ideological conflicts arose within the context of daily experience, where, in the ancient world, religious behavior was precisely a matter of public conduct informed by the standards of a tradition.[88]

Origen's own interaction with the rabbis followed, in some respects, the pattern of disputes of popular philosophers in late antiquity. In private, of course, their relations could be rather peaceable, even convivial, Origen researching those Jewish traditions which would enrich his own scholarship, and at times openly admitting his curiosity--a remarkable, albeit naïve curiosity[89]--about rabbinic hermeneutics. Theologically, too, he could extol the ancient and venerable "Jewish" sages and prophets for their relative proximity to the spiritual truth,[90] and assess the positive place of Judaism in the unfolding history of salvation, in a way unprecedented amid strong the Christian antipathy toward Judaism in his time. Such is the aspect of Origen's relationship with Judaism which is atypical in its ancient context, and which brings the admiration of modern critics anxious to find in him a model for sholarly interchange between Christians and Jews today.[91]

---

[88]See Drijvers, "Jews and Christians in Edessa," p. 89.

[89]One is reminded here of the passage in *Sel. in Ps.* (PG 12.1080B-C) in which Origen concurs with "the Hebrew" that the whole of scripture mysteriously resembles a single house with a number of locked rooms. By each room is a key, but not the one fitting that room, such that the exegete's task is to match keys with rooms and thereby gain access to the Bible innermost secrets. Origen admired the rabbis' sense of the mystical depth of scripture, and sometimes borrowed isolated pieces of haggadah, but he did not venture, beyond his means, into the labyrinth of rabbinic hermeneutics.

[90]Cf., in particular, *C. Cels.* 7.7ff, and the study of P. Gorday in this volume, "Moses and Jesus in contra Celsum 7.1-25: Ethics, History and Jewish Christian Eirenics in Origen's Theology."

[91]I am thinking here principally of de Lange, in the Afterword to his *Origen and the Jews,* p. 135.

Yet, from most indications, Origen's scholarly and theological interest in Judaism did not betray itself openly in his public dispositon toward the Jews. Here Origen's debates with the rabbis over the Bible presented less a scholarly exchange of ideas than a platform for mutual disclaimers.   Origen's anti-Jewish maneuvers in his homilies and commentaries reflect just this same inflexibility. There was no question here of negotiation in these "philosophers'" debates. The rabbis' exegetical arguments had to be dismissed *in toto* because Judaism continued to be a viable threat to the Christian mission, a live option for those seeking to be faithful to the tradition of the Bible. In this adamant public posture toward Judaism, Origen remained indeed quite typical of the patterns of Christian-Jewish relations in late antiquity.

ORIGEN AND THE *SENSUS LITERALIS*

Charles J. Scalise
Southern Baptist Theological Seminary

Origen's allegorical exegesis presents a major difficulty to the modern reader. Fantastic allegory--simply incredible exegesis to modern eyes--appears in the midst of biblically-grounded, textually sensitive, historically perceptive interpretation. One has the impression that Hanson's dramatic characterization of "exegetical suicide"[1] may not be too far from the mark in describing these allegorical flights of fancy.

This brief paper attempts to take a first step towards understanding Origen's allegorical exegesis by examining his use of the *sensus literalis* in its hermeneutical context. The paper argues that Origen's depreciation of the literal sense of Scripture contributes to a loss of hermeneutical control in his exegesis. Thus, Origen's rather rigid view of the *sensus literalis* is a significant factor underlying his allegorical interpretation of Scripture.

---

[1]R.P.C. Hanson, *Allegory and Event* (London: SCM Press, 1959), p. 258.

The Problem of Defining *"Sensus Literalis"*

Raymond Brown has offered the following modern definition of *sensus literalis*: "The sense which the human author directly intended and which his words convey."[2] In defending this definition, Brown cites Origen as the classic example of the consequences of rejecting this view:

> . . . the intention of the author and the sense conveyed by the words cannot be separated. Such a separation has been responsible for what historically has been one of the great confusions about the literal sense. . . . Many of the Church Fathers, e.g., Origen, thought that the literal sense was what the words said independently of the author's intent. Thus were Christ spoken of as "the lion of Judah," the literal sense for these Fathers would be that he was an animal. That is why some of them rejected the literal sense of Scripture.[3]

Brown's modern definition of *sensus literalis* reflects the exclusive focus of post-Enlightenment historical critical scholarship upon the intentionality of the human author.[4] This view, however, has also

---

[2]Raymond E. Brown, "The Literal Sense of Scripture," in *The Jerome Biblical Commentary*, ed. Raymond Brown, Joseph Fitzmeyer, and Jerome Murphy (Englewood Cliffs, N.J.: Prentice-Hall, 1968), p. 606.

[3]Ibid., p. 607.

[4]Cf. Hans Frei's detailed chronicling of the development of this emphasis upon the author's intention in *The Eclipse of Biblical Narrative* (New Haven: Yale Univ. Press, 1974). Of course, earlier exegetes (e.g., Hugh of St. Victor, Luther, and especially Calvin with his stress upon the *mens auctori*) also place significant emphasis upon recovering the author's intentionality. Yet their stress upon the intentionality of the human author

increasingly come under attack as too narrow and sterile by a wide range of crtitics.[5]

A most helpful corrective to Brown's historical critical definition is provided by Raphael Loewe's work on the *peshat* or "plain sense" in early Jewish exegesis.[6] Loewe has shown that the verb *peshat* in Aramaic and in rabbinic Hebrew has the meaning of "explain" with "authority" as its "central notion."[7] Thus, the noun *peshat* denotes "authoritative teaching,"[8] rather

---

is never incompatible or even in major tension with the divine authorship of Scripture, in contrast to the post-Enlightenment situation. This change from "pre-critical" to critical biblical scholarship reflects a major shift in the understanding of the inspiration of Scripture, which has been greatly influenced by the critical challenge to traditional assumptions concerning the identity of the human authors of the Bible.

[5]David C. Steinmetz, "The Superiority of Pre-Critical Exegesis," *Theology Today* 37 (1980-81), 27-38, offers a controversial critique from a historical point of view. For a balanced critique and exegetical model from the point of view of the new literary criticism see R. Alan Culpepper, *Anatomy of the Fourth Gospel: A Study in Literary Design* (Philadelphia: Fortress, 1983).

[6]Raphael Loewe, "The 'Plain' Meaning of the Scripture in Early Jewish Exegesis," *Papers of the Institute of Jewish Studies London*, ed. J. G. Weiss (Jerusalem: Magnes Press, 1964), Vol. I, pp. 140-185. Loewe points out that the fundamental meaning of *peshat* in Hebrew is "to *strip* [a garment], properly to *flatten* it by so doing," with the meaning "make a raid" as a metaphorical extension. Also, via the cognate languages *peshat* comes to mean "extend" or "stretch out" in later rabbinic Hebrew (ibid., p. 155).

[7]Ibid., pp. 155-160.

[8]Ibid., pp. 155-160. For further explanation of Loewe's view in the context of Christian exegesis and its application to a canonical approach to biblical studies see Brevard S. Childs, "The '*Sensus Literalis*' of Scripture: An Ancient and Modern Problem," *Beiträge zur Alttestamentliche Theologie, Festschrift für Walther Zimmerli zum 70. Geburtstag*, ed. Herbert Donner, Robert Hanhart, and Rudolph Smend (Göttingen: Vandenhoeck und Ruprecht, 1977), pp. 80-93. Following Loewe, Childs maintains that, "The *peshat* is that familiar and traditional teaching of Scripture which was recognized by the community as authoritative" (p. 81), and concludes that,

than the commonly accepted textbook definition of "that straightforward
simple exegesis which corresponds to the meaning intended by its author."[9]
It is Loewe's view of the ancient Jewish definition of *peshat*, rather than
Brown's modern post-Enlightenment definition of the literal sense, which
should be used to critique Origen's understanding of the *sensus literalis*,
especially since Origen had ample opportunity to be exposed to rabbinic
Jewish exegesis during his years at Caesarea (c. 231-255).

Origen's Depreciation of the *"Sensus Literalis"*

During the ancient period of Christian history the fundamental
distinction which shapes the *sensus literalis* of Scripture is that of "the letter
and the spirit." The origin of the distinction between "the letter and the
spirit" in Christian theology may be found in Paul's contrast of these terms
in Romans 2:29 and 7:6 and especially in 2 Corinthians 3:6. As Origen
explains his view of the two senses of the law,[10] he shows how Paul's
distinction between "letter and spirit" underlies his exegesis:

"In terms of classical Christian theology, there can be no genuine *sensus
literalis* apart from a commitment to canon" (p. 93).

[9]Childs, *Sensus Literalis*, p. 81. A clear sense of the "usual
textbook explanation" may be gained by consulting Wilhelm Bacher's
standard work, *Die Exegetische Terminologie der Judischen Traditionsliteratur*
(1905; rpt. Hildesheim: Georg Olms, 1965). Examining the use of *peshat*
in the Tannaitic period, Bacher states, "mit *peshat* ist dann das einfache,
einmalige Recitiren verstanden" (i, p. 86). For a similar definition from the
Amoraic period, see Part ii, pp. 170-173.

[10]Origen's interpretation of the Old Testament law is one of his
major exegetical achievements. For a detailed exposition see Hanson,
Allegory, pp. 288-310. Also, cf. Jean Daniélou, *Origen*, trans. Walter
Mitchell (New York: Sheed and Ward, 1955), pp. 139-173.

We maintain that the law has a twofold interpretation [ὁ νόμος διττός ἐστιν], one literal [πρός ῥητόν] and the other spiritual [πρὸς διάνοιαν] ... and it is not so much we as God speaking in one of the prophets [Ezekiel 20:25], who described the law literally understood as 'judgments that are not good' and 'statutes that are not good'; and in the same prophet [cf. Ezek. 20:19-24] God is represented as saying that the law spiritually understood is 'judgments that are good' and 'statutes that are good.' The prophet is obviously not making contradictory statements in the same passage. It is consistent with this when Paul [2 Cor. 3:6] also says that 'the letter kills,' which is the equivalent of literal interpretation; whereas 'the spirit gives life' which means the same as the spiritual interpretation.[11]

Though Origen takes Paul's contrast between "the letter and the spirit" and Paul's use of allegory as scriptural points of departure, his view of "the letter and the spirit" dramatically alters the Pauline perspective. For Paul, the "historical pattern" of the Old Testament story is preserved, even in the few places where an allegorical approach is explicitly used (e.g., the story of Sarah and Hagar in Gal. 4:22-26).[12] For Origen, however, though much

---

[11]Henry Chadwick, trans., *Origen: Contra Celsum* (Cambridge: Cambridge Univ. Press, 1965), VII, 20, p. 411. GCS 2, p. 171. Also found in Caroli Delarue and Caroli Vincente Delarue, eds., *Origenis Opera Omnia*, in PG 11.1449.

[12]K. J. Woollcombe, "The Biblical Origins and Patristic Development of Typology," in *Essays on Typology* (Naperville, Ill.: Alec R. Allenson, 1957), p. 53. Other instances of Pauline "allegory" which are significant for Origen include 1 Cor. 9:9-10 (Paul's symbolic interpretation of the law requiring the unmuzzling of oxen treading grain; see quotation

of the Scripture is viewed as historical, the historicity of Scripture is itself unimportant; what matters is the spiritual meaning of Scripture developed by the method of allegory.[13]

In *De Principiis* Origen makes his famous distinction of the three senses of Scripture.[14] Origen seems to have derived this method of interpretation from Philo,[15] though this has been sometimes disputed.[16] Origen first distinguishes between literal and non-literal senses ("the bare

---

below), 1 Cor. 10:1-4 (the Red Sea crossing and baptism), Col. 2:17 (the law as a shadow of things to come), and Eph. 5:32 (marriage in Genesis and Christ and the church). For a good discussion of Origen's use of these and other inner biblical interpretations see M. F. Wiles, "Origen as Biblical Scholar," *The Cambridge History of the Bible*, Vol. I, ed. P. R. Ackroyd and C. F. Evans (Cambridge: Cambridge Univ. Press, 1970), pp. 465-466.

[13]As Hanson (*Allegory*, p. 280) comments, for Origen, "History . . . is meaningless unless a parable is derived from it, unless it is made into an allegory." For a detailed discussion of issues related to the historicity of Scripture in Origen, see Hanson, *Allegory*, pp. 258-288.

[14]As Hanson wryly notes, "The fact that Origen divided the interpretation of Scripture into three senses is almost as well known as the fact that Caesar divided Gaul into three parts" (Ibid., p. 237).

[15]Harry Austryn Wolfson, *The Philosophy of the Church Fathers*, Vol. I, *Faith, Trinity, Incarnation*, 3rd Ed., revised (Cambridge, Mass.: Harvard Univ. Press, 1970), pp. 57-60, 62. Wolfson especially points to Origen's "direct reference" in *Contra Celsum* VII, 20, quoted above, to Philo's twofold sense of the law.

[16]For example, R. M. Grant partially disagrees with this view, instead holding that Origen's most extreme allegorical views are "not Philonic, but derived from Origen's studies of Greek grammar and rhetoric" (R. M. Grant, *The Letter and the Spirit* [London: S.P.C.K., 1957], p. 101). Nevertheless, Daniélou's analysis of Origen's allegory of the Ark (*Genesis Homily II*) clearly demonstrates Origen's dependence upon Philo, down to some of the specific details of his exegesis (Jean Daniélou, *From Shadows to Reality*, trans. Dom Wulstand Hibberd [London: Burns and Oates, 1960], pp. 103-112).

letter [τὸ ψιλὸν γράμμα]" and "the spiritual sense [τὰ πνευματικά]").[17]
The non-literal sense is subsequently divided into "moral" and "spiritual"
senses, thus yielding three levels. Though Origen appeals to Proverbs 22:20-
21 (as translated in the Septuagint---τρισσῶς)[18] for scriptural support of his
threefold method of interpretation, it is Greek anthropology which provides
his primary ground for argument:

> For just as man consists of body [σώματος], soul [ψυχῆς], and
> spirit [πνεύματος], so in the same way [τὸν αὐτὸν τρόπον], does
> the Scripture which has been prepared [οἰκονομοθεῖσα] by God to
> be given for man's salvation.[19]

Often in the actual practice of exegesis Origen's three levels are collapsed
back into two: the literal (bodily) and the spiritual.[20]

Origen holds a rigid, narrow view of the literal level of
interpretation.[21] He rather disparagingly refers to the literal sense of

---

[17]G. W. Butterworth, trans. *Origen On First Principles*, (London:
S.P.C.K., 1936), IV, 2, 2, p. 72. PG 11 (IV, 9), 360.

[18]See G. Kittel, ed., *Biblia Hebraica*, third ed., p. 1181.

[19]Butterworth, *First Principles*, IV, 2, 4, p. 276. PG 11 (IV, ii),
365. Cf. also Origen's emphasis on the harmony or concord (συμφωνία) of
body, soul, and spirit in his *Commentary on Matthew*, XIV, 3 (John Patrick,
trans., "Origen's Commentary on the Gospel of Matthew," *The Ante-Nicene
Fathers*, v. 9, 3rd ed., ed. A. Menzies [New York: Charles Scribner's Sons,
1899], p. 496. GCS 10, p. 278).

[20]Wiles, "Origen," pp. 467-468. Also, N. R. M. de Lange, *Origen
and the Jews* (Cambridge: Cambridge Univ. Press, 1976), p. 109.

[21]M. F. Wiles offers the following analysis: "Despite the great
range of his intellectual gifts Origen was totally lacking in poetic sensitivity.
The literal sense of Scripture is for him the literally literal meaning of the

Scripture as "obvious (πρόχειπον), conceding its necessity, "so that the simple man [ἁπλούστερος] may be edified by what we all the flesh [σαρκός] of Scripture."[22] Origen graphically depicts the literal sense in his first homily on Leviticus:

> I myself think that the priest removes the hide "of the calf" offered as a "whole burnt offering" and pulls away the skin with which its limbs are covered. He who removes the veil of the letter [velamen litterai] from the word of God uncovers its interior parts which are members of spiritual understanding.[23]

---

words. When the Psalmist declares that God's truth 'reaches to the clouds,' Origen feels constrained to say that the clouds cannot be intended literally in such a saying; they must be interpreted spiritually of those who are obedient to the word of God. The literal interpretation of Zech. 4:10 would imply that God had seven bodily eyes" (Wiles, "Origen," p. 470). In contrast, Henri de Lubac attempts to distinguish betwen "the letter" and "literal meaning" in Origen's interpretation. "The letter" is described as "a sort of sterilized literal meaning, stripped of the spiritual potencies which lie, like seeds, within it" (Henri de Lubac, *The Sources of Revelation*, trans. Luke G. O'Neill [New York: Herder and Herder, 1968], p. 18). Such a view unnecessarily complicates Origen's contrasting exegetical levels, proliferating categories which Origen does not seem to acknowledge and which are not warranted by his actual exposition.

[22]Butterworth, *First Principles*, IV, 2, 4, pp. 275-276. PG, 11 (IV, I1), 364. Grant perceptively makes the important point that for Origen, "Condemning literalism does not involve condemning literalists" (Grant, *The Letter*, p. 90). Wiles suggests that a distinction should be made between the literalism of "simple unintellectual believers," which Origen tolerates, and that of "others of a Judaizing tendency," which he bitterly opposes (Wiles, "Origen," p. 472).

[23]*Leviticus Homily I*, 4. Gary W. Barkley, trans., "Origen's Homilies on Leviticus: An Annotated Translation" (Ph. D. dissertation, The Southern Baptist Theological Seminary, 1984), pp. 32-33. PG 12, 409. Also, while expounding Leviticus 6:25, Origen declares that, "Unless we take all these words in another sense [alio sensu] than the literal text [litterae textus] shows, as we already said often, when they are read in the church, they

In *De Principiis* Origen portrays literal interpretation of Scripture for the multitudes as analogous to Paul's "unmuzzled oxen" treading corn! "Is it for the oxen that God is concerned? Does he not speak entirely for our sake?" (1 Cor. 9:9-10).[24] God has given the Scripture so that people may discover its *spiritual* meaning, rather than its literal one.

For Origen "all [Scripture] has a spiritual meaning [τὸ πνευματικόν] but not all a bodily meaning [τὸ σωματικόν]."[25] So, Origen claims that there are passages of Scripture which "make no literal sense at all [τὸ σωματικὸν οὐδαμῶς ἔχουσι]," thus requiring the reader to seek only the moral and spiritual meanings of the words.[26] To take one simple instance[27] from Genesis 1, Origen asks,

---

will present more an obstacle and ruin [*subversionem*] of the Christian religion than an exhortation and edification" (*Leviticus Homily V*, 1. Barkley, *Leviticus*, pp. 100-101. PG 12, 447).

[24]Butterworth, *First Principles*, IV, 2, 6, p. 279. PG 11 (IV, 12), 368. Cf. Deuteronomy 25:4 for the Old Testament law to which Paul is referring.

[25]Butterworth, *First Principles*, IV, 3, 5, p. 297. PG 11 (IV, 20), 385. De Lange traces Origen's view that every word of Scripture has a deeper meaning back through Aquila's Greek version to the rabbinic exegesis of Akiba (de Lange, *Jews*, pp. 107, 110-111).

[26]Butterworth, *First Principles*, IV, 2, 5, pp. 277-278. PG 11 (IV, 12), 365.

[27]Hanson (*Allegory*, pp. 239-241) provides an extensive listing of these passages in Origen's writing. Hanson also suggests that Origen's opposition to eschatological literalism, especially millenarianism, plays a major role in his opposition to literal exegesis (R.P.C. Hanson, "Biblical Exegesis in the Early Church," *The Cambridge History of the Bible*, vol. I, ed. P. R. Ackroyd and C. F. Evans [Cambridge: Cambridge Univ. Press, 1970], p. 418).

Now what man of intelligence [νοῦν ἔχων] will believe that the first, second, and third day, and the evening and the morning existed without the sun, moon, and stars?[28]

Moreover, Origen holds that the Word "has arranged for certain stumbling blocks [σκάνδαλα]" in the literal sense of Scripture, with the primary purpose of leading readers to seek the higher, mystical wisdom[29] and with the secondary purpose of "concealing [κρύψαι]" the higher doctrine from "those who were unable to endure the burden of investigating matters of such importance."[30] Origen maintains that the composition of Scripture involved a process of occasionally "weaving in" mystical meanings in the form of

---

[28]Butterworth, *First Principles*, IV,3, 1, p. 288. PG 11 (IV, 16), 376-377.

[29]Butterworth, *First Principles*, IV, 2, 9, p. 285. PG 11 (IV, 15), 373. Charles Bigg notes the influence of Origen's personal history upon his exegetical method and his strong desire to move beyond the literal sense: "If we compare what he [Origen] says in *De Principiis*, where he treats the command about the two coats as purely figurative, with the passionate asceticism of his youth, we see how the letter had been to him in very truth . . . a stumbling block" (Charles Bigg, *The Christian Platonists of Alexandria* [Oxford: Clarendon Press, 1913], p. 177). In his *Commentary on Matthew* Origen even goes so far as to speak of "the repentance [μετάνοιαν] from the letter unto the spirit" (Patrick, "Matthew," *Ante-Nicene Fathers* X, 15, p. 423. GCS 10, X, 14, p. 18).

[30]Butterworth, *First Principles*, IV, 2, 8, p. 284. PG 11 (IV, 14), 373. Bigg characterizes this as the "rule of Reserve" or "Economy," in both Celement of Alexandria and Origen (Bigg, *Platonists*, pp. 178-184; cf. *Contra Celsum*, III, 52-53. Chadwick, *Contra Celsum*, pp. 164-165. GCS 1, pp. 248-249). Hanson declares that this "method of Reserve" moves Origen towards "an almost Gnostic view" (R.P.C. Hanson, *Origen's Doctrine of Tradition* [London: S.P.C.K., 1954], p. 77).

events which did not correspond to the events of history.[31] As he contends in *Homilies on Genesis*, "I have often said already that in these stories history is not being narrated [*narruntur*], but mysteries are interwoven [*mysteria contextuntur*]."[32]

Once Origen has decided that a passage of Scripture should be taken allegorically in order to be understood at all, he has little patience with other interpreters who want to defend the literal sense of the text. A classical example of this situation occurs in his *Commentary on John* where Origen ridicules Heracleon and "many others" for taking John 4:35 ("There are yet four months and the harvest comes") in a literal sense.[33] It is certainly ironical to see Origen attack a speculative Gnostic like Heracleon for not being mystical (ἀνάγεσθαι) enough!

In an overview of Origen's literal use of Scripture in *De Principiis*, Gary Barkley observes that Origen frequently resorts to a method of prooftexting.[34] Prooftexting exegesis was, of course, quite common in early

---

[31]Butterworth, *First Principles*, IV, 2, 9, p. 286. Migne, PG 11 (IV, 15), 376. Grant (*The Letter*, pp. 95-96) points to Strabo's view of Homeric poetry and Aristotle's *Poetics* as earlier classical parallels.

[32]*Genesis Homily X*, 4. Ronald E. Heine, trans., *Origen: Homilies on Genesis and Exodus*, The Fathers of the Church, v. 71 (Washington, D.C.: The Catholic Univ. of America Press, 1982), p. 164. Cf. Frederic W. Farrer, *History of Interpretation* (London: MacMillan and Co., 1886), p. 198.

[33]Origen, *Commentary on John*, XIII, 40, 41. Carl Moss, "Origen's *Commentary on John*, Book XIII: A Translation with Annotations" (Ph. D. dissertation, The Southern Baptist Theological Seminary, 1982), pp. 111-112 (especialy n. 109). GCS 4, pp. 266-267. Cf also Origen's critique in XIII, 53, of Heracleon's interpretation of John 4:42 (Moss, *John*, p. 150. GCS 4, p. 283).

[34]Gary Barkley, "Allegory and Typology in Origen's *De Principiis*," in *The Role of Institutional Forms in the Early Christian Mission*, ed. E.

Christianity, especially in regard to Messianic ideas. Numerous examples
may be found in the use of the Old Testament in the New. Early Christianity
probably derived this method from Jewish exegesis (e.g., the Habakkuk
pesher from Qumran).[35]

For Origen literal prooftexting was often "a first line of defence
against heretics."[36] Yet due to the rigid narrowness of his definition of the
sensus literalis, the polemical utility of this literal level for Origen is soon
exhausted. He quickly moves on to use either the moral and spiritual senses
of Scripture or rational argument and philosophical speculation against his
opponents. In *De Principiis*, for example, Origen begins by arguing that
God is light and so cannot have a body at all (literally prooftexting 1 John
1:5). Then in the same paragraph (shifting to the spiritual sense) he
immediately goes on to argue that in 1 John 1:5 light is *symbolic* of God's
"spiritual power." He even asks, "For can we possibly think that because it
is termed light, it is like the light of our sun?"[37] Thus, Origen's overly
narrow view of the *sensus liteeralis* forces him to abandon this primary level
as soon as possible in the quest for spiritual meaning.

Conclusion

This paper has sought to examine Origen's understanding of the
sensus literalis of Scripture in its hermeneutical context. It has been argued

---

Glenn Hinson (Unpublished seminar papers, The Southern Baptist
Theological Seminary, Fall, 1981), pp. 9-13.

[35]Cf. Hanson, "Exegesis," pp. 412-413.

[36]Barkley, *Allegory*, p. 13.

[37]Butteworth, *First Principles*, I, 1, 1, p. 7. PG 11, 121.

that Origen's depreciation of the literal sense of Scripture contributes to a loss of hermeneutical control in his exegesis, which in turn underlies his speculative allegorical exegesis.

Origen's rigid, narrow view of the *sensus literalis* should be contrasted to and corrected by a more communally established and canonically grounded notion of the first level of meaning of Scripture, as exemplified by the Jewish *peshat* of his time. For Origen's depreciation of the *sensus literalis*--often to the point of wooden literalism and disparagement--drives him to abandon too quickly the grammatical and historical senses of the text as possibilities in themselves for "spiritual meaning." The text loses its capacity to exercise hermeneutical control over interpretation through its literal sense.

A revitalized understanding of the *sensus literalis* of Scripture, which seeks to unite grammatical, historical, and theological meanings at the primary textual level, is an urgent need of contemporary exegesis. The recent crisis in the historical-critical approach to modern biblical study and the current ferment in biblical theology point to the urgent need for such an exegetical model. A renewal of the *sensus literalis* may function as part of a *"preparatio evangelica"* that will enable Scripture to be heard again clearly as the Word of God in this age.

ALLEGORY AND SPIRITUAL OBSERVANCE
IN ORIGEN'S DISCUSSIONS OF THE SABBATH

Daniel J. Nodes
Old College, Reno

Some of Origen's individual observations on the Sabbath reflect the heat of an anti-Jewish polemist, others give off the chill of one who is unconcerned with the old dispensation, but his collective attitude toward the Sabbath is neither hostile nor indifferent.[1] Perhaps more than any other

Research in the preparation of this paper was facilitated by a Travel to Collections Grant from the National Endowment for the Humanities.

[1]Studies of Origen have shown considerable interest in his attitude toward Jewish traditions. In the past decade, the scholarship on this topic has been enhanced especially by two books: Hans Bietenhard, *Caesarea, Origenes, und die Juden* (Stuttgart, 1974), and Nicholas de Lange, *Origen and the Jews*, (Cambridge, 1976). Both works make progress in developing a clearer picture of Origen's relationship to Jewish tradition as well as his approaches to the Old Testament. We are now in an excellent position to reexamine in detail Origen's attitude toward specific elements of that tradition. It is important to remember the stated intention of de Lange's work in this regard (p. ix), as a contribution to renewed study of Origen's role in the Christian appropriation of the Jewish tradition.

The following studies made during the same decade by Jewish scholars also address the question of Origen's use of rabbinic exegesis: E. Urbach, "Homiletical Intepretations of the Sages and the Expositions of Origen on the Canticles, and the Jewish-Christian Disputation," *Scripta hierosolymitana* 22 (1971): 247-275; R. Kimelman, "Rabbi Yohanan and Origen on the Song the Songs: A Third-Century Jewish-Christian Disputation," *HTR* 73 (1980): 567-595.

element of Jewish tradition, Sabbath observance allowed him to present the
Christian faith as the fulfillment rather than the repudiation of Jewish Law,
and this on every level of meaning that the Sabbath had for him. On the
literal level, although he refused to accept the notion that Christians could
justly divide their loyalty between church and synagogue, he found it possible
to defend the Jewish tradition of sabbath worship when occasions presented
themselves. On the higher levels of meaning, his positive discussions are
manifold. There is the Sabbath that one observes by being at rest from
immorality and worldly cares, which applies equally to Christian, Jew and
pagan, and equally to any day of the week. On a still higher plane, the truly
spiritual Sabbath allows the individual to experience a personal reunion with
God in a way that transfers the idea of observance to the scope of eternity.
Ultimately, there is the eschatological Sabbath, that heavenly rest to follow
the completion of this world, a hope common to rabbinic literature and the
New Testament.[2] In this context Origen interprets the sabbath law as a
promise of the ultimate spiritual communion of all rational creation.

His commentary thus forms a progression of meaning which in sum
contributes to a reappropriation and consequent revalidation of the sabbath

---

[2]*Midrash on Psalms* comments: " 'And he rested on the seventh
day.' God's day is a thousand years, as in Ps. 90:4: 'For a thousand years in
thy sight are but as yesterday.' Just as we observe every seventh year as a
sabbatical year, even so will God observe a Sabbatical year which will
consist of a thousand years. Thus we read, 'And there shall be one day which
shall be known as the Lord's, not day, not night; but it shall come to pass,
that at evening time there shall be light' (Zech. 14:7). The future world and
the resurrection of the dead are referred to here, and the light which the
almighty hid away for the righteous from the beginning, as it is written, 'And
God saw the light, that it was good' (1:4). . . . This refers to the world (the
Hereafter) which is all Sabbath." (Cited in M. Kasher, *Encyclopedia of
Biblical Exegesis*, vol. 1, p. 81). Cf. Heb. 4.9: "There remains therefore a
Sabbath rest for the people of God."

tradition. Moreover, it reveals in a most concentrated form the interpretive process and hierarchy of values that were the guiding principles of his general approach to the Jewish heritage. His discussions on this topic reveal a detailed familiarity with the Jewish heritage, familiarity that centers on but is not restricted to what can be learned from the Scriptures. Sabbath observance is, after all, grounded in the whole Torah, both written and oral. Even when Origen's discussions appear in writings whose main purpose is other than to improve Jewish-Christian relations, they address a wide variety of topics whose positive interpretations for both Christians and Jews are often brought out. It is the purpose of this study to examine those positive interpretations, which give excellent testimony to his ability to appropriate the Jewish tradition.

Among Origen's observations on the Sabbath there are, of course, straightforward polemics addressing this tradition of worship in negative terms. One such passage, so frequently cited that it presents a distorted view of his overall attitude, argues for the divine preference, even from Old Testament times, for the forthcoming Christian Lord's day.[3] He refers in this passage to the account of God's provision of manna to the Hebrews during the Exodus from Egypt. On the Sabbath none was to be collected. Instead, a double amount was to be brought in on the day of preparation. God first began to provide manna for the chosen people on the Lord's day and on the seventh day it ceased. This cessation is a sign of God's preference for the Lord's Day:

> Let the Jews understand that even then the Lord's day was preferred
> to the Jewish Sabbath, that even then it was indicated that on their

---

[3]In his brief treatment of Origen on the Sabbath, N. R. M. de Lange, *Origen and the Jews*, quotes the passage at length (pp. 93-94).

Sabbath none of God's grace descended to them from heaven, none of the heavenly bread, which is the word of God, came to them. For the prophet also says elsewhere: (Osee 3.4) "For many days the sons of Israel will sit without a king, without a prince, without a prophet, without a sacrifice, without a priest." But on our Lord's day the Lord always rains down manna from heaven.[4]

Similarly, Origen attempts to demonstrate the historical end of Sabbath observance with the coming of John the Baptist. He observes that the Christian "day of rest," marking the resurrection of Christ, is celebrated on the first day of the week, acknowledging the new dispensation, not deriving from the Jewish sabbath:

It is not possible that the Savior's rest, which caused those after his death to be molded by his death, and therefore also by the Resurrection, a rest that is after the Sabbath, should have come into existence from the seventh day of our God.[5]

In spite of these and similar claims, however, we observe that Origen did not adhere to the principle that the Lord's Day is unrelated to the sabbath tradition. Although in theory the Lord's Day replaced the Sabbath, it did not actually do so for many Christians of the third century, and in opposing the practice of attending both church and synagogue, Origen himself responded by invoking the sabbath law. He did this with the aid of

---

[4]*Hom. in Ex.* 7.5, PG 14.345-46. All translations of primary and secondary sources are those of the present author unless otherwise noted.

[5]*Comm. in Joh.* 2.27, GCS 4.91.

Philonic metaphor, by interpreting the word of Scripture that is shared during
the worship as the Sabbath meal. To hear and receive the word in both places
is therefore to transgress the law that prohibits the eating of the sabbath meal
in more than one house (Ex. 12.46):

> If you eat the word of God in one house, namely in the church, and
> then leave it on the opinion that you are made a partaker of God in
> the synagogue, although the law says "in one house it is to be
> eaten," you do not eat in one house.[6]

Similarly, he directs the law against those who would discuss in the
synagogue what they learned in the church:

> "And you shall not take from the flesh and carry it out of the
> house." It is not permitted to teach the Church's word outside the
> Church, just as you are not to take meat outside the house.[7]

The context enables Origen to make use of sabbath law in a somewhat naive
yet positive way. The metaphor maintains the validity of the old
dispensation's law in the support of the new dispensation's practice of
worshiping in a new place on a new day. Although Origen surely was not
prepared to invoke this law in the reverse direction and to suggest that the
sabbath meal must be eaten only in the synagogue, his line of reasoning does
establish a positive link with the sabbath tradition, employing and
revalidating rather than abandoning the law.

---

[6]*Selecta in Ex.* PG 12.286.

[7]Ibid.

The opportunity to respond to Celsus enabled Origen to defend the literal Sabbath in a less naive way. The scriptural account of the Creator's rest from all his works on the primordial first Sabbath, the seventh day of creation, provided the topic. In the course of a counterattack on Celsus' efforts to ridicule the biblical creation account, Origen takes issue, for example, with the philosopher's disdain for the mention of God's rest as a childish anthropomorphism:

> Not understanding the meaning of the words: "And God ended on the sixth day his works which he had made, and ceased on the seventh day from all his works which he had made..." [Celsus] makes the remark: "Indeed after this he is weary like a very bad workman who stands in need of rest to refresh himself!" for he knows nothing of the Sabbath day and rest of God which follows the completion of the world's creation and which lasts for the duration of the world, and on which all those will keep festival with God who have done all *their* works in *their* six days, and who because they have omitted none of their duties, will ascend to the contemplation and assembly of righteous and blessed beings.[8]

In this passage accusing Celsus of ignorance of the Sabbath day as a human institution bearing a spiritual promise, to which, it is claimed, the account of God's rest in Genesis is in reality pointing, Origen is able to avoid defending a literal view of the creation story, which he was averse to do, and is instead able to defend the pious institution of the day of rest and to suggest the higher meaning that is in direct relation to the creation account.

---

[8]*Cels.* 6.61, GCS 2.131-32; trans., ANF 4.601.

Here Origen should have been equipped to make observations that would still have refuted Celsus' only charge in this passage, namely that the notion of God's resting is inappropriate, but which would also have repudiated the institution of the sabbath rest had he chosen to do so. The most elmentary knowledge of Hebrew would have enabled him to point, for example, to the Hebrew version of Gn. 2.2: "And on the *seventh* day God finished (E.V.)". This verse troubled the Rabbis because it carried with it the potential for understanding that God did in fact perform work on the first sabbath.[9] Origen's reliance on the Septuagint, which describes God's completion of creation on the sixth day, is consistent with his view of that translation as an inspired text, but his apparent disregard of the Hebrew reading in this context also suggests a readiness to avoid casting unnecessary suspicion on the institution of literal sabbath observance.[10] Jerome, by contrast, gave a fully hostile reaction to the Jewish Sabbath in his commentary on the Hebrew text of Genesis 2.2:

> For "the sixth day" the Hebrew has "the seventh day." And so we
> confound the Jews who glory in the idleness of the Sabbath, because
> even at that time the Sabbath was broken because God worked on

---

[9]The problem of God resting occupied the minds of previous [pre-9th century] generations. Philo as well as the Rabbis explained וישבות and ויהו as causative verbs." (J. Rosenthal, "Hiwi Al-Balkhi: A Comparative Study," *JQR* 38 (1947-48), 333. By Hiwi's time the use of the account of God's rest against Judaism was common to Jewish heretics, such as Hiwi, as well as Gnostics and Christians. In earlier times the Rabbis faced the difficulty in a number of creative ways. See the entries under GN. 2.2-2.3 in *The Encyclopedia of Biblical Exegesis*.

[10]See Sidney Jellicoe, *The Septuagint and Modern Study* (Oxford, 1968), p. 102, and R.C.P. Hanson, *Allegory and Event* (London, 1959), pp. 166-78.

the Sabbath, completing his works on that day and even blessing the day itself, because on it he completed all things.[11]

The Rabbis, also in reaction to the ambiguity of God's activity on the seventh day in the Hebrew, had felt it necessary to offer several defenses in order to uphold the validity of sabbath observance in light of Gn. 2.2. One typical defense argued that God created on the seventh day only in the sense that he created the Sabbath rest itself: "What did the world lack [but] the Sabbath [rest]".[12]

The Rabbis were also aware of the problems inherent in what was Celsus' only real charge, the notion of God's rest. To explain the passage, therefore, they stressed that Gn. 2.2 does not mean that God ceased, for example, from causing natural phenomena to occur, such as the rains, tides, or the exchange of day and night.[13] They also point, as in this passage, to the "works" of justice which God always performs:

Although you read: "Because that on it he rested from all his work which God created to make," He rested from his work of [creating] his world, but not from the work of the wicked and the work of the righteous, for he works with the former and with the latter.[14]

---

[11]*Hebr. Quaes. in Lib. Gn* 2.2, CCSL 72, pt. 1:4.

[12]*Gn. r.* 10, 9, *The Midrash Rabbah*, trans. Freedman and Simon, vol. 1, (London, 1939), p. 78. All subsequent citations are taken from this edition.

[13]Cf. *Gn. r.* 11, 5 (p. 84).

[14]Ibid. 11, 10 (p. 86).

We know that in the *Contra Celsum* Origen consciously sidestepped the issue of God's work on the Sabbath, for it is a theme which he had already used in the *Commentary on Matthew* and the *Commentary on Numbers*. In responding to Celsus' charge he put all his efforts instead upon reinforcing the practice of sabbath observance, patterned after the divine rest, insofar as actual religious worship is concerned, the practice on which his own spiritual interpretations of the Sabbath had to be based.

Where the purposes of exhortation to piety prevail, Origen's discussions do make use of those same rabbinical observations on the sabbath rest which he avoided in the reply to Celsus. He is eager to observe, as the Rabbis do, that although God is said to have rested on the primordial sabbath, he did not rest from his works of justice. Accordingly, Origen adds that as the New Testament shows Jesus also performing works of justice on the Sabbath, we, in imitation of him and his heavenly father, ought to cease from all worldly works while we continue to perfrom works of justice. The *Series Commentary on Matthew* makes the following observation:

> God in six days made the works of the world and rested on the Sabbath. He rested from the works of the world which he began to make. The works of justice, however, he always does and will do without end. Now the races of men did all the works of the world before the coming of Christ and no one rested from them, collectedly keeping a Sabbath from good works. But our Lord came and brought us our Sabbath, his own, so that just as he rested on the Sabbath from the works of the world but did not rest from the works of justice, so also let us through him observe the Sabbath

from worldly, carnal, and harmful works, but let us always perform works of justice.[15]

Here Origen gives to the sabbath observance a moral significance as a rest from sin, and he uses the image of the good work from which God never rests, and which Christ performed equally on the Sabbath as on other days, as a figure of what the transformed Sabbath should signify. In this context, therefore, in considering literal observance supplanted by moral observance, he has again made use of an interpretation to emphasize the moral meaning of the Sabbath that is amenable, on that level, to Jewish teaching.

Moreover, Origen's spiritual interpretation, in which the individual soul's approach to the knowledge of God becomes the central theme, can be witnessed in a passage from his *Commentary on Matthew* inspired by the account of Christ's transfiguration before Peter, James, and John, which is linked to the notion of the Sabbath because it took place "after six days had passed" (Matt. 17.1):

> For after one has passed the six days, as we said, he will celebrate a new Sabbath, overwhelmed with joy upon the lofty mountain, because he has seen Jesus transfigured before him.[16]

Origen reacts to the account in Matthew of the transfiguration of Jesus by connecting the six days prior to Jesus' journey to the mountain with the six days of spiritual journey that precede the Sabbath. This interpretation results

---

[15]*Comm. Ser.* 45 GCS 11, pt. 2, p. 90.

[16]*Comm. in Mt.* 12.36, GCS 10.151-52.

in a transfiguration of the sabbath idea in its own right into a spiritual sabbath that marks the culmination of a gradual process of individual disassociation from the material world. It is indeed a Christian interpretation, but its emphasis on the individual experience--on seeing the transformed Jesus "apart"--places emphasis neither on the communal aspects of Christian worship nor on that of the Jews. Origen's consuming purpose is to employ the concept of the sabbath in an individually positive way, devoid of animosity.

We have thus far witnessed Origen use three different levels of meaning, a literal, a moral, and a spiritual. His most overt reference in his writings to various meanings of sabbath observance suggests that there are only these three levels. Commenting on Exodus 16:23-30, "Tomorrow is the Sabbath, a holy rest (day) unto the Lord," etc., he writes:

> I set forth what is said about the Sabbath, first according to the naked words, in order that they might see what the letter means.

He follows this with a level addressing moral concerns:

> Then according to the spiritual understanding, according to which I would say that the day of the Sabbath weighs upon the just man to negate the works of the world, who glorifies God and lives in peace: nor does he go away from the place in which he stood, doubtless from Christ, nor does he light a fire by sinning, nor does he carry loads. Every sin is a load heavier than a mountain.

Then there is the level that can best be described as the contemplative:

Another explanation of the Sabbath is (Heb. 4.9) "There remains an observation of the Sabbath for the people of God" a holy and sacred rest. Truly, he who has done all his works is held worthy of this Sabbath, being at leisure for no other thing than for contemplating truth and wisdom.[17]

This discussion of the various meanings of the Sabbath is consonant with what he says about the various meanings of Scripture itself,[18] and yet, despite the abundant scholarly recognition of his references to three levels of meaning in Scripture, there is disagreement over what Origen meant by these levels.[19] Three decades ago, this difficulty led Cardinal de Lubac to demonstrate that Origen was the sponsor of two different three-fold classes: one that includes a literal or historical level, a moral level, and a mystical or spiritual level; and another class that contains ostensibly these same three elements arranged as historical, mystical, and moral. The difference between these patterns was seen, however, to lie not only in the ordering, but in the

---

[17]*Sel. in Ex.* PG 12:290.

[18]See *Princ.* 4.2,4; *Hom. in Nu.* 9.7, and *Hom. in Lv.* 5.1-5.8.

[19]J. W. Trigg agrees that what is usually termed the "moral" level is where difficulty arises: "The Bible, Origen argued, contains three levels of meaning, corresponding to the three-fold Pauline (and Platonic) division of a person into body, soul, and spirit. The bodily level of Scripture, the bare letter, is normally helpful as it stands to meet the needs of the more simple. The psychic level, corresponding to the soul, is for those making progress in perfection. *It is hard to say what Origen understood this level of meaning to be. Some scholars have taken the psychic level to be what later interpreters of the Bible called the "moral level of interpretation, the level at which the text provides guidance for conduct, but there is no good reason to think that Origen thought of it in that way. The actual example Origen gave of psychic interpretation indicates that Origen considered the psychic level a non-mystical level of allegory."* Origen: The Bible and Philosophy in the Third-Century Church (Atlanta, 1983), pp. 125-26. [Emphasis mine].

very nature of the moral element. In the first case, the moral sense may be said to concern general ethical principles. In the second, it relates directly to the work of Christ and his redemption of souls through his church:

> In the first case Origen draws from the sacred text diverse "morals" which may contain nothing that is specifically Christian, containing no reference to the mystery of Christ. It is this that we have the habit of calling, with a word that is not very suitable, in fact even contrary to the ancient usage, his "allegorism." In the second case, it is only after he makes reference to the mystery of Christ and in relation to it, that he comes to the spiritual explanation...In this second case, Origen's exegesis, related entirely to the *anima credentis*, to the *anima fidelis*, to the *anima ecclesiastica*, or the *anima in Ecclesia*, is therefore entirely Christian both in form and content, both in its results and its sources.[20]

The section from Origen's *Commentary on Exodus* given above corresponds to de Lubac's first grouping, as do all the individual examples given thus far in this study. Even if one were to argue that the passage from the *Commentary on Exodus* contains two distinct parts, one of truly general morality ("The Sabbath weighs upon the just man to negate the works of the world, who glorifies God and lives in peace") and one that is specifically Christian ("nor does he go away from the place in which he stood, namely from Christ"), neither part would fit the description of de Lubac's other moral level because the ecclesiastical aspect is missing. But the range of Origen's discussion of the Sabbath also includes a level of meaning akin to that sense,

---

[20]Henri de Lubac, *Exégèse médiévale: Les quatre sens de l'Écriture* (Paris, 1959), p. 203.

adding a fourth to our list, which emphasizes a communal, ecclesiastical type of spiritual observance.

This fourth level of sabbath observance returns to the subject of communal worship, the principle of the first level of interpretation. Only now the eschatological context enlarges the idea of communal observance into a Sabbath whose meaning achieves its fulfillment in the future.[21] This level also gives Origen the opportunity fully to incorporate into this topic one of his most inspiring as well as controversial teachings, that of the universal communion of saints at the end of time. And while this, the true Sabbath, is still to come, it will be, for Origen, the culmination in eternity of the observances which the living community, God's faithful on earth, have been celebrating in a continuous tradition. Introducing this theme, Origen draws once again on rabbinical discussion of God's own continuation of work on the Sabbath, and this time he makes reference to it not to support his individual, spiritual interpretation but rather to demonstrate that any sabbath observance must ultimately remain incomplete so long as God is working in his care of the material world. Origen again adds to this the account of Christ's work on the Sabbath, an important issue in the New Testament, to show further that the true Sabbath does not belong to this age:

> The observation of the true Sabbath is beyond this world because it
> is written in Genesis that (Gn. 2.2): "God rested on the Sabbath day
> from all his works," and we see that that did not happen then, on the

---

[21]This description of Origen's scriptural exegesis, with its two distinct moral levels, reveals an affinity between Origen and Clement, his immediate predecessor, who openly writes of four distinct levels according to a similar though not identical pattern: first, the literal; second, as displaying a type; third, as establishing a command for the moral life; and fourth, as giving a prophecy (Clement of Alexandria, *Strom.* 1.27).

seventh day of creation, and that it is not happening now. For we see that God always works, and there is no Sabbath on which God does not work, on which he does not bring forth the sun upon the good and the wicked, and rains upon the just and unjust, on which he does not bring forth the hay upon the mountains and the grass for the domestic animals that obey man, on which he does not afflict and heal, draw down into hell and lead back, on which he does not slay and cause to live. When the Jews persecuted him for working and curing on the Sabbath, our Lord answered them, according to the Gospels (John 5.17): "My father is still working and I am working." Showing through these things that in no Sabbath of this age does God rest from the care of the world and from the provisions of the human race. For indeed he made creation from the beginning, and brought forth matter, as much as he as the creator of the universe knew would suffice for the creation of the world.

Therefore the true Sabbath will be [that day] on which God rests from all his works, the future age, then when pain and sadness, and lamentation will vanish and God will be all and in all.[22]

This view of the eternal Sabbath represents the last word in Origen's theology, in which the ultimate reunion with God is realized, the final step in the process of salvation. We witness that process in each of Origen's four levels of Sabbath observance, which leaves the physical sense, moves to the level of abstract morality, then to the individual spirit, and lastly to the spiritual community. Forceful testimony that Origen thought in terms of this progression is provided by the very passage from his homily just quoted,

---

[22]*Hom. in Num.* 23.4, GSC 7.215-16.

for a discussion of the other three levels immediately precedes his exhortation to look toward that final and only true Sabbath:

> Let us see what kind of observation of the Sabbath there ought to be for a Christian. On the day of the Sabbath, one must do none of the works of the world. If therefore you cease from all secular works and do nothing worldly, but have leisure for spiritual works, you convene at the church, you offer the ear to divine readings and tracts, and you think about heavenly things, you have concern about the future, you have before your eyes the judgment that is to come, you do not have concern for present and visible things, but for invisible and future things. This is observance of the Christian Sabbath. But the Jews too had to observe these things. . . . Whoever therefore ceases from the works of the world and has leisure for spiritual things, that is the one who makes sacrifice of the Sabbath and a feast day of Sabbaths. On the Sabbath each one sits in his place and does not go forth from it. What therefore is the spiritual place of the soul? Justice is his place, and truth, wisdom, holiness, and everything that is Christ. Out of this place it is not necessary to go to keep the true Sabbath and complete the feast day in sacrifices of Sabbaths.[23]

In this one passage he uses all the levels of observation we have heard him use elsewhere. It means physical, communal worship in a church. It means ceasing from the works of the world. And it means remaining at home spiritually, that is to say, remaining in truth, wisdom, and holiness, and

---

[23]Ibid.

"everything that is Christ." We witness Origen's tremendous efforts to translate the validity of the literal meaning of Sabbath observance into moral, intellectual, and spiritual realities.

In closing, let us consider the development of the resulting fourfold meaning of the Sabbath in Origen with reference to two tensions that permeate all of his writings: namely, the tension between the physical and the spiritual on the one hand, and the tension between the worship of the church and the spiritual experience of the individual believer on the other. In essence, there are only these levels of interpretation, the physical and the spiritual, and there are only two modes of Sabbath observance, the communal and the individual. Simply stated, Origen's four levels suggest the various combinations of these elements. The first level interprets the Sabbath observance as it applies to the literal, communal aspects of worship. The second level focuses on the temporal, worldly observance with reference to the individual. The third level marks a view in terms of the individual in the spiritual scope of eternity, and the fourth level focuses on the true and ultimate spiritual community. This hierarchy brings us full circle. Any suggestion, therefore, that Origen devalued the tradition of communal worship in favor of individual spiritual experience must be qualified, for in his discussions of the new and eternal Sabbath, what awaits the individual spiritual pilgrim at the end of his journey is a full, glorious renunion in unending spiritual observance, together, in holy community.

DIVINE DECEPTION AND
THE TRUTHFULNESS OF SCRIPTURE

Joseph W. Trigg
Falls Church, Va

Origen's twentieth homily on Jeremiah deals with Jeremiah 20:7-12,
an intensely lyrical confession in which Jeremiah voiced his personal agony
at the rejection of his prophecy. This is a translation of the Septuagint text
on which Origen preached:

> Thou has deceived me, O Lord, and I was deceived (ʾHπάτησάς με
> κύριε καὶ ἠπατήθην) . Thou art stronger than I, and thou has
> prevailed. I have become a laughingstock. Each day I continue to
> be mocked. So they shall laugh at my bitter word. I shall call upon
> breach of covenant and wretchedness (ἀθεσίαν καὶ ταλαιπωρία
> ἐπικαλέσομαι). For the word of God has become for me a
> reproach and a derision all the day long. And I said, 'I shall not
> mention him, or speak any more in his name.' There is in my heart
> as it were a burning fire, smoldering in my bones, and I am afflicted
> throughout, and I cannot bear it, since I have heard the slander of
> many, whispering on every side, 'Conspire, conspire against him,
> all of us his friends. Watch his actions, and he will be deceived, and
> we can observe him and take our revenge on him.' But the Lord is

with me like a dread warrior, therefore they persecuted me and were unable to understand, they were greatly ashamed and did not comprehend their dishonor, which will not be forgotten forever. For the Lord is with me, approving the righteous things, knowing the reins and hearts.

For Origen, the divine deception of which Jeremiah spoke explains the need for allegorical interpretation of the Bible and justifies a corresponding deception on the part of those who interpret the Bible. Preaching on divine deception required delicacy, but Origen considered himself obligated, as a pastor, to do so. In this case, Origen felt a need to reach persons like his patron Ambrosius, who found Gnosticism attractive because he "could not accept an irrational and ignorant faith (μὴ φέβων τὴν ἄλογον καὶ ἰδιωτικὴν πίστην)."[1] Thus Origen needed to hint at a higher truth about God's behavior in order to counter the Gnostics, who taught that the crude and savage God of the simple was an inferior deity to the loving God and Father of Jesus Christ. Origen could not, however, be entirely open in presenting his criticism of the understanding of God held by the simple, if for no other reason than because the simple, at their stage of progress in the Christian life, needed to be motivated by fear of a wrathful God. Origen's method for meeting the needs of advanced as well as simple hearers is, I intend to show, the method his probable mentor, Clement of Alexandria, set forth in his program for the *Stromata*:

---

[1] See Gunnar af Hällström, *Fides Simpliciorum According to Origen of Alexandria* (Helsinki: Societas Scientiarum Fennica, 1984), esp. pp. 64-69.

Let our reminiscenses, as we have often said, for the sake of those
reading them unrestrainedly or inexperiencedly, be spread out
variegatedly, as their name implies, passing continually from one
matter to another, hinting at one thing while demonstrating another
(καὶ ἕτερον μέν τι κατὰ τὸν εἱρμὸν τῶν λόγων μηνύοντα,
ἐνδεικνύμενα δὲ ἄλλο τι). . . . The quilts of reminiscences
therefore contribute to the expression of the truth for the person who
is able to seek with reason (τῷ οἕῳ τε ζητεῖν μετὰ λόγου).[2]

An echo of Origen's understanding of divine deception, which places
it in a revealing light, occurs in the celebrated correspondence between
Augustine and Jerome.[3] Augustine's chief concern in that correspondence
was with Jerome's interpretation, in his *Commentary on Galatians*, of the
confrontation between Peter and Paul, recounted in Galatians 2, where Paul
"rebuked Peter to his face" for withdrawing under pressure from table
fellowship with gentile Christians. In order to mitigate the scandal of a
confrontation between the two most revered Apostles, Jerome had adopted an
interpretation which he claimed to find in the tenth book of Origen's (now no
longer extant) *Stromata*. In that interpretation Paul and Peter deliberately
simulated a confrontation in order to demonstrate that the Jewish law was no
longer applicable to Gentiles. Augustine could not accept this interpretation,
which struck him as implying deception on the part of the Apostle Paul, a
deception bad enough in itself but compounded in this case by perjury, since

---

[2]Clement of Alexandria, *Stromata* 4.2. All translations are by the
author unless otherwise noted.

[3]See the edition of the correspondence in *Florilegium Patristicum*
12, ed. J. Schmid and the discussion in J. N. D. Kelly, *Jerome: His Life,
Writings, and Controversies* (London, Duckworth: 1975), pp. 263-72.

Paul had written earlier in the letter "In what I am writing to you, before God, I do not lie!" (Gal. 1:20).

Conceivably, Augustine wrote his treatise *On Lying*, which established as normative in our ethical tradition an absolute prohibition of lying, out of an interest piqued by this encounter with Origen's view. Augustine, in his objection to Jerome's Origenist interpretation, appeals to a Western tradition of interpretation of Galatians that goes back to Cyprian.[4] He might have also cited Irenaeus, who accused the Gnostics of making the Apostles hypocrites by interpreting their works as if they on occasion made use of the medicinal lie. Truth excludes lying as darkness excludes light, Irenaeus taught, so that the Apostles, who were disciples of Jesus Christ, who is Truth, could not have employed lies.[5] Augustine's controversy with Jerome vividly illustrates the difference between his understanding of the truthfulness of scripture and Origen's.

The interpretation Jerome cited appears in none of Origen's extant works, but it is entirely plausible. We might expect Origen to find Peter's waffling at Antioch embarrassing, since Peter, as the "rock" upon whom Christ founded his church, was the image of the ideal spiritual man.[6]

---

[4]Augustine, *Letter* 82.24.

[5]Neque discipul ejus alium quemdam Deum nominarent, aut Dominum vocarent praeter eum, qui vere esset Deus et Dominus omnium: quemadmodum dicunt hi, qui sunt vanissimi sophistae, quoniam Apostoli cum hypocrisi fecerunt doctrinam secundum audientium capacitatem, et responsiones secundum interrogantium suspiciones, caecis caeca confabulantes secundum caecitatem ipsorum, languentibus autem secundum languorem ipsorum, et errantibus secundum errorem eorum (Irenaeus, *Adversus Haereses* 1.5.2). Et Apostoli autem discipuli veritatis exsistentes, extra omne mendacium sunt: non enim communicat mendacium veritati, sicut non communicat tenebrae luci; sed praesentia alterius excludit alterum (Ibid., 1.5.1).

[6]See Origen, *Commentary on Matthew* 10 and *Contra Celsum* 6.77.

Furthermore, the exercise of reserve, if not outright deception, was consistent with Origen's understanding of Paul. In his homilies on Leviticus, Origen compared the Apostle Paul to the high priest changing his robe.

> It must be observed that the priest employs one set of vestments when he is administering the sacrifice and another when he goes out before the people. Paul, who was a very knowledgeable and experienced priest, did this also. When he was in the company of the perfect, as if in the Holy of Holies and robed in the garment of perfection, he said: "Yet among the perfect we do impart wisdom, although it is not a wisdom of this age, or of the rulers of this age, who are doomed to pass away. But we impart a secret and hidden wisdom of God," which "none of the rulers of this age understood ... for, if they had, they would not have crucified the Lord of Glory" (1 Cor. 2:6-8). But later, as if going out before the people, he changes his garment and takes another, much inferior to it. What did he say? "I judged it expedient," he said "to know nothing among you save Jesus Christ, and him crucified" (1 Cor. 2:2).[7]

In another homily on Leviticus, Origen spoke of how Apostles do not "cast pearls before swine" (Matt. 7:6), an action which symbolizes talking about inappropriate matters before the simple. In order to avoid doing so, they wear the priestly "linen breeches" (Ex. 28:42), the symbol of chastity, so as not to "engender Christ" (Gal. 4:19) among the unworthy.[8]

---

[7]Origen, *Homilies on Leviticus* 4.6.

[8]Ibid., 6.6 On "casting pearls before swine" see also Origen, *Dialogue with Heracleides* 148-50 and *Contra Celsum* 5.29.

In Homily 20 the deception Peter and Paul alledgedly employed at Antioch has its foundation in the divine deception of "Thou hast deceived me, O Lord, and I was deceived." Origen's argument provides a rationale for such deception on God's part and on the part of human teachers. In the process, Origen himself hinted at one thing while demonstrating another. The discussion of our passage actually begins in the nineteenth homily on Jeremiah, toward the end of which Origen quoted and discussed the entire pericope. There he sets up the problem: was Jeremiah telling the truth, as we ought to expect of a prophet, or was he lying, as we are not permitted to say? Granted that he was speaking the truth, we must assume that God did indeed deceive him. Origen compares God's deception to the deception practiced on small children in order to educate them and finds examples of such pedagogical deception in the Bible's threats of future punishment.[9]

In the twentieth homily Origen establishes the propriety of divine deception and examines its implications. The homily begins with a discussion of the equivocal character of language about God, which Origen describes in terms of Aristotle's *Categories*, from which he quotes, without attribution, the definition of "equivocal" (ὁμώνυμος), "Things are equivocally named, when they have the name only in common, the definition (or statement of essence) being different."[10] The simple will fail to understand that words have different meanings when applied to God. It is necessary to point out this equivocal character of biblical langauge in order to confute the heretics, who use it as evidence against the God of the Old Testament. Origen cites as examples of such equivocal language the words θυμὸς, ὀργή,

---

[9]Origen, *Homilies on Jeremiah* 19.15.

[10]Ibid., 20.1, citing Airstotle, *Categories* 1, tr. Harold P. Cooke in *Loeb Classical Library* 325, p. 13.

and μετάνοια as applied to God, all words open to Marcionite criticism, as well as λόγος. In the case of wrath or anger and repentance, we must recognize the equivocal character of language about God if we are to maintain our belief in the worthiness of God. Origen rejects the notion that God could be angry or repent in the commonly accepted sense of the word. For us to be angry is a bad thing, and for us to repent, while good, implies that we had acted improperly before we repented.[11]

It is crucial, in interpreting Origen's thought here, to determine whether or not divine deception involves an intention on God's part to deceive. Is ἀπατή an equivocal word when applied to God because human deception involves such an intention but divine deception does not? Certainly the use of "wrath" and "repentance" as analogies, both of which imply defects on God's part, suggest such an interpretation, if we assume that it is necessarily bad at all times to intend deception. Thus we might assume that divine deception is simply a necessary result of the incapacity of human language to depict God. Henri de Lubac made that assumption in an article on this text, presenting, as Origen's position, the view that what may appear to be divine deception is entirely a consequence of "*l'infirmité congénitale de la connaissance humaine.*"[12] Origen may have intended to leave this impression, but we cannot accept it as the definitive expression of his thought. Rather, Origen hints that divine deception is deliberate. One such hint is that Origen never explicitly says, as he does in the case of "wrath" and "repentance," that deception is necessarily unworthy of God; all he claims is

---

[11]Ibid.

[12]Henri de Lubac, "Tu m'as trompé, Seigneur, le commentaire d'Origène sur Jérémie 20.7" in Henri de Lubac *Recherches dans la foi: Trois études sur Origène, saint Anselme et la philosophie chrétienne* (Paris: Beauchesne, 1979), p. 24.

that divine deception is "of another sort," ἑτερογενής from our deception. Another hint is that Origen cites God's "word" as another case of equivocal language about God. We are left to decide for ourselves whether the use of "deception" in connection with God necessarily implies a moral defect on God's part, as in the case of "wrath" and "repentance," or if it is morally neutral like "word". If God's deception can be deliberate, how does it differ from ours? How is ἀπατή equivocal? The one way that Origen actually claims that divine deception differs from our deception is that it always benefits the one deceived.

This is the point of the Jewish story μῦθος, involving intentional divine deception, which Origen uses in order to introduce the concept. God does not rule as a tyrant but as a king. He desires, not to compel, but to persuade, so that those over whom he reigns will do his will voluntarily and not by compulsion. God had a prophecy of judgment for Jeremiah to make against his own people. God knew, however, that although Jeremiah would not willingly prophecy against his own people, he would have no qualms about prophecying against other people. God, therefore, deceived Jeremiah. He says to him, "Take from my hand the cup of this unmixed wine, and make all the nations to whom I send you drink from it." Jeremiah understood God to be asking him to make all the other nations drink from the cup of God's wrath and punishment, without imagining that his own would be the first nation to drink from it. Having accepted the cup, he realized he had been deceived when God said, "And you shall first make Jerusalem drink from it." He accepted the cup with the expectation of one mission, but he ended up with another.[13]

---

[13]Origen, *Homilies on Jeremiah* 20.2.

Origen compares this tradition with another from the same source which compares the two occasions in the Book of Isaiah where the prophet receives a call. In Isaiah 6 the prophet eagerly responds to the divine question, "Whom shall I send, and who will go for us?" with the words "Here I am, send me." He receives a message of God's judgment against his own people, a message to be received with incomprehension and anger. Later, in the fortieth chapter, Isaiah hears "A voice said cry," but once burned is twice shy; he responds "What shall I cry?"[14]

Origen expresses his concern, not simply to pass on this tradition, but to employ it fruitfully. In doing so, he brings forward two classical *topoi* where deception is permissible, a father deceiving his children and a physician deceiving his patient.[15] The father deceives his son by concealing his affection while disciplining him, so that the child will do the right thing out of fear.[16] The physician deceives the patient by hiding the scalpel beneath a sponge or a bitter medicine in honey, so that the patient may accept needed treatment he otherwise would refuse. God acts like the physician, who hides the bitter in the sweet, when he allows people to believe that they can expect to attain a heavenly rest at their death if all they do is avoid committing the notoriously wicked sins of idolatry and fornication, hiding from them the cleansing punishment they must undergo for such sins as gossip and overindulgence. If God did not do this, Origen argues, the

---

[14]Ibid.

[15]Ibid., 20.3 See also Origen, *Contra Celsum* 4.18. For classical examples, see Plato, *Republic* 2.382c and 3.389b; Xenophon, *Memorabilia* 4.2.17; and Maximus of Tyre, *Lectures* 13.3.

[16]Ibid. See also Origen, *Homilies on Exodus* 1.2, where Origen compares God to a schoolmaster who employs the same ruse.

majority of believers would lose all hope and make no effort to maintain even a modest level of morality.[17] Origen then offers an example of divine deception. What he is doing, he admits, may be risky. (Presumably the risk is that he may undeceive persons who are beneficially deceived.) A widow may have the mistaken belief that she will be damned if she remarries, and therefore remain celibate. Surely, given the preferability of celibacy to the married state, this is a beneficial deception.[18]

Origen contrasts the putatively beneficial deception of the celibate widow to the bad effects of a premature awareness of the truth. Some who have "found out the truth about punishment and have supposedly passed beyond deception" (εὑρόντες τὸ περὶ κολάσεως ἀληθὲς καὶ διελθόντες δῆθεν τὰ τῆς ἀπάτης), have fallen into a worse manner of life. It would be better for them if they still believed literally in such Biblical texts as "their worm does not die and their fire is not quenched" and "they shall be an abhorrence to all flesh" (Is. 66:24) and "the chaff will be burned with unquenchable fire" (Matt. 3:12).[19] This statement, under scrutiny, provides an example of Origen's own deceptiveness. Although Origen states that those who have "found out the truth about punishment" have only "supposedly (δῆθεν) passed beyond deception," his statement, in the context of a discussion of the beneficial effects of divine deception, does not follow logically unless Origen believed that such persons had indeed glimpsed a higher truth behind the deceptive words of the biblical passages he quoted, which, of course Origen himself did not accept as literally true.

---

[17] Ibid.

[18] Ibid. 20.4.

[19] Ibid.

What is that higher truth? De Lubac has argued that the illusion from which the unfortunate persons Origen refers to had disembarrassed themselves was simply a gross and superficial representation of divine punishment, a representation that, presumably would involve real worms and real fire.[20] However, Origen, in the next lines of the homily, alludes to Romans 2:4, stating that the persons in question "presume upon the riches of the goodness of God and upon his forbearance and patience (καὶ τῆς ἀνοχῆς κὰ τῆς μακροθυμίας)." The words "forbearance" and "patience" would seem to indicate that the truth in question is that the punishments after death are not necessarily permanent. It is easy to see how most Christians, who still need to be inspired to do good by fear, since they have not attained to love as a motivation,[21] might, if aware of God's ultimate salvific purpose, misguidedly put off until after death a purification they should begin in their earthly life. Origen draws the moral that, while we ought vigilantly to avoid being deceived by Satan, we ought to lower our guard toward divine deception, if we are certain that God is speaking to us, because such deception will always benefit us.[22] This is the quality that makes divine deception ἑτερογενής and language about it equivocal. So concludes Origen's discussion of the verse, "Thou hast deceived me, O Lord, and I was deceived."

In his discussion of the rest of the pericope from Jeremiah Origen justifies human deception for similarly beneficial purposes. The Jewish tradition he had received went on to relate how Jeremiah himself used deception. Jeremiah lived in an extremely sinful time, so sinful that the exile

---

[20]De Lubac, "Tu m'as trompé, Seigneur," p. 45.

[21]See Origen, *Contra Celsum* 5.16 and *Homilies on Genesis* 8.4.

[22]Origen, *Homilies on Jeremiah* 20.4.

and captivity occurred then. Because the people mocked when he said "Thus saith the Lord," Jeremiah presented God's word deceptively. Rather than putting forward the oracles he had received as the Lord's word, he offered them as his own words. That is why the book of Jeremiah, in Hebrew, begins "The words of Jeremiah, the son of Hilkiah," instead of "The word of the Lord to Jeremiah, the son of Hilkiah," as the Septuagint has it. Origen, in this case as in others, prefers the Hebrew reading to the Septuagint.[23]

Origen then recounts how he himself employed beneficial deception:

> And we ourselves do such things when it appears useful (καὶ ἡμεῖς ἔσθ' ὅτε τοιαῦτα). Whenever we address words to pagans in order to lead them to the faith, if we see that they have been prejudiced against Christianity and despise the name and hate to hear it, just because it is the teaching of Christians, we act as if we were presenting a useful teaching that is not Christian, but when the teaching has been established according to the best of our ability, and we deem it possible to acquire the listener for our party, since he has not just been listening indifferently to what has been said to him, then we confess that our praiseworthy teaching is Christian doctrine. In that case we do something similar to what Jeremiah did when he said "Hear my words, those of Jeremiah," instead of "Thus saith the Lord."[24]

Arguably, Origen's Socratic method of teaching was itself pervasively deceptive. According to the student who wrote the *Speech of Appreciation*,

---

[23]Ibid., 20.5.

[24]Ibid.

Origen often deliberately concealed his true opinion about philosophical doctrines in order to encourage his students to exercise their own logical capacities.[25]

The interpretation of a subsequent verse, "I shall call upon breach of covenant and wretchedness" (ἀθεσίαν καὶ ταλαιπωρίαν ἐπικαλέσουαι), provides another example of laudable human deception couched in deceptive terms. To call upon breach of covenant and wretchedness, as if calling upon God, sounds sinful. However, if we made covenants wickedly, we should indeed call upon breach of covenant, and such a breach of covenant will entail wretchedness, "since strait is the way and narrow the gate that leads to eternal life," as opposed to the wide and easy way that leads to destruction. Judith, who agreed to sleep with Holophernes, but broke her covenant with him, rightly "called upon breach of covenant."[26] Origen is less than straightforward in presenting Judith's situation; he makes it sound as if she simply refused to sleep with Holophernes after heedlessly agreeeing to do so. Inquiring minds, familiar with the story, will recognize that Judith's agreement to sleep with Holophernes is, in fact, part of a carefully planned deception that culminates in his assassination.

A bit later on, Origen discussed the words, "There is as it were a fire, shut up in my bones." Origen interprets this as the fire of repentance which Jeremiah feels immediately upon having said, "I shall not mention him, or speak any more in his name." In the course of his interpretation of this part of the lament, Origen says "The word is about to be audacious (Μέλλει τι ὁ λόγος τολμᾶν) and I do not know if it will be useful to some sections of the congregation." He then describes the fire of repentance,

---

[25]Gregory Thaumaturgus, *Speech of Appreciation* 7.103-06.

[26]Origen, *Homilies on Jeremiah* 20.7.

which burns in the heart, and which is necessary for the cleansing of sin.
Those who experience repentance immediately upon sinning receive that fire
in this life, but those who do not do so will experience it in a way that will
be far more painful in the life to come than the sensible fires of any earthly
torturer.[27]

What could be audacious about Origen's interpretation? Perhaps it is
audacious to speak about the necessary purification to come, since such talk
might cause ordinary Christians to lose heart. It is also audacious, however,
to talk about the fires which await sinners in the afterlife as spiritual and
purificatory rather than physical and penal. In *On First Principles* Origen
describes the "eternal fire" as the fire of conscience. This is interpreted as the
purgatorial fire of I Cor. 3:12, a verse to which Origen refers in this homily
and deals with in some detail earlier in the series.[28] In the homily Origen
leaves the question open whether or not these fires are permanent, but, in
doing so, he is concealing his own opinion that they are not. This we can
tell from a revealing passage in the *Contra Celsum:*

> The Logos, accommodating himself to what is appropriate to the
> masses who will read the Bible (οἰκονομούμενος δ' ὁ λόγος
> ἁρμόζοντα πλήθεσιν ἐντευξομένοις τῇ γραφῇ), wisely utters
> threatening words with a hidden meaning to frighten people who
> cannot in any other way turn from the flood of iniquities, Even so,
> however, the observant person (ὁ τηρῶν) will find an indication of
> the end for which the pains and threats are inflicted on those who
> suffer. . . .We have been compelled to hint at truths which are not

[27]Ibid., 20.8.

[28]Ibid. 20.3 and 16.5-6. See Origen, *On First Principles,* 2.5.4-5.

suitable for the simple-minded believers who need elementary words
which come down to their own level (τὰ μὴ ἁρμόζοντα τοῖς
ἁπλούστερον πιστεύουσι καὶ δεομένοις τῆς ἁπλουστέρας
ἐν λόγοις οἰκονομίας αἰνίξασθαι), in order that we may not
seem to allow Celsus' attack to pass without refutation when he
says *When God applies the fire like a cook.*[29]

This is not an isolated passage. It is consistent with Origen's treatment of
eternal punishment elsewhere in his homilies, his allegorization of "eternal
fire" and other punishments of the afterlife, which Origen presents as
beneficial to those punished, in *On First Principles* and his suggestion that
the Greeek word αἰώνιος may refer only to the present αἰών in his
Commentary on Romans.[30]

Origen, in his discussion of divine chastisement that closes the
homily, must have been exercising deception, "hinting at one thing while
saying another." He interprets the parables of the unforgiving servant and of
the rich man and Lazarus as statements about punishment in the afterlife.
He suggests that the "torturers" to whom the servant is delivered and the
torment of the rich man in Hades represent a state of divine purgation before
purgation by the Logos, who "tries the reins and hearts." Origen's
juxtaposition of the two texts is significant. The unjust servant is handed
over to torturers "until he should pay all his debt," implying that his torment
is temporary. By interpreting the parable of the rich man and Lazarus in the

---

[29]Origen, *Contra Celsum,* tr. Henry Chadwick (Cambridge: The
University Press, 1965), p. 276.

[30]See Origen, *Homilies on Exodus* 6.6, *On First Principles* 2.10.6-
8, and *Commentary on Romans* 5.5, as well as *Commentary on John*
19.13.82.

same context, Origen implies that the rich man's torment is also temporary. He states: "That rich man was not worthy to be given to him who tries the hearts and reins; therefore he was tortured by many. Whether or not he might be able to undergo it later is a question I reserve for someone who can answer it (ὕστερον δὲ εἰ καὶ ἐκεῖνος τοῦτο πάσχει ἢ μή, ὁ δυνάμενος ἐξεταζέτω)."[31] Having provided an example of God's acting like a physician who hides the bitter in the sweet earlier in the homily, Origen now provides, for "the person who is able to seek with reason", the balancing example where God acts like the father who hides the sweet in the bitter, when he allows the simple to believe in literal and everlasting fires of judgment.

The first substantive chapter in Henri de Lubac's epochal study of Origen's biblical interpretation, *Histoire et esprit*, is entitled "Griefs contre Origène." Are we to add a new accusation, one which de Lubac himself endeavored to obviate, that of systematic duplicity on Origen's part? On the basis of our study of the twentieth homily on Jeremiah, we must conclude that Origen considered deliberate deception a part of God's strategy for winning back erring souls. We must also conclude that he considered such deception acceptable on the part of spiritual Christians in their dealings with simple believers and employed it himself. I wish to suggest four responses to these conclusions.

(1) In discussing divine deception, we must distinguish "truth" from "truthfulness." This is a point which Sissela Bok makes in her excellent book, *Lying: Moral Choice in Public and Private Life*, which is helpful in clarifying issues involved here.[32] Bok begins her study by separating "truth"

---

[31]Origen, *Homilies on Jeremiah* 20.9.

[32]Sissela Bok, *Lying: Moral Choice in Public and Private Life* (New York: Random House, 1978).

as an epistemological issue from "truthfulness" as a moral issue. A typical
dodge for liars, Bok asserts, is to claim that, since it is impossible to arrive
at absolute truth, their own truthfulness is of small moment. In our case, the
equivocal character of language about God is an epistemological issue; the
intention to deceive is a moral issue. Origen, perhaps deliberately, confuses
the two by opening his homily with a discussion of the equivocal character of
divine language, but he does provide a reasonable moral justification for such
deception, its always beneficial character. God can presumably be trusted to
know when it is in our best interest to be deceived, whether divine deception
is indeed compatible with human freedom, as Origen seems to assume, is a
more difficult issue, but not to the point here. It is when he uses divine
deception to justify deception on the part of fallible human beings that the
issue becomes morally problematical. Unfortunately, because of the
philosphical confusion which surrounds the issue, this is a question which
Origen does not address, although the implication is that the spiritual man
participates in divine deception.

(2) We should, by Origen's account, expect deception in scripture;
the words of the Bible, taken literally, are not always true, and there is no
reason they should be. Origen's discussion of divine deception does indeed
constitute, in de Lubac's words, "a theory of divine allegorisation." Given
his concern with the Bible's literal truthfulness, Augustine was indeed on to
something when he questioned Jerome's Origenist interpretation of Galatians.

(3) Deception is admissible in the spiritual interpretation of the
Bible. We must, therefore, read Origen as Origen read the Bible. This does
not mean that we can simply read into Origen any out-of-the way speculation
we would like to. When Origen expressly denies that he holds an opinion
and never indicates otherwise, we must take him at his word. Nevertheless,

we must pay close attention to what Origen actually says, and follow carefully the logic of his arguments and the implications of the analogies he draws and the scriptural texts he cites. He does leave hints of his real position while suggesting another to edify the simple or to avert their suspicions.

(4) Most importantly, we must not condemn Origen's duplicity, but understand it sympathetically, in his own terms. Although he was a resolute opponent of heresy, Origen's primary commitment was to the Bible as an instrument for personal transformation; truth, for Origen, is not factual information but saving knowledge. Augustine's primary commitment, on the other hand, at least in his years as a bishop, was to the Bible as an instrument for maintaining institutional integrity. It is, I contend, unfortunate that Augustine's frankly inerrantist approach came to dominate the Western tradition, and it may be held responsible for many of the difficulties which still plague biblical hermeneutics. We must not assume naively that a respect for the literal sense is compatible with a modern approach to the Bible. Augustine had a great concern for the literal truthfulness of the Bible and, arguably, a better sense of history than Origen, but his approach to the Bible can easily lead to a sterile inerrantism. It is no accident that B. B. Warfield, the father of Fundamentalism, was a distinguised scholar of Augustine. Augustine raises the point in his letters to Jerome that, if the Bible contains untruths, it cannot be used to confound heretics. How might Origen have responded? I suggest that he would say that we should read the Bible and argue from it as he did. We should, in other words, read the Bible as Henri de Lubac wisely recommended that we read Origen, by massive utilization of the available texts.

POETIC WORDS, ABYSMAL WORDS:
REFLECTIONS ON ORIGEN'S HERMENEUTICS

Patricia Cox Miller
Syracuse University

In an essay entitled "Is there a Fish in this Text?," the literary critic Robert Scholes reflects upon an anecdote by Ezra Pound that deals with a particular kind of relationship between a writer, writing, and what is written about. Here is the anecdote.

> No man is equipped for modern thinking until he has understood the anecdote of Agassiz and the fish:
> A post-graduate student equipped with honours and diplomas went to Agassiz to receive the final and finishing touches. The great man offered him a small fish and told him to describe it.
> Post-graduate student: "That's only a sunfish."
> Agassiz: "I know that. Write a description of it."
> After a few minutes the student returned with the description of the Ichthus Heliodiplodokus, or whatever term is used to conceal the common sunfish from vulgar knowledge, family of Heliichthinkerus, etc., as found in textbooks of the subject.
> Agassiz again told the student to describe the fish.

The student produced a four-page essay. Agassiz then told him to look at the fish. At the end of three weeks the fish was in an advanced stage of decomposition, but the student knew something about it.[1]

Underlying this anecdote by Pound are stories by students in the mid-nineteenth century who actually experienced such ritual initiations at the hands of the biologist Louis Agassiz. Into what were they being initiated? Scholes points out that, in the paradigm enshrined by Agassiz, there is a strong presumption that we learn by *looking* and that, further, we live in "a real and solid world in a perfectly transparent language" which is thus able to communicate that world "as it really is." Yet, as Scholes goes on to remark, "To 'speak the fish' as a biologist or a fisherman or a poet is to speak in a particular discourse."[2] Our post-graduate friend with his rotten fish was being initiated into a specific discourse, a structure within which he could "see" the fish.

Scholes, however, wonders whether the student *knew* that he was being initiated into a conceptual framework, that nothing can be " 'seen' apart from the concept that gives it status." He argues that it is time--indeed, past time--to abandon the uncritical assumption that has informed Western thinking and writing, which is that "a complete self confronts a solid world, perceiving it directly and accurately, always capable of capturing it perfectly in a transparent language."[3] "The way to see the fish and to write the fish,"

---

[1]Robert Scholes, "Is There a Fish in this Text?," in *On Signs*, ed. by Marshall Blonsky (Baltimore: The Johns Hopkins University Press, 1985), p. 309.

[2]Ibid., p. 310.

[3]Ibid., pp. 315, 310.

rather, "is first to see how one's discourse writes the fish. And the way to see one discourse is to see more than one. To write the fish in many modes is finally to see that one will never catch *the* fish in any one discourse."[4]

I have stayed with this fish for some time because I think that, decomposed or not, the fish and structures of perception that one brings to bear upon it may function as figures for one of the focal points of Origen's hermeneutical work. The problem of looking--that is, of interpretation--was central to his writing, and it is that problem that I wish to address.

Scholes' perspective on interpretation is double-edged. To use the terms in the title of this essay, a text offers to an interpreter both abysmal and poetic possibilities, abysmal as in the Greek $\ddot{\alpha}\beta\upsilon\sigma\sigma\sigma\varsigma$, without bottom, no end to meaning, no chance of catching *the* fish, yet also poetic as in the Greek $\pi o\acute{\iota}\eta\sigma\iota\varsigma$, a working relationship with words that discloses not only multiple dimensions of the fish but also multiple dimensions of the interpreter's stance toward the fish.

"Abysmal" and "poetic" are not really two different kinds of interpretation; rather these terms indicate how the mood of the interpreter is valenced when faced with "the often problematical process of meaning multiple things simultaneously with one word."[5] Origen's approach to his fish, the Bible, shows awareness of the double-edged quality, the abysmal and poetic dimensions of any interpretative act.

Origen's awareness of $\pi o\acute{\iota}\eta\sigma\iota\varsigma$, of the imaginative working of Biblical words, is evident in the opening sentence of his first *Homily on Exodus*: "I think each word of divine scripture is like a seed whose nature is

---

[4]Ibid., p. 318.

[5]Maureen Quilligan, *The Language of Allegory: Defining the Genre* (Ithaca: Cornell University Press, 1979), p. 26.

to multiply diffusely. . . . Its increase is proportionate to the diligent labor of the skillful farmer or the fertility of the earth."[6] Words are alive, explosive, diffuse--but only if they fall on the fertile ground of a mind alive to multiple meaning. In a change of metaphor, Origen remarks in his *Commentary on Matthew* that words act as goads, prodding the beast, the interpreter, to move in the nuanced world that they offer.[7] In yet another change of metaphor, Origen pictures words in his *Commentary on the Song of Songs* as beguiling and seductive, inflaming their reader with desire.[8] In the *Philocalia*, words are shepherds; in the *Homilies on Genesis* they are springs; in the *Homilies on the Song of Songs* they are, simply, mysteries.[9] Yet under whatever metaphor Origen discusses words--agricultural, erotic, bestial--it seems clear that words are active, that there is a play or an energy packed into language. The interpreter's task is to let words speak, not to

---

[6]Origen, *Homilies on Exodus 1.1,* in *Origen: Homilies on Genesis and Exodus,* trans. by Ronald E. Heine, The Fathers of the Church, vol. 71 (Washington, D.C.: The Catholic University of America Press, 1982), p. 227.

[7]Origen, *Commentary on Matthew* 2, in *Philocalia* 6.1, *Origène Philocalie, 1-20, Sur Les Écritures*, trans. by Marguerite Harl, SC 302 (Paris: Les Éditions du Cerf, 1983), p. 309. See Harl's discussion of this passage on p. 316.

[8]In his *Commentary on the Song of Songs*, Origen has offered a sustained figuration of the Bridegroom as word. This word smites with passionate love and flirts with, beguiles, and seduces the Bride, a figure for a text's reader. See the discussion of this figuration in Patricia Cox Miller, "'Pleasure of the Text, Text of Pleasure': Eros and Language in Origen's *Commentary on the Song of Songs*," *Journal of the American Acaaemy of Religion* 54 (Summer, 1986).

[9]Origen, *Philocalia* 6.1 (Harl, p. 309); *Homilies on Genesis* 13 (Heine, pp. 185-95); *Homilies on the Song of Songs* 1.4, in *Origène: Homélies sur le Cantique des Cantiques*, trans. by Dom Olivier Rousseau, SC 37 (Paris: Les Éditions du Cerf, 1966), p. 81.

perform an exegetical dissection upon them. It is a question of interpretative attitude, as expressed, for example, by the philosopher Martin Heidegger: "Words are not terms, and thus are not like buckets and kegs from which we scoop a content that is there. Words are wellsprings that are found and dug up in the telling, wellsprings that must be found and dug up again and again, that easily cave in, but that at times also well up when least expected."[10]

The interpreter is not, however, merely a passive observer who watches as meaning wells up out of language. There is work to be done. In one of his most extended figures for interpretative labor, Origen shows Isaac dwelling at the wells of vision.[11] As a type of the interpreter as well as a type of Christ, Isaac *digs* the wells of vision and does not merely dwell there. Actually Isaac is *re*-digging the wells of his father, which had been filled in by envious Philistines.[12] As Heidegger noted, words are well-springs that must be found and dug up again and again, for our ability as interpreters to dwell in the mobile realm of figures easily caves in, blocked and choked by the wish for an end, for a word to end all words, for a final truth that will make things clear, for the hope that, as a poet said ironically, "They will get it straight one day at the Sorbonne."[13] Isaac kept on digging--indeed, his digging *was* his dwelling. On this point Origen is uncompromising: just as language is agonistic, so too is interpretative activity.

---

[10]Martin Heidegger, *What Is Called Thinking?*, trans. by J. Glenn Gray (New York: Harper and Row, 1968), p. 130.

[11]Origen, *Homilies on Genesis* 13 (Heine, pp. 185-195).

[12]Ibid., 12.4 (Heine, pp. 180-181).

[13]Wallace Stevens, "Notes Toward A Supreme Fiction," in *The Collected Poems of Wallace Stevens* (New York: Alfred A. Knopf, 1977), p. 406.

In his commentary on the story of the Witch of Endor in I Samuel, Origen says that there is "a great struggle ($\dot{\alpha}\gamma\dot{\omega}\nu$) in the language of God."[14] Biblical texts are agonistic because the literal works on the page are figures, icons that hold a plenitude of meaning. Thus the literal quality of every text is metaphoric, and the interpreter's task is to "wake up what is useful in all the icons."[15] In Origen's view the Bible is a "texte crypté," as Marguerite Harl has put it, and its words are radical metaphors, or catachreses, which are "violent, forced, or abusive" uses of a word "to name something which has no literal name."[16] Words are violent; so also is interpretation.

We have just heard one of Origen's forceful descriptions of interpretative work: to wake up what is useful in the icons, to give a jolt to a slumbering word which will not willingly disclose its dreams, its interior visions. Elsewhere Origen resorts to more violent images. In his *Homilies on Genesis*, Origen takes the Christ of the Gospels as his model interpreter. More specifically, it is the story of the feeding of the five thousand with just a few loaves of bread that engages his interest. "Notice that the Lord in the Gospels breaks a few loaves, and notice how many thousand people he refreshes. . . . While the loaves are whole, no one is filled, nor do the loaves themselves appear to be increased."[17] As Origen goes on to say, the loaves

---

[14]Origen, *De Engastrimutho* 4, in *Origenes, Eustathius von Antiochien und Gregor von Nyssa über die Hexe von Endor*, Kleine Texte 83, ed. by Erich Klostermann (Bonn: A. Marcus & E. Weber's Verlag, 1912).

[15]Ibid., 2.

[16]Harl, "Introduction" *Origène: Philocalie*, p. 135; on catachresis see J. Hillis Miller, "Stevens' Rock and Criticism as Cure," *The Georgia Review* 30 (Spring, 1976), p. 28 and Harl, ibid., p. 129.

[17]Origen, *Homilies on Genesis* 12 (Heine, p. 182).

are the words of Scripture, which must be broken, "crumbled into pieces . . . unless the letter has been discussed and broken into little pieces, its meaning cannot reach everyone."[18] Like the Christ who broke the loaves, the interpreter breaks the word, rending its letters in the service of meaning.

In the *Philocalia*, Origen offers yet another image of the interpretative process. And once again the Christ is the paradigm of the interpreter. Scripture as a whole, says Origen, is "the musical instrument of God, letting a single melody be heard by way of different sounds."[19] The maestro of this symphonic production is the Christ, the Word which can hear harmony in discord, identity in difference. The human interpreter works exactly in this way, playing the discordant notes so that the harmony might become apparent. The presiding figure for all this is astonishingly strong: David played the lyre to appease the evil spirit of Saul.[20] Although he does not spell out the ramifications of this image, its place in the musical setting is clear: as David, the interpreter appeases evil spirits, the words themselves, since his musical ability consists, according to Origen, in smiting or striking the cords at the appropriate moment.[21] Striking and smiting, the interpreter approaches an equally adversarial text. The musical metaphor would be quite beguiling, lulling one to sleep, had Origen not revealed its foundation in difference and discord.

Finally there is Origen's well-known metaphor of interpretation in *De Principiis*, where words are likened to a field in which treasure is buried.

---

[18]Ibid., pp. 182-183.

[19]Origen, *Philocalia* 6.2 (Harl, p. 311).

[20]Ibid.

[21]See the discussion by Harl, *Origène: Philocalie*, p. 321.

One knows that the treasure is there, but how to expose it? Using a metaphor of hell, Origen says: "These treasures require for their discovering the help of God, who alone is able to 'break in pieces the gates of brass' that conceal them and to burst the iron bars that are upon the gates..."[22] "God," in this case, is the descendent Christ harrowing hell, who is in his turn image for the interpreter whose work is one of breaking and transgression.[23] However polysemous their potential, words are gates of brass that must be broken by active interpretation; unless so engaged, they remain like iron bars. The problem, however, is this: how, exactly, does the interpreter go about his violent task while still respecting the depths of meaning in words?

The refusal of words to reveal their depths easily is an agony for the interpreter. Language is not transparent to meaning; on the contrary, as Origen notes often, Biblical language is frequently opaque. The letters--that is, the literal words on the page--are sometimes absurd and they present the reader with conundrums.[24] As Harl has pointed out, for Origen the "semantic habits" of the Christ as Word, as language itself, are obscure,

---

[22]Origen, *De Principiis* 4.3.11, in *Origen: On First Principles*, trans. by G. W. Butterworth (New York: Harper and Row, 1966), p. 306.

[23]Origen also speaks about Christ as a transgressor of boundaries in *De Engastrimutho*. For a discussion see Patricia Cox, "Origen and the Witch of Endor: Toward an Iconoclastic Typology," *Anglican Theological Review* 66 (April,1984): 137-147.

[24]On the literal absurdity of some Biblical words, see Origen, *De Principiis* 4.3.5 and *Philocalia* 2. In his *Commentary on John*, Origen remarks that the intention of Biblical authors was "to speak the truth at once spiritually and bodily when that was feasible"; but it was not always possible (text and translation in *Origène: Commentaire sur Saint Jean*, 4 vols., trans. Cecile Blanc [Paris: Les Éditions du Cerf, 1966-1982], 2:395). See the discussion of this issue in Harl, "Introduction" to *Origène: Philocalie*, pp. 94-100.

enigmatic, ambiguous, riddling, dark.[25] Words may indeed reveal what Origen calls "the depths of the wisdom of God,"[26] but do they not also conceal those depths as well? Is there, in other words, a "bottom", an end to the poetic display of verbal polysemy?

With such a question, we begin to slide into the abysmal aspect of interpretation, with its quandary concerning not only whether one can catch *the fish*, but whether there is a fish to be caught at all. In his work *Against Celsus*, Origen remarks that "the gospel so desires wise men among believers that, in order to exercise the understanding of hearers, it has expressed certain truths in enigmatic forms, and some in the so-called dark sayings, some by parables, and others by problems."[27] In view of such statements, Harl argues that because it is precisely those obscure passages of the Bible that give access to wisdom, the paradoxical fact is that for Origen wisdom arises from the *silence* of the text.[28] Interpretation is founded on the refusal of speech! Such silence is related to another passage in *Against Celsus* where Origen develops an extended image comparing the unknowability of God with Biblical texts: the obscurantist words of the Bible are like the "great deep" that covers God like a garment, like the darkness that is God's hiding-place, like the "depth of the knowledge of the Father."[29] Is there a God in this text?

---

[25]Marguerite Harl, "Origène et la Sémantique du Langage Biblique," *VC* 26:161-187.

[26]Origen, *De Principiis* 4.3.4 (Butterworth, p. 296).

[27]Origen, *Against Celsus* 3.45, in *Origen: Contra Celsum*, trans. Henry Chadwick (Cambridge: Cambridge University Press, 1965), pp. 159-160.

[28]Harl, *Origène: Philocalie*, p. 460.

[29]Origen, *Against Celsus* 6.17 (Chadwick, pp. 330-331).

One way to look at this question from Origen's perspective is to examine his famous comment in the first *Homily on the Song of Songs*.

> The bride beholds the Bridegroom; and He, as soon as she has seen Him, goes away. He does this frequently throughout the Song; and that is something nobody can understand who has not suffered it himself. God is my witness that I have often perceived the Bridegroom drawing near me and being most intensely present with me; then suddenly He has withdrawn and I could not find Him, though I sought to do so. I long, therefore, for Him to come again, and sometimes He does so. Then, when He has appeared and I lay hold of Him, He slips away once more; and, when He has so slipped away, my search for Him begins anew.[30]

This statement has typically been used to show Origen as a mystic--or, in Dodds' phrase, a "mystic manqué."[31] The soul is the Bride longing for mystical union with the Christ as Bridegroom. There is, however, another way to understand this statement, for in both the *Commentary* and the *Homilies* on the Song of Songs Origen develops a picture of the Bridegroom as *Logos*--as language--who woos, entices, and seduces the Bride, a figure for a reader or interpreter of texts.[32] In this case, Origen's lament about the

---

[30]Origen, *Homilies on the Song of Songs* 1.7, in *Origen: The Song of Songs, Commentary and Homilies*, trans. by R. P. Lawson, Ancient Christian Writers 26 (New York: Newman Press, 1956), pp. 279-280.

[31]E. R. Dodds, *Pagan and Christian in an Age of Anxiety* (New York: W. W. Norton, 1970), p. 98.

[32]See note 8.

disappearing Bridegroom, more present when he is absent, can be read as hermeneutical comment. The word that slips away at the moment when one thinks that one has "laid hold of it," only to return with promise of renewed meaning, and so on *ad infinitum*, forms a precise picture of the deferral of final meaning characteristic of the interpreter's abyss. The *Logos*/Bridegroom works to de-center or defer the interpreter's tidy structures of meaning in consonance with the poetic character of words, as we have seen.

Origen wrote in the *Philocalia* that if " 'the world is unable to contain the books that would be written' [Jn. 21:25] concerning the divinity of Jesus, it is not because of the number of books but because of the greatness of the realities which can't be said in human language."[33] Ironically, Origen uses words in order to say that he can't use words! The irony of this kind of statement has been called in contemporary literary criticism by a French phrase, *mise en abyme*. *Mise en abyme* is a "name for the enigma of the nameless," an "impasse of language which is that however hard one tries to fix a word in a single sense it remains indeterminable, uncannily resisting attempts to end its movement."[34] The paradox of the *mise en abyme* is that "without the production of some schema, some icon, there can be no glimpse of the abyss, no vertigo of the underlying nothingness. Any such schema, however, both opens the chasm, creates it or reveals it, and at the same time fills it up, covers it over by naming it, gives the groundless a ground, the bottomless a bottom."[35] Any word at once creates the "ground" of meaning, names it "properly," so to speak, reveals the

---

[33]Origen, *Philocalia* 15.19 (Harl, pp. 437-438).

[34]Miller, "Stevens' Rock," p. 11.

[35]Ibid., p. 12.

ground, and covers it over. What is the interpreter to do in the face of this abysmal paradox?

Origen's response to the silence and the absence at the center of words is allegory, that interpretative strategy most appropriate to his abysmal interpretative consciousness. In the fragment on I Cor. 2.13, he says: "It is by examining together this and that word and by reuniting those that are similar that the sense of Scripture reveals itself, as one might say."[36] Anyone who is familiar with the first book of Origen's *Commentary on John* knows what this procedure is: all the names of the Christ as *Logos* and Wisdom are assembled and become successive metaphors for each other.[37] The "ground," the Christ, is named, but no one name suffices; each in turn becomes the figure for yet another "ground" in a constant displacement of terms that one modern critic has called the "lateral dance" of allegory.[38] This lateral dance is "an incessant movement from one displaced figural point to another," an attempt to find the final figure, the trope of tropes.[39] Origen describes allegory's lateral dance thus: as soon as the interpreter "has discovered a small fragment of what he is seeking, he again sees other things

---

[36]Origen, fragment on I Cor. 2.13, cited in Harl, *Origène: Philocalie*, p. 143.

[37]Origen follows a similar procedure in *De Principiis* 1.2 and 4.4.1-2.

[38]J. Hillis Miller, "Fiction and Repetition: *Tess of the d'Urbervilles*," in *Forms of Modern British Fiction*, ed. Alan Warren Friedman (Austin: University of Texas Press, 1975), p. 68. See also Miller's "Stevens' Rock," pp. 18-19, and the discussion of Miller's concept of "lateral dance" in Vincent Leitch, *Deconstructive Criticism* (New York: Columbia University Press, 1983), pp. 190-197.

[39] Leitch, *Deconstructive Criticism*, p. 191.

that must be sought for, and if in turn he comes to know these, he will again see arising out of them many more things that demand investigation."[40]

In Origen's hands this interpretative strategy is a kind of repetition, an "interplay of opaquely similar things, opaque in the sense of riddling."[41] The "similar words" that Origen unites as he interprets texts are opaquely similar; for how, logically, can one really say that "way," "door," "light," "shepherd," and so on are "similar," except insofar as they are all figures that both cover and reveal the silence and absence of God? Origen's word for this aspect of allegory--this "other-saying"--is *metalepsis*: "transposition," "alternation," "succession," "the use of one word for another."[42] Not only does Origen so characterize his work, but such scholars as Crouzel and Harl have noted about his work its operation by *glissement*--the sliding of words into other words characteristic of his handling of a text's meaning.[43] Thus, for example, in the passage from the *Philocalia* concerning the Christ as musician, the maestro is displaced by the peacemaker, who is displaced by the shepherd. Only through such displacement or deferral or discord can meaning appear.

What, then, is allegory? As one critic has suggested, allegory names an exegetical perspective which affirms "the possibility of an

---

[40]Origen, *De Principiis* 4.3.14 (Butterworth, p. 311).

[41]J. Hillis Miller, *Fiction and Repetition: Seven English Novels* (Cambridge: Harvard University Press, 1982), p. 8.

[42]See the discusion of this word, with many texts, by Harl, *Origène: Philocalie*, pp. 133-135.

[43]Harl, *Origène: Philocalie*, p. 312; Henri Crouzel, *Origène et la 'Connaissance Mystique'* (Paris: Desclée de Brouwer, 1961), p. 58.

otherness, a polysemy, inherent in the very words on the page."[44] But there is more to allegory than this: in the hands of such an interpreter as Origen, allegory is the name of interpretation as such, provided that one brings to interpretation the kind of poetic and abysmal recognitions that Origen expressed so well. Consciousness of the perceptual structures that one brings to words entails the recognition that all writing is allegory, a fall into a poetic abyss.

The critical stance that allegory names has been well expressed by Vincent Leitch: "Reading uncovers and confronts a language that vacillates uncontrollably between the promise of referential meaning and the rhetorical subversion of that promise. Truth is permanently threatened. A disruptive tropological language endlessly repeats that threat. Whatever wisdom the language of the text offers is undermined through a continuous slide or displacement from figure to substitute figure."[45] Recall the subversive activity of the *Logos*-Bridegroom, endlessly threatening loss of meaning, yet at the same time promising it! Abysmal and poetic at once, the Christ as *logos* is for Origen a figure for allegory itself, both in the Biblical text as well as in texts that displace that text by interpreting it. The *Logos* bestowed on Origen the hermeneutic awareness that we have been exploring here. As Origen's Agassiz, the word initiated him not only into looking, but into consciousness about his *stance toward* looking. The gift of *Logos* to Origen, and his gift to us, is allegory, a poetics of the abyss.

---

[44]Maureen Quilligan, *The Language of Allegory: Defining the Genre* (Ithaca: Cornell University Press, 1979), p. 26.

[45]Leitch, *Deconstructive Criticism*, p. 184.

II. Spirituality--Philosophy--Theology

ORIGENIAN UNDERSTANDING OF MARTYRDOM AND ITS BIBLICAL FRAMEWORK

Pamela Bright
Concordia University, Montreal

Introduction

The title of the paper is indicative of two underlying questions,

1. What characterizes the specifically Origenian concept of martyrdom?

2. What is the role of scripture in the development and the elucidation of this concept?

Methodologically, I shall concentrate on the treatise, *An Exhortation to Martyrdom*, but shall draw upon other Origenian works to test both the consistency of the concept and of its Biblical framing.

The paper will consider:

I.   The genre, structure and content of the treatise.

II. The function of dominant biblical images.

III. An analysis of the specifically Origenian concept of martyrdom in relation to its Biblical frame.

It will be argued that Origen's understanding of martyrdom is elaborated within a soteriology that is, at once, eucharistic, ecclesial, eschatological and, above all, Christological.

These are the very elements that characterize the martyr literature of the early Christian communities.[1] Origen stands firmly within that tradition. But what makes for the specifically Origenian concept of martyrdom is the way in which these elements are woven into a systematic whole, focussing upon martyrdom as a "special kind of death" (τὸ ἰδίως τὸν ἐν μαρτυρίῳ θάνατον),[2] a death "for religion" (ὑπὲρ εὐσεβείας).[3]

It is in this context of martyrdom as an act of pure worship that Origen develops the concept of martyrdom as a privileged moment in which salvation is recognized, celebrated with thanksgiving, and shared with others in union with the saving death of Christ, in fulfillment of "the entire citizenship of the gospel (XII)."

I. Genre, Structure and Content

GENRE

The *Exhortation* is a work of Origen's maturity. Written in the mid-230's, during the persecutions of Maximin and the overthrow of the Severan dynasty, the work is one of his rare "occasional" pieces, in this case addressed to his friend and patron, Ambrose, and to Protoctetus, a priest of Caesarea.[4] Rich in content and intense in emotion, the treatise is the fruit of long years of prayerful reflection.

---

[1]See Section III.

[2]*Exhortatio ad martyrium* L, GCS 1.47.1. An English translation of the text is provided by Rowan Greer in *Origen: An Exhortation to Martyrdom, Prayer & Selected Works,* Classics of Western Spirituality (New York, 1979).

[3]Ibid. V, GCS 1.6.26.

[4]Eusebius, *Church History*, 6:28.

As an "exhortation," the work is often classified among the spiritual writings of the early church rather than among those of more immediate theological interest. Nevertheless this text affords significant insights into Origen's soteriology--what might be termed his "psychic" view of salvation. In it we find echoes of the theory of the transformation of the "psyche" into "nous" in his comment on Mt. 16:24, the paradoxical "losing" and "saving" of the soul: "If we wish to save our soul in order to get it back better than a soul let us lose it by our martyrdom" (XII).[5]

But it is not enough to mine the text for citations illustrating Origen's thinking on various aspects of theology. I would argue that the *Exhortation* not only fulfills its immediate purpose of providing encouragement to his friends in their "present straits" (LI), but is a finely-honed work elaborating a theological reflection on martyrdom which calls for careful attention to the structure and the content of the work as a whole.

STRUCTURE AND CONTENT

The argument of the *Exhortation* moves forward in a kind of insistent rhythm with passages of dramatic urgency alternating with other sections more reflective, even didactic in tone.

Broadly, the text may be divided into seven sections, distinguished by these changes in tone, the announcement of a new topic, or by literary devices such as inclusions.

1. *Introduction*. I-V describes the terms of the contest to which the martyrs are called. Weaving his argument around the prophetic announcement of "affliction upon affliction" and "hope upon hope,"[6] Origen

---

[5]Cf. *Hom. in Lucam* XXXVI; *De Principiis* II 8:3.

[6]Is. 28:9-11, LXX.

asserts that this is no ordinary contest, no ordinary death (V). It is reserved for "those of God's portion" (V).

> . . . the only people to join the contest for true religion is the chosen race, the royal priesthood, the holy nation, the people for his own possession (V). 1 Pet 2:9; Ex 19:6; Is 43: 20-21.

It is the privilege of the martyr to make the "holy proclamation" of salvation, "Thanks be to God through Jesus Christ our Lord" Rom. 7:25 (III).

2. In VI-XI Origen argues against those who would suggest any form of expediency or compromise with idolatry, or with anything that would distract from the fullness of the martyr's confession of faith in the true God. By such a confession, one belongs "totally to God and to life with Him, and near Him, as those who will join in communion with His only Begotten Son and His fellows" (XI).[7]

3. XII-XVII forms a literary inclusion, framed by the relation of martyrdom to the "agreements about religion" [αἱ περὶ θεοσεβείας συνθῆκαι] in baptism (XVII):[8]

> . . . among our agreements with God was the entire citizenship of the Gospel which says, "If anyone would come after me, let him deny himself and take up his cross and follow me. . . (XII)

---

[7]Cf. Heb. 3:4.

[8]GCS 1.16.15.

> . . . what must be said of those who by denying make null
> and void the agreements they made with God, and who run back to
> Satan, whom they renounced when they were baptised? (XVII)

The renunciations in the "agreements" entail the following of Jesus
in whom we have a great High Priest who has passed through the heavens,
Heb. 4:14, and following him,

> . . . you will pass through the heavens, climbing above not only
> the earth and earth's mysteries, but also above the heavens and
> their mysteries (XIII).

4.   In XVIII-XXVII, Origen announces the summons to the contest
in the sight of the whole cosmos (XVIII). He calls upon the example of the
martyrs of 2 Maccabees who died "for true religion" (XXII, XXVII).

> I think it extremely useful for what lies ahead to tell the story I
> have summarized from scripture so that we may see how much
> power against the harshest sufferings and the deepest tortures there
> is in religion and in the spell of love for God . . . (XXVII)

5.   In XXVIII-XXX Origen further develops the priestly character of
this "perfection in martyrdom" (XXVIII). The martyr at the threshold of
eternity offers up the "cup of salvation." It is a "cup" of thanksgiving, as
well as a "cup" of expiation "for the many":

> . . . who else is the blameless priest offering a blameless sacrifice
> than the person who holds fast to his confession, and fulfils every
> requirement the account of martyrdom demands? (XXX)

6. In XXI-XLVI Origen develops a series of exhortations to
perserverence in this "present winter," and warnings against the slightest
compromise.

> You must keep in mind that you cannot hear, "The winter is past"
> (Cant. 2:11), any other way than by entering into this contest
> with all your strength and might and main (XXI).

He concludes the section with a reflection of the arguments of those
who regard the offering of burnt sacrifice to the demand or invocation of their
names as matters of indifference (XLV, XLVI).

7. *Conclusion*. In XLVII-LI a final exhortation is made to be true
to the inner "yearning for true religion and fellowship with him"[9] instilled by
our maker; to withstand the wintry blasts (XLVII); to receive the word of
God, "bear fruit, keep the work to the end by endurance, bearing a hundred-
fold" (XLIX).

Typically, for Origen the climax is couched in Christological terms.
The "precious blood of the martyrs" cries to God. This "special kind of
death" is an "exaltation" in the Johannine sense of the death/exaltation of
Jesus (Jn. 12: 32; 21:19).

---

[9]πρὸς αὐτὸν εὐσεβείας καὶ κοινωνίας, *ad Mart*. XLVII, GCS
1.43.2-3.

II.   The function of the dominant biblical images

The question of the role of scripture in the thought of Origen belongs to the larger question of the relationship of philosophy and theology in the framing of his thought. The present study is too narrow to attempt to draw inferences in such a complex area, but it may be useful to observe how scripture functions within the confines of a particular topic and within a specific treatise.

The *Exhortation* is a veritable tissue of biblical material--literally hundreds of direct quotations, let alone allusions and conflated texts. But what is of particular significance from the point of view of the question of the *function* of the scriptural texts is to observe how the argument is woven around a number of dominant images, e.g. the "cup," and that this image becomes a focus for a network of texts, the exegesis of which forms the framework of the theological consideration.

THE CUP OF SALVATION

Origen begins a consideration of the significance of martyrdom in XXVIII with the image of the "cup of salvation." Drawing attention to the perplexity expressed by the Psalmist, "What shall I give back to the Lord for all his bounty to me?" (Ps. 116:12), he notes the immediate response, "I will take up the cup of salvation and call upon the name of the Lord" (v. 13).

That the "cup" mentioned here is to be interpreted as martyrdom is clear, he argues, from the consistent use of "cup" as image for martyrdom in the Gospel narratives. Origen points to Mk. 10:38 ("Are you able to drink the cup that I am to drink?") and to the "cup" in the prayer of Jesus in the garden, ("Father, if it be possible, remove this cup from me." Mk. 14:36; Mt. 26:39).

Finally, he argues that this is indeed the sense intended by the Psalmist, as demonstrated by the subsequent verse, "Precious in the sight of the Lord is the death of his saints" (v. 15).

In the *Homily on Leviticus*, 2:2, when commenting on the eucharistic offerings, Origen notes that the sacrifice of salvation is offered by those aware of their own salvation. This point is made clearer in the lines of the argument in the *Exhortation*. Martyrdom is *the* day of salvation,

> . . . and God says through the prophet, "In an acceptable time I have heard you, and on the day of salvation I have helped you." What other time, then, is more acceptable than when for piety toward God in Christ we are led in procession before the world . .
> What other day is so much a day of salvation as the one when we gain such a deliverance. . . ? (XLII)

Again in the *Exhortation*, speaking of the desire for "deliverance" from the earthly body, Origen comments:

> Who among those who groan in this tabernacle because they are weighed down by the corruptible body will not first give thanks saying: "Who shall deliver me from this body of death?" He sees that by his confession he has been delivered from the body of death and with holy lips will cry: Thanks be to God through Jesus Christ our Lord!" (III)

The "holy proclamation" of thanksgiving is witnessed to constantly in the martyr literature of the early church. We hear it as Cyprian receives the death sentence. The *Martyrdom of Polycarp* records the prayer of the martyr bishop of Smyrna:

> . . . I bless thee because you have deemed me worthy of this day and hour to take my part in the number of the martyrs, in the cup of Christ . . . for this and everything I praise you, I bless you, I glorify you, through the eternal High Priest, your beloved servant. . .[10]

In Origen, this eucharistic aspect of martyrdom is set within his broader perspective of Christian perfection for the whole of life to be lived eucharistically. In the *Exhortation*, he speaks of this daily interior martyrdom,

> "Daily" he poured out his "soul" by himself, rebuking it again and again for being sorrowful and disquieted in its weakness, and saying, "I will enter the place of the marvellous tabernacle up to the house of God, with the voice of rejoicing and of the thanksgiving of a festal sound" (III).

However, while all are called to live (and die) eucharistically, yet, according to Origen, it is especially the martyr, in that "precious death," who performs the priestly act of the offering of the "sacrifice of salvation." Commenting on Ps. 116, Origen claims that the saint, searching out "what he can do for the Lord in return for everything he has obtained from him . . .

---

[10]C. Richardson, *Early Christian Fathers*, Library of Christian Classics I, (New York, 1953), p. 154.

finds that nothing else can be given to God from a person of high purpose that will so balance his benefits as perfection in martyrdom" (XXVIII).

At that "acceptable time," on that "day of salvation," (XLII) in vivid awareness of the gift of salvation (*Hom. Lev.* 2:2), the martyr is privileged to utter the "holy proclamation" - "Thanks be to God!" (III; XXVIII).

"MINISTERING FORGIVENESS"

The image of the "cup" leads to a second consideration, martyrdom as expiation for sin. Stressing again the evangelical source of his exegesis, Origen notes that the same verse that spoke of martyrdom as a "cup," now speaks of it in terms of a "baptism." "Are you able to drink the cup that I drink or to be baptized with the baptism with which I am baptised?" (Mk. 10:38).

> Consider well whether baptism by martyrdom, just as the Savior's brought cleansing to the world, may not also serve to cleanse many. For just as those who served the altar according to the Law of Moses thought they were ministering forgiveness of sins to the people by the blood of goats and bulls so also the souls of those who have been beheaded for their witness to Jesus do not serve the heavenly altar in vain and minister forgiveness of sins to those who pray (XXX).

The final comment in XXX links this concept of martyrdom as a "ministry at the heavenly altar" to the Christological theme dominating the *Epistle to the Hebrews*--the sacrificial death of Jesus imaged as the entry of the High Priest into the sanctuary on Yom Kippur.

Origen's understanding of the atoning character of martyrdom is witnessed in a number of his writings. In his *Homily on Leviticus* 214, he includes martyrdom among the seven "remissions for sin." In the *Homily on Numbers* 10:2, he speaks of the martyrs as precious victims of the propitiation for sinners.[11] The *Exhortation*, itself, concludes with a reference to the expiation of martyrdom:

> . . . and perhaps just as we have been redeemed by the precious blood of Jesus, who received the Name above every name, so some will be redeemed by the precious blood of the martyrs . . . (L).

At the beginning of the *Exhortation*, Origen had insisted that martyrdom was the prerogative of the true believer: ". . . the only people to join the contest for true religion is the chosen race, the royal priesthood, the holy nation, the people for his own possession" (V). Thus martyrdom is an act of true worship and priestly in character. The image of the "cup" thus introduces the "priestly" aspect of the Origenian concept of martyrdom in terms of the offerings of the "sacrifice of salvation"--the thanksgiving sacrifice, and of the sin offering.

THE JOURNEY/ASCENT OF THE SOUL

The "day of salvation" on which the "cup" is offered is also the day of the glorious departure from this world, when the painful following of the crucified Jesus is transformed into the ascent through the heavens in the company of the great High Priest (Heb. 4:14).

---

[11]See also *Hom. on John* 6:54.

. . . and if you do not shrink from what following him means you
will pass through the heavens, climbing above not only earth and
earth's mysteries, but also above the heavens and their mysteries
(XIII).

The *Exhortation* is filled with Biblical allusions, depicting
martyrdom as a "journey/ascent" of the soul, so characteristically an
Origenian theme.

"Delivered from the body of death" (III), the martyr hears not the
command to Abraham, "Come out of your land," but "Come out of the
whole earth" (V). Losing, yet, paradoxically, saving the soul for the sake of
the Gospel (XII), the martyr climbs the heavens (XIII), "returning like an
eagle to the house of the master" (XV). In suffering, "travelling the narrow
and hard way of winter," the martyr hears the voice of the Beloved, "Arise,
and come away . . . the winter is past" (XXI). "You go in procession bearing
the cross of Jesus and following him . . . and he is with you to show you the
way to the Paradise of God, past the cherubim, the flaming sword to the tree
of life" (XXXVI). The Word of God, "living and active, sharper than any
two-edged sword" now draws a sword "between the image of the man of dust
and the image of the man of heaven" so that "by taking our heavenly part at
this time, he may later make us entirely heavenly, if we are worthy of not
remaining cut in two" (XXXVII).[12]

Just as the image of the "cup of salvation" is the referent around
which Origen develops the concept of the priestly aspects of martyrdom, in
the Biblical images of the journey/ascent, the eschatological dimensions are

---

[12]Heb. 4:2; 1 Cor 15:47.

explored. Within this eschatological perspective, two elements can be discerned, first the emphasis on the salvation of the soul--a "psychic" soteriology--and secondly, the relation between martyrdom and "gnosis."

The drama of the "return of the soul" dominates Origen's eschatology and leaves its imprint on his concept of martyrdom. As "foreigners from the body" (XLVII) and "true Hebrews in exile from our homeland" (XXXIII), we are encouraged to look upon martyrdom as the blessed moment of separation, not only from the earthly body, but also from every corporeal thing (III). This concentration on the salvation of the soul altogether subordinates the eschatological expectation of the resurrection of the body--so central in the expressions of faith of the early church--and when he does make such a reference it is phrased in the "spiritualized" language of 1 Corinthians 15, ". . . that later he may make us entirely heavenly" (XXXVII).

The second element of Origen's eschatological view of martyrdom is its relationship to "gnosis"--the revelation of mysteries.

> . . . it is clear that just as each one of our members is constituted by nature to preserve a relation proper to it, the eyes in relation to what is intelligible and to God who transcends the intelligible order . . . why do we hesitate to put off the perishable body . . . By the true and unceasing Light of knowledge our minds will be enlightened to gaze upon what is by nature to be seen in that Light with eyes illumined by the Lord's commandment (XLVII).

Exploring the "deeper insights" of Is. 43:3-4 in the context of the ransom given for our soul in the "most precious blood" of Christ, Origen bids the martyr to hasten to Christ, and being received as a friend, "face to face," "beyond the enigmas," beyond the "third heavens,"

> . . . you will consequently know more and greater things than the unspeakable words then revealed to Paul, after which he came down from the third heaven. But you will not come down if you take up your cross and follow Jesus whom we have as a great High Priest who has passed through the heavens . . . (XIII)

THE EPISTLE TO THE HEBREWS

Again and again, at the points of intersection of all these lines of argumentation--eucharistic, propitiatory, eschatological--there occurs a constant biblical image, the High Priest of the *Epistle to the Hebrews*.

The great High Priest, the revealer of the heavenly mysteries, the priest and victim offering his own "most precious blood" for the remission of the sins of "the many" is the obvious focus for the various lines of thought as Origen contemplates the meaning of Christian martyrdom.

At the beginning of the discussion of the function of the biblical material in the *Exhortation*, attention was drawn to the richness of the scriptural content in the treatise, not only in direct citation, but also allusions. This richness is further enhanced by the wide range of the biblical texts over which Origen's thought roams so freely--an obvious witness to the long years devoted to the exposition of scripture. However in the development of the various aspects of his teaching on martyrdom, this paper has suggested that certain images have been vehicles for his reflection. I would suggest that the significance of the *Epistle to the Hebrews* for the *Exhortation* lies not so much in the frequency of its citation--though this is considerable--but in its function within the text. Its function lies both in providing a focus for the lines of thought developed in the images of the "cup" and the "ascent" of Christ, the High Priest, as well as in providing a general ambiance for the treatment of the topic. It is this ambiance that distinguishes Origen's treatment of martyrdom within the martyr literature of the early church.

III. The Origenian Concept of Martyrdom and its Biblical Frame

THE TRADITIONAL ASPECTS

An important aspect of the Origenian concept of martyrdom is the degree to which it shares the traditional features of the martyr literature of the very early Christian communities.

The *Exhortation* presents the familiar image of the contest with the triumphal witness of the "noble athletes" (I) set against a backdrop of cosmic proportions:

> A great theatre is filled with spectators to watch your contests and your summons to martyrdom . . . the whole world . . . the angels of the left and the right . . . all those of God's portion . . . those of the other portions . . . the floods . . . the mountains . . . the trees . . . the powers below . . .(XVIII).

We hear the same heightened language and sense the dramatic interplay of cosmic forces in the *Letter of the Martyrs of Lyon* half a century before:

> The Adversary hurtled down in full force . . . taking the field against him was the Grace of God protecting the weak . . . and

> setting up sturdy pillars . . . to draw upon themselves the attacks
> of the Evil One.[13]

Again, in the long section (XX-XXVII) Origen recounts the exploits of the Maccabean martyrs, Eleazar, and the mother and her seven sons, 2 Macc. 7: 18-42. This inclusion demonstrates once again the church's enthusiasm for this material as well as the rootedness of its understanding of martyrdom in the eschatological aspects of such writings as the Maccabees and the Wisdom of Solomon.

Origen's concept of martyrdom shares the eucharistic and Christological character of the early literature. The eucharistic overtones of the narrative of Polycarp's death have already been noted,[14] and the petition of Ignatius is justly famous:

> I am the wheat of God, and let me be ground by the teeth of wild
> beasts, that I may be found the pure bread of God.[15]

The Christological focus of Origen's concept of martyrdom is also shared by the early literature. That martyrdom is "true discipleship" and a form of Christ-likeness is evident in the Letter of the Lyon community. The young advocate, Vettius Apagathus, was only too glad "to lay down his life for his fellow Christian" (I John 3:16) for he was a true disciple of Christ,

---

[13] Charles Kannengiesser, ed., Pamela Bright, trans., *Early Christian Spirituality* (Philadelphia, 1986), 39.

[14] Supra page 188.

[15] *Ep. to Romans* 4.

"following the Lamb wherever he goes" (Rev. 14:4).[16] In the same work, there is a striking picture of the young slave, Blandina.

> All the while, Blandina, hanging from a stake, was exposed as bait for the wild beasts which had been loosed for the attack. She seemed to hang there in the form of a cross and continued to inspire with great enthusiasm those still struggling in the combat. In the midst of their anguish, through their sister it seemed to them that they saw with the eyes of their bodies, him, who was crucified for them so that he might convince those who believed in him that all who suffer for Christ's glory will have eternal fellowship with the living God.

It is interesting to compare the writer's reflection on the "exodus" of Blandina with the exodus/ascent theme in Origen.

> As for the blessed Blandina, last of all, like a noble mother [2 Macc. 7:20ff] having encouraged her children and sent them on before her in triumph to the King, she herself set out on the path of her children's suffering, hastening towards them, rejoicing and exulting because of her own exodus as one being invited to a bridal feast [Rev. 19:9] rather than as one being thrown to the beasts.[17]

---

[16]Kannengiesser & Bright, *Early Christian Spirituality*, 45.

[17]Kannengiesser & Bright, *Early Christian Spirituality*, 48.

Granted the differences in the purpose and style of the two works, the Lyon letter speaks of the "exodus" solely in Biblical terms allusive of Maccabees and Revelation, while Origen integrates his own anthropological viewpoint with that of scripture. It is this systematic integration of his own "psychic" anthropology[18] with the traditional spirituality of the church that so distinguishes the Origenian concept of martyrdom.

MARTYRDOM AND ECCLESIOLOGY

The ecclesiological implications of martyrdom for the early church can hardly be exaggerated. The complexity of the issues surrounding atonement and remission of sin are all too evident in the literature of the North African Church. In fact it may be argued that the martyr debate was instrumental in the bias towards ecclesiological reflection which characterized the North African communities.

The question of the ecclesiological dimension of Origen's concept of martyrdom calls for a more elaborate analysis than that allowed by the scope of this paper. Of primary importance is his insistence on the concept of the "ecclesia"--the "people of God" as a priestly people, the holy nation--"the only people to join the contest for true religion" (V). From that premise he develops his concept of the priestly dimensions of martyrdom in relation to the atoning death of Christ. It is the full citizenship of the Gospel" (XII).

But this aspect of "full citizenship" in martyrdom is related to the vexed question of the "gnostic" levels of spirituality in the church. At the beginning of the *Exhortation* Origen insists that the martyrs have advanced beyond the milk of a "babe in Christ," and have grown in spiritual stature.

---

[18]"Why do we hang back and hesitate to put off the perishable body, the earthly tent that hinders us, weighs down the thoughtful mind?" (Wis. 9:15) (XLVII).

The distinction in spiritual levels does not stop here. He further insists on
the different levels within the martyr ranks!

> Therefore, one of those already martyred and who possessed
> something more than many martyrs in their Christian love of
> learning will ascend quite swiftly to those heights (XIV).

The martyrs offer the "cup of salvation" in thanksgiving for the gift
of "perfection in martyrdom" (XXVIII). This correlation of martyrdom,
perfection and salvation he shares with the author of the *Epistle to the
Hebrews* (Heb. 2:10; 5:9; 7:28; 10:14), and he integrates this concept within
the Alexandrian theme of Christian gnosis. Following the crucified Lord
who came to perfection in suffering, according to Hebrews (Heb. 5:8), the
martyrs cross over the threshold of death and ascend towards the heavenly
sanctuary with Christ, the High Priest of Salvation. "Then you will know as
friends of the Father and teacher in heaven" (XIII). There ". . .washed of
every sin, we may press our existence with our fellow contestants near the
altar in heaven" (XXXIX). Perfected in the contemplation of the mysteries of
God (XIII), they are united in the saving purpose of Christ, crucified and
exalted (L). At one and the same time, the martyr and "gnostic" ministers at
the heavenly altar--at the same time perfect in contemplation and most active
on behalf of the church. More precisely, such a one is at the heart of the
Church. This concept of the ecclesial role of martyrdom is deeply rooted in
the martyr literature. In the closing comments of the Letter of the martyrs of
Lyon we read:

> They did not boast over the ones who had fallen. On the contrary,
> of their riches they gave to those in need, and with motherly

tenderness went and pleaded with the Father on their behalf. They asked for life, and He gave it to them, and they shared it with their neighbor when they went forth to God in complete triumph.[19]

Profoundly in touch with the spiritual vision of the early Christian communities in their affirmation of the significance of martyrdom, Origen, as exegete and theologian, probes the meaning of what he terms "this special kind of death" (L). The *Exhortation* reveals him to be in a creative tradition of scriptural interpretation, in a living tradition of Christian spirituality, and contributing his own genius of speculative and systematic thought to a very rich area of Christian experience.

---

[19]Kannengiesser & Bright, *Early Christian Spirituality*, 50.

THE ROLE OF PRAYER IN ORIGEN'S HOMILIES[1]

Daniel Sheerin
University of Notre Dame

Into God's Word, as in a palace fair,

Thou leadest on and on, while still beyond

Each chamber, touched by holy wisdom's wand,

Another opes, more beautiful and rare;

And thou in each art kneeling down in prayer...

-- from *Origen* by Isaac Williams in *Lyra Apostolica*.

---

[1]This discussion is, to a degree, anticipated by and is to be supplemented by the sketch of Origen's preaching by Thomas K. Carroll, *Preaching the Word, Message of the Fathers of the Church*, 11 (Wilmington: Michael Glazier, 1984), 42-62, esp. 43-47, "The Liturgical Dimension." References to Origen's homilies are made simply by the standard Latin siglum (from the Stuttgart Vulgate) for the book of Scripture involved, followed by the number of the homily and of the paragraph within it; reference to the GCS editions is made in parentheses. Origen's homilies on the Psalms are cited with the siglum Ps followed by the number of the psalm with the number of the homily and its internal division after a slash; reference to PL 12 is given in parentheses. The *Tractatus in Psalmos* recently ascribed to Origen (see CPG #1429) are cited as TrPs with the appropriate number; reference to CCSL 72 is given in parentheses. Origen's commentaries are cited with the siglum Com prefixed to the siglum for the book of Scripture, with GCS reference in parentheses.

Origen's homilies, for all the problems associated with their transmission, still place us in the milieu of the living word, the word living in the congregation, and we find in the homilies, not only exegesis, however learned, however insightful, however devout, but *viva voce* exegesis presented to the church, encompassing, in varying degrees, all three of the *nutrimenta spiritus* which Origen lists when urging his people to frequent attention to the word of God in church: *divina lectio, orationes assiduae,* and *sermo doctrinae.*[2]

My topic is the role of prayer in Origen's homilies. Let me first make clear what I will not be addressing. Origen provides in his homilies many comments on the nature and practice of prayer;[3] and these observations and practical exhortations, as well as Origen's euchological praxis in the homilies, support and supplement, but in some respects seem to disagree with his theoretical treatment of prayer in *De oratione.*[4] Many of the prayers

---

[2]Lv 9.7 (432.5-6); on study, preaching, and prayer as priestly functions, see Lv 6.6 (369.17-370.11).

[3]See Appendix, "Origen's *obiter dicta* on prayer in the homilies," and details of euchological praxis excerpted by V. Saxer, " 'Il étendit les mains à l'heure de sa Passion': Le thème de l'orant/-te dans la littérature chrétienne des IIe et IIIe siècles," Augustinianum 20 [1980]) 335-365, *re* Origen, 352-357; and by W. Schütz, *Der christliche Gottesdienst bei Origenes* (Stuttgart: Calwer, 1984), *passim,* esp. 136-42.

[4]Any treatment of Origen on prayer which focuses on the *De oratione* to the virtual exclusion of the homilies is bound to provide a point of view distorted in some respects, just as the *De oratione* itself gives a distorted view. Note, e.g., apropos of the subordinationism perceived in the *De oratione,* the remarks of A. Hamman (*Early Christian Prayers,* tr. W. Mitchell [Chicago: H. Regnery, 1961], 43, n. 1), of C. Riggi ("Tipi di preci liturgiche e struttura eucologica nel trattatello origeniano 'Sulla preghiera'," *Ephemerides liturgicae* 88 [1974] 370), and of A. Bouley (*From Freedom to Formula: The Evolution of the Eucharistic Prayer from Oral Improvisation to Written Texts* [Washington: Catholic University of America Press, 1981], 138, n. 217) on prayer addressed to Christ in the homilies.

which conclude the homilies, in particular the collect-like prayers, have drawn the attention of liturgical historians, and some have been included in the collections of Cabrol and Leclercq, of Hamman, and of Lodi,[5] though these concluding prayers have been only partially studied in detail.[6] Some of the phenomena which I will be describing and illustrating occur in Origen's commentaries as well,[7] but I have chosen to focus on Origen's homilies, to see the archetypal exegete at work as preacher, *in medio ecclesiae,* presenting the Scripture to a popular audience, and I wish to consider two principal aspects of the role of prayer in Origen's homilies:

I.   the role of prayer in the homiletic encounter with Scripture, and, related to this,

II.   the paradigmatic role of prayer in the homilies.

Origen the homilist describes a number of considerable problems in his ministry, problems additional to those faced by a learned commentator who is drawn to rise above the letter in his exegesis. Origen finds himself working in a scope at once more narrow and more broad than that of the commentator. He has only the limited time[8] of the homilist, not the *otium*

---

[5]F. Cabrol and H. Leclercq, *Monumenta Ecclesiae Liturgica,* 1.1, (Paris: Firmin Didot, 1895-1902), 114-30; A. Hamman, *Early Christian Prayers,* 40-43; E. Lodi, *Enchiridion euchologicum fontium liturgicorum* (Roma: Edizione liturgiche, 1979), 151-54.

[6]See H. Crouzel, "Les doxologies finales des homélies d'Origène selon le texte grec et les versions latines," *Augustinianum* 20 (1980), 95-107.

[7]For example, ComMt 16.9 (503.5-8), 16.29 (574.28-33); ComIo 1.15 (19.32-34), 20.1 (327.2-11), 28.1 (389.20-390.3), 32.1 (425.5-6); ComRm pr (PL 114.833AB); compare *Contra Celsum* 1.71, 2.79, 4.99, 5.1, 6.81, 7.1, 8.1, 8.76, *Peri archon* 1.4.2; *De oratione* 2.6.

[8]For some of Origen's remarks about constraints due to time, see Ex 1.1 (145.20-146.5), Ex 2.4 (159.26-28), Nm 6.1 (31.4-10), Nm 27.2 (258.5-7, 19-21,) TrPs 89 (26-30), Ez 11.5 (431.19-27).

scribentis.[9] He is not writing for the motivated and diligent,[10] but speaking to that net cast into the sea, a congregation in church, and must take their impatience and relative lack of capacity into account: ". . . since there is not time enough to discuss all aspects individually--for the listeners in church value brevity--nonetheless, either discussing a few of the text's main points, or gathering blossoms from it here and there, we will attempt to provide some consolation for the listeners," etc. (Idc6.1 [498.21-26]).[11] Moreover, Origen seems to express genuine reservations about baring the mysteries of Scripture before the unsophisticated.[12] But the edification and consolation[13] of his audience are Origen's goals, and he is prepared to be selective,[14] and to run the risk of divulging things perhaps

---

[9]Work of homiliist contrasted to that of commentator: Lv 1.1 (281.23-26), Nm 14.1 (120.1-10), Idc 8.3 (510.24-27); see also Rufinus' contrast of the two genres in the preface to his translation of Origen's Homilies on Numbers (in GCS ed 1.21-2.2).

[10]Origen complains of the difficulty of motivating his hearers, even the young among them, to the study of Scripture in Ez 13.3 (448, 18-21).

[11]On this point see also Gn 2.6 (38.26-27), Ex 1.1 (146.4-5), Nm 27.4 (261.24-262.3), TrPs 7 (41-43), Ez 11.5 (431.19-27); for a more detailed account see Schütz 107-114.

[12]See, e.g., Nm 22.2 (206.21-24), Ez 1.3 (325.2-16), Lc 35 (201.4-6).

[13]See Nm 5.3 (28.29-29.2), Nm 24.1 (224.18-23), Ios 20.1 (415.7-12).

[14]Gn 2.6 (38.23-27), Ex 1.1 (146.3-5), Ex 2.4 (159.28), Nm 6.1 (31.4-10), Idc 6.1 (498.23-26), Idc 8.3 (510.24-27).

better left hidden[15] (though a decent obscurity must be maintained),[16] in the hope of achieving them.

For his own effectiveness in understanding the word of God and presenting his understandings prudently and effectively to his audience, Origen must rely on divine help, and he must have recourse to prayer to obtain it. Compact allusions to his reliance on God's help occur, too frequently to cite, in parenthetical absolute constructions (*revelante Deo, αὐτοῦ διδόντος τοῦ λόγου*, etc.), in conditional constructions (*Si gratia Domini nos visitare dignetur, ἐάν ὁ θεὸς διδῷ*, etc.), and in limiting and relative constructions (*prout dominus dederit, ἢ ἔδωκεν ὁ λόγος*). That this aid is associated with prayer is made clear by Origen's allusions to the necessity of his prayer for his own illumination at important junctures in the *viva voce* delivery of his homilies, in prologues, and at transitions, e.g.: "For I truly consider myself unequal to explaining the mysteries which this book of Numbers contains, and far below explaining those enclosed in the book of Deuteronomy. And therefore we hasten to come to Joshua/Jesus, not the son of Nave, but to Jesus Christ." (Nm 1.3 [727.20-8.1]).[17]

Origen also acknowledges the necessity of divine help, and of prayer to obtain it, for his congregation. It should be noted parenthetically that discernment of reference to preacher from reference to congregation in such passages is complicated by Origen's frequent use of the first person plural to refer both to himself and to his audience. The ambiguity arising from this

---

[15]Nm 5.3 (28.29-29.2), Nm 22.2 (206.21-24, Ez 1.3 (325.2-4).

[16]Nm 4.3 (23.1-6), Ez 1.3 (325.2-16).

[17]See also Gn 2.3 (30.4-7), Gn 4.6 (56.17-19), Ex 3.2 (164.23-25), Lv 5.5 (343.15-18), Lv 5.8 (348.5-8), Lv 6.1 (359.10-14), Nm 13.4 (112.8-11), Ex 11.1 (424.13-16).

hinders the construction of a nice taxonomy, but must have had the happy effect, from a rhetorical and pedagogical point of view, of including the congregation in their teacher's quest for meaning in Scripture and of inculcating the correct, God-ward attitude of the devout reader. Homily is, after all, in Origen's view, the common endeavor of preacher and people, whether it be portrayed as a common enquiry, or as a common endeavor with preacher and people fulfilling their various roles in liturgico-homiletic activity.[18] But I think we can see Origen teaching the people the necessity of prayer for divine aid in their encounter with Scripture in the following examples: "From this it is clear that we must not only bring study to bear on the learning of Scripture, but we must also pray and beseech the Lord day and night, that the Lamb from the tribe of Juda may come, and deign to take up the book that has been sealed and open it." (Ex 12.4 [266.20-23]), or "We must pray to the Lord, we must pray to the Holy Spirit, that He may deign to take away every cloud, every darkness," etc. (Lv 1.1 [281.18-20]), or ". . . but let us be turned to the Lord, that He may take away the veil of the letter for us, that the countenance of Moses may appear to us not misshapen, but glorious and beautiful" (Nm 7.2 [40.27-29]).[19]

Origen repeatedly links the receipt of divine aid for his effective preaching and his audience's fecund reception of the word to the people's prayers; he acknowledges the contribution of their prayer as a necessary pre-

---

[18]Common enquiry, Ios 7.3 (330.12-16), and see Carroll p. 43; for roles of priest and people see TrPs 9 (1-6).

[19]See also Gn 6.1 (66.12-18), Gn 12.1 (106.20-25), Nm 27.1 (258.2-5), Is 5.2 (264.5-12).

condition and accompaniment to the homilist's understanding of Scripture and fruitful preaching of it.[20]

It should come, then, as no surprise that we find Origen requesting the prayers of the people, both for his own work, e.g.: "And so, while she is still speaking, the Bridegroom comes. She points Him out with her finger, and says: 'Behold He comes, leaping upon the mountains.' . . . Pray that I too may be able to say 'Behold He comes.' For if I am able to explain the word of God, in a certain way I too say 'Behold He comes.' " (Ct 2.10 [55.28-56.6]),[21] and for preacher and people together, e.g.: "And now one pericope is completed; let us begin the second. And indeed, from the very beginning it contains extraordinary matters, and as we approach the text, let us ask Jesus to come, and urge him to come quite manifestly and clearly, that coming He may teach all of us. . . ." (Ier 19.15 [173.3-7]).[22]

The second aspect of the role of prayer in Origen's homilies which I wish to discuss is the paradigmatic character of prayer. We have seen that Origen teaches by instruction, example, and exhortation the prayerful attitude

---

[20]This acknowledgement can be found in prologues, Gn 3.1 (39.18-19), Gn 9.1 (86.25-27), Ex 9.2 (237.20), Lv 5.2 (335.17-20), Lv 6.1 (359.10-14), Nm 20.1 (185.14-15), Nm 26.3 (249.14-16), Ios 8.3 (338.4-7), TrPs 9 (1-6), Ct 1.1 (28.19-20); at cruces in the scriptural text, Gn 3.5 (44.15-23), Lv 12.4 (460.8-11), Lv 14.4 (484.10-11), Ios 26.2 (458.24-459.6), Ez 4.3 (363.29-364.2), Ez 7.9 (399.29-400.6), and in Origen's portrayal of the preacher's work in Ps 36/4.3 (1357AB).

[21]Other examples of requests for people's prayer for preacher, in prologue Nm 19.1 (176.23-26), Is 5.1 (263.23-26), Is 7.1 (279.13-17), Is 9.1 (288.11-13), Lc 32 (182.3-16), in transition, Nm 26.3 (248.26-249.1), in excursus, Ps 36/4.4 (1358B), Ez 2.5 (347.19-23).

[22]See also, in prologue, Gn 7.1 (70.12-14), Lv 13.1 (468.4-7), Is 5.2 (264.5-12), Lc 35 (196.3-11), Lc frg 125 (278.4-6); in transition, Lv 6.4 (365.28-366.4), Lv 13.2 (468.20-23), Nm 12.4 (104.2-4), Nm 26.3 (248.26-249.1, 249.14-19); at crux, 1 Rg 1.3 (5.8-15); in excursus, Is 6.3 (274.4-6); in concl. Lv 6.6 (370.4-11).

with which one should approach the word of God. He also provides, through exhortation and example, instruction, both as to pattern and content, in the appropriate, prayerful response to the word of God in general, and in quite specific situations.

This is, in a sense, an integral part of Origen's homiletic instruction, for in his teaching, meditation on the Law of the Lord and prayer are inextricably linked,[23] prayer being the necessary prelude, as we have seen, and the necessary response to the reading/hearing of Scripture as well. He teaches this by example in the prayerful conclusions of many of the homilies, expecially those of the *surgentes* type: "And so, rising up, let us pray that we may find always ready this sword of the spirit by which to destroy the seeds and the very seedbeds of sin, and that God may be propitious to us through the true Phineas, Himself our Lord Jesus Christ: to Him be glory and dominion unto the ages of ages. Amen." (Nm 20.5 [198.21-25]).[24] Indeed, in Homily 11 on Numbers, Origen portrays immediate, intense, prayer as the necessary fruit of an effective encounter with Scripture:

> For even now God's angels, the cultivators and farmers of our hearts stand in attendance, and they are trying to find if in any of us there is a soul so concerned, so attentive, that it has received the divine seed with all eagerness, and if it shows fruit immediately, when we rise to pray, that is, if it prays to God with its thoughts collected

---

[23]For the general association of Scripture and prayer, see Lv 9.7 (432.5-6), Ps 36/2.1 (1330CD), Ios 1.7 (295.18-19), Ios 16.5 (400.2-3, 8-9).

[24]See also Ct 2.13 (60.19-21), Is 1.5 (248.6-10), Is 3.3 (257.15-20), Lc 12 (76.16-20), Lc 15 (94.23-28), Lc 38 (216.12-23), Lc 39 (222.10-13).

and gathered within it, if it does not wander about in mind and fly
away in thought. . . (Nm 11.8 [92.30-93.4]).

In this connection we should bear in mind that Origen's homilies
are, among many other things, paradigms, for it is clear from a number of
passages that Origen views his homilies as paradigms for the individual,
extra-congregational encounter with Scripture.[25] That the prayers within the
homilies serve, among others, a similar paradigmatic function is nowhere so
clearly stated, but it seems a safe inference. The hortatory prayers are surely
intended to instruct as well as to exhort to prayer. And we must ask what is
the point of Origen's own prayers if not to instruct and edify. Consider this
comment from Homily 10 on Numbers:

> But there are two altars, that is, an inner one and an outer one.
> Since an altar is a sign of prayer, I think that it means what the
> Apostle says: 'I shall pray in spirit, I shall pray in my mind.' For
> when I pray in my heart, I go in to the inner altar. . . . But when
> someone pours out his prayer to God in a clear voice and with words
> produced with sound, as if to edify his hearers, he prays in spirit,
> and seems to offer his victim on the altar which was set up outside
> for the holocausts of the people (Nm 10.3 [73.21-74.2]).

This is not to deprive these prayers of their status as prayers, nor yet
as components of Origen's exegesis, for many of them do contain clear and

---

[25]See Gn 10.5 (100.10-17), Gn 12.5 (112.15-21) Gn 13.4 (119.1-
7), Lv 8.1 (393.18-394.19), Nm 5.3 (30.20-23), Nm 11.2 (79.21-23), Nm
27.13 (280.5-18), Ios 20.1 (415.12-16), Ios 20.2 (420.3-15), Ps 36/5.1
(1360AB), TrPs 95 (34-37), TrPs 131 (25-28); see also Rufinus' observation
cited supra in n. 9.

effective exegetical features. I merely wish to focus on their instructional, paradigmatic role.

What I want to call paradigmatic prayers can be seen in various forms, in a variety of locations within the homilies, in a variety of responses to Scripture and its explanation. Origen interrupts himself in mid-homily to bid the prayers of the people in response to what has been said, e.g., to take a prayer with particular application to the troubled times of the church in which Origen was living: responding to Judges 6.1   ("But the sons of Israel did evil in the sight of the Lord who gave them over into the hand of Madian for seven years"), and amplifying it through recombination with a prayer text from Psalm 73.19 ("Do not give over to the beasts the soul which confesses to you"), Origen urges his congregation to prayer as follows:

> Wherefore, then, brothers, let us beseech the Lord, confessing our frailty to Him, that He may not give us over into the hands of Madian, that He may not give over to the beasts the soul confessing to Him, that He may not give us over into the power of those who say 'When will the time come when we will be given power against the Christians? When will those men who say that they have and know God be given over into our hands?' But if we are given over, and they receive power over us, let us pray that we may be able to endure, that our faith may be even brighter in persecutions and tribulations, that we may overcome their wantonness by our patience, and, as the Lord said, we may win our souls by our patience. . . (Idc 7.2 [506.22-507.3]).[26]

---

[26]Some other examples of Origen's pausing in mid-homily to bid prayers in response to Scripture: Ios 6.4 (326.13-19), Ios 12.2 (369.6-9), Idc 1.1 (467.13-16), 1 Rg 1.1 (1.9-12), Ps 36/4.2 (1352C), TrPs 95 (175-179), TrPs 103 (136-137), TrPs 106 (118-121), TrPs 119 (49-52), TrPs 127 (225-

Origen sometimes incorporates into his exegesis an exhortation to pray in the words of Scripture, especially in the homilies on the Canticle of Canticles, in his remarks on prayers within the biblical texts, and in his paraphrases of the prayers of the prophets and the Psalmist. For example, at the conclusion of the second homily of Psalm 37, he incorporates Psalm 37.23 as follows:

> Unhappy the man from whom God has withdrawn, but blessed is he with whom God abides. 'Look to my aid, O Lord, God of my salvation!' So let us also pray and say: Look to my aid, for the struggle is great and mighty are my adversaries. The enemy is dangerous, the unseen enemy makes his attacks through these visible ones. Look, then, to our aid, and help us through your holy Son, our Lord Jesus Christ, through whom you have redeemed us all, through Him is glory and power yours unto ages of ages. Amen. (Ps 37/2.8 [1388BC]).[27]

The exhortations to prayer which conclude many of the homilies respond to Scripture in various ways: a) most respond to the text taken up in the latter part of the homily; b) a few are general recapitulations of the entire

---

233), Is 5.2 (264.5-12, 265.14-22), Is 5.3 (267.8-9), Is 6.3 (274.4-6), Ier II.12 (300.9-15), Ier 5.7 (47.7-9), Ez 13.1 (442.22-25), Lc 13 (81.10-15).

[27] See also, e.g., Ct 2.4 (49.9-14), Ct 2.12 (58.4-7, 12-16), Ps 37/1.6 (1380BC), Ps 37/2.8 (1388BC), Ps 38/2.10 (1409AB), TrPs 66 (172-74), TrPs 89 (51-57); see comments on the OT canticles in Ct 1.1 (27.15-28.18), discussion of the Canticle of Hannah in 1 Rg 1.8-19; see also Ps 36/5.1 (1360AB) where vocal prayer, in part in the words of Scripture, serves as a *meditatio sapientiae* for the unlearned.

homily; c) some respond to a specific text from outside the pericope brought in to explain, amplify, or apply the reading; d) some prayers relate to a concluding moral reflection; and e) some are prayers for divine aid in the growing understanding of Scripture.[28]

Origen goes beyond exhortation to prayer and himself delivers prayers in the place of the people, invoking God directly, e.g. " 'And the sons of Israel did evil before God (Judges 2.11).' O Almighty God the Sovereign, grant that it may never happen to us that Jesus Christ, after He has risen from the dead, dies again in us." (Idc 2.2 [473.16-18]), and indirectly, e.g. "But may the Lord grant us to be sons of Abraham and Isaac and Jacob, heirs according to the promise, and raise us up from the stones to be sons of Abraham, by Christ Jesus our Lord, etc." (Ios 22.6 [438.18.21]).[29]

We must close with a glance at Origen's prayers *in propria persona*, which manifest his personal reaction to Scripture and his own spiritual longings. Some of these pertain to his role as homilist,[30] and are not

---

[28]E.g., of type a: Gn 14.4 (126.23-32), Nm 20.5 (198.21-25), Ios 9.9 (357.8-15), Ios 20.6 (427.7-9), Ios 21.2 (432.4-10), Idc 9.2 (522.6-10), Ps 37/2.8 (1388BC) TrPs 5 (256-260), TrPs 89 (226-241), TrPs 149 (133-144), Ct 2.13 (60.19-21), Is 3.3 (257.15-20), Ez 10.4 (423.8-19), Ez 11.5 (432.12-21), Ez 12.5 (439.18-22), Lc 6 (40.9-17), Lc 27 (160.11-22), Lc 30 (174.22-25), Lc 37 (212.22-25), Lc 38 (216.8-23); of type b: Gn 2.6 (38.27-39.3), TrPs 89 (226-241), TrPs 106 (175-178), Lc 15 (94.23-28), Lc 18 (113.13-22); of type c: Ex 2.4 (161.12-15), Is 1.5 (248.6-10), Ez 2.5 (348.14-17), Lc 12 (76.16-20), Lc 26 (156.13-17); type d: Ex 4.8 (183.3-8), Lv 15.3 (491.16-21), Ios 17.3 (405.19-24), TrPs 91 (259-263); type e: Ex 10.4 (252.7-10), Lv 6.6 (370.4-11), Nm 16.9 (153.1-8), Ier 6.3 (51.6-12).

[29]See also Gn 3.7 (50.11-15), Lv 5.12 (358.12-17), Ios 12.2 (368.19-24), Ios 22.6 (438.18-21), TrPs 1 (279-284), TrPs 89 (51-57), TrPs 119 (279-282), TrPs 132 (69-71), TrPs 147 (170-172), Ez 6.10 (388.19-20), Ez 6.11 (391.1-3).

[30]See Ex 13.1 (270.2-6), Ios 8.7 (343.18-23), Idc 8.5 (514.24-515.23), TrPs 111 (94-97), Is 6.3 (273.2-4), Ier 19(18).4 (170.8-9).

necessarily paradigmatic, save for other preachers and pastors, and they are paralleled by the prayers which are found in the prefaces of various books of Origen's commentaries and treatises.[31] Many are prayers or heartfelt wishes on behalf of the congregation;[32] many seem to include both the congregation and Origen himself.[33]

But perhaps the most striking and most instructive, if the least numerous of Origen's prayers are those which portray his personal response to Scripture. As with other of his prayers, some are direct invocations, others are indirect prayers, or expressions of longing. The best we can do here is to offer a few abbreviated examples: "Would that the Lord would give his blessing to me too, that I might deserve to dwell at 'the well of vision' " (Gn 11.3 [105.3-4]); "Lord Jesus, grant to me to have some memorial in your tabernacle. I would have liked, were it possible, that there be something of mine in that gold from which the mercy-seat is made," etc. (Ex 13.3 [273.22-274.5]); "There is a certain spiritual embrace, and would that it might come to pass that a closer embrace of the Bridegroom would enclose my bride as well, that I too could say what is written in this same book: 'His left hand is under my head, and His right hand embraces me.' " (Ct 1.2 [31.19-22]). "I pray that the Seraph be sent to me as well, and taking a coal with tongs may cleanse my lips. . . . But I fear that by running after evil I have soiled my feet. . . . Who then cleanses me? Who washes my

---

[31]See supra note 7.

[32]See Nm 27.13 (280.12-18), Ios 11.6 (366.15-20), Lc 32 (184.17-23); for priests, 1 Rg 1.7 (13.5-9).

[33]See Gn 15.7 (135.24-136.3), Ios 12.2 (368.19-369.12), Ps 37/2.1 (138 2B).

feet? O Jesus, come, I have soiled feet. Become a slave on my account, put your water in a basin, come, wash my feet." (Is 5.2 [264.12-27]).[34]

Against great odds, a large portion of Origen's homiletic corpus has come down to us. These homilies are, to be sure, precious as monuments of exegesis. But may I venture to say that they are of even greater and enduring value as examples of a technique for the community's and the individual's encounter with the word of God? *Spatiis iniquis exclusus,* I have been able to give only a brief account of the important role of prayer in these homilies and a sketchy catalogue of the kinds of prayers. Detailed study of these phenomena, both in their broader ramifications (relationship of theory of *De oratione* to practice of homilies, sacerdotal role of preacher, role of prayer in hermeneutics), and in the interactions within the homilies of prayers and calls-to-prayer which have, in some case, been artifically sundered from one another in this treatment for the sake of classification, remains to be done, but it is hoped that this sketch may provide a first step in these directions.

Appendix

Origen's *obiter dicta* on prayer in the homilies:

only Christians able to invoke angels, God, Christ, Nm 13.5 (114.23-115.8);

prayer through the Spirit, Ex 5.4 (189.11-20), Ios 9.2 (347.29-348.7);

---

[34]See also Nm 18.4 (174.25-175.4), Nm 22.4 (209.27-210.9), Ios 12.3 (370.9-16), Ios 13.3 (373.6-13), Ios 18.3 (410.8-11), Idc 8.5 (514.24-515.23), TrPs 66 (160-162), TrPs 95 (16-28), TrPs 147 (40-43, 134-138), TrPs 149 (95-99; NB, cannot be Origen's in current form), Is 1.4 (247.7-8), Jer 17.5 (149.3-17), Lc 16 (99.26-31).

unceasing prayer, Nm 23.3 (214.22-27), 1 Rg 1.9 (15.10-16.5), Ios 16.5 (400.8);

intense prayer the necessary fruit of encounter with Scripture, Nm 11.8 (92.33-94.4);

liturgical rituals, Nm 5.1 (26.14-27.3);

in psalms, hymns, canticles as *meditatio sapientiae*, see n.27;

in persona of biblical figures, see n.27;

prayer and meditation on Scripture as *arma spiritalia*, Ios 16.5 (399.18-400.3, 7-12);

prayer offered by angel to Christ the High-Priest, Nm 11.8 (93.4-10);

purity in prayer, Lv 13.5 (475.24-476.9), Ps 37/2.3 (1384AB), Ier frg 68 (230-231), Ier 14.14 (119.10-26);

tears in prayer of repentance, Ps 38/2.10 (1409AB);

posture for prayer, arms extended, Ex 3.3 (170.19-25), Ex 11.4 (255.16-256.19), 1 Rg 1.9 (16.2-6), body bowed Nm 11.8 (93.3);

silent and vocal prayer, Nm 10.3 (73.21-74.2), Nm 11.8 (92.26-30), silent prayer, Ex 5.4 (189.11-20);

power of prayer, Nm 25.2 (234.15-17);

sin as obstacle to prayer, Ps 36/2.1 (1330D-1331A), Ps 37/2.3 (1384AB), Ier 10.10 (164.9-27);

incorrect prayer, Ier 17.6 (150.9-13), Ez 7.4 (394.15-22).

LOOKING ON THE LIGHT: SOME REMARKS ON THE IMAGERY OF LIGHT IN THE FIRST CHAPTER OF THE *PERI ARCHON*

John Dillon
Trinity College, Dublin

This essay is an attempt to address a general question, that of Origen's relation to the Greek philosophical tradition, by concentrating on one particular issue, which I hope will prove adequately illustrative.

As we all know, the battle has long raged between partisans of Origen the systematic philosopher, such as Adolf von Harnack, Eugène de Faye, Hal Koch and Hans Jonas, and those who see him as essentially an exegete of scripture and Christian apologist, such as Walther Völker, Henri de Lubac, Henri Crouzel, or Marguerite Harl. To a certain extent one's attitude is conditioned by how far one concentrates on a text such as the *Peri Archon,* or rather on the *Homilies* and such works as the *Exhortation to Martyrdom* and the treatise *On Prayer,* but these emphases are themselves plainly conditioned by the overt or covert prejudices of the authorities concerned, in their anxiety to maintain either the originality and philosophical standing of Origen or alternatively, if not his orthodoxy, at least his essential Christianity. Part of the problem, I think, has been that the alternatives are stated too starkly. Either Origen is presented as a Platonist with a superficial veneer of Christianity, or he is not to be a systematic philosopher at all. The truth may rather be that he is indeed a philosopher, but one who, rather than adopting Platonism or the doctrine of any other Hellenic school, has forged a system of his own out of the Christian scriptures and tradition, to which he lays Platonism tribute for concepts and formulations which he finds useful, without surrendering to the Greeks any principle whatever.[1] I would suggest that Origen's relation to primitive Christianity is somewhat analogous to that of Plotinus to Plato and earlier Platonism. He draws his inspiration from the tradition, and genuinely aspires to be faithful to it, but his genius drives him to the creation of a new system, built upon what he has inherited. In a word, Origen only wishes to be a Christian, as does Plotinus to be a Platonist, but if we persist in calling Plotinus, in recognition of his achievement, a Neoplatonist, then we must denominate Origen a 'Neochristian'.

What I want to do in this paper is to consider one dominant image of which Origen makes much use in his discussion of the nature of God in

---

[1]We may recall that, as he tells it himself (*ap.* Eusebius *HE* VI.19, 12-13), Origen only began to attend the lectures of "the teacher of philosophy" (sc. Ammonius Saccas) when he himself was already an established, if precocious, teacher of Christian doctrine. He went to Ammonius, not to be converted to Platonism, but rather to pick up useful technical information, to aid in his apostolate to the Alexandrian intelligentsia, a number of whom, such as Heraclas and his brother Plutarch, he actually lured away from Ammonius. This he could not have done, I submit, without a system to offer. The system need not be worked out in every detail, nor even free of contradictions, but one cannot reasonably deny, I think, that it is there. Without going into details, I see it as involving, above all, the concept of a cosmic process of procession (or 'fall') and return, involving the pre-existence of souls and, inevitably, some form of reincarnation and sequence of worlds (though I doubt that Origen ever quite made up his mind on these questions). All other aspects of his thought seem to me to be conditioned by this grand conception, which is itself the product of his concern with the problem of God's providence and our free will. To that extent I remain sympathetic to Hal Koch, in *Pronoia und Paideusis* (Berlin and Leipzig, 1932), and even to Hans Jonas.

the *Peri Archon*, and see how his use of Platonic imagery and doctrine may

be seen to support my thesis.[2]

On the vexed question of the nature of the *Peri Archon*, on which

much has been written in recent years,[3] I must say that I am inclined to view

---

[2]Origen's use of light imagery in general is comprehensively examined in a thesis by M. Martinez-Pastor, *Teologia de la luz en Orígenes* (Comillas, 1962), but Martinez does not address himself to the particular problem that concerns me here. See also H. Crouzel, *Origène et la 'Connaissance mystique'* (Paris/Bruges, 1961), pp. 130-154, for a good account of the uses to which Origen puts the imagery of light.

[3]Cf. B. Steidle, "Neue Untersuchungen zu Origenes" περὶ Ἀρχῶν', *ZNW* 40 (1942), 236-243; M. Harl, "Recherches sur le περὶ Ἀρχῶν' d'Origène en vue d'une nouvelle édition: la division en chapitres," *Studia Patristica* 3 (= TU 78; Berlin, 1961), pp. 57-67; H. Crouzel, Intro. to *Origène Traité des Principes*, Tome 1 (SC 252), pp. 15-22. The precise meaning of ἀρχαί intended by Origen in this context has been the object of some uncertainty (Cf. Crouzel's discussion *op. cit.* pp. 12-15, and "Qu'a voulu faire Origène en composant le Traité des Principes?," *BLE* 76 (1975), pp. 161-186, and 241-260). It seems probable to me that he sees himself as meaning what any Platonic philosopher would mean by this, viz. a discussion of the three acknowledged "first principles", God, Idea(s), Matter, together with topics arising out of those, and that is the subject-matter of the first section of the work (to II.3), *mutatis mutandis* (e.g. for "Ideas", we have "rational beings", for Matter, the World). How well the title fits the other portions of the work is more problematic (a reference back to the discussion of free will in III.1 in the *Comm. in Rom.* (VII.15, PG XIV 1145A) as a separate *libellus* would seem to indicate that Origen thought of the work rather as a collection of essays).

Some light may be thrown on what particular connotation Origen attaches to the term ἀρχαί by his remarks at *Comm. in Joh.* XIII.46, 302, where he presents the ἀρχαί of any science or art as what the first discoverer, or "sower", lays down, to be developed further and brought to completion (τέλος) by later generations ("reapers")--all this by way of exegesis of John 4:36. This "dynamic" concept of the ἀρχαί of a science imports another dimension, I think, into the traditionally static philosophical meanings of the term, as immutable basic principles, or ultimate principles of reality. Certainly Origen is to some extent "transposing" the traditional Platonic meaning of the term, as Crouzel suggests; the connotation "principles of the Christian faith" is superimposed on the basic meaning "first principles of reality." Cf. also *De Princ.* 4, 1.7, where ἀρχή is significantly glossed by στοιχείωσις.

the work as an attempt by Origen to state a reasoned Christian position on the topic of $\dot{a}\rho\chi a\acute{\iota}$, or 'first principles', arising out of his attendance at the lectures of Ammonius Saccas. I am led to this view, not just by a consideration of the subject matter; but by looking at the very way in which the work starts out. Origen begins abruptly, not with a positive statement of God's nature,[4] but with an answer to an accusation, plainly from a Platonic source, that Christians regard God as having a *corporeal* nature.[5] In combating this accusation he has to face a series of passages of Scripture which seem to attribute to God material substance or characteristics.[6]

For instance, Moses says at Deut. 4:24: "Our God is a consuming fire",[7] and Jesus says to the Samaritan woman at John 4:24: "God is spirit ($\pi\nu\epsilon\hat{\upsilon}\mu a$), and those who worship him must worship in spirit and in truth". Now Origen's general line of defense is plainly that such passages must be taken figuratively, but that is not the first point that he makes. This first

---

[4]As one would expect in a statement of First Principles. On the immateriality of God, Cf. Aetius, *Placita* I.7, 31 (p. 304 Diels, *Dox.Gr.*), Apuleius, *De Plat.* I.5, 190-1; Numenius, Fr. 3 des Places. (Albinus in *Did.* ch. 10 asserts, certainly, God's immateriality, but only at the *end* of his discussion).

[5]In the Preface, also, he begins, rather defensively, by identifying himself with Moses, who preferred, in the words of the author of Hebrews (11:24-26), "the abused state ($\dot{o}\nu\epsilon\iota\delta\iota\sigma\mu\dot{o}\varsigma$) of Christ to the treasure-houses of the Egyptians", these latter being the much-vaunted doctrines of contemporary philosophy.

[6]These passages may well have been adduced by anti-Christian polemicists, (and even by Ammonius, whom Porphyry, at least, maintained to have started as a Christian himself), though here Origen only says that they *might* do so (*scio quoniam conabuntur*).

[7]He also describes him there as "a jealous God", but Origen leaves that aside in the present context.

point I find rather interesting, and it is that which I wish to start from, since I think that it serves as a good instance of Origen's complex relationship to contemporary Hellenic[8] philosophy.

"These men," says Origen, "will have it that fire and spirit are body and nothing else. But I would ask them what they have to say about this passage of Scripture: 'God is light,' as John says in his epistle (1 John 1:5), 'and in him is no darkness.' "

The point of adducing this passage about light is presumably that, in later Platonism, light is agreed to be incorporeal. But this is, strangely enough, not a point which Origen cares to make explicit. Instead, he goes on:

> He is that light, surely, which lightens the whole understanding of those who are capable of receiving truth, as it is written in the Thirty-fifth Psalm, 'In thy light shall we see light.' For what other light of God can we speak of in which a man sees light, except God's spiritual power ($\delta\acute{v}\nu\alpha\mu\iota\varsigma$) which when it lightens a man causes him either to see clearly the truth of all things or to know God himself, who is called the truth? (trans. Butterworth).

Origen here has slipped unobtrusively from making one point to making another. The original purpose of introducing the example of light, to counter the references to fire and to $\pi\nu\epsilon\hat{v}\mu\alpha$, has been passed over in favour of an argument which applies to all three epithets equally, that they are not to be taken literally but metaphorically.

---

[8]I use "Hellenic" here instead of the commonly-used term "pagan," which I find objectionable.

Why should Origen make such an apparently inconsequential move? I wish to propose two reasons, both of which illustrate his complex relationship to contemporary Platonism. The first is that, while he was well aware of contemporary Platonic doctrine on the incorporeality of light, he did not necessarily accept it himself; the second is that he also has very much in mind the Sun Simile of *Republic* VI (507a-509c), which certainly since Alexander of Aphrodisias had been brought into conjunction with Aristotle's doctrines of the Active Intellect in *De Anima* III.5 and of the Unmoved Mover in *Metaphysics* XII, and had thus been incorporated in a coordinated Peripatetic and Platonist doctrine of God as Pure Activity (ἐνέργεια) and as the *noetic* analogue of the Sun, bestowing both intelligibility and existence on all things, as well as knowledge on rational souls.

Let us explore each of these points in turn. First of all, the incorporeality of light. This is not a Platonic doctrine--neither in the *Republic* nor in the *Timaeus* is light presented as something incorporeal--but it is at least derivable from Aristotle, who, in *De Anima* II.7, declares light to be "the actuality of the transparent *qua* transparent."[9] Aristotle simply wants to make the point that light is not a substance of any kind, but a condition of a substance (countering the doctrine of Empedocles), but for later Aristotelians and Platonists this incorporeality of light became something rather special, being connected with its preeminent role in the operation of the sense of sight, the most 'honourable' of the senses (cf. Plato, *Tim.* 45B-D), and then being used as an analogy for the role of the Good (or in Alexander's theory, *Nous*) in the activation of the human intellect in its cognising of True Being.

---

[9]148b9-10: φῶς δέ ἐστιν ἡ τούτου ἐνέργεια, τοῦ διαφανοῦς ᾗ διαφανές.

Thus it is that in Alexander's *De Anima* we find, first, at pp. 42, 19-43, 11 Bruns, a straightforward paraphrase of Ar. *De An.* III.7, but then, at 88, 26-89, 6, the use of the analogy of light to illustrate the principle that "whatever is eminently some kind of being imparts this kind of being to everything which is less eminently the same kind of being," to quote Philip Merlan's formulation.[10]   The Active Intellect, being preeminently intelligible, imparts intelligibility to the "material" intellect (that is, the immanent human intellect), which becomes intelligible by intelligising the proper objects of intellect, the forms in matter. Similarly, light, being preeminently visible, is the cause of the visibility of everything visible, as well as of the seeing ability of the eyes.

This comparison of Alexander's plainly owes much to the Sun Simile of the *Republic*, and it in turn can be seen to have had considerable influence on Plotinus' view of the status of light in such passages as *Enn.* IV.5, 6-7, II.1,7 and I.6,3.[11] The evidence of Origen would seem to indicate that this identification of light as $\dot{\alpha}\sigma\dot{\omega}\mu\alpha\tau o\nu$, against the indications of Plato's doctrine in the *Timaeus*, goes back to Middle Platonism, perhaps to Numenius, or at least to Ammonius Saccas.

For a Platonist, Aristotle's doctrine as presented in *De An.* II.7 is not satisfactory, since Aristotle declares light not to be a body, not for the purpose of exalting it, but simply to deprive it of any independent existence. Quite a different connotation can be put upon this bodilessness of light if one

---

[10]In *Monopsychism, Mysticism, Metaconsciousness* (The Hague, 1969[2]), p. 39.

[11]See A. H. Armstrong, *The Architecture of the Intelligible Universe in the Philosophy of Plotinus* (Cambridge, 1940; repr. Hakkert, 1967), pp. 54-57; F. M. Schroeder, "Light and the Active Intellect in Alexander and Plotinus," *Hermes* 112 (1984), pp. 239-245.

chooses to take this, as does Alexander, and later Plotinus, as indicating that light is pure Form without an admixture of matter. In Alexander this is actually only implied in the comparison of light with the Active Intellect, but in Plotinus it is quite explicit.[12] For Plotinus, ordinary, physical light is, by reason of its freedom from admixture with body, the noblest element in the material universe.

Now as I say, Origen seems to recognize the existence of this doctrine of light, but he is not prepared to approve it. When it comes to employing the similies of the Sun and the Cave of the *Republic*, however, he has no such hesitation, although he employs them in a suitably disguised form. At *De Princ*, I. 1.5, we find the following:[13]

> Having then refuted, to the best of our ability, every interpretation which suggests that we should attribute to God any material characteristics, we assert that he is in truth incomprehensible and immeasurable.[14] For whatever may be the knowledge which we have been able to obtain about God, whether by perception or reflection, we must of necessity believe that he is far and away better than our thoughts about him. For if we see a man who can scarcely look at a glimmer or the light of the smallest lamp, and if we wish to teach such a one, whose eyesight is not strong enough

---

[12]E.g. *Enn.* I 6, 7, 17-18: light is ἀσώματον καὶ λόγος καὶ εἶδος.

[13]I use Butterworth's translation, unless otherwise noted.

[14]*Incomprehensibilis* here translates ἀκατάληπτος; *inaestimabilis* may render ἀπερίμετρος, an epithet, which, though Greek, is only found in Apuleius' *De Plat.* ch. 5, but ἀδιεξήμντος or ἀπεριόριστος are also possibilities.

to receive more light than we have said, about the brightness and splendour of the sun, shall we not have to tell him that the splendour of the sun is unspeakably and immeasurably better and more glorious than all this light he can see?

Here, and in what follows, the influence of the Simile of the Cave is palpable enough, I think,[15] but there is another element here also, which is not present in Plato's image. Plato stresses the shock and discomfort of being brought from one's comfortable viewing of the shadows on the wall cast by the fire, first to the realization that the fire is only a fire, and the figures only cardboard cutouts, and then to a view of the outside world dominated by the sun, but the end result is that one *can* view the sun, one *does* attain to a knowledge of the Good. For Origen, God is of such a nature as "the human mind, however pure or clear to the very utmost that mind may be, cannot gaze at or behold" (*ibid.*).

Now this is very much a part of the Christian doctrine of the "invisibility" of God, but it finds an echo also in a passage of Numenius' dialogue *On the Good* (Fr. 2, des Places), a work which Origen certainly knew (since he quotes from it in the *Contra Celsum*),[16] to the effect that we can gain the notion of anything bodily from comparison with things of a similar nature, but in the case of the Good, "no object present to us nor any

---

[15]Though long since formalized in Middle Platonic tradition, the Sun Simile is given by Albinus in *Did.* ch. 10 as prime example of the "way of analogy", while of the "way of ἀναγωγή" (*via eminentiae*), of which the Cave is certainly an instance, he actually gives Diotima's speech in the *Symposium* as the example. Origen uses the comparison of the light of a lamp with the light of the sun elsewhere, at *Comm. in Joh.* II.120-121 and *C.Cels.* V.II.

[16]I.15; IV.51.

sensible object similar to it gives us any means of grasping its nature."
However, Numenius is actually leading up here to his lively description of
the mystical vision of the Good, which he compares with a little fishing-
boat which by close attention one can just pick out bobbing between the
waves. Origen gives no such promise of a mystical vision in this life. The
important thing is, though, that Numenius seems here to be giving an
interpretation of the negative aspect of the Sun Simile--after all, Socrates
does emphasize at the outset, in 506 C-E, that he cannot give an account of
the Good itself, but only a series of images.

In the very next section (I.1.6), Origen seems to make further use of
the Cave Simile, though sufficiently altered as to make identification less
than obvious:

> But it will not appear out of place if to make the matter clearer still
> we use yet another illustration. Sometimes our eyes cannot look
> upon the light itself, that is, the actual sun, but when we see the
> brightness and rays of the sun as they pour into our windows, for
> example, or into any small openings for light, we are able to infer
> from these how great is the source and the foundation of physical
> light.

This seems to owe something to *Rep*. VII.515e-516b, where the prisoner,
newly freed from the Cave, cannot yet look upon the sun or bear the
sunlight: "he would find it painful to be thus dragged out, and would chafe
at it, and when he came out into the light, his eyes would be filled with its
beam so that he would not be able to see even one of the things which we
call real," and a gradual process of habituation is required. The difference, of
course, is, once again, that in Plato one does come eventually to a vision of

the Good, whereas in Origen one does not, at least in this life.[17] In fact, Origen has here subtly blended the imagery of the Cave with the later Stoic argument for the existence of God from the contemplation of his works (cf. Sextus Empiricus, *Adversus Mathematicos* IX.75-87), which suits him rather better, especially as St. Paul himself had referred to it at *Rom.* 1:20: "Ever since the creation of the world his invisible nature, namely, his eternal power and deity, has been clearly perceived in the things that have been made." But for Origen the force of this argument, in relation to the Cave Simile, is that we can get no further than inference from God's manifestations and effects to His nature; we cannot know Him as He is.

Origen certainly approves of the central images of the *Republic*, as we can see from *Contra Celsum* VII.45-6, where he first quotes Celsus making use of the Sun and the Line, and then says, "We are careful not to raise objections to good teachings, even if the authors are outside the faith," but he is not committed to the full implications of the doctrine behind them, nor does he feel constrained from modifying them with other doctrines of his own. For instance, in the next chapter of Book I (2, 7) dealing with the Son or *Logos*, he identifies the process of habitation (συνήθεια) mentioned in *Rep.* VII.516 a with the activity of the *Logos* (who is, after all, "light from light"):[18]

> . . . for it is through his brightness that the nature of the light itself
> is known and experienced. This brightness falls softly and gently on

---

[17]There seems almost an explicit contradiction of *Rep.* VII.516B, αὐτόν καθ' αὐτόν ἐν τῇ αὐτοῦ χώρᾳ δύναιτ' ἀν κατιδεῖν in I.1, 6: *mens nostra ipsum per se ipsum deum sicut est non potest intueri.*

[18]*Splendor ex luce* (presumably translating ἀπαύγασμα ἐκ φωτός) a phrase inspired by Wisdom of Solomon 7:26 and Hebrews 1:3.

the tender and weak eyes of mortal man and little by little trains and
accustoms (*adsuescens*) them to bear the light in its clearness; and
when it has removed from them all that darkens and obstructs their
vision, . . . it renders them capable of enduring the glory of the
light, becoming in this respect even a kind of mediator (μεσίτης, 1
Tim. 2:5) between men and the light.

Here, indeed, it seems as if, through Christ, we *are* enabled to see the Father,
which would be fully in the spirit of the imagery of the Cave, but in fact
Origen is allowing himself to be carried away slightly. This impression is
severely qualified in what follows (sects. 8-10), particularly by the striking
image of the immense statue, which is too big for us to view, and the
miniature statue which is its faithful copy, which we can see, and which
gives us a true image (εἰκών, *similitudo*), but still only an image, of what
we cannot see.[19]

In all this we cannot, unfortunately, be sure that Rufinus is not
indulging in a certain degree of censorship and "laundering" of the text (as he
certainly is seen to be doing in the few places where the original is available
to us), but Origen seems to be struggling with the problem of how far God is
knowable or unknowable, and to what extent Christ is the means to that
knowledge, and Platonic imagery is both a help and a hindrance to him in
this.

This is not quite the whole story, however. Origen gives ample
indication, in ch. 1 of the *Peri Archon*, that he is aware of the considerable
development that had taken place over the previous centuries in the Platonic

---

[19]This is very much in the spirit of Origen's view of Christ as the
"image of the invisible God" (Col. 1:15)--one of Origen's favorite texts (119
citations listed in *Biblia Patristica* 3).

doctrine of the nature and the knowability of God. He is influenced not only by his knowledge of the speculations of such Pythagoreanising Platonists as Moderatus and Numenius, and also possibly of the more "main-line" Platonist Albinus, but also by his acquaintance with the works of Philo, who was himself influenced by contemporary Platonism. The consensus that appears to have been reached by 200 A.D. or so was that God was both absolute Unity (μονάς, εἷς, ἕν) but also an Intellect--an Intellect, however, which is to be distinguished from a second, active, demiurgic intellect or λόγος (Moderatus, Numenius and Albinus favour a second νοῦς, Philo, Plutarch and Atticus a λόγος), by being "static" (Num. Fr. 15 des Places) as opposed to "in motion", a fount and first principle of νοῦς, or, more vaguely "something higher" (ἀνωτέρω) than νοῦς (Albinus, *Didaskalikos*, ch. 10).

Such an entity can be known, if at all, only in some rather special way. Plato's famous dictum at *Timaeus* 28c about the difficulty of discovering the nature of God and the impossibility of communicating it to the general public gave much stimulus to negative theology of various kinds in later times, but it was not until the second part of the *Parmenides* was given a metaphysical interpretation, from the 1st century A.D. on, that the problem of how the First Principle could be cognised became an acute one for Platonists. At the end of the first hypothesis (142A), we reach the conclusion about the One that "it cannot have a name or be spoken of, nor can there by any knowledge or perception or opinion of it. It is not named or spoken of, not an object of opinion or knowledge, not perceived by any creature."

If it is to be cognised at all, then, it cannot be by any 'normal' cognitive process, such as αἴσθησις, δόξα, or ἐπιστήμη. It will require a distinct supra-noetic faculty, termed poetically by the *Chaldaean Oracles* (Fr. 1.1*DP*) "the flower of the mind" (ἄνθος νοῦ), recognized by Plotinus as the νοῦς in a state of sober intoxication (*Enn.* III 5, 9; VI 7, 35), and also perhaps by Numenius in his eloquent description of the vision of the Good in Fr. 2 (mentioned above).

Origen, however, does not seem to have arrived at a formula for this special faculty. In his exhaustive study of Origen's terminology and doctrine of the modes and levels of knowledge (*Origène et la 'connaissance mystique'*),[20] despite the promising title (which he does, admittedly, enclose in inverted commas), Henri Crouzel cannot come up with any clear reference to a direct vision of God himself *in this life*. The term which best expresses the sort of direct intellectual contact envisaged by Origen for the beatific vision to be enjoyed by the saints after death is προσβολή,[21] but the significant thing here is that this same term is used by Plotinus, along with ἐπιβολή and ἐπαφή, for the sort of supranoetic contact which is attainable by the νοῦς while still in the body.[22] This is not to deny that Origen had mystical experience (Crouzel makes an eloquent case for his having had some, quoting in particular his first Homily on the Song of Songs (sec. 7),[23] but the fact remains, I think, that for theological reasons he denied that

---

[20]Paris/Bruges, 1963, pp. 496-508.

[21]Interesting passages are *Fragm. In Joh.* XIII (GCS, IV p. 495), κατ᾿ προσβολὴν νοήσεως, *Exh. ad Mart.*. XIII, where the "friends of God" will enjoy direct knowledge ἐν εἴδει, προσβάλλοντες τῇ τῶν νοητῶν φύσει καὶ τῷ τῆς ἀληθείας κάλλει; *P. Euch.* XXV, 2 ὁ νοῦς προσβάλλει τοῖς νοητοῖς.

[22]E.G. *Enn.* III.8, 10, 33 προσβολή; VI.7, 35, 21 ἐπιβολή; V.3, 10, 42 ἐπαφή.

[23]*Origène*, pp. 162-4. Even here, though, as Patricia Cox points out to me, Origen may after all only be talking about the frustrating experience of having at one moment a vision of the spiritual meaning of a certain text, only to lose it again on further reflection.

the human soul or mind, while still in the body, could achieve the equivalent, in Platonic terms, of looking directly at the sun.

* * * * * *

This has been, I fear, a rather superficial study, based only on one particular series of connected passages in one work (though a major one), of a very prolific and many-sided thinker, but, such as it is, it serves to bear out Crouzel's characterization of Origen as a "transformer" of Platonism, rather than a crypto-Platonist of any sort. One could, obviously, pursue this theme much further, in various directions. One direction that occurs to me is the paradoxical presentation of God as "darkness" ($\sigma\kappa\delta\tau\sigma$) in the *Commentary on John* (II.172), arising out of the exegesis of John 1:5, where precisely God is, after all, declared to be "light shining in darkness". By way of going one better, it would almost seem, than the traditional Platonic image of God as light and standing it on its head, but also in order to explain certain troublesome passages of the Old Testament, such as Exodus 19:9, 16, and 20:21, where God is described as enveloped in a thick cloud, and Psalm 18:11: "He made darkness his covering around him, his canopy thick clouds dark with water" (passages which, it seems, Gnostics such as Marcion had fastened on to support their argument that Jahweh was an evil Demiurge), Origen presents this "darkness" and "cloudiness" as a symbol of God's unknowability to the human intellect; in himself, of course, he remains Light.[24]

But this is just by way of coda to my main theme. It seems suitable that a discussion of Origen's use of light imagery should end, paradoxically, with a discussion of God as darkness. My main purpose has

---

[24]Cf. Crouzel, *Origène et la 'connaissance mystique'*, pp. 91-95.

been to suggest that Origen, while making extensive use of Platonic images and formulations, is never enslaved by these, but subordinates them always to his own independent purposes. In view of that I would like to substitute for the misleading notion of Origen the Neoplatonist what I hope is the more accurate picture of Origen as "Neochristian".

DIVINE TRINITY AND THE
STRUCTURE OF *PERI ARCHON*

Charles Kannengiesser
University of Notre Dame

The purpose of this paper is to inquire about the possibility of a systematic motivation lying behind the literary features of Origen's work *On First Principles*. Two main redactional scenarios seem to be the most likely, if one tries to justify the actual context of the work. Either the author composed *Peri Archon* as a consistent unit, framed by an appropriate preface and a final conclusion; or the author was compelled to a more modest procedure, in adding complementary parts to an initial section, the whole work being given the appearances of a unified project by some literary devices. In both cases, the question remains: Is there a key notion in Origen's mind for his arranging the various themes, as he knotted them together in one way or another in *Peri Archon*?

1. The literary division of *Peri Archon*

The four "books" of the work were probably a division going back to Origen himself.[1] They reflected editorial techniques of late Antiquity,[2] as

---

[1] *Origenes. Vier Bücher von den Prinzipien*, ed. Herwig Görgemanns and Heinrich Karpp, Texte zur Forschung, 24 (Darmstadt, 1976) p. 16. *Origène. Traité des Principes*, I, ed. Henri Crouzel and Manlio Simonetti, SC 252 (Paris, 1978) p. 15-16.

well as a sequence of main focuses, each of the "books" concentrating on one central issue, respectively God, the World, Freedom, Biblical Revelation.[3] Thus people have been used for a long time to justify the four books as a division *de facto* of *Peri Archon* from a doctrinal viewpoint. The thematic analysis of their contents seemed to secure for each book a clear and consistent view of their inner coherency and of their logical links to each other. Adolf von Harnack illustrated such a view in the editions of his *Dogmengeschichte* from 1885 on through 1909.[4] In 1913, the editor of *Peri Archon* in the corpus of the Academy of Berlin, Paul Koetschau, limited his remarks on the structure of the work to considering the antiquity of its division into four books and of their subdivision into nineteen chapters.[5] These "chapters" had been witnessed by Photius in the 9th century[6] as well as by the extracts from "book IV" collected in the *Philocalia* before the end of the 4th century.[7] As a matter of fact, one must admit a distinction in the

---

[2]"An erster Stelle buchtechnisch bedingt." Karpp, *Origenes. Vier Bücher von den Prinzipien*, p. 16; the division in four books "est d'ordre éditorial. Un tome c'est la quantité de texte que contient un rouleau de papyrus", Crouzel, *Origène. Traité des Principes*, I, p. 16. On books in classical and Christian Antiquity, Tönnes Kleberg, *Buchhandel and Verlagswesen in der Antike* (Darmstadt, 1969).

[3]In his Introduction, H. Karpp insists rightly on this thematic sequence, *Origenes. Vier Bücher von den Prinzipien*, p. 10-15.

[4]In the edition of 1909, repr. Darmstadt 1964, p. 662-663, no. 2.

[5]GCS 22: Origenes Werke V, *De Principiis* (Leipzig, 1913) p. CXVIII-CLII.

[6]*Bibliotheca or Myriobiblos*, Codex 8.

[7]In J. A. Robinson's edition of *The Philocalia of Origen* (Cambridge, 1893), see p. xiiiff.

style and in the dogmatic focus proper to each of the *four* books of *Peri Archon*, even if more recent research has established the overlapping of certain themes from one book to another. Thus book IV has obviously been added to the other three as a complementary introduction into Origenian hermeneutics. Book III offers six essays on theological anthropology, which seem to build up a body of doctrine written out in its own right, properly speaking a σύγγραμμα elaborated for itself, but harmoniously adjusted to books I and II. Even these first two books of *Peri Archon* differ from each other, in so far as book I presents a more synthetic and metaphysical teaching on God, whereas book II becomes, at least from chapter 4 on, more polemical and engages the reader in a plurality of open questions.

But beyond the distinction of the features proper to each of the four books, another structure of *Peri Archon* has increasingly appealed to scholars in the recent past. A broad consensus indeed among Origen students welcomes today the suggestions made in 1941 by Basilius Steidle, a Benedictine monk of Beuron, who claimed in the *Zeitschrift für die neutestamentliche Wissenschaft*,[8] that the division of the *four* books of *Peri Archon* was merely a material editorial necessity imposed in third century Alexandria, and that their content represented actually a threefold bulk of teachings: "drei Stoffmassen." There one finds a first exposition including book I and the first three chapters of book II. Then comes a "second" and longer "exposition," running from book II, chapter 4, to book IV at the end of chapter 3. Thirdly, in book IV, chapter 4 one finds a last independent section which recapitulates the whole work. The benefit of Steidle's

---

[8]"Neue Untersuchungen zu Origenes' Peri Archon": *ZNW* 40 (1941): 236-243. For a critical evaluation of Steidle's article, see M. Simonetti, "Osservazioni sulla struttura del De principiis di Origene," *Rivista di filologia e d'istruzione classica* n.s., 40 (1962): 273-290, 372-393.

observations was not so much, should I say, to reduce the division of *Peri Archon* from four to three. Certainly more important was the reason given by Steidle for imposing a threefold structure, namely that it was fitting Origen's teaching position.

In fact, Steidle had discovered what he calls "surprising parallels between *Peri Archon* and the contemporary teaching of philosophy" in his reading of Hal Koch's magisterial survey *Pronoia und Paideusis*, published in 1932, in the "Arbeiten zur Kirchengeschichte," a series edited in particular by Hans Lietzmann. Koch, a Danish scholar from the University of Copenhagen, had dedicated the longest chapter by far of his "Studien" to "Origen and the contemporary teaching of philosophy".[9] He had, for instance, underscored the structural affinities of *Peri Archon* with chapter 8, on theology and first principles, in Albinus' *Didaskalikos*, better known under the title *Epitome of Plato's Doctrines*, a middle-Platonic schoolbook of the second century C.E. Thanks to Koch's illuminating data, Steidle succeeded in shifting the critical consideration of *Peri Archon's* inner divisions from a theological viewpoint to a more secular and historical one. Henceforth the cultural setting of Origen's work opened a new access to its interpretation. Unfortunately, in a rather speculative and unconvincing way Steidle imagined that the threefold division of *Peri Archon* resulted from three courses in which Origen would have treated the same basic questions on different levels and for different audiences. But despite this blunder he opened a bright future. In the sixties and the seventies Italian and French critics, like Manlio Simonetti, Marguerite Harl and Gilles Dorival, adopted his conclusions and refined them. Finally, the threefold structuring of *Peri*

---

[9]*Pronoia und Paideusis. Studien über Origenes und sein Verhältnis zum Platonismus*, Arbeiten zur Kirchengeschichte 22 (Berlin and Leipzig, 1932), pp. 225-304.

Archon was reproduced by Henri Crouzel and Manlio Simonetti in the Sources Chrétiennes edition.[10] In this edition, two of the three main divisions of *Peri Archon* were respectively entitled "Premier cycle de traités" and "Second cycle de traités," the third of Steidle's divisions being simply called "Récapitulation." This editorial structure reflects the greater importance given since Steidle to the subdivision of *Peri Archon* into a continuous series of smaller "treatises", as witnessed already by Photius.[11]

In response to all the fruitful inquiries completed during the past three decades on the literary structure of *Peri Archon*, many observations could be made from a literary, critical, and historical point of view.[12] But for now, I would like to raise only one question concerning the methodological presuppositions implied in these studies. They seem to admit that the inner logic commanding the composition of *Peri Archon* finds itself articulated with enough critical awareness, when discussed from an "external" standpoint. Dorival evaluates his own contribution in terms highly significant of that admission. I quote him in translation: "One sees the limits of our study; far from trying to catch the original value of *Peri Archon*, it belongs to a point of view which one may specify as external."[13]

---

[10]M. Harl, "Structure et cohérence de *Peri Archon*," *Origeniana* Quaderni di "Vetera Christianorum" (Bari ,1975) p. 11-32. G. Dorival, "Remarques sur la forme du *Peri Archon*," Ibid., pp. 33-45. The SC edition includes a first volume (no. 252) quoted above note 1, and vol. II, no. 253 (1978). III, no. 268 (1980). IV, no. 269 (1980). V, no. 312 (1984).

[11]P. Kübel, "Zum Aufbau von Origenes 'De Principiis' ": *VC* 25 (1971): 31-39.

[12]The discussion on this issue is still going on, as witnessed by G. Dorival's paper, "La récapitulation du *Traité des Principes* d'Origène," at the Tenth International Conference on Patristic Studies, Oxford, 24-29 August 1987.

[13]"Remarques sur la forme du *Peri Archon*," p. 33.

2. The doctrinal motive for the distinction between the two expositions in Peri Archon

The question of method imposed on the student of Origen by Dorival's restrictive self-appraisal may be following: How far can we actually go in the study of the logical articulations and of the literary divisions in *Peri Archon* without taking into account its original motivation? In other words, would it be mistaken to ask for a clearer understanding of Origen's theological originality in the light of this fresh approach to his work which claims to be only an "external" one? Or should the exclusively contextual viewpoint, on which such a claim rests, alienate us from Origen's original creativity and from what is proper to his doctrinal message? As a matter of fact, from a more "internal" and systematic viewpoint, a whole range of fundamental questions seem to be waiting for their answers in the wave of the recent investigations concerning the literary structure of *Peri Archon*. Let us only look, for instance, at the distinction originating from Steidle and now currently made between a "first" and a "second exposition."

The "first exposition," from 1:1 to the end of 2:3, develops Origen's theory of what he calls in his Preface "matters briefly discussed in order"[14] and which he considers as "questions that are great and important,"[15] namely "on the nature of God or of the Lord Jesus Christ or of the Holy Spirit, and in addition on the nature of those created beings, the dominions and the holy

---

[14] 4:1, p. 95. For the quotations from *Peri Archon* in English, I am referring to G.W. Butterworth, *Origen. On First Principles*. New York, 1966.

[15] 1:2, p. 1.

powers."[16] In the same first part of the preface of *Peri Archon*, Origen
announces also the axiomatic character of his "first exposition." In his own
words he intends, "to lay down a definite line and unmistakable rule in regard
to each of these [questions],"[17] a rule which would secure for them "the
truth," which is "the doctrine of Christ." And he makes it quite clear that in
his present exposition "the truth . . . in no way conflicts with the tradition of
the church and the apostles."[18]

Not the slightest doubt seems allowed here on the dogmatic and
properly ecclesiastical nature of the "matters" included by Origen in the
program of his "first" exposition. It would be misleading to oppose them, as
it happens sometimes, to the doctrines discussed in the "second exposition",
for being more philosophical and less concerned by the apostolic tradition.
And probably it would be rather inaccurate to qualify them like mere
generalities or preliminaries, before the "second exposition" starts in 2:4. In
fact, what is at stake in the so-called "first exposition" of *Peri Archon* is no
less a task than what may be seen as Origen's greatest achievement as a
theologian. Here he builds up the central notion of his theology, which is
the notion of a Christian, Trinitarian God, and in doing so he completes the
unfinished apologetical program of his teacher and predecessor Clement. By
the same way he justifies the title *Peri Archon* given to the four "books" of
his work, but which fits, properly speaking, only the so-called "first
exposition", from book I to book II, chapter Three, and its final
"recapitulation". For it is Origen's epoch-making initiative as a Christian
theologian to have integrated the middle-Platonic traditions on divine

---

[16]Ibid.

[17]1:2, p.2.

[18]Ibid.

principles (*ἀρχαί*) into his notion of a Trinitarian godhead. Before discussing this initiative against its broader philosophical background, let me explore very briefly the relation of Origen to Clement on this matter, my guess being that by his initiative about the first principles Origen filled precisely a metaphysical gap never bridged by Clement as a Christian theologian.

3.   Clement of Alexandria on First Principles

Clement flourished in Alexandria during the last two decades of the second century. He was a contemporary of Celsus in that same town. He belonged to a generation of Christian apologists among which we find Irenaeus, Athenagoras, Melito and Tertullian. He left Alexandria during the persecution of Septimus Severus probably in 202-203, and continued his intellectual activity in the church of Jerusalem for another couple of decades. These biographical data serve here one purpose only. They highlight the fact that today's historians generally agree that Clement, freed from many pastoral duties in Jerusalem under the protection of bishop Alexander could elaborate there more at ease the 6th and the 7th *Stromates* as well as the treatise *Quis dives salvetur* and the doxographical compilation of the *Hypothyposeis*.[19]

---

[19]Johannes Munck, *Untersuchungen über Klemens von Alexandria*, Forschungen zur Kirchen-und Geistesgeschichte, 2 (Stuttgart, 1933) pp. 84-109: Kap. III. Die Fortsetzung der Stromateis. André Méhat. *Étude sur les 'Stromates' de Clément d'Alexandrie*, Patristica Sorbonensia, 7 (Paris, 1966) pp. 148-175: Chap. VI. Le programme des Stromates. Pierre Nautin, "La fin des Stromates et les Hypotyposes de Clément d'Alexandrie," *VC* 30 (1976): 268-302.

Now, in the first chapter of the first *Stromates* Clement announces the main topics on which he would comment in this series of, as he called them, philosophical "Tapestries," or "Miscellanies."[20]

After a treatise on ethics, there would follow his "theory on physics" (φυσικὴ θεωρία) [1:15.2]. In the third *Stromates* the bias of the still announced physics is unmistakably anti-Marcionite. I quote: "But against those people [the Marcionites] we shall argue as pointedly as possible when we grasp the treatise *On Principles*."[21] And, I quote again; "When we treat *On Principles*, then we will examine those objections invented by the philosophers and believed by the Marcionites (ἐπειδὰν δὲ περὶ τῶν ἀρχῶν διαλαμβάνωμεν . . .).[22] A few years later, at the start of the fourth *Stromates*, he repeats once more a similar announcement: "Then, later on, . . . we must expose the theory on physics about principles (τὰ περὶ ἀρχῶν φυσιολογηθέντα) proper to the Greek and to the other Barbarians, when opinions have come down to us, and we must discuss the main doctrines of the philosophers" (καὶ πρὸς τὰ κυριώτατα τῶν τοῖς φιλοσόφοις ἐπινενοηγένων ἐγχειρητέον).[23] This discussion, Clement adds, would include "the summary of the theory on God (τὴν ἐπιδρομὴν τῆς θεολογίας) . . . When we will have completed our whole project in the books which, according to the Spirit, we have to dedicate to that urgent need (namely: refuting all sorts of heresies) . . . , then we will go over to the

---

[20]Otto Stählin ed., G.C.S. 15 (Leipzig, 1906); I am quoting actually L. Früchtel, ed., *Clemens Alexandrinus* II: *Stromata* I, 3d ed. (Berlin, 1960) 15.1: p. 11, l. 16-17.

[21]*Stromata* III. 13. 1: p. 201, l. 12-13. Translation mine.

[22]21.2: p. 205, l. 11-13.

[23]*Stromata* IV. I. 2.1: p. 248, l. 15-19.

truly gnostic theory on physics (τὴν τῷ ὄντι γνωστικὴν φυσιολογίαν
μέτιμεν) . . . For the theory on physics ruled by the truth of the gnostic
tradition, or better the highest grade of initiation, starts with the teaching on
cosmogony and climbs up from there to the theological pattern" (Ἡ γοῦν
κατὰ τὸν τῆς ἀληθείας κανόνα γνωστικῆς παραδόσεως
φυσιολογία μᾶλλον δὲ ἐποπτεία, ἐκ τοῦ περὶ κοσμογονίας
ἤρτηται λόγου, ἐνθένδε ἀναβαίνουσα ἐπὶ τὸ θεολογικὸν εἶδος).
Clement concludes his outline of the planned essay on first principles in
announcing that the start of the "truly gnostic physics" would be given in the
form of a commentary on Genesis 1.[24]

In the midst of a lively discussion based on the presumption that the
Greek philosophers have stolen their doctrines from Moses and the prophets,
the author of the fifth *Stromates*, still writing in Alexandria, claims that
more arguments would be added, "when we shall collect the opinions on first
principles circulating among the Greeks" (ὁπηνίκα ἂν τὰς περὶ ἀρχῶν
δόξας τὰς παρ' Ἕλλησι φερομένας ἀναλεγώμεθα).[25] In the sixth
Stromate, probably composed after his move to Jerusalem, Clement still
makes anticipatory remarks of the same sort, like this one, about what more
should be said concerning the "mysteries" alluded to in the symbolic
language of the Greeks: "I have postponed making a clear statement on it,
until we have refuted the opinions of the Greeks on first principles."[26]

Finally, we come very close to the promised refutation, when we
read a reference to it in *Quis dives salvetur*, chapter 26, an essay from the last
period of Clement's prolific writings. About the exegesis of Mark 10:25, "It

[24]2.2: p. 248, l. 19-20, and 3.1-2: p. 249, l. 4-13.

[25]*Stromata* V. XIV. 140, 3: p. 420, l. 24-25.

[26]*Stromata* VI. II. 4.2: p. 424, l. 4-5.

is easier for a camel to pass through a needle's eye" the author remarks: "The 'higher meaning' of the 'camel' leading the 'rich' along the narrow and restricted way may be found in the exposition 'On Principles and Theology.' "[27]

In short, Clement advertising for a lifetime his forthcoming work *On Principles* prepares us to welcome Origen's achievement. There would be a discussion on theoretical physics, including their theological foundations. The work would justify Christian apologetics mainly aimed against the Marcionites and the philosophers at large. It would rest on the evidence of doxographical data and on an exegesis of Genesis. Probably less than a decade after his old master had passed away, Origen wrote his *Peri Archon*. He mentions in it that he was already engaged from an earlier time on in a commentary on Genesis. His main adversaries through the whole work are the Marcionites. And he discusses thoroughly a whole set of questions illustrating his theory on physics. But now it should be the more obvious, at the end of our comparison with Clement, that Origen's outline of a treatise *On First Principles* escaped completely the frame of the Clementine project. There, in Clement's *Stromates* composed through at least two decades, the author was engaged in a doxographic retrieving of classical doctrines on first principles. Clement's expressed purpose was to show that the partial truth contained in such doctrines had been stolen by the oldest Greek philosophers from Genesis and from the Biblical tradition. There also, Christian apologetics culminated in identifying consequently "the principle of all things" (ἡ τῶν ὅλων ἀρχή), also called "the first and oldest principle" (ἡ πρώτη καὶ πρεσβυτάτη ἀρχή),[28] with God Almighty in the Jewish

---

[27]26.8 CGS 17, *Clemens Alexandrinus* III, ed. O. Stählin, p. 177, l. 25-26.

[28]*Stromata* V. XII. 81.4: p. 380, l. 16.

scriptures. And there the Logos, Son of God, was called a divine ἀρχή in his own right (*Strom.* 5:38.7, 6:141.7, 7:2.2, 9.3).[29]

4. Trinity and First Principles in *Peri Archon's* First Exposition

With Origen we move over into a pre-established doctrine on Trinity which overrules the traditional notion of first principles. In *Peri Archon* chapter 1 of book I, God is introduced at once as Father and Son and Holy Spirit, the latter being precisely called "an intellectual existence, with a subsistence and being of its own" (ed. Butterworth, p. 9). The Three altogether are one and the same spiritual reality of a transcendent simplicity, which Origen calls a *Monas*, or "Unity," and a *Henas* or "Oneness," in any case "the mind and fount from which originates all intellectual existence or mind" (p. 10). This triune God as such is repeatedly called Father, Son and Holy Spirit in the first chapter of *Peri Archon*, for the reason that "the relations between [them] are such as pertain to the nature of deity. . . ."[30] There is much more said about the Son and the Spirit in relation to the Father, than about the Father Himself, in the initial chapter of *Peri Archon*. Thus the category of an ultimate cause and first principle of all things used in this chapter in regard to the Father is applied to him as to one of the Trinity. Thus Origen's basic notion of the Christian godhead explicitates its potential

---

[29]*Stromata* V. VI. 38.7: p. 353, 1. 1; VI. XVI. 141. 7: p. 503, 1. 32; VII.I.2.2: p. 4, 1. 6; II. 9.3: p. 8, 1. 17.

[30]Ed. Butterworth, p. 13. GCS 22, 26.5 quod vero ad naturam pertinet deitatis.

rationality from the start on as a trinitarian category established with the help of a middle-Platonic notion of first principles.

Before having a closer look at this middle-Platonic notion as assimilated by Origen in his theory on God, let us secure all the needed evidence in order to locate correctly the Origenian teaching on Trinity in the so-called "first exposition" of *Peri Archon*. In chapter 2 of book I the Christological titles, mainly those of Wisdom, Logos and Eikon, given to the Son of God, serve to distinguish diverse modes of divine causality: efficient, exemplaristic, final, etc. This diversity of causal modes of acting reveals what Origen calls God's "original goodness itself" (p. 27), whose Trinitarian nature he underscores instantly: "the original goodness must be believed to reside in God the Father, and from him both the Son and Holy Spirit undoubtedly draw into themselves the nature of that goodness existing in the fount from which the one is born and the other proceeds" (p. 25). The very condensed phrasing of this conclusion signals at least clearly enough that the second chapter of *Peri Archon*, like the first, focusses on the Trinitarian nature of the godhead. The same conclusion is true of chapter 3, on the "Holy Spirit," whose peculiar efficiency is shown as exercised, I quote, "with the authority of the whole most excellent Trinity, that is by the naming of Father, Son, and Holy Spirit" (p. 30). For, as Origen insists, "he who is born again through God (I Peter 1:3) to salvation has need of both Father and Son and Holy Spirit and will not obtain salvation apart from the entire Trinity" (p. 33). Therefore Origen covers the largest section of chapter 3 in discussing "the unity of Father, Son, and Holy Spirit" (p. 38), his purpose being to celebrate "the ceaseless work on our behalf of the Father, the Son and the Holy Spirit, . . .as ever our hearts grow in fervour and eagerness to receive and hold fast the Father, the Son and the Holy Spirit" (p. 39). In chapter 4 Origen engages the consideration of the rational natures by discussing their original fall, but his goal remains adamantly "to explain the divine blessings which are bestowed upon us by the Father, the Son and the Holy Spirit, that Trinity which is the fount of all holiness" (p. 41). In chapter 5, the loss of Lucifer and of his angels makes sense only, as an apostasy of opposing and fugitive powers, when one acknowledges that "to be stainless is a quality which belongs essentially to none except the Father, Son and Holy Spirit" (p. 50). In chapter 6, the consummation and ultimate restoration of all things means that they would be "restored, through God's goodness, through their subjection to Christ and their unity with the Holy Spirit" (p. 53). This mysterious process will tend to a sort of bodiless existence of all things in analogy "to the nature of God, that is of the Father, the Son and the Holy Spirit. . . . But exactly how it will be is known to God alone, and to those who through Christ and the Holy Spirit are the 'friends' of God" (p. 58). This is Origen's last word on Trinity in the "first exposition" of *Peri Archon*. He rests on it in the following chapters on the material cosmos, for instance in repeating at the start of book II chapter 2 that only "the Father, Son and Holy Spirit" are bodiless and "that life without a body is found in the Trinity alone" (p. 81).

Enough immediate evidence has thus been given, I hope, about the absolute priority of Trinity as a ruling category in Origen's vision, as deployed throughout the first exposition of *Peri Archon*. What is striking in this regard is that the "Recapitulation" of *Peri Archon*, in book IV, chapter 4, parallels exactly the Trinitarian characteristics of the first exposition. Origen starts by stating that nothing bodily can be conceived in the Father, the Son and the Holy Spirit. He insists on their eternity: "the statements we make about the Father and the Son and the Holy Spirit must be understood as transcending all time and all ages and all eternity. For it is this Trinity alone which exceeds all comprehension, not only of temporal but even of eternal intelligence" (p. 316). "Having briefly repeated these points concerning the doctrine of the Trinity," as Origen observes it at the beginning of paragraph 3, there follows a short note on "the mystery of the Trinity in the creation of the universe" (p. 317), and a longer one on the incarnation of the Logos, entirely considered from above, namely from a Trinitarian viewpoint. In paragraph 5, the recapitulating remarks on the salvation of human souls focus on their ability "to receive a share of the Holy Spirit, who is the Spirit of the Father and the Son, since the nature of the Trinity is one and incorporeal" (p. 320). The vision is enlarged to the noetic world as such: "for every rational nature needs to participate in the Trinity" (ibid). Again the summary on the material universe leads to a similar affirmation of divine Trinity: "there is nothing that was not made except the nature of the Father, the Son and the Holy Spirit" (p. 323). At last, the same Trinity plays a key role in the final paragraphs of the "Recapitulation": in paragraph 9, "since the nature of Father, Son and Holy Spirit, to whom alone belongs the intellectual light in which the universal creation has a share, is incorruptible and eternal . . ." (p. 326); in paragraph 10: "God the Father, with his only-begotten Son and the Holy Spirit, stand alone in his knowledge . . ." (p. 327).

What comes out of this long analysis may be formulated in two thesis:

1. Origen's "first exposition" and final "recapitulation" in *Peri Archon* offer an access to his systematic theology on Trinity. Origen entitled his presentation of such a theology by a phrase, taken over from the middle-Platonic school, namely "On First Principles."

2. Trinity assumes the function of "first principles" in Origen's theology, so that the *very notion of "first principles" becomes analogical in its Origenian status.* For the Christian theologian Origen deity and universe

are both to be considered exclusively in regard to the mystery of our salvation, in which both play a decisive role. Thus there are three first principles in one Godhead, according to Origen, the Holy Spirit being also a first principle of salvation, like the Father and the Son.

5. The background of *Peri Archon*

If I am right, my two thesis may allow a few new insights into the significance of *Peri Archon*. I wondered about the possiblity of uncovering a doctrinal ground on which the inner division of *Peri Archon* would rest. Now there is no surprise if, divine Trinity seeming to offer such a gound, one has to position Origen's work against the two major cultural figures in its immediate background.

First and foremost, in regard to Clement, the distinction between the two expositions in *Peri Archon*, with the first one resulting from a Trinitarian articulation of the author's thought, illuminates remarkably the proper motivation of Origen. He wanted to have the numerous questions debated in the second exposition framed by a substantial dogmatic statement on divine Trinity, a Trinity considered in itself and in view of a universal salvation. The first exposition and the corresponding recapitulation serve such a purpose. In other words, by such an arrangement of his rather complex work *On First Principles*, the still young theological author shows up with a central motive of his own. He does not just implement a promise of his predecessor, which would mean addressing a Christian response to the Hellenic notion of first principles. Far from doing so, Origen lets first principles play a key-role in the logical framing of his work. However, as Mozart was eager to absorb musical motives of his contemporaries in carefully transposing them into a Mozartian composition, so did Origen. He transferred the middle-Platonic theory of first principles into the properly Origenian notion of Trinity. The work which he himself may have entitled *Peri Archon*[31] was first of all in his mind a theological synthesis *Peri Triados*.

Secondly, in regard to the broader philosophical context of the Middle-Platonists, Origen structured *Peri Archon* as he did by witnessing even more his true identity as a Christian theological thinker. For Robert M. Berchman, *From Philo to Origen. Middle Platonism in Transition*,[32] "Origens' thought represents the consummation of Middle Platonic thought" (p. 100), "the final chapter in the history of Middle Platonic thought" (p. 105). And when Berchman undertakes to interpret the meaning of first principles in *Peri Archon*, he declares boldly: "We want to show how Origen formally argued his first principles, and demonstrated a Middle Platonic theoretic and epistemology from the premises of this sacred scripture. The purpose of such a study is to illustrate the strategy of philosophical debate in the Middle Academy, and to gain an insight into the situation out of which philosophical postulates were formed. This permits us to more accurately reconstruct the intellectual world of Middle Platonism" (p. 251).

The announced purpose implies a perplexing notion of Origen's position in regard to the Academy of his time. He never considered himself as belonging to the Middle Academy. Nor did he ever intend to articulate a proper argument about first principles. In reality, Berchman's Origen looks like a Middle Platonic travesty, more precisely like a hypothetical philosopher, stripped of his theological identity, or like a metaphysician

---

[31]In Eusebius, *Church History* VI. 24 (καὶ τὰ περὶ ἀρχῶν . . . γράφει), the title is enumerated among others in a conventional way.

[32]Brown Judaic Studies, 69 (Chico, Ca., 1984).

gone lost in the very contradictions which the true Origen firmly and expressedly avoided.[33] Even in his grasp of the traditional notion of first principles, the ghostly Origen depicted by Berchman would have run into some helpless contradictions: "the Father is . . . the necessary first principle of all things" (p. 118), but there are "two Ones": "The first "One" is a transcendent *monas* and *henas*. The second 'One' is a *monada* and *henada* (*sic*, p. 118); the Holy Spirit was by no means a first principle, but nevertheless: "As such, the Father, Son and Holy Spirit are the *protai ousiai* or the non-material primary forms of the universe . . . They are the *protai ousiai* and the *archai* of all things in the universe" (p. 153).

If Berchman's approach to Origen should yield any help at all for further studies, it would probably, I think, address a challenging call to the historians of Christian thought. For Berchman shows how urgent indeed appears the task of reevaluating Origen's original speculation in the line of a more carefully explored philosophical setting. But he attests also, be it in a negative and contradictory way, how the task of interpreting Origen ends in serious trouble if the interpreter ignores what historical theology means in this case. Only as a Christian theologian, bound to his own theological

---

[33]Thus Berchman states that according to Origen: "The Logos subsists like the Father . . . but does not exist like the Father, . . . the Logos exists contingently" (p. 127), "The Son . . . is the first of created beings . . . . The Son is created. The Father is eternal" (p. 128), "Like the Son, the Holy Spirit is something created or begotten" (p. 128). But Origen clearly states: "The Holy Spirit is an intellectual existence, with a subsistence and being of its own" (1.1.3). "God was always Father of his only-begotten Son. . . . This is an eternal and everlasting begetting. . . . For he does not become Son in an external way through the adoption of the Spirit, but is Son by nature" (1.2.4). "The Son's existence springs from the Father himself, yet not in time, nor from any other beginning except, as we have said, from God himself" (1.2.11). "There is absolutely no dissimilarity between the Son and the Father" (1.2.12). "We have been able to find no passage in the holy scriptures which would warrant us in saying that the Spirit was a being made or created" (1.3.3).

tradition, and passionately seminal for the theological future of the
Alexandrian Christianity, is Origen asking for his critical appraisal, in
particular in his understanding of metaphysical principles. Berchman reduces
him exclusively to a final figure of a dying Middle Academy, where he
should at least have given some weight to Origen's foundational and
paradigmatic achievement in the line of his own Christian tradition. Origen
was, so to speak, indebted by a double allegience, to both cultural and
religious trends, the one linked with the Academy, the other ecclesial. For
that reason his apropriation of the philosophical notion of first principles, in
the line of Clement's intuitions, resulted in a central category of his own
"physics". Thus he secured for the appropriated notion a new and quite
paradoxical Trinitarian understanding. The same sort of subversion, or of
sublimation if someone prefers, was being practiced by Origen in his use of
the classical "allegory". A literary and philosophical device, basic in the
Hellenistic culture, became in his mind a Christological procedure of
hermeneutics applied to Scripture. With the Greek philosophers, Origen
would refer to "first principles" according to the common use of the phrase,
but as a Christian theologian he would identify them with a divine Trinity,
source and cause of the universe,[34] but even more so in the singular and in
the plural, source and cause, of universal salvation.

---

[34]"But God, who is the beginning of all things, . . . the first
principle himself" (I.1.6; ed. Butterworth, p. 11, GCS 22, 22.4 Deum vero,
qui omnium initium est . . .). Rufinus' "initium" may easily translate $\dot{\alpha}\rho\chi\dot{\eta}$,
with its allusion to Prov. 8: 22. Cp. *Peri Archon* I. 2.5: Sapientiam vero
dei . . . subsistentiam habentem non alibi nisi in eo, qui est initium
omnium" (CGS 22, 34. 4-5).

SACRIFICE IN ORIGEN
IN THE LIGHT OF PHILONIC MODELS

Jean Laporte
University of Notre Dame

Philo of Alexandria has long been recognized as a predecessor of Origen as an allegorist, with a similar tendency to spiritualize scripture. However, Origen inherits from Philo more than a method of exegesis. More important theologically are the models provided by Philo which inspire Origen's notion of sacrifice.

Recent scholarship on sacrifice in Origen includes the following studies:

R. J. Daly wrote *Christian Sacrifice* as preparation for a study of sacrifice in Origen. He gives an up-to-date analysis of the data found in scripture and the early Christian tradition, and has an important section on Philo, but the promised study on Origen is not yet published.[1]

---

[1]R. J. Daly, *Christian Sacrifice: The Judeo-Christian Background Before Origen*, Studies in Christian Antiquity 18 (Washington, 1978).

V. Nikiprowetsky treats the spiritualization of sacrifices and worship in Philo, but he is not interested in the sacrificial system of Philo, and does not deal with the Christian tradition.[2]

L. Lies, in his *Wort und Eucharistie bei Origenes*, similarly deals with the spiritualization of the Eucharist in the early Christian tradition and in Origen. He has a large section on Philo, but does not consider the Philonic models in his sophisticated analysis of the Origenian Eucharist.[3]

F. M. Young, in *The Use of Sacrificial Ideas in Greek Christian Writers from the New Testament to John Chrysostom*,[4] shows a commendable interest in methodology but, in my opinion, this study suffers from the fact that the models used for the analysis of the biblical and Christian tradition, chiefly focussed on Origen, are borrowed from the Greek religion. The use of biblical and Philonic models, those which Origen himself follows, would have led to many different positions, particularly concerning the notion of propitiation.

I find that these authors, and generally the respected scholarship of the beginning of this century, have been too negative regarding Philo's faithfulness to the actual practice of the Law, particularly in liturgical matters. Too often scholars tended to consider Origen and Philo as twisted minds trying to teach Greek philosophy under the cover of scripture, and they simply used their writings as sources for the knowledge of Greek philosophy.

---

[2]V. Nikiprowetsky, "La spiritualisation des sacrifices et le culte sacrificiel au temple de Jerusalem chez Philon d'Alexandrie." *Semitica* XVII (1967), pp. 96-110.

[3]L. Lies, *Wort und Eucharistie bei Origenes. Zur Spiritualierungstendenz des Eucharlstieverstandnisses* (Munich, 1978).

[4]F. M. Young, *The Use of Sacrificial Ideas in Greek Christian Writers from the New Testament to John Chrysostom* (Philadelphia, 1978).

We must first admit the fact that, together with the New Testament, Philo is the chief source of Origen's teaching on sacrifice as on many other things. Philo provides the basis of Origen's doctrines of the Eucharist and of forgiveness, which are closely related to sacrifice.[5] We must also understand that Origen does not only make an occasional use of Philo, but relies on the Philonic models for his explanation of the Eucharist and of forgiveness, therefore, of sacrifice.

Moreover, we must go beyond the disgust of the uninitiated for the Philonic allegory. Many scholars have been, as it were, dazzled by Philo's spiritual exegesis. However, a long acquaintance with Philo shows that, through allegory, Philo does not actually empty the precept, but extends it to the realities which are proper to the soul. Philo thinks that the Law provides the right concept and reasoning for the treatment of these matters as well. For Philo, it is still the Law of Moses, the will of God, which rules the life of the soul.

Therefore, the Philonic allegory does not propose to reduce the Law and its ritual to a pretext to extol Truth and Love and other Platonic Forms as Augustine does. It provides, on the contrary, a way to remain faithful to the Law, to become more faithful to the Law, to resist assimilation of Hellenism. Through meditation on the Law and its practice, the Philonic allegory aimed, in a world impregnated with the Hellenistic "psychologism," at putting the Law and its observation into people's faith and life.

---

[5]J. Laporte, "Philonic Models in Origen's Doctrine of Forgiveness," paper presented at the North American Academy of Liturgy (January, 1986); "Sacrifice and Forgiveness in Philo of Alexandria," paper presented at the Oxford Patristics Conference (September, 1983); *Eucharistia in Philo of Alexandria* (New York, 1983); "Philonic Models of Eucharistia in the Eucharist of Origen," *Laval théologique et philosophique*, 42, I (fevrier, 1986), pp. 71-91.

The same remark can be made about Origen's exegesis. First, Origen inherited the Philonic teaching. Secondly, he refused to see the Christian understanding of scripture, of God, of Christ, of baptism, of the Eucharist, of forgiveness, etc., mutilated by a kind of Christian fundamentalism emptying Christian exegesis of the theology attested in the Gospels and in Paul.

We do not need to forage in the various fields covered by the History of Religions, not even Greece, in order to define our Philonic models of sacrifice. We just have to open the book of Leviticus. There we find the three principal forms of sacrifice in which Philo is interested: whole-burnt offerings, sacrifices of salvation, and sacrifices for sin. These are the models to be considered here in both Philo and Origen.

First, we deal with the first-fruits, which were brought to the altar, and were represented in most sacrifices by the vegetable offering. Then, we deal with holocaust, sacrifice of salvation, and sacrifice for sin, particularly at Yom-Kippur. We add to the section on sacrifice of salvation a discussion of the Jewish Passover and of the Last Supper, and make some remarks on the relevance of the covenant sacrifice as a regular model of sacrifice. And we complete the section on sacrifice for sin with a discussion of the meaning of the incense-offering at Yom-Kippur and with remarks on sacrificial purifications.

Three components of sacrifice require our attention: the victim, the priest, and the altar. They can be considered literally, with moral implications, and allegorically. In the allegorical interpretation, the sacrifice is internalized: the soul is the altar, or temple, as well as the priest, and the victim.

First Fruits

The first fruits, by extension but properly, can be considered as sacrifices because they are brought to the temple and given to God. Such is the opinion of Philo who, significantly, uses the term ἀπαρχή, not only for the ordinary gift of first fruits to the temple, but also for the vegetable offerings brought to the altar and considered as part of a sacrifice.

Vegetable offerings are found in a holocaust, a sacrifice of salvation, a sacrifice for sin. For Philo the show-bread and other offerings of unleavened bread, the loaves offered at Pentecost, the sheaf, the basket--all are ἀπαρχή.[6] We read in *Spec. Leg.* I, 152, that the first fruits are first brought to the temple as thank-offering (χαριστηρίους ἀνάγειν ἀπαρχάς), and then received by the priests as bestowed by God.

For Philo the laws concerning first fruits have moral implications.[7] More particularly, the best inclinations of our soul are first fruits, not, Philo says, because they are earlier in time, but because they are first in value.[8] Philo completes this moral interpretation with an allegorical development.[9] Commenting on Lev. 2:14, the offering of wheat ears νέα, πεφρύγμενα, χίδρα ἐρικτά, Philo explains that, 1) νέα figures "new, fresh, blessed thoughts from the ever ageless God;" 2) πεφρύγμενα ("roasted") means "tested by the might of reason, as gold is tested by the furnace;" 3) χίδρα ("sliced") refers to the division of the εὐχαριστία into its proper sections;

---

[6]Laporte, *Eucharistia*, pp. 77-88.

[7]Ex. 23:19; 34:26; Lev. 19:24; 23:9-11, 15-17; Num. 18:12; 28:2.

[8]Philo, *Sacr.*, 73-76; 106-114; *Sp. Leg.* I. 117-161; Laporte, *Eucharistia*, pp. 70-72.

[9]Philo, *Sacr.*, 76-84.

4) ἐρικτά ("pounded") is the result of "lingering over the thoughts presented to our mind."

On a more humble level of intellectual sophistication, the first fruits are also the offering of ordinary people consisting in the virtues and good deeds of common life and activity, for instance the exercise of a craft.[10]

Origen's teaching on the first fruits follows Philo very closely. For Origen the Christians must certainly offer the first fruits of their labor in the material sense.[11] Origen repeats Philo on the vegetable offerings connected with sacrifices, show bread, etc., when he comments on the same texts.[12] For instance, for Origen as for Philo the fine-flour offered by the poor is the offering of their daily life: agriculture, sailing, a craft, etc.[13] Like Philo, Origen interprets the feast of Pentecost as the feast of First-Fruits. But, because of Acts of Apostles ch. 2, he lays the emphasis on the "fruits of the Holy Spirit," which are joy and love.[14] Origen also refers to Christ, the Apostles, the Christian martyrs, even the Gospel of John among other books of the New Testament, as first-fruits.[15] Here we find a Christological interpretation.

---

[10]Ibid., 112-117.

[11]L. Vischer, *Tithing in the Early Church* (Philadelphia, 1966); Origen, *Hom. on Num. XI, 2*, SC 29, pp. 207-209, PG XII, 644.

[12]Origen, *Hom. on Lev. I, II, passim* SC 286, pp. 68-118.

[13]Origen, *Hom. on Lev. II*, SC 286, p.96.

[14]Origen, *Hom. on Lev. II, 2*, SC 286, p. 98. *Hom. on Num. XI, 8*, SC 29, pp. 227-233, PG XII, 654.

[15]Origen, *Hom. on Num. XI, 3*, SC 29, pp. 210-220, PG XII, 645-647; *First Principles* I. 3, SC 252, pp. 148-154; *Comm. on John I, 12-23*, SC 120, pp. 64-70.

The developments of Origen on the manna as the bread of the word
of God, and on the Christological interpretation of this bread, which are
related to the vegetable offering, are typical of the way Origen repeats Philo,
and then completes his teaching with a Christological interpretation. The
bread is *carnem verbi*, the flesh of the word, and the wine is the redeeming
blood of Christ.[16]

This is the pattern of reasoning in Origen. Origen generally repeats
Philo in his interpretation of the literal meaning and of its moral
implications, with or without the help of allegory. With the allegorical
method, he deals with the life of the soul, which as well ought to be ruled
according to the Law. Such developments are the consequence of the
Hellenistic interest in psychology. But Origen adds the Christian
component: a Christological interpretation, and its implication in Christian
life.

Holocausts

Philo interprets the whole-burnt offering as $\epsilon\dot{v}\chi\alpha\rho\iota\sigma\tau\dot{\iota}\alpha$ in the
sense of praise and confession of God's gifts. It is not bare thanks. $\Theta\upsilon\sigma\dot{\iota}\alpha$
is the proper term for sacrifice, and remains the basic term for the holocaust
together with the more specific term $\dot{o}\lambda o\kappa\alpha\dot{\upsilon}\tau\omega\mu\alpha$, "whole-burnt offering."
In Philo, the altar of whole-burnt offerings ($\theta\upsilon\sigma\iota\alpha\sigma\tau\dot{\eta}\rho\iota o\nu$) suggests
$\epsilon\dot{\upsilon}\chi\alpha\rho\iota\sigma\tau\dot{\iota}\alpha$ for the products of the earth, and allegorically for the body.[17]
The flame on the altar is seen by Philo as consecrating ($\kappa\alpha\theta\iota\epsilon\rho o\tilde{\upsilon}\nu\tau\alpha\iota$) and

---

[16]Origen, *Hom. on Gen. X, 3*, SC 7 bis, pp. 262-264; *Hom. on Num. XXIII, 8*, SC 29, pp. 448-449, PG XII, 752; *Comm. on Mat. 26:26-30, Comm. Ser. 84*, GCS XI, p. 197.

[17]Philo, *Sp. Leg. I.* 169-171; *Q.E. II*, 100-102.

uniting all sacrifices into the same $\epsilon\dot{v}\chi\alpha\rho\iota\sigma\tau\acute{\iota}\alpha$. The accompanying vegetable offering is eucharistic as seen above.[18]

The moral implications of the holocaust are best seen in the Philonic symbolism of the division of the holocaust, which reflects a well-structured Eucharistic prayer for the gifts of creation. After a recognition of God's existence, thanks are given for the Cosmos, then for the individual person, body and soul and all their parts.[19]

We find nothing in Philo about an atoning use of the daily holocaust.

The figure of the high-priest, who is the Priest par excellence, is deeply connected with the sacrifice of praise and gratitude. Philo distinguishes: 1) the high-priest ministering in the temple of Jerusalem, 2) the high-priest Logos involved in the creation of the universe and giving thanks for it together with the heavens and the human mind. This second symbolism is represented by the high priest wearing the so-called "cosmic"robe.[20] Another version of this same cosmic $\epsilon\dot{v}\chi\alpha\rho\iota\sigma\tau\acute{\iota}\alpha$ is given in the story of the Muses and their mother Mnemosyne, "Memory," the memory of the works of God.[21] 3) The high-priest entering the temple in his linen tunic only, without his solemn robe, figures the spiritual sacrifice of the Logos pouring himself as a libation before God.[22] 4) The double

---

[18]Philo, *Sp. Leg. I*, 172-176, 286; II   161, cf.; Laporte, *Eucharistia*, pp. 65-88.

[19]Philo, *Sp. Leg. I*, 208-211.

[20]Philo, *Mos. II*, 109-130; *Q.E. II*, 107.

[21]Philo, *Plant.*, 126-131.

[22]Philo, *Som. II* 108-183, 249.

appearance of the high-priest with his cosmic robe, or with his simple tunic, respectively figures our common human εὐχαριστία under the form of both a cosmic praise and under the form of the spiritual sacrifice.

In this spiritual sacrifice the intermediary of the high-priest Logos may no longer be needed. We are put "in place of the Logos." As an intermediary--a minister only--the divine Logos seems to vanish, and the human λόγος, our reason, becomes the high-priest and performs the offering of the self.[23]

Εὐχαριστία as praise of God is also expressed by εὐλογεῖν, τιμεῖν, ὑμνεῖν, αἰνεῖν, ἐχομολογεῖσθαι, μακαρίζειν, which are not sacrificial terms, although somehow they may by extension share in the connotation of sacrifice in the way prayer can be understood as sacrifice.[24]

Origen repeats the terminology and teaching of Philo about the whole-burnt offering: the altar, the flame, the victim, the priest are eucharistic.[25]

But Origen always refers to Christ when he deals with sacrifice. For instance, the bull of the holocaust in Lev. 1 is Christ, the *saginatus vitulus*. Like the he-goat of the sacrifice for sin, Christ perished outside the camp. He was chosen a "blameless male", i.e., a virtuous man who, like the suffering-Servant of Isaiah 53, died for the remission of our sins, not because of sins of his own. Annas and Caiphas laid their hand on him, charging on him the

---

[23]Philo, *Q.E. II* 37-40; *Conf.* 58-63; 145-149.

[24]Laporte, *Eucharistia*, pp. 26-47.

[25]Origen, *Hom. on Lev. IV, 6-10*, SC 286, pp. 108-200; *Hom. on Lev. II, 2*, p. 78.

sins of mankind. His sacrifice reached beyond the veil of the flesh unto the heavenly altar, thereby purifying both those on earth and those in heaven.[26]

The dismembering of the holocaust in Origen cannot simply, as in Philo, figure a eucharistic prayer for the parts of the cosmos and the anthropos. It becomes the symbol of the various manners of touching Christ. The Canaanite woman touched his garments; Magdalen washed his feet with her tears and then she anointed his head with perfumes; John leaned on his breast.[27]

Just as there is a progress towards intimacy with Christ in the manner of touching him, there is a progress in the type of spiritual food we can assimilate. The word of God is given, according to our capacity, as milk, vegetable, or solid food.[28] This progress attests that we are aiming toward a spiritual perception of Christ beyond the flesh, to a communication with Christ as the divine Logos in the manner of the prophets.[29]

The idea of communicating with Christ on a higher level of faith leads to the consideration of a mediation of Christ as the divine Logos similar to the eucharistic mediation of the divine Logos in Philo.[30] For Origen, Christ is not simply mediator as man, but also as the divine

---

[26]Origen, *Hom. on Lev. I, 2-3*, SC 286, pp. 73-78.

[27]F. Bertrand, *Mystique de Jesus chez Origène* (Paris, 1951).

[28]Origen, *Hom. on Ex. VII, 8*, SC 16, pp. 177-181.

[29]Origen, *Hom. on Lev. I, 4*, SC 286, pp. 80-84; *Comm. on John II, 1-11*, SC 120, pp. 208-215.

[30]Origen, *Contra Celsum* VIII, 28, SC 105, p. 232; 67, pp. 328-330; Laporte, "Philonic Models of Eucharistia in the Eucharist of Origen," pp. 81-85.

Logos.[31] For this reason, more than once, Origen insists on the necessity of making the Eucharistic prayer not to the Son only, but to the Father through the Son, or to the Father and to the Son who will carry it to the Father. The most striking of these texts is found in Origen's treatise *On Prayer* 15-18.[32]

Origen's dependance on the epistle to the Hebrews (5:1-11) for the notion of Christ, "mediator as man", i.e., as the victim and priest of a sacrifice for sin, does not prevent him from considering, together with Philo, the divine Logos as the high-priest of $\epsilon \vec{v} \chi \alpha \rho \iota \sigma \tau \iota a$. Origen differs from Philo in that for him the Logos, Christ, is a person properly speaking. Therefore, the mediation of the Logos between us and God can never vanish as it does in Philo. Although Philo paved the way to the Christian Logos and Trinity, his theory of the divine Powers does not imply for them the possession of an individual existence.

Sacrifice of Salvation

Leviticus 3 deals with the communion sacrifice, which Philo calls "sacrifice of salvation", $\theta \upsilon \sigma \iota \alpha \nu$ $\mathring{\eta} \nu$ $\mathring{\omega} \nu \acute{o} \mu \alpha \sigma \epsilon$ $\sigma \omega \tau \acute{\eta} \rho \iota \upsilon \nu$.[33] This kind of sacrifice gives thanks for the gifts of God, first of all, when we are enjoying material and moral prosperity. If we benefit of such a prosperity, we offer a

---

[31]Origen, *Contra Celsum* VIII, 26, SC 150, p. 232; 67, pp. 328; Laporte, "Philonic Models of Eucharistia in the Eucharist of Origen," pp. 81-85.

[32]Origen, *On Prayer*, 15-16, ACW 19, pp. 57-62; cf. *Contra Celsum* VIII, 26, SC 150, p. 132; 66-67, pp. 326-330.

[33]Philo, *Sp. Leg. I* 196; 212-225.

special sacrifice of salvation which is called the "praise-offering", ἡ θυσία ἡ λεγομένη τῆς αἰνήσεως, the biblical *todah*.[34]

Philo enlarges on the symbolism of the victims accepted in sacrifices of salvation, on the meaning of the limitation of time imposed for eating the victim, and on the symbolism of the portion of the priest: the shoulder and the breast, in whose removal Philo sees a symbol of ἀπάθεια.[35] We may add to the list of sacrifices of thanksgiving in Philo the references to χαριστήριον, to εὐχαριστίαι (in the plural), to ἀνάθεμα, etc.[36]

Most interesting is Philo's understanding of the communion sacrifice as a common meal in which God is the host, and where he treats us as his guests with the flesh of the victim.[37] The best illustration in Philo is probably the reference to the "ancient sacrifices with their banquets", where the ancient Sages--Philo probably means the ancient Israelites, or perhaps the ancient Greek men mentioned by Aristotle--enjoyed the pleasure of friendship after a sacrifice, and sang hymns to God in the warmth of a "sober drunkenness."[38]

At first sight, Origen does not have much to say about sacrifices of salvation, at least from what appears in his commentary on Leviticus 3 where he repeats Philo.[39] Elsewhere Origen makes use of the category of

---

[34]Leviticus 3; 7:11-21; Philo, *Sp. Leg. I*, 251-252.

[35]Philo, *Leg. Al. III*, 114-150.

[36]Laporte, *Eucharistia*, pp. 36-47.

[37]Philo, *Sp. Leg. I*, 231.

[38]Philo, *Plant.* 161-163; Aristotle, *Nic. Ethics* VIII, 11, 25-30.

[39]Origen, *Hom. on Lev. I*, SC, 286, pp. 232-246; *Hom. on Lev. II, 2*, SC 286, p. 96.

the sacrifice of communion in relation to the Eucharist. In Origen's opinion, the most interesting of all sacrifices of salvation celebrated with a banquet and hymns is certainly the Last Supper.

Before dealing with the Last Supper in Origen, we must say a few words about the Paschal sacrifice in Philo, which is a foundation for the teaching of Origen on the Last Supper.

The Pasch is an interesting kind of sacrifice in Philo, who interprets it literally as a spontaneous sacrifice offered by the people of Israel in order to give thanks for the liberation of their from the bondage of Pharaoh in Egypt and for their establishment in the land of Canaan. This pious gesture turned Israel into a priestly nation in which everyone is basically a priest, although an institutional priesthood was established later on for the service of the altar and of the tabernacle.[40]

As a moral implication, Philo sees in the Pasch a passage, διαβατήρια - διάβασις from the bondage of the body and the passions to the acquisition of self-mastery and the other virtues.[41]

Origen repeats this last teaching of Philo on the symbolism of the Passover as a pilgrimage from sin toward perfection. The best illustration of this theme is the twenty-seventh homily on Numbers which comments on the spiritual meaning of each station in the desert.[42]

Origen also repeats the Philonic theme of the priesthood of the faithful. First, like Philo, Origen shows that all the faithful are priests of

---

[40]Philo, *Sp. Leg. II*, 145-149; *Q.E. I.* 10.

[41]Philo, *Sp. Leg. II*, 147; *Q.E. I*, 13-19; *Leg. Al. III*, 165, 172; *Sacr.*, 63.

[42]Origen, *Hom. on Num. XXVII, passim,* SC 29, pp. 5ll-557, PG XII, 780-801.

their own sacrifices, whether sacrifices of thanksgiving, or sacrifices for sin.[43] He invites the fathers present in the congregation to be, like Abraham, ready to offer up to God the sacrifice of their child. This makes sense when we remember that infant mortality affected every family in the past.[44]

In addition, like the apostles, the martyrs, and the priests of the Church, the Christians share in the priesthood of Christ. Origen acknowledges the value of their modest sacrifice as praise or atonement, and the quasi-priestly ministry of good Christians who care for their weaker brethren and do not hesitate to warn sinners.[45]

The most important aspect of the Pasch, as usual with Origen, is Christological. Origen likes to repeat the statement of Paul, "Christ, our Pasch, has been sacrificed" (1 Cor. 5:7) and that of John the Baptist in the Johannine Gospel, "Behold, the Lamb of God, who takes away the sin of the world" (1:39). Origen also refers to similar statements in Jeremiah (Jer. 11:19), and in the poem of the Suffering Servant, concerning the lamb of God innocent but slaughtered because of our sins.[46] In addition, Origen interprets the Last Supper as following and fulfilling the prophecy of the meal of the Jewish Passover. Many references could be brought forth. The best texts are the *Commentary on Matthew* 26:17-30 on the Last Supper, and

---

[43]Origen, *Hom. on Lev. II, 4*, SC 286, pp. 110-112; *Hom. on Ex. IX, 4*, SC 16, pp. 213-220; PG XII, 366-369.

[44]Origen, *Hom. on Gen. VIII, 7*, SC 7 bis, pp. 224-226.

[45]Origen, *Hom. on Num. X, 2*, SC 29, pp. 193-196, PG XII, 638-40: *Hom. on Lev. V, 4*, SC 286, p. 224.

[46]Origen, *Hom. on Num. XXIII, 6-7*, SC 29, pp. 448-450, PG XII, 752-753; *Contra Celsum* VIII 43, SC 150, p. 268; *Hom. on Jer. X, 1*, SC 232, p. 398.

because the section of the *Commentary on John* 6 is missing, a series of passages dealing with the Bread of Life.[47]

Origen does not seem to be troubled by the twofold definition of the sacrifice of Christ, the one based on the feast of Passover in March, the second on the feast of Yom-Kippur in September. Origen favors a diversity of approach to the mystery of Christ, and sees in such diversity a way provided by Scripture to complete our understanding of it. Moreover, the Last Supper and the Epistle to the Hebrews--which develops the theme of Yom-Kippur--have in common two basic affirmations which characterize the sacrifice of Christ: the blood of Christ is poured out 1) for the remission of our sins, and 2) for the conclusion of the New Covenant with God.

More than once, Origen refers to the covenant in the blood of Christ.[48] He is invited to do so by the clause of the Last Supper: "the New Covenant in my blood," and by the emphasis of the epistle to the Hebrews on Christ as the mediator of a new and perfect covenant. Christ is both the priest and victim of the sacrifice lying at the foundation of this Covenant

Philo enlarges on the sacrifice of the covenant with Abraham, from which he derives allegorical teachings on the duty of εὐχαριστία,[49] but he does not provide Origen with a model of covenant sacrifice because such a sacrifice, in principle, is unique, and does not figure among the regular and usual forms of sacrifice in Leviticus.

---

[47]Origen, *On Mat.*: GCS XI, *Comm. Ser. 79-86*, pp. 189-200; cf. *Hom. on Lev. VII. 5*, SC 286, pp. 336-338; *Hom. on Gen. X, 3*, SC 7 bis, pp. 262-264; *Comm. on Mat. X, 24-25, XI, 1-7*, pp. 258-302; *Comm. on John X*, SC 157, pp. 438-449.

[48]Origen, *Comm. on Rom. 4:23-25*, J. Scherer, *Le Commentaire d'Origène sur Romains III; 5 - V:7* (Cairo, 1957), p. 222; *Hom. on Gen. III, 7*, SC 7 bis, pp. 140-142.

[49]Philo, *Q.G.* III 3-7, *Her.*, 125-137.

The Sacrifice for Sin

We may retain as the chief terms pertaining to the "sacrifice for sin" in Philo--the same as in Septuagint--the name ἡ θυσία περὶ ἁμαρτίας, or περὶ πλημμελείας, and the verb ἰλάσκεσθαι ("to wash off," "to cover," in the sense of forgiveness), together with connected terms: ἵλαος (propitious), ἱλαστήριον (the mercy-seat, the kapporeth), and ἱλασμός (expiation, propitiation). The Latin parallels are "to make God propitius, propitiatio, repropitiatio, placare, expiare."[50]

Philo deals both with ordinary sacrifices for sin and with the lost solemn sacrifice for sin in the ritual of propitiation by the high-priest at Yom-Kippur. A sacrifice for sin regularly included a ritual of propitiation by blood, and was considered as a holy sacrifice, since the priests, eating their portion of the victim, attested that it was offered by a repenting and thereby forgiven sinner.[51]

For Philo, repentance was the most necessary component of a sacrifice for sin, and required a confession of sin before God and, to some extent, before the priest. It also eventually supposed the reparation of damage caused to neighbor, and restitution.[52]

The sacrifice of the he-goat at Yom-Kippur with the pouring of blood on the mercy-seat and the ritual of incense at the same place, beyond

---

[50]K. Grayston, "*Hilaskesthai* and related words in LXX," *New Testament Studies* 27 (1980-1981), pp. 640-656; *Sp. Leg. I* 194, 226-246 (ἡ θυσία περὶ ἁμαρτίας περὶ πλημμελείας).

[51]Philo, *Sp. Leg. I*, 242-243.

[52]Ibid., 236-237.

the veil of the Holy of Holies, was a magnified form of the sacrifice for sin. Philo enlarges on the solemnity of the Fast and on the willingness on that day of all Jews, even the least zealous of them, to fast and to humble themselves, to confess their sins, to engage a moral conversion, and thus obtain, through the propitiation made by the high-priest, the remission of their sins, both voluntary and involuntary.[53]

An ordinary sacrifice for sin included all these elements in a reduced form, particularly repentance and confession of sin. These elements reappear elsewhere in Philo without the context of a sacrifice for sin, and they seem to be sufficient by themselves for obtaining forgiveness from God.[54] This observation simply attests that the sacrifice for sin purified the conscience from moral sins and not simply from "levitical" sins, or impurities. Since the emphasis was laid on moral sins, it was proper to consider the possibility of their "atonement" through moral means.

Origen is very interested in the sacrifice for sin generally and in its magnified form at Yom-Kippur, which had already been exploited by the epistle to the Hebrews in a Christological sense. In regard to this Christological meaning, I select two instances among many.

In *Homily 2 on Leviticus* 4,[55] Origen answers the objection that, after baptism, the Christians have no recourse to the sacrifice for sin as did the ancient Israelites. Origen answers that there are seven remissions available to the Christians, each corresponding to one of the victims of the biblical sacrifice for sin. The young bull figures baptism; the he-goat martyrdom; the young goats figure forgiveness granted to others; the sheep

---

[53]Ibid., 188-193; II 196.

[54]Philo, *Som.* I, 87-91; II, 289.

[55]SC 286, pp. 106-112.

and lamb figure remedy to anger; the dove figures the remission obtained through meditation on Scripture (probably when we convert a sinner); the pair of turtle-doves figure charity (as do also the fine flour baked in oil, and the the dove's little ones).

The seventh and last remission is the hard way of penance, which includes confession to the priest, repentance with tears, mortification of the flesh, eventually public confession in order to obtain the intercession of the community or, at least, in order to make it clear that we are our own accuser, and that we accept shame now in order to escape the condemnation and shame of the tribunal of God at the Last Judgment.[56]

We can consider these remissions as moral implications of the sacrifice for sin in the manner of Philo. They also represent classical remissions known in Philo, in Palestinian Judaism, and in early Christian writers. Just as in Philo, they preserve in Origen a link with the actual sacrifice for sin. For Origen, of course, this link is with the sacrifice of Christ.

The connection between the sacrifice of Christ and the remission of sins is the object of *Homily 9 on Leviticus* and parallels,[57] where Origen exploits the image of the ritual of propitiation by the high-priest at Yom-Kippur. This theme had already been developed by the epistle to the Hebrews. Origen follows Hebrews. At the same time, he also reflects Philo's comment on the ritual of Yom-Kippur.

Origen clearly defines the death of Christ as a sacrifice for sin. He interprets II Cor. 5:21, "Christ has been made sin for us" in the sense of a

---

[56]Origen, *Hom. II in Ps. 37*, PG XII, 1381.

[57]Origen, *Hom. on Lev. IX*, SC 287, pp. 70-126.

sacrifice for sin.[58]   The application of the remission resulting from this sacrifice is clear in baptism.   In the case of sins committed after baptism, the remission is no longer the simple and joyful gift of forgiveness to an already well disposed catechumen,[59] but requires proper repentance: that is, the hard way of penance with tears, fasting, confession before God, and eventually the shame of a public confession before the community.   The term "mortification" adequately explains the link between penance and the death of Christ.[60]   Paul, Origen notes, gave this interpretation of penance when he spoke of "being crucified together with Christ," and of "putting to death the old man in ourselves in order to become a new man in Christ."   It is not that Christ is crucified again for a fallen Christian, but that repentance and hard penance for purposes of forgiveness are an assimilation to the death of Christ.[61]

Both Philo and Origen see in the process of forgiveness for grievous sins the necessity of mastering ("mortifying") the flesh, or of moral conversion.   Both Philo and Origen resolve the problem of the quasi-impossibility, according to the teaching of Leviticus, for a grievous sin to be forgiven.   According to Leviticus 4:2; 5:15-16, only involuntary sins can be forgiven. How is it then possible to obtain the remission of voluntary sins by way of sacrifice, even at Yom-Kippur, as it was then generally assumed?

---

[58]Origen, *Hom. on Lev. III, 1*, SC 287, p. 121.

[59]Origen, *Contra Celsum* III 78-79, SC 136, pp. 176-178.

[60]Origen, *Hom. on Lev. IX, 3*, SC 287, p. 82; *Hom. on Lev. X, 2*, ibid., p. 138; *Hom. on Lev. XI, 2*, ibid., pp. 156-158; *Hom. on Lev. XIV, 4*, ibid., p. 242; *Hom. on Jer. XIII-XVIII*, SC 238, pp. 52-214.

[61]Heb. 9:26-28; 10:26.

The answer is the same in Philo and Origen, and relies on the interpretation of the notion of involuntary sin. According to Philo, if such a sinner:

> ... after having apparently escaped conviction by his accusers, but now, convicted inwardly by his conscience, becomes his own accuser, reproaches himself for his disavowals and perjuries, makes a plain confession of the wrong he has committed and asks for pardon, the lawgiver orders that forgiveness be extended to such a person on condition that he verifies his repentance not by a mere promise but by his actions, i.e., by restoring the deposit or the property which he has seized or found or in any way usurped from his neighbor, and by paying an additional fifth as a solatium for the offence. And when he has thus propitiated (hilasetai) the injured person, he must follow it up, says the lawgiver, by proceeding to the temple to ask for remission of his sins, and the sacrifice prescribed for him is a ram, as also for the offender in sacred matters.[62]

Origen gives the same interpretation of the voluntary sin (Lev. 5:4-5). When a grievous sin becomes the object of awareness at the tribunal of the moral conscience, and thus the object of repentance, reparation and forgiveness, in some regard this sin enters the class of sin by inadvertance, or involuntary sin.[63]

---

[62]Philo, *Sp. Leg.* I, 235-238.

[63]Origen, *Hom. on Jer. XIII - XVIII*, SC 286, pp. 52-214; *Hom. on Lev. IX, 8*, SC 287, p. 112.

Origen declares that, if we become our own accuser, the devil has no case to make against us at the last judgment, and that, according to David (Ps. 31:5), "to confess one's sins is to deserve forgiveness."[64] In his *Homily on Psalm 37*, Origen enlarges on the remission of grievous sins, the advantage of confession, and the process of public penance.[65] It is noteworthy that Origen not only speculates on the free-will in the manner of the Greeks, but, like Philo, discusses the problem of the remission of grievous sins, i.e., voluntary sins, in the light of the rules for the sacrifice for sin.

For Philo, the high-priest Logos, who is essentially a mediator of thanksgiving, does not become priest or victim of a sacrifice for sin as does Christ in Origen.

Following the epistle to the Hebrews, Origen affirms the mediation of Christ as man for the remission of sins because a man is expected to suffer and die.[66]

There is in Philo a kind of adjustment of God to the weakness and sin of men which is comparable to the Incarnation. It is Philo's theory of the powers and his interpretation of the biblical anthropomorphisms.[67] But the Philonic Powers are physicians, pedagogues, even judges: neither intercessors nor victims. And biblical anthropomorphisms are simply a form

---

[64]Origen, *Hom. on Lev. III, 4*, SC 286, pp. 140-142, cf. Lev. 5:5-6.

[65]Origen, *Hom. on Ps. 87*, 1-2, PG XII, 1367-81; *Hom. on Lev. XI and XIV*, SC 287, pp. 150-159, 226-248.

[66]Origen, *Hom. on Ex. IX, 1*, SC 16, p. 206; *Hom. on Lev. II, 3-4*, SC 286, pp. 102-106; *Hom. on Lev. III, 1*, ibid., p. 120.

[67]Philo, *Fug.*, 100-106; *Q.G.* IV, 51; *Q.E.* II, 21, *Som. I*, 235-236.

of divine language adjusted to our carnal understanding or to the hardness of our heart, for instance when they speak of divine wrath and revenge.[68] They invite us to answer with the language of expiation. But they deal with correction, not sacrifice.

The language of sacrifice reappears in the allegorical representation of the internal sacrifice of the soul. We have seen above that we are invited by both Philo and Origen to offer the sacrifice of prayer and the first fruits of our good thoughts, of virtue and self. Similarly we must offer on the altar of our soul the sacrifice for sin. Origen insists on this latter aspect more than Philo.

For instance, in *Homily 5 on Leviticus*, Origen reminds us that there are in our soul spiritual bulls, sheep, goats, birds ready for sacrifice. In the temple of our soul we must offer both whole-burnt offerings and sacrifices for sin. We offer sacrifices for sin when we offer up to God a contrite heart, a broken spirit in a holy place, and the soul of a repenting sinner is a holy place. We offer this sacrifice before the Lord, i.e., in a sincere confession.[69]

But Origen soon passes to a Christological interpretation. The victim offered for sin, and very holy, is the only Son of God, our Lord Jesus Christ, who alone is "victim for sin."[70] The priest also is Christ, who offered himself to God, and now, like the priest eating the sin (victim) of a repenting sinner, "eats the sins of the people." Following Christ the high-priest, his sons, the priests of the Church, also "eat the sins of the people"

---

[68]Philo, *Deus*, 59-69; *Q.G.* II, 54; *Contra Celsum* IV, 71-72, SC 136, pp. 359-365.

[69]Origen, *Hom. on Lev. V, 2*, SC 286, pp. 210-214.

[70]Origen, ibid., 3, pp. 214-216.

when they purify from their sins the hearts of their listeners. The priests of the Church offer the propitiation for sinners when they take them apart, warn, exhort, teach, and bring them to repentance.[71]

Incense-offering, Purifications

Under the heading of sacrifice, we also find incense-offering and purifications. A few remarks will be enough.

Incense-offering is connected with the vegetable-offering generally accompanying sacrifices. It is placed on the incense altar in the temple every morning and evening, and on each sabbath day on the table of the show-bread. Relying on the cosmic symbolism of the composition of incense, Philo interprets the incense-offering in the sense of praise and $\epsilon \dot{\upsilon} \chi \alpha \rho \iota \sigma \tau \dot{\iota} \alpha$. The incense-altar is also the symbol of the offering of virtue and self.[72]

Origen seems to innovate only in that he interprets the incense-offering as a symbol of prayer according to Ps. 141:2:

Let my prayer rise like incense before you,
The lifting up of my hands like the evening sacrifice.[73]

More significant for the parallel between Philo and Origen is the role of incense in the ritual of propitiation at Yom-Kippur. We read in Leviticus 10 that the smoke of incense, like a cloud, prevents the death of the high-priest. Although propitiation properly speaking consists in atonement

[71]Origen, ibid., 3, SC 286, pp. 218-220.

[72]Philo. *Congr.*, 114; *Her.*, 199, 226.

[73]Origen, *Hom. IX on Lev. 8*, SC 287, pp. 106-112.

with blood on the mercy seat, in speaking of the incense-offering in the ritual of Yom-Kippur Philo and Origen both make use of the vocabulary of propitiation.[74] Incense refers to the gesture of intercession of Aaron standing with his censer between the living and the dead in order to stop the plague (Ex. 30:11-16). At Yom-Kippur also the high-priest seems to stand in the midst of the people of Israel as a mediator and an intercessor in order to appease the wrath of the justice of God and to obtain reconciliation. Origen and Philo retain this idea, and Origen recognizes Christ as the intercessor par excellence.[75]

Since by themselves purifications are not sacrifices, they only belong to our present topic in so far as they represent a preparation, a requirement for sacrifice. I have dealt elsewhere with purifications in Philo.[76] In Origen, the topic deserves a special inquiry. Probably here again such an inquiry would show that, to a large extent, Origen follows Philo in his literal and moral interpretation of the laws on purifications in so far as they do not mean a return to the practice of ancient sacrifices.

Early Christian literature reveals the permanence of many levitical purifications in the Christian practice, for instance, a washing of hands before prayer, to say nothing of the custom of fasting on certain days. There are also specifically Christian purifications such as the sign of the cross. All these purifications are loaded with moral implications.[77]

---

[74]Origen, *Hom. IX on Lev., 9-10*, SC 287, pp. 112-122.

[75]Origen, *Hom. on Num. IX, 2-5*, SC 29, pp. 168-176, PG XII, 612-617.

[76]Laporte, "Sacrifice and Forgiveness in Philo of Alexandria," paper at the Oxford Patristic Conference, 1983.

[77]Origen, *Contra Celsum* I.6, SC 132, pp. 90-92, V.49, SC 147, pp. 140-142; VII.4, SC 150, pp. 20-22; *Hom. on Gen X, 1*, SC 7 bis, p.

The most interesting of these purifications, because it is directly connected with the celebration of the Christian Eucharist, is the recommendation to abstain from intercourse the night before sharing in the sacrifice.[78]   Origen even goes so far as to suggest reserving a room for prayer in order not to pray in the bedroom and thus offend the Holy Spirit.[79]

We must acknowledge that this restriction is never presented as important, and communion or prayer in that situation as a fault deserving condemnation. Purification with water, even with the moisture of the breath, is enough to remove the impurity, and is not obligatory.[80] This observation confirms that the Levitical forms of sacrifice, and certain forms of purification of the same kind, really served as models for the Christian understanding and practice of sacrifice.

Conclusion

For the explanation of Origen's doctrine of sacrifice the best methodology is to recognize his real models in his sources, i.e., Leviticus as interpreted by Philo. Origen repeats Philo's teachings on sacrifice without much alteration. He completes them with a Christian development already

---

254-258; *Hom. on Ex. XI, 7*, pp. 243-244, PG XII, 381; *Hom. on Lev. VII, 4-5*, SC 286, pp. 326-334.

[78]Origen, *Hom. XI on Ex., 7*, SC 16, pp. 242-244. PG XII, 381; *Hom. on Num. VI, 3*, SC 29, pp. 129-130, PG XII, 610; *Hom. on Num. XXIII, 3*, ibid., p. 442, PG XII, 740.

[79]Origen, *On Prayer*, 31, 4, ACW 19, p. 133.

[80]*Didascalia*, Connolly, pp. 242-254; Origen, *Hom. on Num. XXIIl, 3*, SC 29, pp. 439-442, PG XII, 749; *The Apostolic Tradition of Hippolytus*, ed. G. Dix and H. Chadwick (London, 1968), p. 66.

prepared by Paul and the Epistle to the Hebrews. Thereby Origen offers a Christian theology of sacrifice, in which the sacrifice of Christ is given its capital importance in the mystery of our redemption. Yet our own sacrifice--martyrdom, forgiveness, almsgiving, or whatever--is not emptied by the power of the sacrifice of Christ. It remains valid as interpreted by Philo and Origen according to biblical models, and by its association with the sacrifice of Christ.

Since Origen was among the first exegetes who wrote continuous commentaries on biblical books, he is also the best interpreter of the Christian doctrine of sacrifice which the reflection of Christian faith discovers in these books. All other statements found in the Christian tradition before Origen are occasional and deal with particular aspects as, for instance, the deliverance from the devil, or the ransom. They do not directly deal with the levitical notion of sacrifice which is the basis of the Christian notion. Furthermore since Origen's models of sacrifice are biblical, we must be very critical of the use of other models, such as those elaborated more or less artificially by the History of Religions school, when applied from the outside to Origen's notion of sacrifice.

This study of Origen's theology of sacrifice is of great importance for liturgical theology, since it casts new light on the sacrament of the Eucharist and, complemented by his notion of forgiveness,[81] on the sacrament of penance.

This leads me to suggest a last remark concerning the way the Middle Ages and modern theology have approached the question of the real presence of Christ in the sacrament of the Eucharist. Out of the desire to stick to a literal interpretation of the words of consecration and to give them

---

[81]Laporte, "Philonic Models in Origen's Doctrine of Forgiveness."

their full meaning, as if other considerations might endanger their awesome character, Christian theology came to adopt a kind of Eucharistic fundamentalism, a short-sighted view of the real presence, which can and must be completed with the consideration of a biblical theology of sacrifice.

The gift of the body and blood of Christ is not the mere conveyance of the real presence of Christ to the believer, for Christ is believed to be present in the hearts of the believers before the communion. But it is properly and directly sharing in Christ's sacrifice according to the biblical rule of sacrifice, which prescribes eating our own portion of the victim. Christ's interpretation of the bread and wine as his body and blood made it clear that we share in the victim offered for our redemption and in the blood poured out in propitiation for our sins. Therefore, whatever be the advantage and relevance of the painstaking proof for the real presence in classical theology, a good understanding of the biblical notion of sacrifice provides both a more simple and more complete understanding of the Christian Eucharist.

It also reminds us that the Eucharistic blood is sharing in the propitiation made by Christ for our sins. For, as Origen points out in his homily on Matthew 26, the bread refers to Christ as spiritual food, whereas the wine refers to the blood poured out for the remission of our sins.[82] The "blood of propitiation," combines the blood of the lamb or of the Suffering Servant in the narrative of the Last Supper with the blood poured by Christ the Priest on the altar in heaven, according to the interpretation of the ritual of Yom-Kippur in the epistle to the Hebrews. We joyfully celebrate the memory of Christ, and give thanks for these divine gifts.

---

[82]Origen, *On Mat. 26: 26-30*; *Com. Ser. 85*, GCS XI, pp.196-199.

ORIGEN'S ECCLESIOLOGY AND THE BIBLICAL METAPHOR OF THE CHURCH AS THE BODY OF CHRIST

Verlyn D. Verbrugge
University of Notre Dame

In his masterpiece on theology, *Peri Archon*, Origen discusses the vital topics of his intellectual and philosophical age: for example, the nature of God, the rational soul, the creation of the world, free will, and the end of all things. In contrast to later theological treatises, he undertook no formal discussion of the doctrine of the Church. What Origen thought about the Church we can only glean from incidental references throughout his writings.

It is not as if he had little to say about the Church. In 1974, Josef Vogt published an in-depth analysis of Origen's ecclesiology, *Das Kirchenverständnis des Origenes*.[1] This was no easy task since, as Eric Jay indicates, with no systematic treatment, "Origen's doctrine of the Church is . . . difficult to interpret."[2] Joseph Trigg warns against "drawing too many

---

[1]Josef Vogt, *Das Kirchenverständnis des Origenes* (Köln: Bohlau-Verlag, 1974).

[2]Eric Jay, *The Church: Its Changing Image through Twenty Centuries* (Atlanta: John Knox Press, 1978), p. 64.

conclusions from [Origen's] understanding of the church's leadership, the sacraments, and ecclesiastical discipline." After all, he goes on to say, "ecclesiology . . . was not a major issue for theologians in the Greek Christian tradition, least of all for Origen."[3] Several decades ago, Emile Mersch published a book on the historical development of the doctrine of the Mystical Body; he too asserted that the exposition of Clement and Origen on this doctrine was not easy:

> The difficulty lies in bringing the different texts [of Origen] on the Mystical Body into one single plan. For our part, we confess our failure to discover any key to a synthesis of the whole.[4]

With this in mind, I have no intention of attempting to systematize the teaching of Origen on the Church. What I propose to do in this article is simply to take one specific metaphor that the Bible uses for the Church--that of the Church as the "body of Christ" as found in Rom. 12:4-5; I Cor. 10:17; 12:12-27; Eph. 1:22-23; 4:4; 5:30; and Col. 1:18--and examine all the known passages in which Origen draws upon this imagery in his discussions of various issues.[5] Two specific questions will be addressed: 1) What does

---

[3]Joseph Trigg, *Origen: The Bible and Philosophy in the Third Century Church* (Atlanta: John Knox Press, 1983), p. 199.

[4]Emile Mersch, *The Whole Christ: The Historical Development of the Doctrine of the Mystical Body in Scripture and Tradition*, trans. John R. Kelley (Milwaukee: The Bruce Publishing Co., 1938), p. 249.

[5]For the passages that I deal with in this analysis I have used Volume III of *Biblia Patristica*, ed. Allenbach, et al. (Paris: Éditions du Centre da la Recherche Scientifique, 1983). All references to the Bible will, for the sake of consistency, be to standard English chapters and verses, rather than to the Septuagint, Vulgate, or Biblia Hebraica.

Origen *teach* about the Church as the Body of Christ?   2) How does he *use* the above passages to bring important messages to his hearers/readers?

1. The Teaching of Origen on the Church as the Body of Christ

When Origen reflects on the metaphor of the Church as the body of Christ, he stresses two separate, though related, ideas: a strong sense of unity between Christ as the head and Christians as members of his body, and an equally strong sense of unity that the members of the body of Christ have with one another.

With respect to the former, when Origen discusses Jesus' teaching on divorce in Matt. 19:3-10, he interprets the passage to be speaking, among other things, of Christ and the Church. Christ left his Father in heaven to be joined to his wife, the Church, and the two have become μία σάρξ. He substantiates this by pointing to I Cor. 12:27:

> "you are the body of Christ and members in particular." . . .God has joined these together, not becoming two but becoming one flesh [cf. Eph. 5:31-32], commanding that no man [later, no principality or power] should put asunder the Church from the Lord.[6]

Likewise, as Origen comments on the frequent use of ἕν in John 17, he insists upon the unity between the ἕν σῶμα of I Cor. 12:13 and Eph. 4:4

---

[6]*Commentary on Matthew*, 14.47; GCS 10, p. 326.

and the head, Christ (Col. 1:18).[7] The same emphasis occurs in *Contra Celsum* VI.79.[8]

In another section of *Contra Celsum* (VI.48),[9] Origen uses the analogy of the human body and soul to describe the integral relationship of Christ and the Church: just as the soul gives life to and moves the human body, so the Logos, the Son of God, animates the body of Christ, the Church. In the seventh homily on Leviticus, Origen stresses that Christ wills to dwell in his body the Church as a soul.[10] In a similar vein, as Origen formally discusses Eph. 1:22-23, he probes the relationship between Christ as head and the Church as his body. After proposing two options--is the body a mere instrument for the head or is it analogous to the human body, with the Church being animated (ψυχομένου) by his divinity and filled by his Spirit?--Origen chooses the latter.[11] In *Peri Archon* II.vii.5, this unity between Christ and his Church is expressed, in a more limited way, in reverse form. In referring to Matt. 26:38, "My soul is sorrowful even unto death," Origen suggests, via I Cor. 12:27, that the *apostles* as a unit,

---

[7]*Fragment of Commentary on John*, GCS 4, p. 574.

[8]SC 147, p. 378.

[9]Ibid., p. 300.

[10]*Homilies on Leviticus* 7.2; GCS 6, p. 379. Procopius attributes the same thought to Origen while commenting on the Song of Songs 1:16; see GCS 8, p. 175.

[11]See *JTS* 3 (1903): 401. We ought to take note of the role of the Spirit here. Commenting on Rom. 12:6, Origen says that those who do not have the *gratia* (gift, grace) of the Spirit cannot be members of the body of Christ; see PG 14.1215B.

differentiated from and better than the rest of believers, may be considered the soul of Christ.[12]

Emile Mersch is rather critical of Origen's idea of the Mystical Body because of a "lack of realism":[13] "this union seems to be a participation in Christ's divinity rather than an incorporation in His humanity."[14] He does acknowledge, however, that to interpret Origen properly, one must "*presuppose* that the unity between Christ and Christians, between the Head and the members, is so close that the Scriptures can attribute to the one that which is strictly true only of the other."[15]

Secondly, Origen stresses the unity that the members of the body of Christ have with one another.   In his discussion of Eph. 4:3, he points out that this unity among fellow believers is assured when love binds them together and gathers them into one body of Christ.[16] Origen makes allusions to the same theme in a fragment of a commentary on Ps. 122:3: whenever the $\kappa\alpha\rho\delta\iota\alpha$ and $\psi\upsilon\chi\eta$ of believers are one (cf. Acts 4:32) and the members express the same care for one another (I Cor. 12:25), they are Jerusalem whose communion ($\mu\epsilon\tau\delta\chi\eta$) is together.[17] There is, in other

---

[12]SC 252, p. 330.

[13]Mersch, *The Whole Christ*, pp. 253, 255.

[14]Ibid., p. 248.

[15]Ibid., p. 261 (italics mine). Mersch's own emphasis is on our union with each other as it takes place in Christ. He does not seem to be aware of the many passages in Origen that stress this relationship (cf. the next section of this article).

[16]*JTS* 3 (1902): 412.

[17]PG 12.1632D-1633A. Though the word $\sigma\tilde{\omega}\mu\alpha$ is not used, this passage quotes I Cor. 12:25.

words, a loving unity among the members of the body of Christ. This unity is similarly alluded to in the healing of the righteous man in Ps. 30:2: those who believe are one body in Christ, and members of a member.[18] Thus, if one member suffers, all the members do and the whole body of Christ needs healing.[19]

The above reference to one heart and soul is repeated in Origen's ninth homily on Ezekiel. Here Origen alludes to the Platonic axiom that unity is better than diversity. God, according to Plato,[20] is τò ʽΕν. Indeed, in *Peri Archon* I.i.6, Origen himself states clearly that God is Unity and Oneness (*μονας* and *ἕας*).[21] To Plato and his followers, this teaching had ethical implications. In the *Republic* 4, 445c, Plato says that virtue is of a simple piece whereas vice is multitudinous; similar thoughts can be found in Plutarch (*De virtute morali* 444B) and Plotinus (*Enneads* VI. ix.3-4). Even Clement of Alexandria cites a Pythagorean formula in *Stromata* IV.151.3 that the man who wishes to become one must suppress the passions.[22] As an heir to this Platonic thinking, therefore, Origen asserts in the ninth homily

---

[18]The text reads *ἐκ μέλους* here, rather than *ἐκ μέρους*. This has probably been altered in copying to correspond to the Western text reading, since elsewhere (e.g., GCS 4, p. 209 and 574), the text reads *ἐκ μέρους*. In Leviticus Homily 7, 2, Origen gives a unique explanation of what is undoubtedly *ἐκ μέρους*, *ex parte* cf. below.

[19]PG 12.1292D-1293A. Cf. *Commentary on Matthew* 24:21 (GCS 11, p. 92), where Origen likewise acknowledges that one person's suffering or sin affects the other members.

[20]Cf. John Dillon, *The Middle Platonists* (Ithaca: Cornell University Press, 1977), pp. 3-4.

[21]SC 252, p. 100.

[22]These last four references are cited in M. Harl's comments on *Philocalia*, Chapter 8 (SC 302, pp. 347-48).

on Ezekiel: "where there are sins, there is multitude, there are divisions, heresies, dissensions; however, where there is virtue, there is singularity, unity, out of which there is one heart and soul for all believers."[23] He correlates this unity of principle with I Cor. 1:10 ("that we may be perfectly joined together in the same mind and in the same judgment") and with Eph. 4:4, ("that we may be one body and one spirit").[24] The notion of the spiritual and ethical unity of members of the body is prominent here.

The unity Origen sees in the Church extends to both "time" and "space". Spatially, the saints who have already departed retain their unity with the body of Christ on earth. In *De oratione* 11.2, Origen acknowledges the value of intercessory prayer "by someone who has some greater boldness." Those who pray for us need not be living Christians but may also be saints who have fallen asleep--in fact, the latter have a more perfect love for us than those who still struggle in this life. To them also Origen applies the body of Christ imagery of I Cor. 12:26: "if one member suffers, all the members suffer together and if one member is honored, all the members rejoice together."[25] Like Paul in II Cor. 11:28-29, they have anxiety (μέριμνα cf. μερίμνωσιν in I Cor. 12:25) for all the churches.

Temporally, Origen relates the concept of the body of Christ to the Church from the time of Israel to the end of history. In his *Commentary* on John 2:18-19, Origen interprets both the "temple" and the "body" as τύποι of

---

[23]GCS 8, p. 406.

[24]M. Harl, in SC 302, p. 346, briefly discusses this Ezekiel homily and correlates it with a similar treatment by Origen in a homily on I Kings 1:1 (GCS 8, pp. 5-6).

[25]GCS 2, p. 322. Significantly, when Origen goes on to talk of the ministry of angels on our behalf (11.3-5), he makes no such reference to the "body" metaphor; only departed saints may properly be called "fellow-members of the body of Christ."

the Church. The resurrection on the third day, recorded in this passage, refers to the new heaven and the new earth when these bones, the whole house of Israel (cf. Ezekiel 37), will be raised on the great day of the Lord. This will be the day of the resurrection of τοῦ πάντος χριστοῦ σώματος.[26] A few lines later Origen reiterates this by suggesting that when the resurrection of the true and more perfect body of Christ occurs, then finally the many members will be the one body of Christ.[27]   Similarly, when Origen discusses the awaited "redemption of our body" in Rom. 8:23, he does not view this individually but, via I Cor. 12:27, as the *corpus totius Ecclesiae*.[28] That is, the Apostle is not looking forward here to a time when perfection will be given to individual members, but to the *universum corpus in unum . . . congregatum*. Finally, in the seventh homily on Leviticus, Origen once again unites the idea of perfection (here especially as recorded in Heb. 11:39), the vision of Ezekiel on the bones of Israel, the final day of days, and the body of Christ. "There is one body that is said to rise in judgment. . . . Then there will be full joy when you lack no member of the body."[29]

It would be incorrect to say, however, that Origen sees only the unity in the body--with Christ and with one another. In his *Commentary* on Rom. 12:3-5, for example, Origen acknowledges the diversity of the members of the body with respect to function. God divides to each person according to the measure of faith--Origen suggests that some of his gifts are "the work of love, the act of visiting, mercy to the poor, care of the weak,

---

[26]*Commentary on John* 10.223; GCS 4, p. 209.

[27]Ibid., 10.236-67; GCS 4, pp. 210-11.

[28]*Commentary on Romans* 7.5; PG 14.1116D-1117A.

[29]*Homilies on Leviticus* 7.2; GCS 6, pp. 378-79.

works for widows and the defense of orphans, and hospitality." These (and many others) all occur in the body of Christ, and each one uses his *gratia* for all the others, and all the others use their individual gifts for him. Drawing heavily on I Cor. 12:22-24, Origen insists upon the inappropriateness of speculating whether some members are more or less honorable; every gift, according to the will of God, is important.[30]

2. The Use of Origen Makes of the Church As the Body of Christ

We turn now to the second section of our analysis, inquiring into how Origen takes this metaphor of the Church as the body of Christ and uses it for parenesis and for exegesis.

In a parenetic manner, Origen exhorts his readers to mutual love and care in the church. In his comments on Matt. 18:19, concerning two or three agreeing on anything they shall ask, Origen encourages such harmony when he writes:

> If we are the body of Christ and God has set members, each one of them, in the body so that they have the same care for one another and harmonize with one another. . ., we ought to practice that harmony (συμφωνία) that springs from the divine music in order that when we gather together in the name of Christ, Christ may be in our midst.[31]

---

[30]*Commentary on Romans* 9.2-3; PG 14.1211A-1213C.

[31]*Commentary on Matthew* 14.1; GCS 10, p. 277.

In a similar vein, in the homily on the Passover (Exodus 12), Origen, after alluding to I Cor. 12:20-21 and 10:17, exhorts his hearers to "guard the harmony (ἁρμονία) of the members lest we be accused of tearing asunder the body of Christ."[32] The same idea comes across in a comment on Ps. 119:105, "Thy Word is a lamp to my feet and a light to my path." Origen relates this to "the lamp of the body is the eye" in Matt. 6:22, suggesting that the eye of the body, the church, is that man endowed with a spiritual view and possessing the Logos. But, he goes on to warn, such an important member of the body may still not say of the other members (e.g., the hand) "What will it do? nor may the hand say to the eye, 'I have no need of you.' "[33] Origen draws on the same text (I Cor. 12:21-25) to plead for concord between the perfect and the imperfect in the Church, the body, when explaining the instruction of Paul in Rom. 14:3-4, that Christians ought not to judge one another.[34]

In a rather strange twist, however, Origen reverses the above exhortation to mutual love and concern to allow for different degrees of love for different people. In Book III of the *Commentary on Song of Songs*, he first acknowledges through Eph. 4:3 that we ought to have a similar and equal love for all. But seeing that Paul speaks in I Corinthians 12 of more honorable and important members and less honorable and inferior ones, Origen goes on to say, "I think that the mode of love ought to be adjusted to the merit and honor of the members." He continues by suggesting that

---

[32]*Sur la Pâque* 1.32, ed. and trans. O. Guéraud and P. Nautin (Paris: Beauchesne, 1979), p. 216.

[33]SC 189, p. 360; cf. fragment of a commentary on Luke 11:33, GCS 9, p. 306.

[34]*Commentary on Romans* 9.36; PG 14.1236B-C.

someone who labors in the Word of God and instructs our souls is much
more worthy of being loved than someone who does not.[35] Origen drops
this issue here and, to my knowledge, does not take it up elsewhere.

As a corollary of mutual care and concern, Origen uses the "body of
Christ" metaphor to call the members to mutual discipline. In dealing with
the Achan episode in Joshua 7, he points out how one sinner polluted the
entire people. "Therefore, let us mutually observe ourselves and let each
one's manner of life be noted," especially by church leaders. After all, we are
the body of Christ, and no part of the body can be indifferent to the sickness
or suffering of another.[36] In his *Commentary on Matthew*, Origen also
applies I Corinthians 12 to the matter of discipline, but this time with a
significantly different thrust. In discussing Matt. 18:18-19 (note the use of
"hand," "foot" and "eye" here, as in I Cor. 12:15-16) and after asserting that
the eye should not say to the hand, "I have no need of you," he goes on to
insist that if anyone in the whole σῶμα of the congregation of the ἐκκλησία
becomes a stumbling block, then "let the eye say to such a hand, 'I have no
need of you' and cut it off and cast it from himself."[37] This is not the time
and place to delve into Origen's view of church discipline.[38] Suffice it to say
that, in his comments on John 2:18-19, he ultimately leaves it in the hands
of God to make judgment of the members.[39] Vogt says on this passage,

---

[35]GCS 8, p. 187.

[36]GCS 7, p. 333.

[37]*Commentary on Matthew* 13.34; GCS 10 p. 245.

[38]An excellent analysis of Origen's attitude to sinners and
repentance is K. Rahner's "La doctrine d'Origène sur la pénitence," *Recherches
de science religieuse* 37 (1950): 47-97, 252-86, 422-56.

[39]*Commentary on John* 10.237; GCS 4, p. 211.

Die Auferstehung dieses Leibes Geschieht durch das Gericht hindurch, das nur Gott selbst vornehmen wird, wenn er scheidet zwischen den edleren und unedleren Teilen. Wer keine Harmonie zu den anderen Gliedern aufweist, der wird nicht eingehen in den Leib des Vollalters und der Reife.[40]

Secondly, Origen consistently draws upon this metaphor of the church as the body of Christ as an exegetical tool. For example, he asks how it is possible in Matt. 24:36 for Jesus, the Son of God, to say he does not know the day or the hour of his return. Later theological interpretations of this text have often made reference to the humanity of Christ--as man, Jesus did not know everything. But Origen draws on the unity of the body of Christ with her Lord: "For as long as the church, which is the body of Christ, does not know the day or the hour, so the Son himself is said not to know, so that he will be understood to know at the time when all of his members also know."[41]

Immediately preceding the above quotation is a reference to I Cor. 15:28, a text that speaks of the Son's future subjection to the Father. Origen quotes this section of I Corinthians approximately fifty times in his works, since it is so important in his eschatology.[42] But Origen notes a problem here: how can Paul say the Son is not yet subject to the Father? He attempts to explain this in his seventh homily on Leviticus: whenever I sin,

---

[40]Vogt, *Das Kirchenverständnis*, p. 242.

[41]GCS 11, pp. 126-27.

[42]See the article on this by Henri Crouzel, "Quand le Fils transmet le Royaume à Dieu son Père," *Studia Missionalia* 33 (1984): 359-384.

I am not subject to the Father. We read in Scripture, "We are the body of Christ and members in particular." Therefore, though in himself (*ipse*) the Son is subject to the Father, "in me in whom he has not yet consummated his work, he is said not to be subject."[43] Christ will be totally subject to the Father, in other words, when all his members are healthy and subject to God--that is, when we obey God in all things.[44] In the same vein, Origen draws on I Cor. 12:27 to explain how Jesus can say in Matt. 25:42-46, "I was hungry and you gave me to eat." Just as a soul dwelling in a body can be said to be hungry when the body is hungry, "so the Savior suffers when his body, the Church, suffers."[45]

In interpreting I Cor. 9:24, Origen again employs the concept of the unity of the body. He asks whether Paul means that we all run but only one receives the prize and the rest are lost. No, this is not Paul's meaning, according to Origen. Since "all those who are saved are one [Gal. 3:28] and one body [Eph. 4:4], and since "we all are one bread and partake of the same bread, [I Cor. 10:17] and all of you are the body of Christ [I Cor. 12:27], therefore all those who are saved are the one ($\epsilon \hat{\iota}s$) who receives the prize."[46]

---

[43]*Homilies on Leviticus* 7.2; GCS 6, p. 376. In this homily, Origen gives a unique explanation of *ex parte* ($\dot{\epsilon}\kappa$ $\mu\dot{\epsilon}\rho ous$) in I Cor. 12:27. He suggests that as long as one has to struggle against the flesh he is subject to God only partially, *ex parte*. Hence, "we are the body of Christ and members *partially*." Later in the homily, he relates this to I Cor. 13:9, "now we know in part and prophesy in part" (*ex parte*, Greek, $\dot{\epsilon}\kappa$ $\mu\dot{\epsilon}\rho ous$).

[44]Origen gives the same interpretation in a homiletical comment on Ps. 37:7; PG 12.1330B.

[45]GCS 11, p. 172.

[46]*JTS* 9 (1908): 514. The unusual changes of person come because of the quotations from Scripture.

The rest who run the race and who do not receive the prize are Jews and those who follow heresies and the teachings of the Greeks.

Not unlike this is Origen's insistence that in Ezekiel 14:14-20, we become "a child of Noah, Daniel, Job and Abraham [all seen as one] to the adoption of God," presumably if we follow in their pattern of a virtuous life. His basis for this peculiar interpretation is, as one might expect, I Cor. 12:27 (as well as the Savior seeking and saving the *one* sheep who was lost cf. Luke 15:45, 19:10).[47]   In a homily on Jer. 50:17, Origen also refers to the Parable of the Lost Sheep.[48]   In this fragment, Jeremiah seems to be struggling with why the sheep of Israel are destroyed here, whereas in the parable, the wandering sheep is brought back. The key seems to be in the concept of unity--we are all ἕν σῶμα and ἕν πρόβατον. God has united us all together by his own Word. We are all one body and one bread and partake of one spirit (I Cor. 10:17, 12:13).   But if we defy this unity by disobedience, we no longer can expect the protection of the Lord; we become food for the lions (Jer. 50:17; that is, the devil, cf. I Peter 5:8).

This concept of unity Origen uses to solve even textual problems. In the *Philocalia,* he questions why there is a switch from the plural to the singular in (the Septuagint version of) Hosea 12:4: "*they* cried and prayed to me and found me in the House of God and there I spoke with *him*." Should we not read, Origen asks, "there I spoke with *them*"? No, he answers: when "they" cried and prayed to God, they are individuals; when they find God, they become one:

---

[47]*Homilies on Ezekiel* 4.6; GCS 8, p. 367.

[48]GCS 3, pp. 212-13.

for the many have become one in finding God and in hearing his Word. For the one is multiple when he sins. . . ., but the many become one when they keep the commandments of God, as also the apostle bears witness when he says, "We who are many are one bread and one body" [I Cor. 10:17]; and again, "There is one God and one Christ and one faith and one baptism" [Eph. 4:5-6]; and in another place, "We are all one in Christ" [Rom. 12:5, Gal. 3:28]; and again, "I have espoused all of you to present you as a holy virgin to one husband, the Lord" [II Cor. 11:2].[49]

Finally, Origen draws upon the imagery of the body of Christ in several of his allegorical interpretations of the Old Testament. For example, Origen speculates regarding "horses" in Song of Songs 1:9. He eventually turns to Rev. 19:11-14 where the Word of God sits upon a white horse. This white horse is the Church which is his body (Col. 1:24), whom he has sanctified for himself without spot or wrinkle (Eph. 5:25-27, 30).[50] He carries this further in Song of Songs 1:10, where he notes the cheeks of the Bride have become lovely because the kisses of the Bridegroom have cleansed her (Eph. 5:25-27)--these cheeks symbolize those members of the Body that

---

[49]*Philocalia* 8.1 and 3; SC 302, pp. 336, 338, 340. It is interesting to note that both Biblia Hebraica and the Septuagint have textual variants with the plural that Origen is either unaware of or ignores. In the same section of *Philocalia*, Origen uses the same argument for a textual problem in Gen. 2:16-17.

[50]GCS 8, p. 152. In the *Commentary on Romans*, Origen uses this same description of Christ as the Head of the Church, his body, whom he cleansed to be without spot and wrinkle. This is the body of the new man, in contrast to the "body of sin" (Rom. 6:6) that must be destroyed, or which the devil is the head (*Commentary on Romans* 5, 9; PG 14.1045D-1046A).

exercise chastity, modesty, and virginity. There are, of course, other members of the Church: eyes (those who have the light of understanding and knowledge), ears (those who hear the word of teaching), and hands (those who do good works).[51]

In his allegorizing of Lev. 1:4, that the priest shall put his hand on the head of the burnt offering "as a symbol of the placing of sins on the animals," Origen interprets this as Christ placing the sins of the human race on his own body, "for he himself is the head of his body, the Church."[52] Here the body of Christ metaphor of Eph. 1:22-23 becomes crucial for his christological understanding of this Old Testament law. Likewise, in an allegory of the Parable of the Good Samaritan (Luke 10:30-37) that Cramer attributes to Origen, Origen understands the beast on which the wounded traveller is placed to be Christ's body. He elucidates this further by saying, "For he carries us ἐν ἑαυτῷ because we are members of his body."[53]

Conclusions

What conclusions can we draw from this analysis of Origen's teaching and use of the metaphor of the Church as the body of Christ? First and most obvious, let us observe the rich and variegated ways in which this Alexandrian Church Father employs this image--from a philosophical

---

[51]GCS 8, pp. 154-55. One other brief reference to the Church as the body of Christ is in the commentary on Song of Songs 1:7 (GCS 8, p. 135).

[52]*Homilies on Leviticus* 1.3; GCS 6, p. 284.

[53]*Catanae Graecorum Patrum in Novum Testamentum*, ed. J.A. Cramer (Oxford, 1841), Vol. 2, p. 88. Note the consistency in these allegories: the Church, Christ's body, is the white horse in Rev. 19, the sacrificial animal in Lev. 1, the beast in Luke 10.

emphasis on unity to a moral exhortation to holy living, from an answer to the pagan critic Celsus to homilies delivered to members of Christ's body.

Taking just this one biblical metaphor, however, we noted several inconsistencies and even outright contradictions in the way Origen explicates this image; for example, 1) a greater love for more important members of the body versus a refusal to speculate who is more important and an insistence on equal love for all; 2) the appropriateness or the inappropriateness of saying to a particular member, "I have no need of you"; 3) the Church defined as the body of Christ animated by Christ as the soul versus the suggestion that the apostles may be defined as the soul of Christ. If this is true for Origen's reflections on just this one image, we can readily understand why the task of a logical systematization of *all* that Origen says about the Church is well nigh impossible.

On the other hand, however, general patterns have emerged in our analysis. First, in asserting the mystical union between Christ and the Church, Origen sees this union is so intimate that what is ascribed to the Church can also be ascribed to Christ: For example, lack of perfection (as in the seventh homily on Leviticus) or lack of knowledge (as in his comments on Matt. 23:36). Conversely, that which describes Christ can be said to be descriptive of his body, the Church: for example, Christ's visible body nailed to the cross is the whole body of Christ's saints nailed to the cross;[54] or again, Christ's divine rebirth through death and resurrection is the rebirth of believers.[55] From the standpoint of the texts we have been discussing, what serves as the intermediary between God and believers is Christ *as body*. A two-way communication between God and man takes place not through

---

[54]See *Commentary on John* 10.230; GCS 4, p. 210.

[55]See comment on John 17:11; GCS 4, p. 574.

Christ as a God-man mediator, but through the intimate union that believers have with Christ's body, Christ himself being the head. In this regard it may be said that Origen is paving the way for *nulla salus ex ecclesia*.

Secondly, believers--members of the Church, the body of Christ-- maintain a mystical union with one another. This unity begins with the Old Testament saints and extends until the eschaton. No believer will experience *perfecta beautitudino* and *plena laetitia* as long as there are members struggling against sin in this life.[56] This sense of an intimate union among Christians inspires Origen, as we have noted, to draw numerous ethical implications on how believers ought to conduct their lives: he encourages Christians everywhere to love one another, to support one another, to help one another until that day when God shall be all in all (cf. I Cor. 15:28).

In sum, therefore, Origen's teaching regarding the body of Christ is living and dynamic. It flows with the biblical data, and the ambiguities in his explication are the ambiguities of the Scriptures. We must certainly endorse the conclusion of Gustave Bardy:

> le catholicisme d'Origène n'est pas celui d'un intellectual, qui s'efforce de penser les enseignements de l'Église et de les exprimer en termes d'école; c'est celui d'une âme religieuse qui ne cesse pas de chercher Dieu pour s'unir toujours plus intinement à Lui.[57]

---

[56]See *Homilies on Leviticus* 7.2; GCS 6, p. 378.

[57]Gustave Bardy, *La vie spirituelle d'après les pères des trois premiers siècles*, rev. by A. Haman (Tournai: Desclée et Cie, 1968), p. 65.

THE PLACE OF SAINTS AND SINNERS AFTER DEATH

Lawrence R. Hennessey
Washington Theological Union

Origen's ideas about the place of the saints and the sinners after death can be conveniently arranged around three headings. The first, which can serve as a prelude to the whole of this present discussion, concerns the descent of Christ into Hades, which is understood as the abode of all the saints and repentant sinners who died before the time of Christ's death and resurrection. Origen carefully distinguishes Hades from Gehenna, which is the abode of the Devil, his demons and all hardened, unrepentant sinners. Christ descends into Hades, not into Gehenna, and liberates all the souls confined there; henceforth, Hades is closed as a place where souls might go after death.

The second heading of this discussion concerns the purifying fire through which the soul passes, and also the dwelling of the blessed. Origen observes that everyone must pass through the eschatological fire of purification. This fire is equated with God Himself, and is applied primarily to all of those destined for Paradise--the saints and repentant sinners, who pass into blessedness. This passage brings the person first to the *schola animarum*, the school for souls, where the person begins to learn all about the things God has done and the reasons for them. Then Christ leads the soul on a gradual ascension into the heavens and to the contemplation of the Father face to face.

The third heading, Gehenna and the punishment of the damned, concerns the very different fate that awaits the wicked, hardened sinner. Such a one is cast into the eternal fire of Gehenna, as Origen understood it, there to suffer eternal punishment and torment. It remains an open question whether or not Origen teaches the eternity of Gehenna. Some texts reflect a final restoration of everyone; some do not; others are unsure.

One important presupposition should be stated at the outset. Origen understood the condition of the soul after death sometimes as in an incorporeal state, and sometimes as clothed with a corporeal ὄχημα, i.e., a corporeal vehicle composed of a light, fine invisible matter. This vehicle is luminous for the just and the repentant, but dark and murky for sinners. A full exposition of Origen's ideas about this corporeal vehicle is beyond the scope of the present study; however, the use of the term "soul" in this discussion presupposes Origen's second sense, the soul clothed with a corporeal vehicle.[1]

I. Prelude: the Descent of Christ into Hades

In developing his own understanding of the Christian theology of the resurrected body, Origen opposed certain ideas of Jewish and pagan origin,

---

[1]For a full discussion of the corporeal or incorporeal condition of the soul after death and of Origen's use of the "corporeal vehicle" see: M. Simonetti, "Alcune osservazioni sull' interpretazione origeniana di Genesi 2, 7 e 3, 21," *Aevum* 36 (1962): 370-381 and H. Crouzel, "Le thème platonicien du 'véhicule de l' âme' chez Origène," *Didaskalia* 7 (1977): 225-238.

which nevertheless, still prevailed among many Christians of his own day.[2] One notable example is found in the *Dialogue with Heraclides*, in the context of the dispute with the Thnetopsychites, who identified the soul with the blood and maintained that the soul thus stayed in the tomb after death. This idea is rooted in a Semitic anthropology.[3] As a result of this view, the Christian bishops who held it expressed surprise that Origen actually taught that the soul was immortal.[4] Other Christians believed that the souls of the dead continued to hover around their tombs, an idea explicity expressed long before in Plato's "ghost-story" in the *Phaedo* (81d). This idea persists for centuries after Origen, and even receives official sanction: the Spanish Council of Elvira (c. 306) in its thirty-fourth canon forbids the lighting of candles in cemeteries during the day for fear of "disturbing the spirits of the saints"--which, of course, presupposes that the souls of the dead are hovering nearby--and refusal to comply was to be punished by excommunication.[5]

An even more pervasive and persistent idea among Christians of Origen's time is that the soul indeed survives between death and resurrection, but in a sort of Sheol, like the one in the Old Testament. The common Greek word for this place is Hades. The only exception to this rule was made for the martyrs: they alone are admitted to Paradise immediately upon their

---

[2]H. Crouzel, "Mort et immortalité selon Origène," *BLE* 79 (1978): 188-89. (Hereafter cited as "Mort").

[3]*Dial. Herac.* 10, 16: SC 67, 76; F. Refoulé, "Seelenschlaf," *LThK* 9 (1964): 575-76.

[4]*Dial. Herac.* 24, 19; SC 67, 102.

[5]F. Lauchert, *Die Kanonen der wichtigsten altkirchlichen Concilien* (Freiburg i. B. and Leipzig: Mohr, 1896), 19.

deaths; the rest of the just wait for the final resurrection in Sheol/Hades.[6] After Clement of Alexandria, Origen seems to have been the first Christian thinker to open up Paradise to all the saints--not just martyrs--before the final resurrection.[7] This difference of opinion from the previous understanding of this point was grounded, in part, on the way Origen perceived the role of Sheol/Hades in the Christian tradition.

First of all, Origen carefully distinguishes Hades/Sheol from Gehenna: Hades (Greek, $\H{A}\iota\delta\eta\varsigma$: Latin, *inferus, infernus, infernum*) directly corresponds to the Old Testament Hebrew, *Sheol*; he uses the Hebrew word only in quoting Scripture, otherwise he adheres strictly to Attic usage by employing the word only in the genitive case to designate the place of the dead.[8] Hades is constantly referred to as a place: the place ($\chi\omega\rho\acute{\iota}o\nu$) of souls,[9] or the region ($\chi\acute{\omega}\rho\alpha$) of the dead.[10] It is situated at the heart of the earth, and it is the place to which one descends.[11] Hades is also the place where the "saints" of the Old Testament were sent prior to Christ's passion and descent there: This includes the patriarchs and prophets, Abraham and

---

[6]Tertullian, *De anima*, VII, 4; LV, 2-4; LVIII, 1: CCSL II, 790; 862-863; 867-868. *De resurrectione*, XVII, 2; XLVIII, 4: CCSL II, 941, 978-979.

[7]H. Crouzel, "L'Hadès et la Géhenne selon Origène," *Gregorianum* 59 (1978): 330 (English summary). Hereafter cited as "L'Hadès").

[8]Ibid., 294: e.g., $\dot{\epsilon}\nu$ $\H{a}\delta o\nu$; $\epsilon\dot{\iota}\varsigma$ $\H{a}\delta o\nu$; $\dot{\epsilon}\xi$ $\H{a}\delta o\nu$; $\chi\omega\rho\acute{\iota}o\nu$ $\H{a}\delta o\nu$. In classical usage, these expressions referred to the place of the underworld god, Hades.

[9]*Comm. Jn.* XXVIII, 6 (5), 43: GCS IV, 395, 32; *Frag. Jn.* 79: GCS IV, 546, 10.

[10]*Comm. Jn.* XXVIII, 7 (6), 54: GCS IV, 397, 17.

[11]Crouzel, "L' Hadès," 304.

Lazarus in his bosom (cf. Lk. 16:23), Samuel, who was called up by the witch of Endor (1 Sm. 28), Lazarus before Jesus raised him (Jn. 11), and even John the Baptist.[12] The reason that all these people went to Hades was the first, or the "original" sin, which had closed the gates to Paradise.

Because of the effects of this sin, the descent of Christ into Hades holds an important place in Origen's understanding of the redemption. By His descent, Christ destroys the Devil's dominion over captured humanity; humanity, in a complete reversal of its previous condition, now becomes Christ's own "spoils of salvation":

> After having vanquished the demons, His enemies, Christ led the people, who were under their sway, as if these people were the booty of victory and the spoils of salvation. So it was written about Him elsewhere: *Ascending on high, He led captivity captive* (Eph. 4:8). This was the captivity of the human race, which the Devil had captured for its destruction. Christ led it into captivity in an opposite sense: He recalled humanity from death to life (*Hom. Nb.* XVIII, 4).[13]

This descent is really accomplished by Christ, it is not something purely allegorical;[14] it opens up for the Old Testament saints the road to Paradise, which, until then, had been closed. Henceforth, the just ones who now die

---

[12]Ibid., 295; *Hom. 1 Rg. (1 Sm.) 28* : GCS III, 283-294; *Frag. Jn.* 78: GCS IV, 545, 9; *Hom. Lc.* IV, 5: GCS IX2, 27, 20; SC 87, 134.

[13]*Hom. Num.* XVIII, 4: GCS VII, 174, 25.

[14]*Comm. Jn.* XXXII, 32 (19), 394-400: GCS IV, 479, 28.

after Christ's suffering, death, descent, and resurrection, will no longer go to Hades, but to Paradise with Christ and God:

> We too will pass through the flaming sword, and we will not descend into the region of those who fell asleep before the coming of Christ, awaiting His arrival (*Hom. 1 Rg. (1 Sm.) 28*, 10).[15]

And so, by Christ's descent, Hades as a place is now closed.

II. The Purifying Fire and the Dwelling of the Blessed

The "flaming sword" in the text just cited--"We too will pass through the flaming sword"--is the fire of judgment, the purifying fire through which every soul must pass, even the just. Origen discusses this idea primarily in his exegesis of 1 Cor. 3:11-15.[16] This doctrine of purification is closely allied to the doctrine of the "first" and "second"

---

[15]*Hom. 1 Rg. (1 Sm.) 28*, 10: GCS III, 294, 11.

[16]See H. Crouzel, "L'exégèse origénienne de 1 Cor. 3, 11-15 et la purification eschatologique," in *Epektasis. Mélanges patristiques offerts au Cardinal Jean Daniélou* (Paris: Beauchesne, 1972): 273-283. Hereafter cited as "L' exégèse."

resurrections;[17] even though everyone passes through the fire,[18] only those stained by sin--those who have built on "wood, straw, or stubble" (1 Cor. 3:12)--will be touched by it.[19] This fire is also called the "baptism of fire" and the one who will undergo it, is the one who has need of the "second" resurrection:

> On account of this, Jesus baptizes--perhaps now I have found the reason--*in the Holy Spirit and in fire* (Lk. 3:16). It is not that He baptizes the same man *in the Holy Spirit and in fire*: the saint He baptizes *in the Holy Spirit*, while the other man, after believing and being judged worthy of the Holy Spirit, sins again--this one He bathes *in fire*. And so, it is not the same man that Jesus baptizes *in the Holy Spirit and in fire*.
>
> Blessed is he who is baptized in the Holy Spirit, and who has no need of the baptism of fire. And thrice unhappy is the other man who needs to be baptized *in fire*. . . .

---

[17]Origen equates the "first" resurrection with the grace of Baptism, which if kept unstained during life, allows a person to pass painlessly through the purifying fire. A repentant sinner will experience a painful passage through the fire as the dross of his/her sin is burned away. Origen calls the completion of the purifying experience of the repentant sinner the "second" resurrection. For a fuller discussion of this theme, see H. Crouzel, "La 'première' et la 'seconde' résurrection des hommes d' après Origène," *Didaskalia* 3 (1973): 3-19. Hereafter cited as "La 'première'."

[18]E.g., the apostles, Peter and Paul: *Hom. Ps. 36*, III, 1: PG 12, 1337B, an ambiguous text.

[19]E.g., an apostate in time of persecution: *Exhor. ad Mart.* 36: GCS I, 33, 20. The images of wood, straw, and stubble refer to all kinds of sins: see Crouzel, "L' exégèse," 276 f.

And blessed is he *who has a share in the first resurrection* (Rev. 20:6), the one who has kept the baptism of the Holy Spirit. Who is it that is to be saved in the second resurrection? It is the one who needs the baptism of fire: when he comes to this fire, the fire will try him (cf. 1 Cor. 3:13), and this fire will find wood, straw, and stubble (1 Cor. 3:12) to burn (*Hom. Jer.* II, 3).[20]

Everyone, saint and sinner, will pass through the fire, because the fire is God Himself,[21] or else it is related to Christ.[22] Nevertheless, only those in need of purification will feel anything painful. These latter are the dead, that is, the dead in Christ: they are sinners who have lost life, but having repented in this world or the next, they only receive total purification and salvation in the second resurrection, which is accompanied by this baptism of fire.[23] The living, those who pass through the baptism of fire unscathed, are conversely those who died to sin and rose with Christ in the

---

[20]*Hom. Jer.* II, 3: GCS III, 29,9; SC 232, 244.

[21]*Hom. Jos.* IV, 3: GCS VII, 311, 22; SC 71, 154: "Remember what is written: Those who draw close to me, draw close to fire." This is an *agraphon*, a word attributed to Christ, but not found in the text of the canonical scripture. It is also found, in a different form, in Didymus the Blind, *Expos. in Ps. 88, 8* : PG 39, 1488D: "He who is close to me is close to fire; he who is far from me is far from the Kingdom." This same form is found in the Nag Hammadi *Gospel of Thomas*, logion 82: J.-E. Ménard, *L' Évangile selon Thomas* (Nag Hammadi Studies V: Leiden: Brill, 1975): 70, 15; 182-184. See A. Jaubert, *Origène: Homélies sur Josué* (SC 71: Paris, 1960), 154, n. 1, and M. Simonetti, "Note sull' interpretazione patristica di Deuteronomia 4, 24," *Vetera christianorum* 5 (1968): 131-36.

[22]*Hom. Ez.* I, 3: GCS VIII, 324, 20 à propos Lk. 12:49.

[23]Crouzel, "La 'première'," 18-19.

first resurrection--their sacramental baptism in the Holy Spirit--and kept the baptismal grace pure and intact.

Generally in Origen's discussions, the eschatological purification is spoken of as in the future. Sometimes, however, in connection with the life of a faithful Christian, it is spoken of in the present: God, who is fire, consumes evil thoughts, shameful actions, and the desires of sin,

> when He inserts Himself into the minds of believers, and when He indwells, along with His Son, in those souls that have been made capable of receiving His Word and His Wisdom (*De Princ.* I, 1, 2).[24]

It does not seem, however, that the eschatological purification should be distinguished from the final judgment. In Origen's writings there is no difference between the particular judgment and the general judgment, nor is there any speculation about the intermediate period between time and eternity, which would extend from the death of the individual until the general resurrection. This will be the preoccupation of later theology.[25] Rather, after death, each person passes through the process of purification, the baptism of fire: the saints and repentant sinners--the former unscathed and the latter painfully purified--pass on afterwards to heaven, while the hardened, unrepentant sinners are sent to the "eternal fire" of Gehenna.

While a soul is undergoing this process of purification, it is also a time of instruction. Origen gives two opinions on where this might

---

[24]Crouzel, "L' exégèse," 278. *De princ.* I, 1, 2: GCS V, 17, 26; SC 252, 92, 33.

[25]Ibid., 282.

occur:[26] in the first, the saints will dwell in the air between heaven and earth; in the second, they will dwell in a special place on earth identified with the earthly Paradise (Gn. 2:8:LXX).[27] In both places, they do the same thing: they gain full knowledge of the things they have seen, and the reasons why things are so. The second opinion--the dwelling place somewhere on earth--is more developed; the place is called a *schola animarum*, a school for souls. In this place of instruction, the well-trained and alert soul will quickly pass from there into the air, and from the air into the heavens. The heavens have many stages through which the soul passes--the "many mansions" of Jn. 14:2--and it stops and observes each one and learns the reasons for what goes on there. The soul learns all about the stars; and most specially, it learns about the "invisible" things (cf. 2 Cor. 4:18) it never knew before. The presence of Christ pervades everywhere, since He is not confined to His corporeal body. When the soul attains the perfection of this knowledge, it is led by Christ to contemplate the Father "face to face" (cf. 1 Cor. 13:12).

This second opinion, then, involves ascension through the air, the realm of the planetary spheres,[28] to which, following ancient astronomy, Origen attaches the seven "wandering stars" or planets, i.e., the Sun, the Moon, Mars, Mercury, Jupiter, Venus, and Saturn. The planetary spheres explain the movements of these seven planets. To the seven spheres is added an eighth, the sphere of the stars, which, when seen from earth, is apparently

---

[26]*De princ.* II, 11, 6-7: GCS V, 189, 9; SC 252, 406, 186.

[27]Origen habitually allegorizes Paradise as the original place of rational creatures, and the future place of the blessed, which, according to some texts, is more than a determined place; it is the state of supernatural joy: *Hom. Lv.* XVI, 15; *Hom. Nb.* XII, 3; *Hom. 1 Rg. (1 Sm.)* I, 1; *Comm. Ct.* I. See H. Crouzel and M. Simonetti, *Origène: Traité des principes* (SC 253: Paris, 1978), 250, n. 43.

[28]*De princ.* II, 11, 6: GCS V, 190, 9; SC 252, 408, 224.

unmoving, with its stars placed together. It is beyond these eight spheres that Origen adds a ninth, an additional sphere, which recalls the one imagined by the astronomer, Hipparchus (190 B.C.E.), to explain the phenomenon of the "precession of equinoxes."[29] In this ninth sphere is set the "good land," the dwelling of the blessed, where they will pass to the "heritage of the heavenly kingdom."[30]

III.   Gehenna and the Punishment of the Damned

When the souls pass through the eschatological baptism of fire, a clear distinction is made between the repentant sinners, whose faults and sins God will consume, and the hardened sinner who will be swallowed up by death:[31]

> But God, the Fire, consumes human sins; He crushes, devours, and purifies them, just as He says elsewhere: *I will refine you with fire, until you are pure* (Is. 1:25). This is how He eats the sin of the one who offers sacrifice for sin. He Himself has taken on our sins (cf. Mt. 8:17), and within Himself, in so far as He is fire, He eats them and destroys them. And so, on the contrary, those who remain in their sins are said to be swallowed up by death, as it was written:

---

[29]Crouzel, "Mort," The precession was Hipparchus' greatest discovery; see G. J. Toomer, "Hipparchus," *Oxford Classical Dictionary* (1970): 516-17.

[30]*De princ.* II, 3, 7: GCS V, 125, 12; SC 252, 272, 337.

[31]Crouzel, "L' exégèse," 280.

Death prevails over them and will swallow them up (Ps. 48 (49):15.
Hom. Lv. V, 3).[32]

If the saints and repentant sinners eventually dwell in the heavens,
above the eight planetary and stellar spheres, the wicked--unrepentant and
hardened sinners--are damned to Gehenna, the place of fire. This is not the
"devouring fire" (cf. Dt. 4:24) which is equated with God, but the "eternal
fire" (Mt. 18:8; 25:41; Jude 7), the "unquenchable fire" (Mt. 3:12; Lk. 3:17;
Mk. 9:43), and finally, the "exterior darkness" (Mt. 22:13; 25:30).[33] This
eternal fire is different from material fire, simply because a material fire goes
out, but eternal fire does not. It is invisible and burns invisible realities.
Nevertheless, there is an analogy between the two kinds of fire: the terrible
suffering of a person who dies in a fire gives some idea of what can be
suffered in the eternal fire.[34]

When Gehenna is called the "exterior darkness," it signifies at least
two things: profound ignorance of God and His saving knowledge, and the
murky dark bodies of the damned that are outward signs of this ignorance.[35]
It is also the dwelling of demons, the "abyss" to which they return upon their
exorcism by Jesus (cf. Lk. 8:31).[36]

---

[32]*Hom. Lv.* V, 3: GCS VI, 338, 36.

[33]*Hom. Jr.* XII, 5; XIX (XVIII), 15: GCS III, 92, 30; 176, 1; SC
238, 28, 47; 246, 119. *Hom. Jos.* IX, 7: GCS VII, 352, 7; SC 71, 256.

[34]Crouzel, "L' Hadès," 317. *Ser. Mt* 72: GCS XI, 171, 25.

[35]*De princ.* II, 10, 8: GCS, V, 182, 3; SC 252, 392, 265.

[36]*Hom. Jos.* XV, 6: GCS VIII, 390, 23; SC 71, 350.

The "premier" demon in Gehenna is, of course, the Devil. When Origen personifies death in his writings, it is identified with either sin or the devil. In other words, it is the evil death because of sin that is Death *par excellence*, and the Devil is the personification of this death.[37]

While the "eternal fire" of Gehenna is often thought of as the abyss into which the wicked demons and the damned are cast, Origen also interprets this fire in a psychological or spiritual sense, as something kindled within the individual and fed by his/her own sins:

> If, then, such is the quality of the body that will rise from the dead, let us now see what is meant by the threat of eternal fire (cf. Mt. 25:41). And we find in the prophet Isaiah that it is attested that each person is punished by his own fire, for he says: *Walk in the light of your own fire and in the flame which you all enkindle in yourselves* (Is. 50:11). By these words, it seems to be indicated that each sinner kindles himself with his own fire, and is not immersed in another fire, which was previously kindled by someone else, or which pre-existed. The food for and the material of this fire are our sins, which the apostle Paul calls *wood, straw, and stubble* (cf. 1 Cor. 3:12). And I think that just as in the body an excess of nourishment, and the unrestrained quality or quantity of food produces fevers--of diverse kinds and frequencies, according to the measure in which the cumulative intemperance has amassed the materials and stimulated the fever (which quality of material amassed

---

[37]E.g., *Comm. Rm.* VI, 6: PG 14, 1067D-1068B - the Devil; *Hom. Jr.* XVII, 3: GCS III, 146; SC 238, 166, 37 - Sin; *Com. Mt.* XII, 33: GCS X, 143, 27 - Sin; *Hom. Lv.* IX, 11: GCS VI, 439, 19 - the Devil; *Hom. Jos.* VIII, 4: GCS VII, 340, 14; SC 71, 228 - the Devil.

from all kinds of intemperance, is the cause of more serious or longer illnesses)--so too the soul, when it has amassed in itself a large number of evil works and an excess of sins. At a suitable time, this whole mass of evils ferments into punishment and kindles into torments. Moreover, when the mind of the conscience, by divine power, recalls all the actions, whose various imprints and forms were impressed on it when it was sinning, will see set out before its eyes a kind of story (*historiam*) of every single evil deed, of every foul, disgraceful or impious act that it has done. Then the conscience is agitated and pricked by its own stings, and becomes the accuser and witness against itself. And I think that the apostle Paul thought likewise when he says: *Among themselves, their thought will accuse or defend them on the day on which God, according to my Gospel, will judge the secrets of men through Jesus Christ* (Rm. 2:15-16). From this, it is understood that in what concerns the very substance of the soul, the noxious passions (*affectibus*) of sinners generate certain torments (*De princ.* II, 10, 4).[38]

This spiritual interpretation of the "eternal fire" is apparently an adaptation on Origen's part of some Stoic ideas, especially of Chrysippus' (c. 280--207 B.C.E.) doctrine of "affections" or "passions."[39] In the Stoic

---

[38]*De princ.* II, 10, 4: GCS V, 177, 1; SC 252, 382, 22.

[39]H.-J. Horn, "Ignis aeternis: une interprétation morale du feu éternel chez Origène," *Revue des études grecques* 82 (1969): 79. Cf. *C. Cels.* I, 64; VIII, 51: GCS I, 117, 15; SC 132, 254, 22; GCS II, 266, 18; SC 150, 286, 19.

tradition, the passions are constantly compared with a burning fever.[40] According to Galen (c. 129-199 C.E.), Chrysippus used this image to explain the mental illness of passions: this illness corresponds to the body's disposition for the fever of passion.[41] Chrysippus, in line with his general intellectualism, interpreted Zeno's primitive definition of passion--"an irrational movement of the soul, which is against nature ($\pi\alpha\rho\grave{\alpha}$ $\phi\acute{\upsilon}\sigma\iota\nu$)," and "an exaggerated impulse"--as a movement of the soul, consisting of a disordered judgement of reason:[42]

> A passion is an exaggerated impulse, which is also disobedient to the controlling reason ($\lambda\acute{o}\gamma\psi$) or an irrational movement of the soul against nature ($\pi\alpha\rho\grave{\alpha}$ $\phi\acute{\upsilon}\sigma\iota\nu$) (for all passions belong to the authoritative part ($\acute{\eta}\gamma\epsilon\mu\omicron\nu\iota\kappa\acute{o}\nu$) of the soul) (Stobaeus, *Eclogai*, II, 88, 6.W.).[43]

The pivot of Chrysippus' theory is the interpretation of the passions as a negative disposition ($\nu\alpha\chi\epsilon\xi\acute{\iota}\alpha$), and, therefore, as a state of soul, i.e., as a way of existing in which the individual can only act in a delirious or passionate manner.[44] When the traditional definition of fever is compared with this definition of passion, an essential affinity can be ascertained:

---

[40]Horn, "Ignis aeternis," 80.

[41]Galen, *De Hippocratis et Platonis placitis*, V, 2: SVF III, 465, p. 116.

[42]Horn, "Ignis aeternis," 80.

[43]Stobaeus, *Eclogai*, II, 8, 6.W: SVF III, 378, p. 92.

[44]Horn, "Ignis aeternis," 81.

Fever was defined in different ways; but Empedocles and Zeno and
most of the Hippocratics have described it as an unnatural warming
(παρά φύσιν θερμασίαν), leaving the heart and spreading by the
arteries and veins throughout the whole body, and harmful, in an
obvious way, to the natural energies (Alexander of Aphrodisias (fl.
early 3rd c. C.E.) *De febribus* 2).[45]

The analogy between the definitions is in the generic part, the expression
παρὰ φύσιν, unnatural, appears in both, and in both, refers to excess.
Furthermore, the "passion" is a movement of the soul; in the description of a
fever as a θερμασία, a warming, movement is also implied. However,
these two points are not the whole comparison. Chrysippus' ethics are
primarily intellectualist: if virtue has the character of a knowledge of the
good, its contrary is ignorance. Since every human being has a natural and
unlimited desire to know, and consequently to be good, the Socratic idea that
"No one does evil deliberately," is true. However, most people act, at least
in part, out of involuntary ignorance. (Origen, for his part, does not accept
that absolute identification of sin/evil with ignorance.)[46]

The comparison, of course, is partly metaphorical. However, the
physicians of the *Corpus Hippocraticum* did not distinguish precisely
between feverish delirium and mental illness. It seems, then, that the
ancients considered the comparison to be partly literal, without, however,
having a clear and distinct idea of how this could be explained. In any event,

---

[45]Alexander of Aphrodisias, *De febribus*, 2; Greek text in Horn,
"Ignis aeternis," 82, n. 23.

[46]Horn, "Ignis aeternis," 82-83, and n. 29; *Comm. Jn.* XX, 40:
GCS IV, 382, 35.

the ancient physician understood the essence of health to be a measurable harmony for both the body and the soul. The dissolution of this harmony by fever in the body, or passion in the soul, puts the being of the person in danger.[47]

These ideas are exactly suited to Origen's purpose: the evil passions and sins of the soul cause a dissolution of the soul's harmony, in effect, a decomposition of its being. A loss of spiritual being is, in fact, estrangement from God. A hardened sinner is one who, by definition, is estranged from God. Thus, it is this decomposition of the soul, its loss of being, which constitutes for Origen the real punishment for sin. The punishment is hardest for the ignorant: the ignorance of the sinner is not lack of instruction, but a conscious refusal of the truth, which consists in self-knowledge. Whoever is not ready to know oneself will not see in oneself a participation in the image of God.[48]

One final point. In elaborating the nature of the punishments for sins, Origen was sensitive to the (primarily Gnostic) charge that God, especially in the Old Testament, was cruel and vindictive.[49] This sensitivity is, in part, responsible for the ambiguity his work displays on the question of the eternity or non-eternity of punishment. One thing seems clear: Origen presents his doctrine of the $ἀποκατάστασις$, the restoration of all things in Christ (cf. 1 Cor. 15:23-28), not as a dogma, but as a profound and secret hope; he has definite doubts and hesitations.[50] Sometimes it seems even the

---

[47]Ibid., 83-86.

[48]Ibid., 86-88. See also, H. Crouzel, *Origène et la philosophie* (Paris: Aubier, 1962), 72.

[49]E.g., *Hom. Lv.* XI, 2: GCS VI 450, 26.

[50]P. Nemeshegyi, *La paternité de Dieu chez Origène* (Tournai: Desclée, 1960), 214.

Devil will be restored to grace;[51] other times it seems that the fate of the hardened sinner is more or less definitive;[52] and sometimes Origen doesn't seem to know, although he inclines in the direction of repentance and restoration.[53]

---

[51]*De princ.* III, 6, 5: GCS V, 286, 10; SC 268, 244, 134.

[52]*Hom. Jr.* XVIII, 1: GCS III, 151, 7; SC 238, 176, 14. *Comm. Jn.* XIX, 14 (3), 88: GCS IV, 314, 8.

[53]*Frag. Eph.* 26 (Eph. 5:14): *JTS* 3 (1902): 563.

MOSES AND JESUS IN *CONTRA CELSUM* 7. 1-25: ETHICS, HISTORY AND JEWISH-CHRISTIAN EIRENICS IN ORIGEN'S THEOLOGY

Peter J. Gorday
Atlanta, Ga.

The gospel, then, does not lay down laws in contradiction to the God of the law, not even if we interpret literally the saying about a blow in the jaw. And neither Moses nor Jesus is wrong. Nor did the Father forget when he sent Jesus the commands which he had given to Moses. Nor did He condemn His own laws, and change His mind, and send His messenger for the opposite purpose.[1]

Origen has been described as a *mystic* for whom the lifetime process of the ascent of the soul to God begins with ethical purification but then, quickly transcending ethical concerns, passes to inward contemplation and the vision of God.[2] Origen has also been labeled an allegorist for whom the

---

[1]All citations of the *Contra Celsum* are from the *Origen: Contra Celsum*, translated with an introduction and notes by Henry Chadwick (Cambridge: Cambridge University Press, 1953). The page numbers given with references to *Contra Celsum* are based on this translation.

[2]So, for example, Andrew Louth, *The Origins of the Christian Mystical Tradition: From Plato to Denys* (Oxford: Clarendon Press, 1983

particularities and concreteness of real historical events in Scripture are of little import except as jumping-off places in various ways to timeless spiritual insight and experience.[3] Both pictures, that of Origen as an athlete of the inner rather than the outer life, and that of Origen as a spiritual interpreter of Scripture concerned with the meaning of the text only for the present, draw upon what is seen as the fundamental Platonism of his worldview, even, it is sometimes suggested, the gnosticism of his spirituality.[4] One implication of these pictures of Origen is that he may come to be seen as anti-Jewish, in the sense that as a mystic he thoroughly rejects the earthbound "types and shadows" of Judaism for a higher realm, while as an allegorist he rejects the "letter," including therein the historical and material world, the world of mere contingencies, to which Judaism and its institutions

---

pb), p. 59, who is generally dependent on Henri Crouzel, *Origène et la "connaissance mystique"* (Toulouse: Desclée et Brouwer, 1961), p. 65, and Marguerite Harl, *Origène et la fonction révélatrice du Verbe Incarné* (Paris: Éditions du Seuil, 1958), p. 321.

[3]Typical is R.P.C. Hanson, *Allegory and Event: A Study of the Sources and Significance of Origen's Interpretation of Scripture* (London: SCM Press, 1959).

[4]The classic treatment is Hal Koch, *Pronoia und Paideusis: Studien über Origenes und sein Verhältnis zum Platonismus* (Berlin and Leipzig: De Gruyter, 1932), who argued (p. 278) that Origen is a middle Platonist in his biblical hermeneutic, and thus intellectualist (p. 84) and Platonic (cf. p. 204) in his view of mystical ascent. The view that Origen is fundamentally gnostic in his theology is best known from the history of dogma tradition, represented pre-eminently by Adolf von Harnack, but also in the more recent work of Hans Jonas and, to some extent, Endre von Ivanka.

belong.[5] The final upshot for many is that Origen cannot be viewed as maintaining a real theology of the Incarnation, since incarnation would require in him a fundamental affirmation of flesh and materiality, not only as a dimension in which God works for the salvation of finite spirits, but also as an essential dimension of the divine being itself.[6]

The perspective on Origen thus articulated emerges in different ways both in the work of those who see him as a systematic thinker, as in the tradition of Harnack, de Faye, Koch and Harl, and in the work of those who see him not as systematic but as "coherent" in his teaching about the soul and perfection in Christ, such as Völker and Crouzel.[7] Both stances tend to be highly synthetic, drawing for their presentations upon the whole Origenian corpus, so to speak, rather than as a rule offering exhaustive analysis of individual texts. As something of a methodological shift, therefore, I would like to offer an examination of one passage in Origen which contains within a brief compass several of his major themes, in order to see if the standard

---

[5]The latest study of Origen and Judaism, Guiseppe Sgherri, *Chiesa e Sinagoga nelle opere di Origene*, Studia Patristica Mediolanensia 13 (Milan: Vita e Pensiero, 1982), highlights the antithetical and structurally parallel relationship of church and synagogue in Origen's ecclesiology. The emphasis on the theme of "church and synagogue" necessarily prejudices any view that might emerge in such a study of Origen's stance toward Judaism in a negative direction.

[6]Cf. Louth, *The Origins of the Christian Mystical Tradition*, p. 70, as an example.

[7]See the works cited in nn. 2 and 4, and Walther Völker, *Die Vollkommenheitsideal des Origenes: Eine Untersuchung zur Geschichte der Frömmigkeit und zu den Anfängen christlicher Mystik*, Beiträge zur historishcen Theologie 7 (Tübingen: J.C.B. Mohr, 1931). Included here also must be the work of Adolf von Harnack, *History of Dogma*, vols. 2 and 3, tr. Neil Buchanan (Boston: Little, Brown & Co., 1899), and Eugène de Faye, *Origène, sa vie, son oeuvre, sa pensée*, 3 vols. (Paris: Ernst Leroux, 1923, 1927, 1928).

picture sketched above needs some modification. Such a text is *Contra Celsum* 7. 1-25, where ethics, history, the Jew-Christian relationship and the Incarnation are all addressed, and in a way which suggests a complex set of relationships among all four. I would like to reflect upon these connections and draw out some implications particularly for the relationship between Christianity and Judaism.

I.

The discussion in *Contra Celsum* 7.1-25 opens with a fresh consideration by Origen of the truth of the Old Testament prophecy. Treatments of the nature and truth of prophecy in the earlier parts of the work establish important points: the laws of Moses enable the moral transformation of their hearers by their outward form (this for the multitude) and by their inner spirit (this for those with understanding) unlike the work of pagan philosophers which has been meaningful only for a few (1.18, pp. 19f). The function of the prophets has been to keep the Jews obedient to their law, and consequently the prophets were basically not diviners who foretold the future (1.36, p. 35); prophetic inspiration was by the Logos so that the prophets saw and recorded heavenly things just as did Jesus (1.48, p. 44). Jesus' actual ministry confirmed the divine inspiration of the prophets by functioning as its miraculous "proof," so that the ultimate fulfillment of prophecy by Jesus in his miracles is a kind of warrant for its moral authority and its pointing forward to him as the Christ (1.45, p. 41; 1.49-56, pp. 46-52). Christian initiation must always be a process of studying the law and the prophets (2.4, 6: pp. 69, 71). The continuing existence of the Jewish nation is taken as a sign that their prophets have spoken truth when they have criticized the gods and oracles of the Gentiles as false (3.2, pp. 129f).

Finally, moral reformation as the central purpose of God's providential activity has been fulfilled first for the Jews in the teaching of Moses and the prophets, then for all in the savior Jesus (4.4, p. 186f).

In Book VII, however, Origen again takes up the subject of Jewish prophecy, but this time to defend it against what seems to be a positive argument by Celsus on behalf of the truth of pagan oracles. Celsus appears to have contended that the Christian apologetic for the oneness of God, a God both just and good, based on the fulfillment of Jewish prophecy in Christ, must logically entail the conclusion that all prophecy which has been fulfilled in later events is *ipso facto* true. The example given by Celsus is that of the Pythian at Delphi, who foretold the successful establishment of colonies by the Greek city-states (7.2-3, pp. 395f). Celsus has thus taken up a kind of all-or-nothing approach to the truth of prophecy in general, based on *his* particular view of what constitutes historical fulfillment: namely, that later events confirm what has been foretold. Origen counters with a vindication of specifically Jewish prophecy by his own historical criteria, which are ethical and hermeneutical, the former involving the fitness of prophecy for the attainment of virtue, the latter dealing with the correct literary analysis of prophetic texts.

Origen opens with the view that true prophecy must induce virtue and piety in its hearers, which the Pythian had failed to do because of the vulgar nature of her means of inspiration and by the ecstasy and irrational frenzy that characterize her state of divine possession (7.3, pp. 395-397). He takes the position that her inspiration is demonic (this reflecting his view that the gods of the nations are demons) because of the crudeness and geographical localization of the Delphic cult (7.5-6, pp. 398-400). Prophecy from God, on the other hand, comes through wise and virtuous persons such as the Jewish prophets, whose teaching, as a foretelling of Christ, is credible precisely because the prophets really lived (unlike the Cynic philosophers, cf. 3.5ff., pp. 131ff.) the virtue of which they spoke (7.7, p. 400f.).

We may recall Origen's earlier argument (5.41-44, pp. 296-299) that the high ethical standard of the Jewish law, a standard which in its rejection of idolatry was far superior to the wisdom of the philosophers, justified their claim to be God's "elect portion." This teaching turned the Jews to the reality of God as spirit and did not permit them to confuse the shadow with the reality (4.31, pp. 206-208). Origen mentions specifically Moses, Jeremiah, Isaiah, Daniel, Noah and

> . . . countless others [who] prophesied unto God and foretold the story of Jesus Christ. That is the reason we reckon of no account the predictions uttered by the Pythian priestess . . . whereas we admire those of the prophets of Judaea, seeing that their strong, courageous, and holy life was worthy of God's Spirit, whose prophecy was imparted in a new way which had nothing in common with the divination inspired by demons (7.7, p. 401).

Origen then moves on to the question of the content of prophecy in order to respond to Celsus' charge that much contemporary prophecy is nonsensical and unintelligible, both because of the grandiose claim to divinity on the part of the prophet and because anyone can interpret the prophet's words in the desired fashion (7.9, pp. 402f.). Origen argues that the letter of the teaching of the Hebrew prophets was always immediately understandable to its hearers and was conducive to moral reformation, but that the deeper meaning--and here Origen appeals to a favorite proof-text in his hermeneutical theory, Proverbs 1.6--took the form of riddles, allegories, dark sayings and parables or proverbs (7.10, p. 403). Origen references his own commentaries on Isaiah, Ezekiel and the minor prophets as attempts to elucidate the deeper meaning of prophecies and makes a clear distinction between obscurity and meaninglessness (7.11, p. 404).

Since Celsus does not cite specific passages from the Jewish prophets in order to focus his charges, Origen deals with the general contention that prophecies which point to the sufferings of Christ are blasphemous or nonsensical because God cannot suffer (7.13-15, pp. 405-407). Origen responds to this charge with the view that the prophecies which describe the Messiah's suffering pertain only to his human aspect (7.16, pp. 407f.), as simple Christians would immediately know, and that these same prophecies tell us that:

> he endured as a wise and perfect man what must needs be endured by a man who does all in his power on behalf of the entire race of men and of material beings as well. There is nothing objectionable in the fact that a man dies, and that in his death should not only be given as an example of the way to die for the sake of religion, but also should effect a beginning and an advance in the overthrow of the evil one, the devil, who dominated the whole earth (7.17, p. 408).

We are reminded of Origen's earlier contention (2.40-42, pp. 98f.) that Jesus' death actually strengthened his cause among those willing to consider courage as a virtue.

At this point in the seventh book of the *Contra Celsum* Origen has in effect merged an argument from hermeneutics (only the letter of prophecy deals with Jesus' suffering), from ethics (the suffering of Jesus and the prophets was consistent with their message about virtue) and from historical apologetics (their virtue was actually lived on this earth) into a unity which focuses on the real humanity of the incarnate Logos as the instrument of redemption. This kind of convergence is a remarkable feature of this portion of *Contra Celsum* and leads to the final section of the passage under discussion, where Origen deals from 7.18 to 7.25 with Celsus' view that the teachings of Moses and Jesus on right living (their "laws") are contradictory. Origen must show that the contradictions alluded to by Celsus are only apparent, that in fact a deeper unity of Moses and Jesus really exists.

Celsus points out that Moses taught the importance of becoming rich and powerful, that God's people should fill the earth, and that they should slaughter their enemies, all of this the antithesis to Jesus' teaching that wealth and power are to be rejected, that material goods are not to be desired and that turning the other cheek is obligatory for one who has already been struck once. Origen immediately counters with the charge that Celsus has fallen into a fundamental error of hermeneutics by interpreting the law and the prophets literally, a mistake he could have avoided by recalling what Origen has already noted--that in fact the prophets lived in extreme poverty--and he cites Ps. 33.10, "many are the afflictions of the righteous." Clearly the teaching of the prophets is not to be understood literally, and, further, the Jews themselves know that some teachings are not to be taken at face value. Origen cites as examples Dt. 15.6 and 28.12, which state that righteous Jews shall be the lenders of money to many nations; it would be absurd to imagine that Judaism would ever possess so much wealth. The Jews would never have remained loyal to, or fought for, such nonsensical teaching, nor would they have experienced repentance so often after they had sinned against the law, if that same law were not true (7.18, pp. 409f).

Origen goes on to show that each of the prophetic passages referenced by Celsus on Moses' ethical doctrine is to be understood in some other sense than its obvious one, and he employs several lines of argument:

in one other case, he recalls the fact that Jewish interpreters do not take a verse at its face meaning (7.19, p. 410); he shows that the fulfillment of another prophecy came only in a paradoxical fashion (7.19, pp. 410-11); another verse is so inconsistent with plain reason that it requires the reader to discern the real words and intentions of the speaker in order to discover the deeper sense (7.19, pp. 410-11). Texts from Ezekiel and Paul are marshalled to show that the law has a spiritual interpretation which is life-giving even when the letter is "dead" (viz., nonsensical or contradictory) (7.20, p. 411).

The conclusion is that riches and power and filling the earth and slaughtering one's enemies all refer to spiritual realities that involve the purfication of the soul which hungers for God (7.21-25, pp. 411-415), and Origen devises an exegesis of each prophecy that relates it to individual ascetic discipline and thus to Jesus' teaching about self-denial and leaving all for the sake of the Kingdom. In this way Origen is able to announce triumphantly in 7.25 that neither Moses nor Jesus is wrong: both are saying essentially the same thing and God is shown to be consistent as He has inspired both men with genuine prophecy.

Elsewhere in the *Contra Celsum* Origen of course makes it clear that as a believer in Jesus Christ he is obliged to disagree with the Jewish understanding of Moses and the prophecies (e.g., 2.4, p. 69f.). He subscribes to a christological scriptural hermeneutic--and so he can refer to Jewish rejection of Christ (e.g., 2.8, pp. 71-73, and *passim*) and to Jewish "mythologies" (2.6, p. 71) and to the disbelief of Judaism as present throughout the Old Testament narrative, particularly in their rejection of Moses himself when he gave the first law (2.74-75, pp. 122f). On the other hand, he can use as a warrant for the more philosophical, less literal, understanding of an Old Testament narrative the statements of "the wise men among the Hebrews" who know, as he does, that a Mosaic passage cannot be pointless when Moses himself wanted the people to believe in what he had given them.

Indeed, in this connection, it is evident in numerous passages of *Contra Celsum* and particularly in the seventh book that Origen makes the hermeneutical leap from a literal understanding of a prophetic passage to its New Testament re-interpretation via the use of passages from the wisdom-literature, particularly the book of Proverbs. In *Contra Celsum* 7.1-25 Wisdom of Solomon is cited twice, Psalms four times, and Proverbs four times in key settings where it is the Jewish scriptures themselves that suggest the need for a more "spiritual" interpretation of the very Pentateuchal passages in question. When Moses in Genesis or Exodus or Deuteronomy calls for an emphasis on wealth or power or the massacre of enemies, it is evident from the hermeneutical key provided in Proverbs or Psalms or other Solomonic texts that what he really means, i.e., the spiritual interpretation, is more ethically elevated than first appears and consequently more in line with Jesus' teaching in the gospels. It would be fair to say, I believe, that, in Origen's view of Moses and Jesus, Jew interprets Jew in order to bring Moses to a position of harmony with Jesus, all of this being done to counter the common foe, the pagan Celsus, with his outrageous views on prophecy and the nature of divine truth.

II.

The first implication of the foregoing analysis concerns the status and role of ethical teaching in Origen's total exegetical and theological program as it comes to expression in his debate with Celsus about the $\dot{\alpha}\lambda\eta\theta\dot{\eta}s$ $\lambda\dot{o}\gamma os$, the fundamental truth about God, the world and human existence.

In *Contra Celsum* 7.4 Origen argued that the divine inspiration of the Hebrew prophets is assured because of their *virtue*, because of how they lived; and in 7.7 he described in specific terms the hardships and sufferings which they endured, far more indeed than the pagan philosophers have ever faced. In 7.10 we learn that the thrust of their teaching was toward the planting of virtue in their hearers and readers. Such sentiments, as noted, are virtual commonplaces in *Contra Celsum*, not least when they are constantly applied to Jesus himself, who is declared the most virtuous of all men, as well as the source and origin of all virtue (1.57, p. 52). The ability of Christian teaching to produce in fact real moral conversion in its adherents is an essential criterion of its truthfulness (1.64, pp. 59f.; 2.45-46, pp. 101f.) even if the content of that moral teaching is largely a reflection of what all virtuous people have come to know (1.4, pp. 8f.) and practice.[8] Jesus' sufferings, the object of so much scorn from Celsus, are declared to be not a compromise of the truth of his teaching, but an actual vindication for those who know that courage is a virtue (2.42, p. 99). "Undertaking the life which Jesus taught," which produces "friendship with God and fellowship with Jesus," is claimed to be the right way to experience the truth of the assertion that he is simultaneously human and divine and that in him God intends for human nature to be divinized (3.28, pp. 145f.).

This line of thought then merges by degrees with the more comprehensive argument for the nature of God as infinite moral goodness and

---

[8]Cf. Carl Joachim Classen, "Der platonisch-stoische Kanon der Kardinaltugenden bei Philo, Clemens Alexandrinus und Origenes," *Kerygma und Logos: Beiträge zu den geistesgeschichtlichen Beziehungen zwishen Antike und Christentum: Festschrift für Carl Andresen zum 70. Geburtstag,* edited by Adolf Martin Ritter (Göttingen: Vandenhoeck und Ruprecht, 1979), p. 68-88, for the view that Origen's classification and ordering of the virtues is largely traditional.

for a world order, manifesting itself universally in all races and particularly in the prophets and Jesus, as benignly providential, moving all persons through punishment and reward into a deeper apprehension of virtue and its fundamental rationality. As in Stoic doctrine (cf. *Contra Celsum* 4.29, pp. 204f.; 6.48, p. 365),[9] the virtue to be sought after and enjoyed by human beings is precisely that which God himself practices since the Logos is the essential factor shared by both creatures and Creator.

That this emphasis on virtue in his theology and spirituality is derived ultimately from Stoic sources, both directly and as mediated through middle-Platonist adaptations, is generally agreed upon.[10] What is less clear and more disputable is the *role* played by his ethical reflection in Origen's view of the process of spiritual maturing.[11] A passage which has become a *locus classicus* in the discussion is found in the prologue to Origen's *Commentary on the Song of Songs*, where he makes ethical study the first step in the ascent to God, for it is by ethical study, associated in that text with the book of Proverbs as the first of wise Solomon's books, that the soul acquires "a seemly manner of life" and gains "a grounding in habits that incline to virtue." Then follows the study of physics, that is, the natural

---

[9]Pierre Nautin, *Origène: Sa vie et son oeuvre* (Paris: Beauchesne, 1977), p. 192, n. 15.

[10]As in the works cited of Koch, Chadwick (next note) and Classen.

[11]The opposing positions would be those of Henry Chadwick, "Origen, Celsus and the Stoa," *JTS* 48 (1947), pp. 34-49, who concludes with reference to Clement and Origen: "To both of them Christianity is not a philosophical school or point of view; it is primarily a living religion demanding right conduct"; and Henri Crouzel, *Origène et la "connaissance mystique,"* and *Origène et la philosophie* (Paris: Aubier, 1962), p. 35, n. 123, who complains in his evaluation of Origen and Stoicism that Chadwick's article just mentioned is confined to a consideration of *Contra Celsum* only.

ends for which all things exist, linked to the book of Ecclesiastes, and finally enoptics, that is, the contemplation of God, as taught in the Song of Songs.[12] The frequent conclusion, as noted, is that ethical study is strictly propaedeutic in Origen's scheme, since he is preeminently focused on the mystical vision of God, located beyond the world of sense and time.

Our brief analysis of *Contra Celsum* 7.1-25 ought to caution us against too one-sided an interpretation of the *Commentary on the Song of Songs* passage and its cognates, however.[13] We have seen that an essential criterion of truth for Origen is that it is virtue lived in the world of space and time; otherwise, what passes as truth has no further claim to consideration. His debate with Celsus is in part not so much about the nature of virtue as about who does it, when the talking is over. Consequently, virtue in the broadest sense (especially if we include piety within its compass)[14] must belong to the whole of Christian maturing, not simply to an early or preliminary phase.

It has been shown by Walther Völker that Origen's whole conception of perfection is permeated by an ideal of ethical purity grounded in love for God that is essential to the mystical experience, an experience which Völker claims to be basically different from the Stoic concern for ἀπάθεια, but which, I would contend, is by its very centrality to Origen's thought

---

[12]*Origen, The Song of Songs, Commentary and Homilies*, tr. R.P. Lawson, Ancient Christian Writers 26 (New York and Ramsey, N. J.: Newman Press, 1956), prologue, sec. 3 (pp. 39ff.).

[13]Principally, *Hom. in Gen.* 13 and 14, and *Hom. in Num.* 12, discussed by Crouzel, *Origène et la philosophie*, p. 22-24.

[14]Cf. Classen, "Der platonisch-stoische Kanon, p. 84.

revealing of the influence of the Stoic theological environment.[15] While Völker puts special emphasis on Origen's concern with martyrdom as the highest form of the *imitatio Christi*, and therefore an act of mystical union,[16] I would suggest that Origen's mature focus was simply on the possession of virtue as itself the life of the Kingdom of God;[17] and if we keep in mind the broadest possible conception of virtue, which includes for Origen the practice of a piety which is empowered by divine grace, then the whole range of Christian experience would seem to be comprehended.

To return to the terminology of the prologue to the *Commentary on the Song of Songs*, enoptics must include ethics as a co-terminous dimension of itself, must indeed see itself as ethically conditioned and determined in a

---

[15]Völker, *Die Vollkommenheitsideal des Origenes*, pp. 146ff. But this tendency to look for a fundamental difference between Origen and the Stoics based on the christologically empowered character of Christian virtue and by the ultimate Christian concern with *imitatio Christi* rather than pure ἀπάθεια must be balanced by Chadwick, "Origen, Ceslus and the Stoa," p. 48. See also now Marcia L. Colish, *The Stoic Tradition from Antiquity to the Early Middle Ages*, vol. I: Studies in Classical Latin Literature (Leiden: E.J. Brill, 1985), who, in a general characterization of the early and middle Stoa, makes the point: "*Apatheia* is not virtue but is a necessary precondition for it. It does not denote a state of passivity but the detachment from things evil and indifferent which gives the sage the moral liberty to judge and to act rightly" (p. 44.). Origen would have agreed.

[16]Völker, *Die Vollkommenheitsideal des Origenes*, pp. 176ff.

[17]Cf. *Comm. in Matt.* 12.14, where, in commenting on Mt. 16: 13-19 and Christ's bestowal of the keys of the Kingdom on Peter, Origen says, "I think that, as a reward for every virtue of knowledge, certain mysteries of wisdom, corresponding to the kind of virtue, are opened up to the one who lives virtuously, since the Savoir bestows on those who have not been subdued by the gates of hell as many keys as there are virtues. These keys, in turn, open an equal number of gates, corresponding to each virtue according to the revelation of the mysteries. Perhaps too every virtue is a kingdom of heaven, such that whoever lives by the virtues is already in the kingdom of heaven . . . " (GCS - Origenes Werke 10.96.33-97.17).

way which brings this particular tripartite division of the process of mystical ascent more into line with the conventional Stoic division of studies in which ethics is the highest and last category.[18] It is not that the pursuit of enoptics quickly leaves ethics behind, rather it is that enoptics contains a gathering up and focusing of ethics within itself so that Gregory Thaumaturgus' description of Origen's course of studies as logic/physics/ethics, with the analysis of virtue as the highest stage, may be taken as substantially true and an indication that we are not to take the prologue to the *Commentary on the Song of Songs* too literally here.

III.

A second issue raised by *Contra Celsum* 7.1-25, which is closely related to the question of the relative import of ethics for Origen, is the matter of his "this-worldliness" as it comes to expression in his biblical hermeneutics. It is easy to draw the conclusion that not only does Origen give the lowest place in the scheme of mystical ascent to ethics. but also that precisely for this reason he has little or no concern for an affirmation of, and fundamental commitment to, the historical actuality of the characters and events of the biblical narratives. Again, however, my reading of the seventh

---

[18]On the Stoic order of studies, see Colish, *The Stoic Tradition*, p. 23. Already for Zeno of Citium, the order logic-physics-ethics is in effect, Hans F. A. von Arnim, *Stoicorum veterum fragmenta*, 4 vols. (Leipzig, 1903-24; reprint Stuttgart: Teubner, 1964), I, 46, as reported by Diogenes Laertius. Cf. Gregory Thaumaturgus, *The Thanksgiving Discourse*, esp. IX, 115ff., where Gregory describes ethical teaching as the goal of Origen's educational programme, *Grégoire le Thaumaturge, Remerciement à Origène-- suivi de la Lettre d'Origène à Grégoire*, texte grec. Introduction, traduction et notes, Henri Crouzel, s.j., SC 148 (Paris, Éditions du Cerf, 1969). Père Crouzel, pp. 87ff., agrees with W. Völker that Gregory over-hellenizes Origen's course of study, making it more Stoic than in fact it was.

book of the *Contra Celsum* ought to create hesitation in accepting such a view.

Origen, as I have indicated, was anxious, from the beginning of his argument on behalf of the truth of Jewish prophecy, to establish the fact that these prophecies were actually uttered at certain times in certain places (7.8). Likewise, the prophets were men who really lived, and as a result, their virtue was real (7.7). Moses and Jesus are historical figures, we learn elsewhere in *Contra Celsum* (c.f. the whole argument of 1.42-71, pp. 39-65), the events of whose lives are to be adjudged as actual because of the moral power with which they infuse human lives in the present. That the virgin birth of Jesus and the miracles he worked in fact did occur is part of Origen's demonstration of the veracity of prophecy. Further, we know from at least one passage (3.42, pp. 156f.) that Origen took the Stoic position that bodily nature is in itself morally neutral, the implication being that it is no shameful thing for Jesus as the Son of God to have been real flesh. The suffering of Jesus is in similar fashion not to be seen as disgraceful, for although it was endured by the human nature of Jesus only, the assumption on Origen's part is that the suffering really occurred as part of the virtue that Jesus in fact summed up in his historical person (7.13-17).

These concerns for historical actuality can be paralleled from other of Origen's late writings, particularly the commentaries on Matthew and Romans, but the basic point here is simply that Origen's apologetic in *Contra Celsum* is fundamentally historical in its orientation--i.e., contingent events and persons are the vehicles for eternal truth precisely because they are *actual*. Such a contention takes Origen beyond anything that can be claimed by the allegorizing middle-Platonists in their approach to the poetic texts or even by Celsus.

As Carl Andresen showed,[19] Celsus worked out a concept of history in which the Platonic Logos, that body of ancient and mysterious truth about the essential nature of things, has been revealed to the wise from the beginning, only in the course of time to be submerged and then re-instated in the folk knowledge and custom practiced in many cultures and rearticulated by new wise men. For Celsus it is "antiquity," the παλαιὸς λόγος, that is the heart of ἀληθῆς λόγος. Andresen was wrong, however, in following Hal Koch too closely and assuming on the basis of the fourth book of *De Principiis* that Origen is only another non-historical middle-Platonist, allegorizing the narrative texts of Scripture and reducing them, in Plutarchian fashion, to moral and fundamentally timeless *exempla* which can then be refined into spiritual verities.[20] Whatever may be the case with Origen's hermeneutics in the *De Principiis*, by the time of the *Contra Celsum* he had moved on to a deeper appreciation of the place of contingent event in the very being of the Logos. Indeed, as H. Cornélis has argued,[21] for Origen the moral situation of human beings is basically a reflection of their *physical*

---

[19]Carl Andresen, *Logos und Nomos: Die Polemik des Kelsos wider das Christentum* (Berlin: De Gruyter, 1955).

[20]Ibid., pp. 292-307, for Andresen's summary comparison of the historical consciousness of Celsus with that of Plutarch, who is taken as the quintessential middle Platonist. For Andresen's reliance on Hal Koch's work, in which Origen is seen as a middle Platonist with no sense of history, cf. pp. 373ff.

[21]H. Cornélis, "Les fondements cosmologiques de l'eschatologie d'Origène," *RSPhTh* 43 (1959), pp. 32-80, 201-247, especially the conclusions, pp. 246f. The logic of Cornélis' presentation is that in some sense Origen's espousal of the Stoic doctrine of providence must entail a form of materialism in metaphysics. Origen believes that the cosmos is immanent to God even if God is not immanent in the cosmos. Consequently, souls must have bodies if they are to realize their providential, i.e., eschatological, destiny.

situation, since in his epistemology the intelligible world, the κοσμòς
νοητός, can be known and can come to realization only through the
mediation of concrete, physical entities. The moral quality of these, i.e.,
their historical virtue, will be the channel by which all persons can progress
in the cosmic movement toward eschatological perfection. In this view
corporeality is indispensable to the being of the Logos in a kind of Hegelian
embodiment, so to speak, which fuels all historical movement.

Origen's hermeneutics may indeed be called a hermeneutics of
historical contingence, as Henri de Lubac suggested in his work *Histoire et
esprit*,[22] but one must not state the case in too metaphysical a fashion since
so much of what Origen does is textual and literary in the manner displayed
in the seventh book of *Contra Celsum*. Jewish history and Christian history,
Moses and Jesus, are the same, i.e., have the same inner meaning, but one's
ability to see that fact depends on the use made of the latter history to
interpret the former. The key to the common element--the shared substance,
so to speak--which unites the two histories is provided by the use of texts
from the Jewish wisdom-literature, particularly, as I have indicated, texts
from Proverbs.[23] Here the literary categorizations contained in 1.6 are
essential to Origen's hermeneutics, as H.-J. Vogt has shown,[24] and the use

---

[22]H. de Lubac, *Histoire et esprit: l'intelligence de l'Écriture d'après
Origène* (Paris: Aubier, 1950), pp. 117f.

[23]Cf. W. Völker, "Die Verwertung der Weisheits-Literatur bei den
christlichen Alexandrinern," *ZKG* 64 (1952-53), pp. 1-33, especially 23ff.

[24]H.-J. Vogt, Introduction to *Origenes, Der Kommentar zum
Evangelium nach Matthäus*, Bibliothek der griechischen Literatur 18
(Stuttgart: Anton Hiersemann, 1983), pp. 38f.

of Proverbs-texts generally is omnipresent in Origen's strategies for dealing with a number of passages, especially in the Old Testament homilies.[25]

It is especially noteworthy that the books of the Jewish wisdom-literature are cited in *Contra Celsum*, apart from massive use of the Psalms, primarily in the form of citations from Proverbs, with hardly any use of the Song of Songs. This fact is not surprising in light of the description in the prologue to the *Commentary on the Song of Songs*, in which an essential dimension of ethical study, that provided by logic or "rational science," is precisely hermeneutics. The very name Proverbs suggests that this book contains the clues for distinguishing between what a word openly says and what is inwardly meant, as well as the means for discerning "the meanings and proper significances and their opposites, the classes and kind of words and their expressions."[26] So it is that moral science and hermeneutics, and thus the determination of what is porperly historical in Scripture, go hand-in-hand.

Contra Celsum 7.18-19 shows that the actual meaning of certain prophetic teachings is to be clarified with reference to the actual situations of the prophets themselves *and* to what Jewish interpreters make of these passages, not with regard to what the passages seem to mean, i.e., their letter, which upon examination turns out to be historically nonsensical. A proper procedure of interpretation in which the exegete knows how to penetrate surface obscurity (7.10-11)[27] by means of his faith (he is in

---

[25]Cf. *Biblia Patristica: Index des citations et allusions bibliques dans la littérature patristique,* vol. III: *Origène* (Paris: Éditions du Centre National de la Recherche Scientifique, 1980), p. 201, for a convenient listing of the places where Origen uses Prov. 1.6.

[26]*Commentary on the Song of Songs,* Ancient Christian Writers 26, prol. 3, n. 11, p. 41.

[27]Cf. Marguerite Harl, "Origène et les interpretations partistiques grecques de l"obscurité' biblique," *VC* 36 (1982), pp. 334-371, especially the remarks on 354f.

Christ), his discernment (he compares spiritual things with spiritual) and his knowledge of literary technique (he compares passages for the common significations of words and phrases) will yield, as part of the exegete's own spiritual ascent, the true meaning.

Again, we are warned against an interpretation of Origen's mystical ascent which would involve too hasty a dismissal of ethics and history as fundamental and enduring in the Christian's journey towards God. Furthermore, this portion of *Contra Celsum* should steer us away from too precipitately claiming that Origen does not have a real doctrine of the Incarnation. While by the terms and standards of later Athanasian orthodoxy such a claim may be justified, Origen's own argument would seem to make no sense without a historical Jesus who is at the same time the fullness of the Logos embodied perfectly.[28]

---

[28]The summary comments of Ekkehard Mühlenberg, "Apollinaris von Laodicea und die origenistische Tradition," *ZNW* 76 (1985), pp. 270-283, are, I believe, accurate and helpful. He describes the function and nature of the Incarnation in Origen's theology in these terms (p. 280): "Bei der Gleichgestaltung mit der körperhaft offenbaren Seele Jesu beginnt der Aufstieg zur Gottesschau, also von ARETE in Angleichung an Jesus und sein Handeln bis hin zur noetischen Gotteserkenntnis. Die körperhaft anschauliche Manifestation der logosgestaltigen Seele ist der notwendige und unüberbietbare Anknüpfungspunkt. Denn nur in dieser Gebrochenheit auf der Seinsebene des Menschen ist den sündigen Menschen ARETE zugänglich." Mühlenberg's argument is that the pre-existent union of the Logos with Jesus' human soul in Origen's christology is a real anticipation of the community of being which Athanasius was to insist upon in his christology as the presupposition of the saving union of human and divine in the Incarnation. Origen's christology takes authentic humanity seriously because it insists that salvation have a noetic dimension in which virtue is *learned* by the Savior, even if his human soul is by nature drawn to that virtue.

IV.

The upshot of this examination of the place of ethics and history in the seventh book of *Contra Celsum* is that Origen emerges as a Christian thinker deeply engaged with the Jewishness of Scripture and its interpretation and, therefore, inclined to be eirenic in his view of Judaism. The logic of his view of truth makes him so, requiring the assertion against Celsus that neither Moses nor Jesus is wrong, that both are right with each needing the other to be understood. To state the matter in the simplest possible way, for Origen there would be without Moses (i.e., Judaism, the Old Testament, the letter of Scripture, history and ethics) nothing to be understood--no revelation of God worthy of the name by Celsus' criterion of antiquity--and thus no need for a hermeneutic; but without Jesus, historical and incarnate as fully embodied virtue, there would be nothing with which to understand, no key to the Scriptures that could unlock their true meaning. Moses and Jesus exist in a true dialectic, each absolutely, by his very nature, needing the other in order to be himself and to fulfill his proper revelatory function. Further, as I have argued, this Moses-Jesus relationship comes to expression most clearly when Origen wrestles with history and ethics in his spirituality. The results of such a structure in his thinking are various for his view of the relations between Christians and Jews in his own day, but all point to a profound and genuine, not a posed and condescending, "eirenicism" toward Judaism on the part of the Church.[29]

---

[29]The best general treatment now is N. R. M. de Lange, *Origen and the Jews: Studies in Jewish-Christian Relations in Third-Century Palestine*, University of Cambridge Oriental Publications 25 (Cambridge, England: Cambridge University Press, 1976), pp. 63-85.

A). Without a clearly defensible linkage to Moses and the prophets Jesus' status would become ambiguous because his teaching would be a novelty, unworthy of being considered as real wisdom. Origen cannot proceed simply to "spiritualize" the teaching of Moses in order to conform it to Jesus' statements without seeking a warrant within the Jewish Scriptures and their own procedures of self-interpretation, a warrant whereby the Jews themselves point to a revelation that transcends their particular history and their particular Scriptures. In this way the bearers of antiquity are made to testify to their having been supplanted by a revelation that will go beyond their particularism while, simultaneously, not leaving it behind. It is at this point that the wisdom literature plays the role of intermediary, conveying in a more spiritual, and, in my argument, more timelessly ethical re-interpretation of Moses. In addition, rabbinic interpretation of Moses is sequestered by Origen for the same role, as we see in *Contra Celsum* 7.18-19, where Jewish expositors are claimed to have argued for non-literal exegesis of ethical teaching that cannot be taken at face-value.

B). The consistency which exists between Moses and Jesus is at bottom the consistency of God's activity (and, therefore, an identity), as we learn in *Contra Celsum* 7.25, and, as such, exhibits the character of a temporal manifestation of the eternal, whose revealed content can only be expounded from one age to the next, never definitively and finally articulated. This fact arises from the character of biblical language itself with its polyvalence and obscurity and multi-layered significations, but it comes also from the fact that the very act of exposition is always to some extent contaminated by the imperfection of the expositor who is not yet without sin.

The antidote to this contamination must be an interpretative setting in which the respective custodians of Moses and Jesus, the synagogue and the

Church, debate their differing views and in which the Church, the younger partner who claims to be in the right, is always in the humiliating posture of having to seek insight from the older partner who is seen to be ultimately in the wrong because of the denial of Jesus' messiahship. This denial does not, however, rule out a more proximate kind of insight which the Christian must have from the Jew. In the allegory of Pharoah's daughter and the infant Moses in the second chapter of Exodus, the daughter, who represents the church of the Gentiles, can never cease to take Moses in her arms and to learn from him that the rejection of idolatry is the beginning of righteousness.[30] The Church thus owes a debt in perpetuity to the synagogue and must incessantly listen to it in order to relearn certain basic truths on the one hand and on the other to avid its errors and the blindness that has resulted.

C). Origen does not hesitate to state repeatedly his charges against the Jews even when he cannot stop from appropriating their heritage. There is no question here of a philosemitism or of a softening of Christian arguments against Jewish prerogatives and exclusivism. Rather, there is a sense of kinship, necessary, divinely ordained, and functional within a dynamic of salvation for both Jews and Gentiles, in which neither party as a whole is to give up its claims until the right time. Consequently, Origen can both affirm and contradict Judaism, almost in the same breath and with a seemingly grand inconsistency, a fact which cannot be reduced to mere

---

[30]*Hom. in Ex.* 2.4 (*Origène, Homélies sur l'Exode*, Texte Latin. Introduction, traduction, et notes par Marcel Borret, s.j., SC 321 [Paris: Éditions du Cerf, 1985], p. 82). Such at any rate is the implication of the transaction that takes place between Pharoah's daughter and the Hebrew nurse to whom the infant Moses is entrusted after being found in the river. The payment which is promised to the nurse is that the Gentiles will abandon idolatry, now that they have received the Law in the person of Moses. The Jews in return will be moved by jealousy of the Gentile Church and its virtue to a purified rejection of idols on their own part (p. 86).

apologetics--a device, so to speak, for defending Christianity against Celsus or against Gnostic detractors of the Old Testament. The ethical and historical dimensions of revelation form an adamantine bond between Jew and Christian in which there must be a refusal to dissolve the ascent of souls into an ahistorical spiritualism or an otherworldly mysticism. Ethics and concrete history combine in the seventh book of *Contra Celsum* for an approach to prophecy that in turn provides the logic for a true Jewish-Christian eirenicism.

ORIGEN AND EARLY CHRISTIAN PLURALISM: THE CONTEXT OF HIS ESCHATOLOGY

Jon F. Dechow
Portola Valley, Ca.

Origen (185-254 C.E.), foundational Christian theologian of ancient Alexandria and Caesarea, was not neutral on what we call today the varieties of early Christianity or early Christian pluralism, nor on that toward which Christian faith points, the resurrection. He did not think one type of belief was just as good as another. Research in the modern period tries to respect the self-definitions of religious groups in antiquity, including early Christian groups later deemed orthodox or heretical, but Origen did not share this mentality. Here we shall look at some of the ways he distinguished himself from other early Christians, especially on the subject of resurrection, and offer a positive statement of his enduring importance and value as Christian theologian and religious thinker.[1]

---

[1]An earlier version of this paper was presented March 20, 1986, in a Christian Theology session of the American Academy of Religion/Western Region annual meeting (March 20-22), University of Santa Clara, Santa Clara, California.

1. Early Christian Pluralism

Near the start of his career as a Christian scholar, Origen chose a middle way between those he called "the hard-hearted and ignorant members of the circumcision" (some Jews), "heretical sects" (mostly gnostics), and "the simpler [believers][2] of the church."[3] From historical study he knew that scripture sometimes says things that "did not happen, . . . could not happen, and . . . might have happened but in fact did not."[4] And "the reason why all" three of the error-prone groups "hold false opinions and make impious or ignorant assertions about God appears to be this, that scripture is not understood in its spiritual sense, but is interpreted according to the bare letter."[5]

In the interpretive process, Origen had no qualms about calling wrong those he considered wrong. He believed "the wisest Christian knows the Jewish and Christian heresies."[6] Some gnostic heretics, like Ophites and Cainites, he considered completely outside the pale of Christianity.[7] Unlike modern scholars who hestitate to call Marcion a gnostic, Origen thought him

---

[2]Sigla (in translated ancient texts):
( ) enclose 1) words from the original texts or 2) added Biblical references
[ ] enclose 1) added words for the sake of translation, 2) editorial interpolations, or 3) parenthetical matter already within parentheses
< > enclose editorial emendations to the original texts.

[3]*Princ.* 4.2.1.

[4]*Princ.* 4.2.9; see 4.3.1.

[5]*Princ.* 4.2.2.

[6]*Cels.* 3.12-13.

[7]*Cels.* 3.13.

one of the "dealers in 'knowledge (γνῶσις) falsely so-called (ψευδώνυμος)' (1 Tim 6.20)."[8] The Alexandrian opposed "the schools of Marcion, Valentinus, and Basilides" on the goodness of God and the predestination of rational beings.[9]   The Valentinian Heracleon was a major opponent in the *Commentary on John*. Origen opposed Basilides' "nihilistic" view of the Son of God's origin,[10] which emerged later in different form in Arianism. Anti-Valentinian views about resurrection were also expressed in the (lost) *Dialogue with Candidus*.

In popular Christianity (see Crouzel 1978, 37-38), Origen opposed Montanist ecstatic prophecy[11] and, within the more regularized mainstream, anthropomorphic (e.g., Tertullian), chiliastic/materialistic (e.g., Papias, Justin, Irenaeus, Athenagoras), and literalistic Christianity (especially the "simpler" believers, sometimes taken to mean popular, "institutional" Christianity in general).

Yet Origen was usually irenic in stating his differences with others, seeming to enjoy the interplay of ideas toward the best evidence, interpretation, and argument. He did not use institutional authority to coerce agreement, but the living Word and words were his stock in trade. In contrast to relying on secret books that gnostics possessed, he believed Jesus' words about Jewish lawyers having the "key of knowledge" (Luke 11.52) pointed toward traditional canon as basic.[12] Such scripture could only be understood

---

[8]*Jo.* 5.4.

[9]*Princ.* 2.9.5.; see 3.1.8; also *Cels.* 5.61.

[10]*Princ.* 4.4.1. See Hipp. *Haer.* 7.8-10.

[11]*Princ.* 2.7.3.

[12]*Princ.* 4.2.3.

correctly by those who have "the mind of Christ" (1 Cor 2.12-13, 16), who would interpret it "threefold ($\tau\rho\iota\sigma\sigma\delta\varsigma$)" (Prov 22.20 LXX), i.e., according to its "body, soul, and spirit",[13] an elaboration of the "spirit" over "letter" principle of the apostle Paul (2 Cor 3.6; see Rom 2.29).[14]

He often drew on cultural resources to illuminate sacred tradition, using the principle of correlation long before Paul Tillich and in the process shedding light on the perennial problem of corporeality in the history of philosophy and science. Thus he associated the "incorporeal" of philosophical tradition with the "invisible" of Biblical tradition.[15] In method typical of intellectual Alexandrian Christianity including Clement, he was closer to Plato than Aristotle, but considered himself eclectic, opposing Aristotle on the existence of a fifth element and holding to more "mainstream" cosmological principles of his time that had analogy with or inference from scripture.[16] If (*cum grano salis*) we would make comparisons to moderns, we might consider him culturally less Jungian than Kuhnian, and as a theologian less of Teilhard than of Rahner, with some Merton thrown in.

2. The Resurrection

On the subject of afterlife and resurrection his views were controversial within the church early on, but he believed they were faithful to Christian tradition and posed appropriate options on matters not yet clearly

---

[13]*Princ.* 4.2.4.

[14]*Princ.* 1.1.2; see 1. Pref. 8, 4.2.5, 4.3.6-7.

[15]*Princ.* 4.3.15; see 1.1.7-8.

[16]*Princ.* 3.6.6.

decided. Ancient Judaism also had its variations of resurrection tradition (Nickelsburg 1972; 1981, esp. 599-600), and complicating matters on the whole was the second-century tension between the Jewish emphasis on re-creation of substance and the Hellenistic emphasis on the persistence of identical substance (O'Hagan 1968). Late in his career he affirmed, too, that the resurrection was disputed even in the Pauline letters and that from the beginning believers differed on its interpretation.[17]

His eschatology, well articulated in his *On the Resurrection*, *Commentary on Psalm 1*, and *Patchwork (Stromateis)*, was framed in opposition to Marcion, the Marcionite Apelles, Valentinus, and Mani, but in its distinction from popular Christian literalism ran into the most difficulty.[18] The distinction from the gnostic types seems clearly because of Origen's position in the classical and Christian mainstream, for his view had a stronger philosophical component than those of the other thinkers and was really in the best tradition of intellectual Alexandrian Christianity.

While most of his controversial writings on resurrection were lost or destroyed, the heart of his view still remains on his *Commentary on Psalm 1*, quoted in rebuttal in Methodius' *On the Resurrection* (c. 300-307) and Epiphanius' *Panarion 64* (376).   In the following excerpt from the commentary Origen attempts to interpret the apostle Paul's explanation of the mysterious process involved in the body's resurrection:

> Because each body is held together by [virtue of] a nature that assimilates into itself from without certain things for nourishment and, corresponding to the things added, excretes other things like the

---

[17]*Cels.* 3.10.

[18]*Jer. C. Ioan.* 25 (PL 23:392AB).

[ingredients] of plants and animals, the material (ὑλικόν) substratum (ὑποκείμενον) is never the same. For this reason, river is not a bad name for the body since, strictly speaking, the initial (πρῶτον) substratum (ὑποκείμενον) in our bodies is perhaps not the same for even two days.

Yet the real (γε) Paul or Peter, so to speak, is always the same--[and] not merely in [the] soul, whose substance (οὐσία) neither flows through us nor has anything ever added [to it]--even if the nature (φύσις) of the body is in a state of flux, because the form (εἶδος) characterizing (χαρακτηρίξον) the body is the same, just as the features (τύπους) constituting (παριστάνοντας) the corporeal quality (ποιότητα) of Peter and Paul remain the same. According to this quality, not only scars from childhood remain on the bodies, but also certain other peculiarities (ἰδιώματα) <like> skin blemishes and similar things.

This form (εἶδος) according to which Peter and Paul are endued with form (εἰδοποιεῖται), the (to) corporeal (σωματικόν) [form], when it makes a transition (μεταβάλλον) to the higher [state]--[but] definitely not the present (τόδε) substratum (ὑποκείμενον) provided (ἐκτεταγμένον) for the [soul at] first (πρώτην)--[is what] is put around (περιτίθεται) the soul again in the resurrection. Just as the form (εἶδος) is <the same> from infancy to old age, even if the characteristics (χαρακτῆρες) seem to undergo considerable change, so also the (to) present (ἐπι τοῦ παρόντος) form (εἶδος) must be understood to be the same in the future, when the transition (μεταβολῆς) to the higher [state] will be as great as possible.

In fact, it is necessary that the soul, when it is in corporeal places, use bodies appropriate to the places. And just as we would certainly need to have gills and the other endowment[s] (κατάτασιν) of fish if it were necessary that we live underwater in the sea, so those who are going to inherit [the] kingdom of heaven and be in the superior places must have spiritual bodies. The previous form (εἶδος) does not disappear, even if its transition (trope) to the more glorious [state] occurs (γένηται), just as the form (εἶδος) of Jesus, Moses, and Elijah in the Transfiguration was not [a] different [one] than what it had been.[19]

Using the seed analogy drawn by the apostle Paul, Origen continues:

Moreover, [it is] worthy of note that what is sown in one way is raised in another, "for it is sown a psychic body, it is raised a spiritual body" (1 Cor 15.44). The apostle also adds--teaching that, although the form (εἶδος) is saved, we are going to put away nearly <every > earthly quality (ποιότητα) in the resurrection--"And this I say, brothers, that flesh and blood cannot inherit [the] kingdom of God, nor corruption incorruption." (1 Cor 15.50). Similarly, for (περί) the saint there will indeed be a <a body> preserved by him who once endued the flesh with form (εἰδοποιοῦντος), but [there will] no longer [be] flesh; yet that very thing which was once being characterized (ἐχαρακτηρίζετο) in the flesh will be characterized (χαρακτηρισθήσεται) in the spiritual body.[20]

---

[19]*Sel. in Ps.* 1.5 (Meth. *Res.* 1.22.2-5 [Epiph. *Haer.* 64.14.2-9]); paragraphing added.

[20]*Sel. in Ps.* 1.5 (Meth. *Res.* 1.23. 2-3 [Epiph. *Haer.* 64.15.2-4]).

Shortly after, Epiphanius' excerpt from the commentary concludes when Origen explains how the generative (spermatikos) principle or Word (Logos) transforms the very essence of matter by changing the diverse qualities of the material elements into the future glorious quality of God's own creation:

[64.16.5] Despite the fact that the body is mortal and does not partake of the true life, the [passage] from the apostle, "He will also give life to your mortal bodies" (Rom 8.11), can prove that the corporeal form ($\epsilon\hat{\iota}\delta os$) about which we have spoken, although mortal by nature--"when Christ, our life, appears" (Col 3.4) and changes ($\mu\epsilon\tau\alpha\beta\acute{a}\lambda\lambda\epsilon\iota$) it from being a "body of death" (Rom 7.24)-- is made alive ($\zeta\omega\sigma\pi o\iota\eta\theta\acute{\epsilon}\nu$) through the life-giving Spirit [and], out of the <fleshly>, becomes ($\gamma\epsilon\gamma\acute{o}\nu os$) spiritual.

[64.16.6] In addition, the [passage], "But some will say, 'How are the dead raised, and with what [quality of] ($\pi o\acute{\iota}\omega$) body do they come?'" (1 Cor 15.35)[21] clearly proves that the initial ($\pi\rho\hat{\omega}\tau o\nu$) substratum ($\acute{\upsilon}\pi o\kappa\epsilon\acute{\iota}\mu\epsilon\nu o\nu$) will not rise. [64.16.7] Indeed, if we have understood the illustration correctly, the observation must be made that the generative ($\sigma\pi\epsilon\rho\mu\alpha\tau\iota\kappa\acute{o}s$) principle ($\lambda\acute{o}\gamma os$) in the seed of the grain, after it has taken hold of ($\delta\rho\alpha\xi\acute{a}\mu\epsilon\nu os$) the available ($\pi\alpha\rho\alpha\kappa\epsilon\iota\mu\acute{\epsilon}\nu\eta s$) matter ($\acute{\upsilon}\lambda\eta s$) and permeated ($\chi\omega\rho\acute{\eta}\sigma\alpha s$) it throughout, <and> after it has taken hold of ($\pi\epsilon\rho\iota\delta\rho\alpha\xi\acute{a}\mu\epsilon\nu os$) the very form ($\epsilon\hat{\iota}\delta os$) of the [the matter], imposes its own powers on the previous earth, water, air, and fire;

[21]Thus implying a new quality created by God.

and it subdues and transforms ($\mu\epsilon\tau\alpha\beta\acute{\alpha}\lambda\lambda\epsilon\iota$) their qualities ($\pi o\iota\acute{o}\tau\eta\tau\alpha\varsigma$) into that [future quality] of which it is itself [the] creator ($\delta\eta\mu\iota o\upsilon\rho\gamma\acute{o}\varsigma$).   And so the ear of corn becomes full, exceedingly superior to the original seed in size, appearance ($\sigma\chi\acute{\eta}\mu\alpha\tau\iota$), and adornment.[22]

The detailed interpretation of these excerpts I have given elsewhere (1975, 344-351; 1986, 373-380).   Here we may consider the pluralistic context in the ancient classical and Christian worlds.

Origen's doctrine is analogous to gnostic speculation about the soul's successive material envelopes in the ascent and descent through the heavens.[23] Popular Christianity in this period also retained widespread notions from Jewish apocalyptic about the passage of the soul upward through the heavens to God.[24] But in intellectual Alexandrian Chrisitianity, Clement had already taught the resurrection of a transformed flesh in opposition to gnostic doctrine. The way Clement refers to the resurrection body as flesh[25] could easily be understood by an anti-Origenist as denying the present flesh's perpetuation[26] and as urging, not simply the correction,

---

[22]*Sel. in Ps.* 1.5 (Meth. *Res.* 1.24.4-5 [Epiph. *Haer.* 64.16.5-7]); paragraphing added.

[23]Just. *Dial.* 80.4; Iren. *Haer.* 1.7.1, 5 (Harvey 1:59.1-2, 9-10); Clem. *Exc. Thdot.* 27.3, 64.

[24]See. e.g., the many examples of the "mythological geography of Jewish apocalyptic" in Jewish Christian speculation about the cosmic ladder (Daniélou 1964, 173-81).

[25]*Paed.* 2.100.3, 3.2.3 (GCS 12:217.19, 237.7-8).

[26]*Paed.* 1.36.6-1.37.1 (GCS 12:112.2-11).

but the permanent end of its "affections ($\pi\acute{a}\theta\eta$)." [27] But Clement's view, while framed against the background of Valentinian speculation about Christ's heavenly flesh,[28] is really distinguished carefully from gnosticism.

Typical of the tradition of Alexandrian Christian Platonism, Clement described the purifying of Christ's heavenly flesh[29] and the putting of "immortality on the pure flesh itself." [30] His view seems formulated with awareness of Biblical *idea*-usage. In his *Outlines* ($\Upsilon\pi o\tau\upsilon\pi\acute{\omega}\sigma\epsilon\iota\varsigma$) he gave "concise explanations of all the canonical scriptures."[31] In so doing, according to Photius, he asserted that the doctrine of forms (ideas) is taught by certain passages of (Greek) scripture.[32] Photius does not say what passages are involved, but susceptible to such an interpretation are Genesis 5.3, 32.30-31; Exodus 24.10, 17; Numbers 12.8; Judges 13.6; Ezekiel 1.26; and 2 Corinthians 5.7. In Clement's known writings, however, we do not find the unique combination of elements, especially the *eidos* explanation, that we find in Origen's *Commentary on Psalm 1*.

In the cultural word outside Christiainity, Origen's *eidos* may be associated with both the Platonic *eidos/idea* and the Aristotelian *eidos* (essential form) but is not completely identifiable with either (Crouzel 1972,

---

[27]*Paed.* 1.43.1 (GCS 12:115.25-29); see also 1.47.1 (GCS 12:118.9-10).

[28]For more on the Valentinan view, see Schoeps 1951, 1-8.

[29]*Paed.* 1.46.3 (GCS 12:117.28-118.2).

[30]*Paed.* 2.100.3 (GCS 12:217.9).

[31]Eus. *H.e.* 6.14.1.

[32]*Cod.* 109 (Henry 1959-65, 2:80).

691; 1980, 255; see Dechow 1975, 352-53; 1986, 380-82). According to Crouzel:

> One may . . . define the word *eidos* in this passage [*Commentary on Psalm 1* (1.5)] as the principle of unity, of development, of existence, and of personalization of the body. . . . The *eidos* . . . constitutes the body's essential [nature]. . . . It is associated with the *logos*, which expresses, perhaps better, its dynamism. It is, then, that which will rise and will ensure the substantial identity between the earthly body and the glorious body.

Also, Origen's speculation about resurrection was typical of many philosophical efforts in his time to explain the nature of corporeality. In second- and third-century eclectic Platonism, the notion of an "astral body" was common. The Neoplatonist Proclus (c. 410-485 C.E.) reflects earlier assumptions when he writes in his *Elements of Theology* (Dodds 1963, 182-83):

> The vehicle (ὄχημα) of every particular soul descends by the addition of vestures increasingly material; and ascends in company with the soul through divestment of all that is material and recovery (ἀναδρομῆς) of (εἰς; or "into") its proper (τὸ οἰκεῖον) form (εἶδος).

In explaining a related passage, that "every (πᾶν) intellectual (νοηρόν) Form (εἶδος) is constitutive (ὑποστατικόν) of things perpetual (ἀΐδιον)" (156-57), Dodds writes (293):

[Proclus'] general view is that there are Forms only of species, not of individuals: even human souls, which are imperishable individuals, are derived not severally from separate Forms, but collectively from the Forms of the various divine souls under which they are grouped (cf. prop. 204 [pp. 178-79]). By an exception to the general principle, these divine souls have each a Form of its own, as have also the heavenly bodies. There are no Forms of things which exist only as parts, e.g. eyes or fingers; of accidental attributes like colour; of artifacts (despite [Plato] Rep X); of practical τέχναι like weaving; or of things evil. This part of the matter goes back in part to Middle Platonist tradition (Albin. [Albinus, mid-2nd century C.E.] *Didasc.* c. ix), and does not differ substantially from that given by Plotinus, save in its greater precision.

Dodds (1963[2], 315 n. 1) drawing on e.g., Bidez (1914, 88-97) and Kissling (1922), sketches the origin of the theory of the astral body prior to the Neoplatonists Plotinus (205-270 C.E.) and Porphyry (1963[2], 313-21; see Chadwick 1953, 112 n. 5; Tripolitis 1971, 58 c.n. 168). I shall try to add clarity to the evidence he cites. He believes the theory was well known by the beginning of the third century C.E. and mentions testimonies to its earlier existence, e.g.:

- Sources of later appeal (discounted) are Plato's *Phaedo* (113D), which refers to boats carrying the souls of the dead, and his *Timaeus* (41E, 44E, 69C), where the soul's "chariot" is not clearly designated as a body other than an ordinary mortal one. But in the *Laws* (898E f.), Plato discusses how the stars are "guided by their souls and suggests as one possibility the interposition of a fiery or aerial body as a *tertium quid* ['third entity']" (Dodds, 315).

- Later appeal is also made to Aristotle's *pneuma*, which is comparable to the Platonist ὄχημα ("vehicle") and "is 'analogous to that element of which the stars are made', i.e., to the πεμπτον [fifth] σῶμα [body or element]" (*On the Generation of Animals* 736b 27ff.). But "the Aristotelian pneuma is still far from being an 'astral body'; it is an element in the body as we know it, is common to all animals, and is transmitted in the act of procreation" (Dodds, 315-16).

- " 'The school of Eratosthenes [possibly c. 275-194 B.C.E.; see Dodds, 318, 348] and Ptolemy the Platonist [if Ptolemaeus Chennos of Alexandria, fl. c. 100 C.E.] and others' is appealed to by Iamblichus (c. 250-c. 325 C.E.) for the opinion that the soul is permanently embodied and passes into the earthly body from others 'of finer stuff' (λεπτόπερα)" (Dodds, 317).

- The views of Poseidonius (c. 135-50 B.C.E.) seem to be echoed in the Hermetic literature (mid-1st to end of 3rd century C.E.), which speaks of:

- "certain 'mists' (ἀέρες) which are the incorporeal envelope (περιβόλαιον) of the soul" (in John Stobaeus [5th century C.E.] 1:410.18ff [988H]); and
- "the πνεῦμα as the soul's περιβολή (or ὑπερέτης), in which it ὀχεῖται" (*Corp. Herm.* 10.13, 17; Dodds, 317).

- The *Chaldean Oracles* (2nd century C.E.) speak of a ψυχῆς λεπτὸν σῶμα ("fine [lit., 'of fine husk'] body of [the] soul,") which is identified with τὸ αὐγοειδὲς ἡμῶν σῶμα ("our luminous body") in Hierocles' *On the Golden Verses* 478b (5th century C.E.; Dodds, 347-48).

- Ps-Plutarch (perhaps 2nd century), in *On the Life and Poetry of Homer*, c. 128, "affirms on the authority of 'Plato and Aristotle' that the soul at death takes with it τὸ πνευματικόν which acts as its ὄχημα" (Dodds, 317).

- Alexander of Aphrodisias (Aristotelian; fl. early 3rd century C.E.) objected to the doctrine of the ὄχημα, but is refuted by Simplicius, 6th century Aristotelian, in the latter's *On Physics* 964.19ff (dodds, 317.

- Macrobius (late 4th/early 5th century), in his *On Cicero's 'Sleep of Scipio'* (1.11.12-13), "which almost certainly goes back to Numenius [2nd century C.E.]," tells how "the soul acquires a *sidereum* (ἀστροειδές [starlight-formed]) or *luminosum* (αὐγοειδὲς [sunlight-formed]) *corpus* in the course of its descent through the planetary spheres" (Dodds, 347).

Origen, as Dodds mentions, uses the expression αὐγοειδὲς ("luminous" or "sunlight-formed") σῶμα ("body")[33] to explain "the possibility of apparitions of the dead" (317). Further Origenist development, as I have shown elsewhere (1986, 320-23, 363, 367-68), occurred among the Origenists refuted by Methodius and Eustathius, in the *Macarian Homilies* 1.6-7, and in the writings of Evagrius, who refers to a distinct bodily "organ" (ὄργανον) of the soul.[34]

As far as Origen's own theology is concerned, all that these citations illustrate is the linguistic and cosmological matrix of contemporary discussion. Just as there is affinity between his "doctrine of the Trinity and some later Neoplatonic theories" (Dillon 1978), so there is relationship

---

[33]*Cels.* 2.60. For additional uses of the ochema concept in Origen's writings (not mentioned by Dodds), esp. the *Commentary on Matthew* and (possibly) *On the Resurrection* and the *Commentary on Genesis*, see Crouzel 1977.

[34]*K.g.* 1.67 (PO 28.1:49).

between his eschatology and some views of corporeality held by his philosophical and gnostic contemporaries. But affinity is not identity. Dodds' followup to the Proclus study, a masterly overview of cosmological assumptions in this "pagan and Christian" environment that Origen shared (1965, 1-101, esp. 5-36), unfortunately overstates the Alexandrian's view of rational beings (λογικοί) as "maintaining the substance of the Gnostic view" (17). Rather, in the Alexandrian's world the astral-body theory and both "learned" and popular speculation about the cosmos were commonplace.

But Origen was interpreting Biblical, especially Pauline, eschatology and trying to make sense of the scripture's cosmological and eschatological references. Customarily, as an informed eclectic Platonist Christian, he was using the regular language of philosophical discourse, but for the sake of making intelligible the Biblical meaning. Yet given the common parlance on which he drew, he intentionally went beyond the views of his philosophical and Christian contemporaries to formulate a uniquely complex view that illuminated the Bible and, to him, was "superior" to a strictly Platonic interpretation.[35]

Attention to his philosophical sources needs to be tempered with the awareness that, not simply these sources, but an understanding of them by way of a Biblically-oriented Hellenistic Judaism shaped his thinking. "I do not doubt that Plato learned the words of the *Phaedrus* from some Hebrews," Origen wrote.[36] Following the precedent set by Aristobulus (early 2nd century B.C.E.)[37] and Philo (c. 20 B.C.E.-c. 50 C.E.), he believed the best

---

[35]*Cels.* 4.40. See Dechow 1986, 318, 322, 327-329.

[36]*Cels.* 6.19.

[37]*Cels.* 4.51. See 2 Macc 1.10; Clem. Al. *Str.* 5.97.7; Eus. *H.e.* 6.13.7, 7.32.16-17, *P.e.* 8.10, 13.12.

in Greek thinking had precedent in Jewish scriptures. To Origen, in fact, Philo's *On Dreams,* interpreting Jacob's ladder to heaven (Gen 28.10-22), "is worthy of intelligent and wise study by those who wish to find the truth."[38]

Origen's eschatology, in its own setting, is then an attempt at clear affirmation and articulation of the resurrection against the wide background of late Hellenistic thought. Featuring a sophisticated conception of the corporeal form in the light of ancient philosophy and science, it offered a plausible option to many third- and fourth-century Christians for stressing the manner of the whole body's resurrection--and of the whole flesh properly understood. Analogous to Platonic, Aristotelian, and gnostic views of corporeality, Origen's belief was nevertheless basically a way of professing traditional Pauline/New Testament resurrection doctrine in the contemporary terms of intellectual Alexandrian Christianity.

3. The Ambiguity of Origen

Like the Christ whom he worshiped (σημεῖον ἀντιλεγόμενον, Luke 2.34), Origen was a "sign of contradiction" (Quasten 1950-60, 2:40). He was the greatest Christian theologian between Paul and Augustine, yet sociologically--i.e., in terms of the Christian institution and the anathemas of its conciliar tradition--a heretic (see Dechow 1975, 79-112, 201-2, 380-85, 432-39; 1985a; 1985b; 1986, 93-124, 244, 405-9, 449-58).

It should be clear, however, that, as he "proclaimed the conformity of ancient learning, especially Alexandrian science, with the Christian faith" (Dampier 1948[4], 63-64), his expression of Christian doctrine was not for the sake of philosophical exposition, but vice-versa: he used philosophical

---

[38]*Cels.* 6.21; see 4.51.

language, the language that he knew, to clarify Christian teaching. In the face of the cultural and Christian pluralism of his time, he was often less than subtle about those with whom he took issue. This approach proved most damaging in the fourth century when his theology was less understood and bits of it were taken out of context and used in new situations of fourth-century controversy. Thus his references to "simpler" believers, removed from the matrix of critical discourse, were perceived, e.g., by the heresiologist Epiphanius, as elitist, pejorative and even insulting. "You . . . stigmatize good [people] as your so-called simpler [believers]," Epiphanius accused him, and do not realize that "the message of the truth [is] simple," for "to the most simple 'belongs the kingdom of the heavens' (Matt 19.14)."[39]

If we want to understand Origen, to achieve *das Verstehen des Origenes*, we need to strip away the veneers of Christendom's crisis of modernity, the struggle of Reformation and Counter-Reformation, the medieval endurance of Christianity, the decline of Rome and the political triumph of Christianity, and go back to when Christianity was not yet legal and its prospects were uncertain except by faith, when time itself was still counted by the onward march of the Roman state and respectable thinking was measured in terms of Greek heritage and Alexandrian renaissance. Then, for a person to offer an exuberance of knowledge faithful to the Jewish and Christian Biblical past and credible in terms of the best philosophy and science of the day, was an achievement remarkable indeed. Even in the late twentieth century when both philosophy and religion are often reduced to mere imagination unmirrored in the natural world outside the human mind, the effort remains impressive.

---

[39]*Haer.* 64.67.1, 3.

MODERN WORKS CITED

Bidez, Joseph

>   1913 *Vie de Porphyre, le philosophe neo-platonicien.* Gand: van
>   Goethem/Leipzig: Teubner.

Chadwick, Henry (ed.)

>   1953, repr. 1965, 1980 *Origen, Contra Celsum.* Cambridge:
>   University.

Crouzel, Henri

>   1972 "Les critiques adressées par Méthode et ses contemporains à la
>   doctrine origénienne du corps ressuscité." *Gregorianum* 53:679-716.
>
>   1977 "Le thème platonicien du 'véhicule de l'âme' chez Origène."
>   *Didaskalia* 7 (1977) 225-38.
>
>   1978 Introduction to *Origène, Traité des principes* (Livres I et II).
>   SC 252:33-52. Paris: Cerf.
>
>   1980 "La doctrine origénienne du corps ressuscité." *BLE* 81.3-
>   4:175-200, 244-266.

Dampier, William C.

>   1948[4] *A History of Science and Its Relations with Philosophy and
>   Religion.* Cambridge: University.

Daniélou, Jean

>   1964 *The Development of Christian Doctrine before the Council of
>   Nicaea, 1: The Theology of Jewish Christianity.* Chicago:
>   Regnery.

Dechow, Jon F.

>   1975, 1986 *Dogma and Mysticism in Early Christianity:
>   Epiphanius of Cyprus and the Legacy of Origen.* Ph.D. dissertation.

University of Pennsylvania. 1975. Rev. ed., with preface by Henri Crouzel. Cambridge, MA: Philadelphia Patristic Foundation, forthcoming [late1986?].

1985a "The Heresy Charges against Origen." *4. Internationales Origeneskolloquium*. University of Innsbruck. September 2-7, 1985.

1985b "Origen's 'Heresy': From Eustathius to Epiphanius." *Die Referate des 4. internationalen Origeneskongresses* (Innsbruck, 2-6 September 1985), pp. 405-409. Edited by Lothar Lies. Innsbruck and Vienna: Tyrolia-Verlag.

Dillon, John

1978 "Origen's Doctrine of the Trinity and Some Later Neoplatonic Theories." In Dominic J. O'Meara (ed.), *Neoplatonism and Christian Thought*. Albany: State University of New York Press, 1982.

Dodds, Eric R.

1963[2] (ed.) Proclus, *The Elements of Theology*. London: Oxford.

1965 *Pagan and Christian in an Age of Anxiety*. Cambridge: University.

Kissling, Robert C.

1922 "The ochema-pneuma of the Neoplatonists and the *De insomniss* of Synesius of Cyrene." *American Journal of Philology* 43:318-30.

Nickelsburg, George W. E., Jr.

1972 *Resurrection, Immortality, and Eternal Life in Intertestamental Judaism*. HTS 16. Cambridge: Harvard.

1981 "Enoch, Levi, and Peter: Recipients of Revelation in Upper Galilee." *Journal of Biblical Literature* 100.4: 575-600.

O'Hagan, Angelo P.

    1968   *Material Re-Creation in the Apostolic Fathers.* TU 100.
    Berlin: Akademie.

Quasten, Johannes.

    1950-60 *Patrology.* 3 vols. Utrecht-Antwerp: Spectrum.

Schoeps, Hans J.

    1951   *Vom   himmlischen   Fleisch   Christi: eine*
    dogmengeschichtliche Untersuchung. Tübingen: Mohr.

Tripolitis, Antonia

    1971 "The Doctrine of the Soul in the Thought of Plotinus and
    Origen." Ph.D. dissertation. University of Pennsylvania. Part
    published 1979, "Return to the Divine: Salvation in the Thought of
    Plotinus and Origen." In Don F. Winslow (ed.), *Disciplina Nostra:*
    Essays in Memory of Robert F. Evans (Patristic Monograph Series
    6; Cambridge, MA: Philadelphia Patristic Foundation, 1979) 171-
    78.

THE ANTHROPOLOGY OF EVAGRIUS PONTICUS AND ITS SOURCES

Michael O'Laughlin
Harvard Divinity School

The point of departure for this paper is an article by Henri Crouzel in the *Bulletin de Literature Ecclesiastique* for 1961 entitled "Recherches sur Origene et son influence."[1] In this article Crouzel notes one surprising and important difference between the conceptuality of Origen and that of Evagrius Ponticus, the 4th-century archdeacon of Gregory Nazianzus at Constantinople. While both figures share many spiritual and theological doctrines, their anthropologies are strikingly different. The anthropology of Origen is a hierarchy of the $\sigma\hat{\omega}\mu\alpha$ or $\sigma\acute{\alpha}\rho\xi$, then the $\psi\nu\chi\acute{\eta}$, of which the $\nu o\hat{\nu}\varsigma$ is the higher part, and, finally, the $\pi\nu\epsilon\hat{\nu}\mu\alpha$. Evagrius, by contrast, has a strict $\sigma\hat{\omega}\mu\alpha$-$\psi\nu\chi\acute{\eta}$-$\nu o\hat{\nu}\varsigma$ anthropology.[2] This difference has important consequences.

---

[1]H. Crouzel, "Recherches sur Origène et son influence," *BLE* 62 (1961): 3-15, 105-113.

[2]Crouzel also notes a role for the $\lambda\acute{o}\gamma o\varsigma$ in the Evagrian system. However, here he has been betrayed by a remark in the Hausherr book, *Les Leçons d'un contemplatif* (Paris: Beauchesne, 1960), 17, which is his principle source on Evagrius. In fact, there is no appreciable role in the anthropology of Evagrius for the $\lambda\acute{o}\gamma o\varsigma$.

As you may know, Evagrius's career in Constantinople lasted only slightly longer than that of his bishop Gregory--two years later he had entered the Egyptian desert and become a monk. He lived the rest of his life among the famous desert fathers of the Natron Valley. There he produced a large corpus of spiritual writings and took part in a brief flourishing of Origenist intellectuals among the early monks.[3] His treatises would become extremely influential in the subsequent history of both monasticism and Origenism. Indeed, Antoine Guillaumont has shown that when that doctrine was condemned in 553, the condemnation was focused not so much on Origen's writings as on those of Evagrius.[4]

In the following pages I would like to present these two contrasting anthropologies, especially that of Evagrius, since he is the more obscure, and then offer some ideas concerning the sources and ramifications of the Evagrian system. In consideration of the small scope of this paper, only passing references will be made to "anthropology" in the larger sense of the word, i.e., the origin, nature and destiny of humanity. In this, the larger schematization of human identity and destiny, Evagrius reveals a definite dependence on Origen and the Origenism of his time.[5] Let us however

---

[3]On this phenomenon, see H. Evelyn-White, *The Monasteries of the Wâdi 'n Natrûn, Part Two: The History of the Monasteries of Nitria and of Scetis* (New York: The Metroplitan Museum of Art Egyptian Expedition, 1932), 84ff; G. Bunge, "Évagre le Pontique et les deux Macaire," *Irénikon* 56 (1983): 215-227 and 323-360, especially 350ff.

[4]A. Guillaumont, *Les 'Képhalaia gnostica' d'Évagre le Pontique et l'Histoire de l'Origénisme chez les grecs et chez les syriens* (Paris: Éditions du Seuil, 1962).

[5]As was noted by F. X. Murphy in his paper at the Origen Conference in Manchester in 1981, "There can be no doubt that Evagrius used the cosmological speculations of Origen regarding the twofold creation and the apocatastasis by way of background for his extravagant anthropology." F.X. Murphy, "Evagrios Pontikos and Origenism," *Origeniana Tertia, Papers*

examine that part of anthropology which concerns the makeup of the human person. Here the disciple has evidently abandoned the master.

For Crouzel and the many scholars who have been influenced by him, the anthropology of Origen is centered around the $\nu o\hat{v}s$ which becomes a soul as it distances itself from God and cools. This soul is then the ground of the human person, the center of the personality and of free will. The $\nu o\hat{v}s$ remains a distinguishable element within the soul and forms the higher part of it.[6] As such, it can also be called $\lambda\acute{o}\gamma os$ or $\acute{\eta}\gamma\epsilon\mu o\nu\iota\kappa\acute{o}\nu$.[7] This $\nu o\hat{v}s$ functions as the "eye" of the soul, and is that part of the person capable of mystical contemplation.[8] The other two elements making up the human person--the spirit and the flesh, or body--both represent larger realities, the celestial world and the terrestrial world, respectively. Although they are intrinsic to the human person, they are not central to it.

The spirit and the flesh impose on or influence the core of the human person, the soul. The $\pi\nu\epsilon\hat{v}\mu a$ attempts to guide the soul towards God and away from the distractions of materiality. The entire celestial sphere, including Christ, joins in this effort to influence the human soul for the good. An opposite influence comes from the body and materiality, which connect to the soul through its lower half. The lower part of the human soul

---

of the Third International Colloquium for Origen Studies, Manchester, 1981 (Rome: Dell'Ateneo, 1985), 256.

[6]H. Crouzel, *Théologie de l'image de Dieu chez Origène* (Aubier: Montaigne, 1956).

[7]For a history of these terms and suggestions on how Origen understood them, see Endre von Ivánka, *Plato Christianus* (Eisiedeln: Johannes, 1964), 322ff.

[8]Fragment 53 on Luke (GCS 9,258,15-6), see H. Crouzel, "L'Anthropologie d'Origène dans la perspective du combat spirituel," *Revue d'Ascétique et de Mystique* 31 (1955): 373.

is that part which is subject to deceptive imaginations and passions. Origen thus sees the human soul to be in a state of continual spiritual struggle to choose always the way of Christ and the πνεῦμα, and reject the way of the passions, the Devil and materiality. The center of the human person is here because it is the soul which has the power of choice, and this determines one's spiritual state and destiny.[9]

The πνεῦμα is sent by God to guide the soul. Origen is careful to distinguish between this guardian spirit in the person and the Holy Spirit. They are two separate realities.[10] Whereas the πνεῦμα is a supernatural presence within the person, and, in an extreme case, such as that of a person damned to hell, can be removed by God, leaving the human person fragmented,[11] the body is a necessary component--all beings, even the pre-existent celestial νοῦς, are clothed in some sort of body.[12]

I characterize Origen's core anthropology as a dichotomy, one made up of body and soul with the πνεῦμα acting as a tangental divine element functioning in opposition to the body. Crouzel would call this same schema a trichotomy, and would include the πνεῦμα in the basic hierarchy; it certainly is a trichotomy in many ways--even Origen refers to the *three* parts

---

[9]Crouzel cites many texts in support of this, his main thesis. Chief among them are: *In Rom.* 1: 18 PG14, 866Cff. "*Ponamus esse aliquod domicilium, in quo cum corpore et spiritu velut cum duobus consiliariis habitet anima. . .*" (867B) and *De Principiis* 3.4. See *Théologie*, 133 and "L'Anthropologie," 366, 370ff.

[10]*Dialogue with Heraclides* 6 (SC 67, ed. Scherer, 71); Origen draws on Biblical sources to clarify this distinction, especially 1 Cor. 2:11, see, *On Matthew* 13,2 (GCS 10, p. 180, 17ff).

[11]*De Principiis* 2,10,7; see also, H. Crouzel, "L'Anthropologie," 367.

[12]*De Principiis* 2,2,2; c.f. however 1,7.

of a human being,[13] but, to avoid confusing Origen's schema with other systems which hold that the νοῦς is separate from the soul, I shall call it a dichotomy.

Spiritual struggle between different parts of the soul is a theme developed already in Plato's *Phaedrus*, where the soul is likened to a chariot pulled by two horses of opposite dispositions--one representing the higher impulses of the soul, the other the passions and unruly elements.[14] Indeed, the anthropology of Origen is not unique to him, but is largely present in Irenaeus, who recognizes a σῶμα-ψυχή dichotomy in the human person with the νοῦς and the heavenly πνεῦμα functioning as activities of the soul.[15] The difference between Origen and Ireneaus is the importance which Origen assigns to the soul. Ireneaus, as Orbe tells us, held that,

> The soul, far from constituting the human species, as Platonists or Origenists might teach, practically speaking does not even reach the level of substantive existence.[16]

I believe that there were in fact two basic anthropological schemas in competition with each other in this era, a dichotomous one, which divided

---

[13]E.g., *Commentary on Romans*, 2, 9 (PG 14, col. 893D); see also, H. Crouzel, "L'Anthropologie," 367.

[14]Plato, *Phaedrus* 246B, 253Dff; See also the comments of A.M. Festugière, "La Trichotomie de 1 Thess. 5:23 et la philosophie grecque," *RSR* 20 (1930): 390.

[15]Irenaeus, *Adversus Haereses* 3.29.3; see further, M. Spanneut, *Le Stoïcisme des pères de l'église* (Paris: Éditions du Seuil, 1957), 149.

[16]A. Orbe, *Antropología de san Ireneo* (Biblioteca de autores christianus; Madrid: La Editorial Católica, 1969), 73.

soul and spirit, and a trichotomous one, which saw both the soul and the body as part of worldly being, in contrast to the heavenly element of νοῦς or πνεῦμα.[17] Origen and Irenaeus have elements of both these systems. I believe they are closer to the dichotomous model, however, because they place the human soul in the middle of the personality and the basic division of the human person between the soul and the body.

Didymus the Blind, a contemporary of Evagrius whom Athanasius had appointed head of the catechetical school in Alexandria[18] provides a good example of the dichotomous anthropology at the time of Evagrius. Like Origen, he also saw human beings as a union of soul and body, with the νοῦς forming the higher part of the soul. He even holds that there is a special divine element in human beings, the same notion of πνεῦμα as Origen.[19] Adolphe Gesché found that Didymus uses this presumably Origenist anthropology of body and soul in the *Commentary on the Psalms* when he wishes to be precise and scientific.[20] But he also employs a trichotomous

---

[17]H. Conzelmann, *I Corinthians* (Hermeneia; Philadelphia: Fortress, 1975), 67-8: Excursus: ψυχή, "Soul"; Manuel Guerra, *Antropologías y teología* (Pamplona: Universidad de Navarra, 1976), 117.

[18]See G. Bardy, "Pour l'histoire de l'école d'Alexandrie," *Vivre et Penser* (= *RB*) 2 (1942): 80-109, for the uncertain continuity of this institution.

[19]The clearest text is in the *Commentary on Zachariah* 12. 1-3, SC III 323, 11-29 (p. 892-4). See S. Reynolds, *Man, Incarnation and Trinity in the Commentary on Zachariah of Didymus the Blind of Alexandria*, (Th.D. diss., Harvard University, 1966), 8-25; and ΜΑΡΚΟΥ Α. ΟΡΦΑΝΟΥ, Η ΨΥΧΗ ΚΑΙ ΤΟ ΣΩΜΑ ΤΟΥ ΑΝΘΡΩΠΟΥ (ΑΝΑΛΕΚΤΑ ΒΛΑΤΑΔΩΝ 21; Thessaloniki: Panayotis Christou, 1974), esp. 42-74.

[20]Adolphe Gesché, *La christologie du «Commentaire sur les Psaumes» découvert à Toura* (Gembloux: J. Duculot, 1962), 130.

anthropology in which the νοῦς is separate and can be called by several other names, one of which is πνεῦμα.

Didymus slips into this older[21] framework when speaking less precisely. I believe this indicates that the trichotomy was a more common, less technical conceptualization. This widely-accepted division is found in Plato, of course,[22] and it is also present in Philo,[23] in Justin Martyr,[24] in Plutarch,[25] and in Marcus Aurelius.[26] After Philo it is found next in the Alexandrian tradition in Clement of Alexandria[27] and Plotinus.[28] It was also popular among Gnostics; the Valentinians even divided humanity into spiritual, psychic and matter-oriented people.[29] Its wide popularity and ancient roots are one explanation for its use by Didymus even though he

---

[21]As Conzelmann shows (fn. 17), dichotomous anthropologies are actually oldest. Trichotomous models result from a devaluation of "soul."

[22]Plato, *Timaeus* 30B; *The Laws* 961D-E; *Phaedrus* 247Cff (λογισμός/νοῦς, ψυχή, σῶμα).

[23]Philo, *Legum Allegoria* 1.32, ed. Wendland, 1,69,6ff (νοῦς, ψυχή, σῶμα).

[24]Justin Martyr, *Second Apology* 10 (λόγος, ψυχή, σῶμα).

[25]Plutarch, *Moralia, De facie in orbe lunae* 943A (νοῦς, ψυχή, σῶμα).

[26]Marcus Aurelius, *Meditationes* 2,2,1; 3,16,1; 7,16:1-4; 8,56,1; 12,3,1; 12,3,1; 12,14,4-5 (νοῦς, ψυχή, σῶμα).

[27]Clement of Alexandria, *Stromata* 3, 68, 5 PG 8, 1113Bff (νοῦς/πνεῦμα/ἡγεμονικόν, ψυχή, σάρξ); See M. Spanneut, op. cit., 167 for the variation in the first element.

[28]Plotinus, *What is Man?*, *Enneades* 1,1,4, (νοῦς, ψυχή, σῶμα).

[29]H. Jonas, *The Gnostic Religion* (2nd. ed.; Boston: Beacon, 1963), 44; On the Valentinians, see Irenaeus, *Adversus Haereses* 1.7.

preferred the dichotomous system. His wavering between two models also indicates that ambiguity between dichotomy and trichotomy was accepted and was perhaps typical of the anthropologies of the age.

The Evagrian anthropological model begins, not with the dichotomous system of Origen, but with the more broadly-accepted trichotomy. Evagrius, unlike Didymus, eschews ambiguity. Following a tendency already visible in Marcus Aurelius, Plutarch, and the Gnostics, the νοῦς is presented clearly by Evagrius as independent of the soul and the true center-point of the human person. As Hausherr puts it,

> The νοῦς is not just a faculty of the soul, but the essence itself of the person, of which the body and the soul do not represent anything more than lower gradations.[30]

Whereas the νοῦς in its original unfallen state is clothed by a heavenly body in Origen,[31] in Evagrius it is pure spirit, one of the many rational beings which are gathered around God. When the νοῦς falls from its original position in Origen it becomes cold and heavy,[32] in Evagrius it becomes thick.[33] Even in its thickness the νοῦς remains a spiritual reality, infinite and comprehensible only to God.[34] When this νοῦς descends fully

---

[30]I. Hausherr, "Nouveaux fragments," 73.

[31]*De Principiis*, 2,2,2.

[32]Ibid, 2,8,3.

[33]*Kephalaia Gnostica* 4,6 (PO 28,1, ed. Guillaumont); *Pseudo-Basilius, Epistula* 8, *Saint Basil, The Letters* (4 vols.; Loeb Classical Library; ed. Deferrari) 1,73).

[34]*Practicus* 47 (SC 170,1, ed. Guillaumont).

to the level of practical existence, it expands to include soul. However, in expanding, the νοῦς is not encased within the soul as in Origen. The soul is rather an outgrowth or addition to the νοῦς separate from it.[35] The soul is subject to sickness, to passions and feeling. Yet it also remains immaterial[36] and possesses capacity for growth and progress. The soul remains with the νοῦς even when the νοῦς returns to God.[37]

The soul in Evagrius is divided into three parts, the rational, the irrascible and the concupiscible, as in Origen and most of the Platonic tradition.[38] Together the irrascible and the concupiscible elements make up the passionate half of the soul. In this sphere passions and delusions and vice can hold sway, but the parts of the soul themselves are not evil. As Evagrius puts it,

If all evil indeed arises out of the rational, the irrascible or the concupiscible spheres, and it is through these powers that we are

---

[35]*Kephalaia Gnostica* 3,28: ~The soul is the νοῦς which, due to negligence, has fallen from Unity and which, due to its lack of vigilance, has descended to the level of "πρακτική." (Cf. *Ad Melaniam*, ed., Frankenberg, *Euagrios Ponticus* (Abhandlungen der Königlichen Gesellshaft der Wissenschaften zu Göttingen, Philol.-hist. Kl., neue Folge, Band 13, no. 2, Berlin, 1912), 618, 2-3. Here Evagrius is more concerned to indicate the source of the soul than its relationship to the νοῦς within the human person.

[36]*Kephalaia Gnostica* 1,45.

[37]Ibid, 2,29. The eschatological aspect of this anthropology will be dealt with further below.

[38]*Practicus* 89. He also notes that in angels the νοῦς is predominant, in human beings the ἐπιθυμία is predominant, and in demons it is the θύμος which is dominant-- *Kephalaia Gnostica* 1,68. This means that angels have souls, as in Origen-- *De Principiis* 2,8,1. Indeed, the demons have both souls and bodies-- *Kephalaia Gnostica* 1,24.

able to act well or badly, clearly it is the result of our usage of these parts that evils befall us; and if this is the case, for nothing which God has made is evil.[39]

Nonetheless, the soul is a handicap and a danger for the νοῦς which is attached to it. The νοῦς can be distracted from God by the forces at play in the soul. So we read in the *Kephalaia Gnostica*:

> The νοῦς, if it advances along its own path, is reunited with the holy powers, but if it follows that of *the organ of the soul*, it falls among the demons.[40]

The body, for Evagrius, is of a entirely different order than the νοῦς and the soul. While the νοῦς and its appendage, the soul, can be said to belong entirely to God's first creation (in Evagrian terms, the *first nature*) or to be dependent on it, the body has two parts, two natures, and the lower, visible nature is part of a separate second creation.[41] It and the material world of which it is part were created by God after the fall to be a resting place and ladder through which the fallen νοῦς might refocus itself on God and recover its spiritual stature. Thus the visible body, like the soul, is providential rather than evil; it is a tool provided by God, and one must be

---

[39]*Kephalaia Gnostica* 3,59.

[40]*Kephalaia Gnostica* 2,48.

[41]*Ad Melaniam*, Text in G. Vitestam, "Seconde partie du traité, qui passe sous le nom de «La grande lettre d'Évagre le Pontique à Mélanie l'Ancienne»," (Scripta minora 31; Lund: Regiae societatis humaniorum litterarum lundensis, 1964), 11-14.

grateful for it.[42] The higher, intelligible body appears to function as a bridge between the soul and the lower body. The type of visible body which is "joined" to the soul creates either a human person, an angel or a demon, so being truly human means nothing more than being joined to a human body.[43] As in Origen, there is a gradation of bodies in Evagrius, according to the degree of "negligence."[44] Yet the entrance of the νοῦς into the realm of corporeality is seen overall as a divine intervention and part of the *Heilsgeschichte*, unlike Origen, who specifically says it is a punishment.[45] Without the body, the soul has no way of functioning and has no *locus* for existence.[46]

To fully understand Evagrius's anthropology, we must ask how he came by it. Since it is not inspired by Origen or shared with Didymus, let us consider the influence of Evagrius's teacher and bishop, Gregory of Nazianzus.[47] Evagrius clearly states that his division of the soul into three parts was learned from Gregory,[48] and it is possible that his indebtedness to him in the realm of anthropology was greater still.

---

[42]*Kephalaia Gnostica* 3,53; 4,60, 62, 76; 6,75; *Practicus* 29.

[43]*Kephalaia Gnostica* 1,4, 11, 58, 63, etc.; see Guillaumont, op. cit., 110-1, n. 135. On the body as a hallmark of human existence, see, *Kephalaia Gnostica* 3,29. As noted above (fn. 38), demons also have bodies.

[44]*De Principiis*, 1,7,1-4; *Kephalaia Gnostica* 2,68, 72, 76, 79.

[45]*De Principiis*, 1,8,1.

[46]*Kephalaia Gnostica*, 1,47, 48.

[47]For the strong relationship between Evagrius and Gregory, see A. Guillaumont, *Évagre le Pontique, Traité pratique ou Le Moine* (2 vols.; SC 170,1; Paris: Éditions du Cerf; 1971), 1.22f.

[48]*Practicus*, 89.

In Gregory of Nazianzus, the pneuma-sarx dichotomy is forcefully
presented. For Gregory, there are three separate spheres of being: God, spirit
and matter, and humanity spans both of the latter.[49] Yet the anthropology of
Gregory is trichotomous,[50] or quintachotomous, as *Epistle* 101 shows,
where he says:

> As to intelligible and incorporeal elements, consider that I myself
> contain a soul and a λόγος and a νοῦς and the Holy Spirit.[51]

In Gregory the νοῦς is separate from the soul as in Evagrius. It
rules the soul and body and can be called the strongpoint and center of the
personality.[52] Gregory's tendency, as we see from the quotation, is to
expand the basic three elements to include a fourth, the λόγος, and,
occasionally, he also includes the spirit, which he calls the Holy Spirit.
However, πνεῦμα in Gregory is an aspect of the human person which cannot
be considered a basic constitutive element on the level of νοῦς, soul or body.

I am inclined to see the systematization of Gregory as the basic
source for that of Evagrius. If this is allowed, it appears that Evagrius has
moved from a loose anthropology which could be expanded to include λόγος
and πνεῦμα or as easily reduced to a soul-body dichotomy to a more rigid and
inflexible model. In Evagrius we do not even see a variation in terminology,

---

[49]*Oratio* 7:23; A. Ellverson, *The Dual Nature of Man, A Study in
the Theological Anthropology of Gregory of Nazianzus* (Studia Doctrinae
Christianae Upsaliensia 21; Uppsala, 1981), 13.

[50]*Oratio* 32,9.

[51]*Epistula* 101,38; text from ed. Gallay, SC 208, 52.

[52]*Epistula* 101,43.

let alone in the number of possible elements. This is in keeping with Evagrius's general character and outlook, first recognized by von Balthasar, who wrote of him,

> [Evagrius] has brought the loose flowing and changing system of Origen to a final, mathematically exact precision. In doing this, he has sacrificed Origen's versatile thought to an iron-clad system to which he holds fast, come what may, to its final consequences.[53]

Besides removing the ambiguities of the Origenist or Gregorian conception of the human person, Evagrius is also returning to older traditions going back to Plato. Here we see a manifestation of his tendency to seek answers in earlier figures, which was what led him to become a student of Origen's writings in the first place.[54] It is also possible that the rigid, tripartite division he espouses reflects a gnosticizing conceptuality popular in the Egyptian desert.[55] Evagrius made several trips into remote areas to question the great ascetics. We have an account of his trip to see John of

---

[53]H. von Balthasar, "The Metaphysics and Mystical Theology of Evagrius," trans. *Monastic Studies* 3 (1965): 184.

[54]Evagrius's adherance to earlier monastic tradition is avowed in *Practicus* 91. This does not mean that Evagrius was not an innovator. As Bouyer says of him, "[He was] one of those that not only marked a decisive turning-point, but called forth a real spiritual mutation." *The Spirituality of the New Testament and the Fathers* (History of Christian Spirituality I; New York: Seabury, 1963), 381.

[55]On the popularity of the trichotomy among the Gnostics, see M. Spanneut, op. cit, 150, 176. On the connection between Gnosticism and the monks, see Frederik Wisse, "Gnosticism and Early Monasticism in Egypt," in B. Aland, ed., *Gnosis* (Festschrift for Hans Jonas; Göttingen, 1978): 431-40.

Lycopolis. He tells us he questioned John about the light seen in contemplative ascent--was it the νοῦς itself which emitted this glow?[56] Such a question is only intelligible if "νοῦς" was a sufficiently common anthropological conception among the monks of the desert.[57]

Crouzel was disappointed to find that in the Evagrian anthropology there was no role for the spirit, and hence, a different understanding of spiritual combat.[58] In fact, the element of spiritual combat is present in both Gregory[59] and Evagrius. But, as the previous quotation from the *Kephalaia Gnostica* indicates, the soul in Evagrius is a hinderance and a danger to the νοῦς in this inner struggle. In the best of cases, the soul becomes submissive and obedient to the νοῦς. While getting to this point is a contest of strength for the opposing elements in the human character,[60] the soul is far from being the sole or central area of spiritual combat. Thus Evagrius only partially preserves the insights of Origen.

Perhaps the most interesting aspect of this question is the speculation which Evagrius was able to engage in based on the trichotomous anthropology. In his letter, *Ad Melaniam* we find evidence, which, pieced together, shows that Evagrius believed that the three parts of humanity corresponded to three metaphysical levels of God and noetic reality. The

---

[56]*Antirrheticus*, Acedia 16 (Frankenberg 524, 7-14).

[57]An anthropogical study of the sayings of the desert fathers would be a fruitful area of further study. The sayings are being edited by Dom Lucien Regnault, *Les Sentences des Pères du désert* (Solemnes: Abbaye Saint Pierre de Solemnes, 1966 and continuing).

[58]H. Crouzel, "Recherches," 111.

[59]Gregory, *Oratio* 2,91.

[60]*Ad Melaniam*, Vitestam 13-21.

νοῦς, and the noetic creation it shares in, are the body of God--Father, Son and Spirit.[61] Likewise, there is a divine soul in heaven; it is composite, made up of the Son, or Word, and the Spirit.[62] The divine νοῦς is the Father.[63] Thus the human being is a microcosm of the divine. Perhaps this speculation is another witness to the enormous importance of Genesis 1:26-- "Let us make man in our image," for desert monastics. The interpretation of this verse was central to the Origenist crisis,[64] which Guillaumont speculates may have been caused in part by the publication of Evagrius's work, *De Oratione*.[65]

There is one aspect of Evagrius's elaborate eschatology which also seems to be based on this speculation: Evagrius saw the νοῦς as being freed and naked in the end, while in some sense it also remained tied to the soul and possibly to a purified body. One model for the final relationship of these parts is absorption of the body and soul into the νοῦς:

A time will come when the names and numbers will be removed from between the body and the soul and the νοῦς because they will enter the realm of the νοῦς.[66]

---

[61]*Ad Melaniam*, Frankenberg 614, 31-2 (Spirit and Word), 34-5 (Father); 616, 17-8 (Son and Spirit), 23 (Father).

[62]Ibid, 616,16-7.

[63]Ibid, 614, 33.

[64]As is seen in Cassian, *Conlatio* 10, 2-4 and Socrates, *Historia Ecclesiastica* 6, 7.

[65]A. Guillaumont, *Les Képhalaia*, 61.

[66]*Ad Melaniam*, Frankenberg 616, 20-1.

In fact, the overall model which Evagrius seems to presuppose is a melding of the human person into the Trinity. The νοῦς is attracted to the Father, the Soul and its dependent body (now purified of its lower nature) is joined to the Son and Spirit:

> Rather, as the nature of the νοῦς is joined to the nature of the Father by being his body, thus the names "soul" and "body" will be swallowed up by the hypostases of the Son and the Spirit.[67]

Evagrius claims that his doctrines are based on insights which had occurred to him.[68] It is interesting to note the indirect parallels with Middle and Neoplatonist ideas.[69] That the highest principle or "father" is a "νοῦς" is an idea found also in Numinius, Maximus of Tyre and the pagan Origen.[70] That the lower realm is "soul" is even more widely attested. Plotinus of course taught that the inner realm of the human person corresponded to the hierarchy of the universe,[71] and that humanity is situated on the third and

---

[67]Ibid, 616, 25-7.

[68]Ibid, 616,3; note the emendation of this passage suggested in A. Guillaumont, *Les Képhalaia*, 121 n. 174.

[69]For a Platonist interpretation of Evagrius, see, Stephan Otto, "Esoterik und individualistische Gnosis: Der mönchische Platonismus des Euagrios Pontikos," in, idem, *Die Antike im Umbruch* (Munich: List, 1974), 65-81.

[70]Numinius, *Frag.* 17 and 22; Maximus of Tyre, *Diss.* 9, 8-12; Origen, *In Plat. theol.* 2,4; see further, P.W. Van Der Horst and J. Mansfield, *An Alexandrian Platonist Against Dualism* (Leiden: Brill, 1974), 11ff.

[71]P. Hadot, *Plotin ou la simplicité du regard* (Paris: Études Augustiniennes, 1973), 28.

lowest level of the divine.[72] John Rist has recently established that the two Cappadocian teachers of Evagrius, Gregory and Basil, became somewhat interested in Plotinus in the later parts of their lives, exactly the time when Evagrius was with them.[73] We are also told by the *Historia Monachorum* that Evagrius frequently found himself in debates with pagan philosophers in Alexandria.[74] Thus Middle or Neoplatonist influence is not impossible.

Alexander of Lycopolis is a good example of an Alexandrian Neoplatonic philosopher, albeit a century earlier, with whom Evagrius might have felt some affinity. For Alexander as well as for Evagrius, the highest principle was a celestial $\nu o\hat{v}\varsigma$, matter was produced by that $\nu o\hat{v}\varsigma$ and hence was not evil, and Christ himself was a $\nu o\hat{v}\varsigma$ come into the world,[75] the doctrine for which Evagrius was specifically condemned in 553.[76]

---

[72]Plotinus, *What Is Man?*, *Enneades* 1,1,8; see also A.H. Armstrong, *The Cambridge History of Later Greek and Early Medieval Philosophy* (Cambridge: Cambridge University, 1967), 223.

[73]J. Rist, "Basil's 'Neoplatonism': Its Background and Nature," in P. Fedwick, ed., *Basil of Caesaria, Christian, Humanist, Ascetic* (2 vols., Toronto: Pontifical Institute of Medieval Studies, 1981), 1. 216-20.

[74]*Historia Monachorum* 20,15.

[75]Alexander of Lycopolis, *Critique of the Doctrines of Manichaeus* (ed. Van der Horst and Mansfield, op. cit.), 60, 68ff, 91ff.

[76]A. Guillaumont, *Les Képhalaia*, 147-56.